EARLY PATRISTIC
READINGS
OF ROMANS

ROMANS THROUGH HISTORY AND CULTURES
Receptions and Critical Interpretations

CHRISTINA GRENHOLM AND DANIEL PATTE, SERIES EDITORS

Romans through History and Cultures includes a wealth of information regarding the receptions of Romans throughout the history of the church and today, in the "first" and the "two-thirds" world. It explores the past and present impact of Romans upon theology, and upon cultural, political, social, and ecclesial life, and gender relations.

In each volume the authors contribute to an integrated practice, "scriptural criticism," which takes into account, with contemporary biblical scholars, that different readings can be grounded in the same text by different critical methods; with church historians and practical theologians, that the believers' readings interrelate biblical text and concrete life; and with theologians, that believers read Romans as Scripture.

The cover art skillfully represents that any interpretation of a scriptural text is framed in three ways: (1) by an *analytical frame* that reflects each reader's autonomous choice of a textural dimension as most significant – see the individual studying the text; (2) by a *contextual/pragmatic frame* shaped by a certain relational network of life in society and community – see the people joining hands; and (3) by a *hermeneutical frame* inspired by a certain religious perception of life – see the bread and chalice and the face-to-face encounter.

By elucidating the threefold choices reflected in various interpretations of Romans through the centuries and present-day cultures, the volumes in the series – which emerge from a three-year SBL consultation and an ongoing SBL seminar – raise a fundamental critical question: Why did I/we choose this interpretation rather than another one?

ROMANS THROUGH HISTORY AND CULTURES SERIES

EARLY PATRISTIC READINGS OF ROMANS

Edited by
**Kathy L. Gaca and
L. L. Welborn**

t&t clark

NEW YORK • LONDON

T & T Clark International,
Madison Square Park, 15 East 26th Street, New York, NY 10010

T & T Clark International
The Tower Building, 11 York Road, London SE1 7NX

T & T Clark International is a Continuum imprint.

Cover art by Elizabeth McNaron Patte

Cataloging-in-Publication Data is available from the Library of Congress

Printed in the United States of America

05 06 07 08 09 10   10 9 8 7 6 5 4 3 2 1

Table of Contents

– INTRODUCTION –

Romans in Light of
Early Patristic Receptions

Kathy L. Gaca and L. L. Welborn, Editors

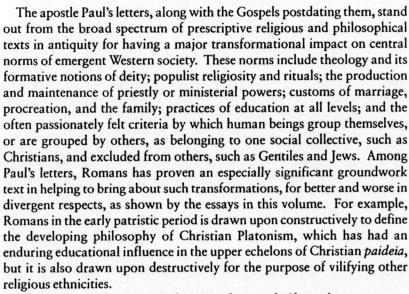

The apostle Paul's letters, along with the Gospels postdating them, stand out from the broad spectrum of prescriptive religious and philosophical texts in antiquity for having a major transformational impact on central norms of emergent Western society. These norms include theology and its formative notions of deity; populist religiosity and rituals; the production and maintenance of priestly or ministerial powers; customs of marriage, procreation, and the family; practices of education at all levels; and the often passionately felt criteria by which human beings group themselves, or are grouped by others, as belonging to one social collective, such as Christians, and excluded from others, such as Gentiles and Jews. Among Paul's letters, Romans has proven an especially significant groundwork text in helping to bring about such transformations, for better and worse in divergent respects, as shown by the essays in this volume. For example, Romans in the early patristic period is drawn upon constructively to define the developing philosophy of Christian Platonism, which has had an enduring educational influence in the upper echelons of Christian *paideia*, but it is also drawn upon destructively for the purpose of vilifying other religious ethnicities.

Paul's letter to the Romans, however, has rarely if ever been transparent in its meaning and significance. Rather, this letter has helped effect central normative changes through the secondary receptions signaled by the title of this Introduction, "Romans in Light of the Early Patristic Receptions." By 'receptions' we the Editors of this essay collection are referring to those hermeneutic endeavors to impart didactic teachings on the basis of Romans that have become influential by virtue of a sector of Christianity granting credibility and authority to the interpreters—Augustine and Luther being among the most well known from the later patristic period and the early Reformation.

This collection of essays, *Early Patristic Readings of Romans*, belongs to the ongoing series titled "Romans through History and Cultures." Each volume in this series shares the common aim of elucidating the hermeneutic strategies and arguments that noteworthy interpreters have used in specific periods and cultures to endorse, explain, construct, and rework Romans as a normative authority. One of the unifying purposes of this multi-volume endeavor is to critically reflect on, and raise awareness of, the steps and assumptions that interpreters of Romans have utilized in their receptions over the centuries to produce such an imposing yet diverse edifice of multi-lingual sermons, treatises, books, and commentaries on Romans. The essays in this present volume are especially pivotal in this overall project, because they go back long before Luther, and on occasion as early as two centuries prior to Augustine, to explore the earliest formative principles on record by which this prescriptive edifice first started to be built.

By the end of the second century CE, the letters of Paul had already established themsleves broadly in early Christianity as authoritative bearers of God's word, along with the Septuagint and the Gospels; and trajectories toward making Paul's words sacrosanct are apparent even in the Apostolic Fathers from the first half of the second century.[1] To name but one striking example dating to the early patristic period, in the years immediately prior to 180 CE, twelve Christians from the North African town of Scillium were already committed to this hermeneutic elevation of Paul's letters as a whole, so much so that they laid down their lives as martyrs in 180 for their conception of his teachings.[2] Similar in conviction was the anonymous author of the *Acts of the Scillitan Martyrs*, whose apparent transcript of their martyrdom narrates their trial so as to reaffirm the Scillitan Christian grasp of Paul's teachings. When put on trial in nearby Carthage for refusing to honor the *genius* or spirit presence of the Roman emperor, the accused Scillitan Christians swore strictly by God "whom no person has seen or can see with mortal eyes," as taught in Paul's letters (1 Tim 6:16). They even brought the writings of Paul with them in a satchel, as a sort of companion script witness, when they were brought before the presiding proconsul, Saturninus. When the proconsul offered to adjourn their case for further questioning in thirty days, the accused instead longed to become martyrs in heaven on the same day, thanks in no small degree to the eschatological tenor that they discerned in Paul's letters, whom they revered, in their own words, as "a just man." Saturninus thereupon changed his verdict to execution through beheading by the sword. In response, the Scillitan Christian martyrs gave thanks to God and were beheaded. Rather, as the narrative puts it, they were "crowned with martyrdom," with the ostensible result that they did not die but "reigned with the Father, Son, and Holy Spirit forever and ever." It is a challenging task to elucidate the hermeneutic principles by which such early interpreters of Paul came to see his letters as teaching that the worship of the unseen God absolutely precludes honoring the emperor's *genius* rather than allowing, say, Christians to reclassify the Roman requirement as a quasi-secular rendering unto Caesar his due. It is similarly worth investigating why the Scillitan Christians thought that Paul regarded Christian martyrdom as a guarantee of a privileged, immediate, and eternally shared rule with the Father, Son, and Holy Spirit, rather than of a more ordinary resurrection on par with the one promised to all faithful Christians alike. The task of comprehending such early conceptions of Paul's teachings is challenging primarily because the interpretive thought world of early Christians is remote, molten, largely oral and as such evanescent, and often puzzling when accessible in texts, such as the purported court transcript of the Scillitan *Acts*.

Secondarily, the task of comprehending early patristic readings of Romans is challenging for a different kind of text-specific reason. The early patristic readings or receptions, which helped to shape the didactic stature of Romans, are almost always selective and allusive in the second and third centuries, for the citations and allusions to Romans are embedded here and there in treatises on a diverse array of topics that need to be appreciated as compositions in their own right before their selective deployment of Romans can be assessed.[3] The now familiar industry of verse-by-verse commentaries to explicate Paul's letters is a genre conspicuous for its absence until the late fourth century, excluding Origen's commentary on Romans, which stands "in splendid isolation" until the next surviving Greek commentaries more than a century later.[4] The essays in this volume have risen to this challenge of explicating significant aspects of the early patristic readings of Romans by revealing a combined sensitivity to Romans and the patristic treatises under their purview.[5]

Kathy L. Gaca opens the essay collection by tracing a radical polemic against Greek polytheism in patristic writers of the 2nd to the 4th centuries to its root in Paul, specifically in Romans 1:18-32. Gaca demonstrates that Paul's understanding of the origin of polytheism represents a significant departure from an older tradition of Hellenistic Jewish polemic, which explained the belief in a plurality of gods as a function of *ignorance*. In a radical revision of this tradition, Paul asserts that an unspecified group of Gentiles, probably the Greeks *willfully suppressed* the truth about God revealed to them in nature. Gaca argues that Paul boldly transfers to Greeks and other Gentiles passages from the Septuagint about rebellious Israel. Thus Paul construes Greek polytheists as *apostates* from the true knowledge of God. Paul's revolutionary theory remained without influence upon the earliest Christian writers who continued to argue, in continuity with the tradition of Hellenistic Judaism, that ignorance motivated polytheism. But, beginning with Tatian in the late second century CE, Paul's theory began to win adherents among church fathers who read Romans in Greek. Gaca demonstrates that Paul's argument proved especially useful to patristic writers such as Athanasius and John Chrysostom

who sought to suppress religious diversity in the interest of shaping a
Christian society.

In "Jewish Salvation in Romans according to Clement of Alexandria,"
Michael Joseph Brown addresses Clement of Alexandria's stance on the
topic of the Jews' salvation in light of Romans 10-11. The main question
here is whether or not Clement interprets these two chapters in Romans
to mean that Christians supersede Jews as God's people or whether he
more amicably takes Romans 10-11 to mean that Judaism and Christianity are two respectable paths to salvation in the eyes of the biblical God.
Brown elicits the most charitable case possible in favor of the latter view.

Laurence L. Welborn likewise works with *Stromateis* 2 in "The
Soteriology of Romans in Clement of Alexandria, *Stromateis* 2: Faith,
Fear, and Assimilation to God." In his study, Welborn shows that
Romans is of premier importance to Clement in his Christian Platonist
construction of faith, fear, and hope. In so doing, Welborn makes
Clement's notion of faith more intelligible and Pauline than has been
appreciated hitherto, and he demonstrates the literary skill with which
Clement uses ancient Greek principles of rhetorical composition to
explore Romans' central themes of faith, fear, and hope.

Building upon recent investigations of Irenaeus's use of Paul in the
Adversus haereses, Susan L. Graham examines Irenaeus's other surviving
work, the *Epideixis*, for evidence that Paul's thoughts on the fate of Jews
and Gentiles in Romans 9-11 may have provided Irenaeus with key
elements of his theology of history. Graham tests this hypothesis by
delineating the major theological features of Irenaeus's demonstration–
election, faith, righteousness, freedom, salvation–and discovers numerous correlations with Paul's arguments in Romans 9-11. Graham also
examines explicit quotations of Romans 9-11 in the *Epideixis*, as well as
reminiscences and paraphrases, and discovers a cluster of Pauline references deriving from Romans 9:6-30 and 10:13-20. The focus of
Graham's investigation is Irenaeus's treatment of the story of Noah's
three sons, who are interpreted as the progenitors of three races–Jews,
Gentile believers, and non-believers. Graham suggests that Irenaeus's
attempt to establish a unified history of divine-human relations is
inspired by Paul's confidence in a faithful and merciful God.

Jeffrey Bingham's essay focuses on Irenaeus's use of Romans 8 in the
anti-gnostic polemic of *Adversus haereses*. Bingham demonstrates that
Irenaeus developed his understanding of Romans 8 in the crucible of
exegetical controversy with the gnostics. Bingham examines the *Gospel
of Philip* as an example of a contemporary gnostic reading of Paul.
Against the Valentinian exegesis of Paul's "olive tree" metaphor, Irenaeus
cites Romans 8 in support of his understanding of the flesh and the spirit.
Irenaeus also draws upon Romans 8 to articulate an eschatological
cosmology. Bingham concludes that Irenaeus's exegetical method

employs a canonical principle in the interpretation of controversial Pauline texts.

In "Origen's Readings of Romans in *Peri Archon*: (Re)Constructing Paul," Ruth Clements elicits and demonstrates the substantive roles that Romans and other Pauline letters play in Origen's treatise, *Peri Archon*. This treatise by Origen concerns his Christian Platonist fundamentals of the Christian faith. Clements shows that Origen presses key proof texts from Romans in particular to support his view that scripture necessarily functions both on the literal and on the more significant–for Origen–spiritual or allegorical level. She further argues the original and more troubling thesis that Origen entwines this bi-level Christian Platonist hermeneutic with a proclivity to enlist Pauline proof texts to identify Judaism with an exclusive and deficient literalism that has served to disenfranchise Jews from God. By Clements' argument, Origen thinks that the spiritual level of the Septuagint and Hebrew Bible manifestly reveals prophecies of the forthcoming Jesus as Christ, but the Jews have failed to grasp these prophecies and hence have not accepted their rightful messiah. This thesis poses a significant challenge to the more common view that Origen found Judaism eminently respectable and worth learning as a justifiable and complete way of knowing God.

Regarding Origen's stance toward Judaism, Sze-Kar Wan's "Jews and Gentiles in Origen's *Commentarii in Epistulam Pauli ad Romanos*" offers a striking contrast with Clements' study of Origen's *Peri Archon*. In Wan's essay, the more familiar view prevails that Origen utilizes Romans to demonstrate an abiding respect for Judaism, especially as he would have known it in Caesarea in his day, even while recognizing its alterity from Christianity. For Wan, Origen's commentary on Romans displays a noteworthy sensitivity to the Jews and Jewish reliosity, even while remaining Christocentric, such as Origen's elucidation of Romans 2:9-10 and 2:17-24.

As Editors of *Early Patristic Readings of Romans*, we have chosen to include response critiques as companion pieces to the essays in this volume. These thoughtful critiques serve to candidly assess the essayists' own interpretive understandings of how Romans is utilized in their patristic sources. We believe that this response format is the most effective way to stimulate greater dialogue and reflection on the hermeneutic methods that have been used to engage with, and teach, Romans from antiquity and the modern day. This enhanced concern and attention to the hermeneutics that informs Pauline authority has been one of the central goals of the Society of Biblical Literature Seminar Panels, "Romans through History and Cultures," from which all the volumes in this series derive. To allow the response critiques to play the strong role that they merit in the present volume, we have kept our above introductory comments about the essays to a minimum, refraining in particular from the evaluative assessments that are the primary function of the response critiques.

As noted above, the essays in this volume, *Early Patristic Readings of Romans*, for the most part originated as peer-reviewed Seminar papers that were debated at the Society of Biblical Literature "Romans through History and Culture" panel sessions spanning from 2000-2002. The papers have since been considerably revised for publication as essays here, and the response critiques have likewise been updated, as necessary, in light of the revisions. The one exception is Kathy L. Gaca's "Paul's Uncommon Declaration in Romans 1:18-32 and Its Problematic Legacy for Pagan and Christian Relations," which originated as a 1999 *Harvard Theological Review* article and was invited as a "Romans through History and Cultures" Seminar paper in 2000. This essay is reprinted here with the kind permission of the *Harvard Theological Review*.[6] The valuable response critiques by Moxnes, Gaca, Bassler, Markschies, Gorday, Cosgrove, and Georgi were commissioned by Executive members of the Steering Committee of the "Romans through History and Cultures" Seminar.

Primary source and other standard abbreviations follow (or , in the interest of clarity, are fuller than) the abbreviations listed in these reference sources:

A Greek-English Lexicon (=LSJ). Edited by Henry G. Liddell, Robert Scott, Henry S. Jones, and Roderick McKenzie, with Revised Supplement edited by P. G. W. Glare and A. A. Thompson. Oxford: Clarendon Press, 1996.

The Oxford Classical Dictionary (=OCD). Edited by Simon Hornblower and Antony Spawforth. New York: Oxford University Press, 1996.

A Patristic Greek Lexicon. Edited by G. W. H. Lampe. Oxford: Clarendon Press, 1968.

The SBL Handbook of Style: For Ancient Near Eastern, Biblical, and Early Christian Studies. Edited by Patrick H. Alexander et al. Peabody, Mass.: Hendrickson Publishers, 1999.

---

[1] Maurice F. Wiles, *The Divine Apostle: The Interpretation of St. Paul's Epistles in the Early Church* (Cambridge: Cambridge University Press, 1967) 4-6.

[2] Their names were Speratus, Nartzalus, Cittinus, Donata, Secunda, Vestia, Veturius, Felix, Aqulinus, Ianuaria, Generosa, and Laetantius. For a readily accessible translation and solid assessment of the trial of the Christian Scillitans, see T. D. Barnes, *Tertullian: A Historical and Literary Study* (Oxford: Clarendon Press, 1971) 60-64.

[3] The same holds true of Paul's other letters as interpreted in this period.

[4] Wiles, *The Divine Apostle*, 6-7.

[5] This collection of essays thus promises to be of great interest to readers of Charles Kannengiesser's *Handbook of Patristic Exegesis* (Leiden: Brill, 2004).

[6] Please see the leading footnote of this essay for full acknowledgment.

– ONE –

Paul's Uncommon Declaration in Romans 1:18-32 and Its Problematic Legacy for Pagan and Christian Relations*

Kathy L. Gaca

———— ◆ ————

Introduction

By the late fourth century, prominent Christian leaders no longer remained content to advocate religious separatism from their poly-theistic social environment. Instead, they started making more strenu-ous efforts in law and in the streets to prohibit Greek and other pagan religious practices in the Roman Empire.[1] This change in policy and practice was the outcome of historical factors that need better explana-tion than that of the unavoidable destiny of Christianity. One important aspect of this change, I will argue here, is a problematic innovation in the tradition of Hellenistic Jewish and early Christian polemic against polytheism. The innovation derives from Paul's letter to the Romans and develops through patristic endorsements of Paul's argument. In Romans 1:18-32 Paul fully reworks the Hellenistic Jewish polemical tradition, yet his argument is not yet recognized in the modern day as the distinctive proclamation that it is. Nonetheless the polemic he wages in Romans 1:18-32 is anomalous in the tradition before, during, and for a century after he lived.

According to current scholarly consensus, Hellenistic Jewish and Christian polemic tediously recites the same diatribe against poly-theistic diversity from the first century BCE through late antiquity, regardless of whether the proponents are Jewish or Christian, such as ps.-Solomon in Wisdom of Solomon and Paul in Romans 1:18-32. The individual expressions of the polemic vary in rhetorical intensity but advocate the following generic position: Ancient Mediterranean poly-theism is an immoral delusion rooted in religiously alien ignorance and

I

false notions of deity. Gentiles, who are either fools of their own accord or duped by demons, would do well to recognize their folly, part ways with their religious heritage, and join the enlightenment of biblical monotheism.[2] As I will demonstrate here, however, this argument represents only one line of the polemical tradition, was originally the most prevalent in early Christianity, and develops in line with Hellenistic Jewish polemic, such as Wisdom 13-14.

A second and distinct argument in the polemical tradition asserts that the ancient ancestors of the Greeks or of the Greeks and other Gentiles once recognized and yet brazenly abandoned biblical monotheism. Unnamed wise persons are to blame for leading the apostate rebellion. The renegade descendants accordingly must reawaken and convert back to monotheism in its Christian form. This argument is far more conducive than the first to a stance of intolerance toward Greek and other Gentile religions. Paul in Romans 1:18-32 is its first and most influential proponent. There is a striking difference between the first argument in its Christian version and the argument motivated by Romans. The first assumes that pagans are genuine religious outsiders and tries to convince them to recognize the biblical God for the first time through Christianity. The second assumes that some or all pagans are rebellious religious insiders and gives a biblically potent rationale for compelling them to return to Christianity.

Paul's argument, as I will also show, is initially a lone voice that does not immediately become prevalent. Starting in the later second century, however, Romans 1:18-32 convinces numerous patristic writers from Tatian through Chrysostom and thereby begins to take hold. One main reason for the shift is that some of the early church fathers come to esteem Paul as a theologian of impeccable authority. Their endorsements of Romans 1:18-32 consequently portray Greeks or Greeks and other Gentiles as apostates. Various Greek philosophers, further, come to be identified as the falsely so-called wise men Paul blames for leading the rebellion against God. This new argument against polytheism reaches a heightened fervor by the late fourth century, when major church fathers such as Athanasius, Augustine, and Chrysostom ardently advocate and elaborate Romans 1:18-32.

It must remain an open question here whether Romans 1:18-32 actually motivated the intolerance in late antiquity or only provided a convenient rationale for it. The success of Paul's argument depends on numerous factors, only a few of which I can explore here: the authoritative stature that Romans 1:18-32 gains over time and the parameters of identity given to the allegedly apostate Gentiles and their leaders. By contrast, the first line of argument against polytheism, though hardly benevolent toward ancient Mediterranean religions, offers neither a formula for suppressing religious diversity nor a smear campaign against Greek philosophers. I will now explore the first argument against polytheism in Hellenistic Judaism, so that it can then become clear how and why the polemic deriving from Romans does present such a formula and campaign.

The First Argument against Polytheism in Hellenistic Judaism

The Hellenistic Jewish argument against polytheism is most thoroughly explicated in Wisdom of Solomon 13:1-14:31.[3] Ps.-Solomon maintains that peoples who think that there is a plurality of gods in the physical world are unenlightened about biblical monotheism and have "ignorance" to blame for thinking there are many gods (13:1-2).[4] There is only one god who at least partially transcends the world and is its craftsman, master, and arranger, in short, its γενεσιάρχης (13:3). As the multivalence of γενεσιάρχης shows, ps.-Solomon's conception of God is grounded strictly in the biblical tradition. The god who commences the genesis of the physical world is identical with the god who appears at the beginning of Genesis, which itself starts with the phrase ἐν ἀρχῇ – hence the term γενεσιάρχης to name the god who "in the beginning made heaven and earth" (Gen 1:1). Gentiles who do not recognize the supreme and solitary power of the creator god in Genesis are religious outsiders who fail to grasp the two aspects of ps.-Solomon's teleological argument for God's existence. First, the world is a magnificently designed and directed work of craftsmanship, so a creator god must have crafted it with the design in mind (13:5). Second, the creator god is to be identified unconditionally as God of the Greek Genesis and laws. Pagans in the main are in a state of culpable ignorance about God because they acknowledge neither that the world has one god who crafted it nor that the creator god is the God of Genesis. They worship multiple icons of false gods and thus show that they are empty-headed about God (14:12-14). Among philosophers, however, the culpability decreases markedly if their cosmologies posit a single creator god. Philosophers with such cosmologies take the first step toward biblical monotheism, or so ps.-Solomon maintains. They fail to take the second step, however, for God as creator in the philosophical cosmologies is not a solitary deity but supreme regent among other genuine gods, as is Zeus to the other Olympians.[5] Ps.-Solomon, accordingly, finds Greek philosophers more commendable than other Gentiles because he interprets their pluralistic monotheism as a step in the right direction toward biblical monotheism (13:6-9). Nonetheless, Gentiles are to blame relative to their degrees of ignorance, for they should have been able to infer biblical monotheism from nature itself without any need for Genesis as commentary. Still, since philosophers have been getting warm in their search for the biblical God, they are nowhere near as cold as their compatriots and the stones that they worship. Ps.-Solomon therefore argues that pagan culture is and always has been religiously

alien and blind to God's manifest existence. He reinterprets the myriad
projects of philosophical monotheism as quests for the biblical God,
and commends the search. Though as yet unsuccessful, philosophers
have at least been groping in the right direction with one eye partly
open. Nowhere does ps.-Solomon contend that any pagans once
knew the creator god of Genesis only to be led astray into polytheistic
idolatry.

Ps.-Solomon's argument that Gentiles are theologically ignorant outsiders is in keeping with the polemic offered in other Hellenistic Jewish
sources. Philo, Josephus, and numerous passages in *Sibylline Oracles*
likewise maintain that biblical monotheism is obviously embedded in
nature, which makes the conspicuous presence of many gods in their
society problematic. Given that one god alone, the biblical one, is naturally to be inferred from the world, why have relatively few made the
inference and so many done otherwise? The solution of these polemicists is to argue likewise that foolish ignorance motivates the Gentiles
to have a diversity of gods, not to reexamine their own premise.
Josephus, reacting to Greek criticisms about Judaism, rounds off his
critique of Greek polytheism by wondering, "What is the cause of such
great error and absence of regulation about the nature of God?" Unlike
Moses, he offers in response, Greek lawgivers simply did not know
about God. Solon, Lycurgus, and the like "did not know the true nature
of God from the start" when they established Hellenic customs and
beliefs. They were "unable to formulate such accurate knowledge." The
ignorance of the Greek lawgivers in turn gave free rein to poets, paint-
ers, and sculptors, who contrived and continue to fashion as gods whatever happens to strike their creative fancy. There are, however, "Greek
philosophers who saw the truth," such as Plato, and they are a noble
exception to the norm of Gentile ignorance. Plato followed the Jews in
formulating his "true and fitting opinion about God," which he pru-
dently refrained from trying to share with the populace at large.[6] The
Greeks are thus well advised to learn better and to honor the biblical
God properly, as Plato does (*Ap* 2.250-54). Josephus therefore agrees
with the Hellenistic Jewish thesis that Gentile ignorance accounts for
the absence of universal belief in the biblical God. Unlike ps.-Solomon,
further, he expresses unreserved admiration for Plato and philosophers
of like mind, because on his view, Plato's θεός is one and the same as
the creator god in Genesis.

Philo similarly resolves the enigma of polytheism by attributing
theological vacuity to Greeks and other Gentiles, and he offers an even
stronger version of this argument. The worship of many gods arises
from "ignorance [ἄγνοια]," "being excessively unlearned [ἀμαθία
ὑπερβάλλουσα]," and from having an "absence of knowledge
[ἀνεπιστημοσύνη]" about God and how to honor him properly (*Spec*
1.15, *Opif* 45, *Ebr* 45). Polytheistic people simply "do not see [μὴ

βλέποντες]" the truth of the Hellenistic Jewish teleological argument and instead elevate the world as "artifact over its artificer."[7] Perhaps pagans in the main are incapable of learning about God, in which case they are blind where the ability to discern the true from false theology is located (*Decal* 59). Alternatively, maybe they are not missing the gene for biblical monotheism. Pagans may simply have an incurable lack of interest in the invisible and transcendent God of Genesis because they find him an improbable cause of the cosmos (*Decal* 59, *Contempl* 10-11). If true, then they are shamelessly mad as well as ignorant, for they openly prefer phenomena to the invisible God and glory in their own sophistry rather than in genuine wisdom (*Opif* 45, *Spec* 1.20-21). Further, Gentiles cannot possibly know God and be polytheistic by Philo's Socratic principle that one cannot possibly know the better and do the worse (*Ebr* 42-5). Therefore, they can only be ignorant, given their worship of many deities. Not all pagans, however, are immersed in blind folly. Plato, the Stoics, and other philosophers have, with God's help, attained the enlightenment of biblical monotheism, thanks partly to tutelage from Moses (*Leg* 3.97-9, *Praem* 41-6). Hence, like Josephus, Philo turns a blind eye to the difference between pluralistic and biblical monotheism. He freely assimilates the former to the latter, and thereby creates a select group of Greek philosophers who know about the biblical God. Aside from this elite, however, Gentiles have always made a diverse muddle of theology.

The *Sibylline Oracles* likewise supports the Hellenistic Jewish argument regarding Gentile ignorance. In book 3.8-9 for instance, the prophetic sibyl wonders why Gentile peoples foolishly worship many gods in iconic form rather than the one great god of Genesis. Like ps.-Solomon, Philo, and Josephus, she attributes the practice to empty-headedness and a lack of education about God's existence (πάντα . . . λαὸν ἀπαίδευτον κενεόφρονα, 3.669-70). The theologically ignorant include Babylonians, Egyptians, Libyans, Persians, Assyrians, Ethiopians, and Romans, to name a few of the peoples she upbraids for their polytheistic folly (*SibOr* 3.207-8, 300-62).[8] In Hellenistic Judaism, therefore, the thesis of Gentile ignorance solves the glaring discrepancy between the theory that biblical monotheism is dictated by nature itself and a social reality that does not fit the paradigm. A number of Greek philosophers, however, are at least on the right track. A few of these philosophers even receive honorary degrees in biblical monotheism from Philo and Josephus.

The Argument against Polytheism in Romans 1:18-32

Paul in Romans 1:18-32 offers a completely distinct explanation of why some or all polytheistic people in the ancient Mediterranean worship numerous gods. The people in question are not theologically blind outsiders but something far more reprehensible in biblical terms. They are knowledgeable about God, Paul asserts, yet have become rebels who worship the created world rather than its creator. Hence, the people know but are suppressing their knowledge about God (1:18-23). In Paul's wording, they are blameworthy "suppressors of the truth" about God and as such they "have no defense" for worshipping their ancestral gods (1:18-20). The possible identities of the people remain to be seen below. Paul advocates this new position because he recasts the teleological argument in Hellenistic Judaism into an active revelation from God to the people in question. God manifestly showed the people through his creation that he is their creator, and the revelation remains part of their awareness in some sense that Paul leaves indeterminate. "That which is knowable about God is obviously in them, for God revealed it to them [τὸ γνωστὸν τοῦ θεοῦ φανερόν ἐστιν ἐν αὐτοῖς· ὁ γὰρ θεὸς αὐτοῖς ἐφανέρωσεν]" (1:19). The content of the revelation is the teleological argument. "God's invisible aspects are visible to the mind's eye through his works since the creation of the cosmos." Nonetheless, the truth-suppressing people have not glorified God or given him thanks even though they are so obliged since they once did recognize him and still know him in some sense. Instead, they actively exchanged biblical monotheism for polytheism under the false pretense of being wise. "They traded the glory of the imperishable God for an image of a perishable human being and of winged, four-footed, and belly-crawling creatures." In so doing, "they traded in the truth of God for falsehood" (1:23, 25). For Paul, therefore, Genesis is so clearly written into nature that the world undeniably beams forth its creator god's existence and his requirement of exclusive worship. The people who have suppressed their recognition of God through polytheistic mores only seem not to know him because they are in deep idolatrous denial. They have been in this blighted condition from the time they exchanged biblical monotheism for polytheistic practices. Ever since their fateful trade-off in deities, further, God has been punishing the people with a retributive affliction that makes them deviant in their reasoning and sexual mores. The people have consequently become a society of sophists and sexual deviants, or so Paul contends (1:21-27).

Paul's accusation in Romans 1:18-32 has a specific and technical biblical force. He boldly classifies the truth-suppressing polytheists as though they were Israel in apostasy, not merely generic rebels against God. If, as Paul maintains in Rom 11:25-27, Israel encompasses all humanity, Jew, Gentile, and Christian alike, then the truth-suppressing polytheists are apostate Israel even though they have this new cultural identity unawares. Paul strenuously reiterates that the people are rebellious Israel through pointed allusions he makes to the Septuagint of Deuteronomy, Psalms, and Jeremiah. The people's polytheistic customs replicate the Israelites worshipping the golden calf at Horeb. Just as the Israelites "exchanged the glory of God for the image of a calf eating grass and forgot God who saved them [ἠλλάξαντο τὴν δόξαν αὐτῶν ἐν ὁμοιώματι μόσχου ἔσθοντος χόρτον. ἐπελάθοντο τοῦ θεοῦ τοῦ σώζοντος αὐτούς]," (LXX Ps 105:20-1) so too have the truth suppressors "exchanged the glory of the imperishable God for an image [καὶ ἤλλαξαν τὴν δόξαν τοῦ ἀφθάρτοῦ θεοῦ ἐν ὁμοιώματι]" (Rom 1:23). Further, Deuteronomy firmly prohibits Israel from "transgressing the law and making any and every carved image and any likeness, be it male or female, a beast that is on the earth, a winged bird that flies under the sky, or a belly-crawling creature that proceeds along the ground [ὁμοίωμα ἀρσενικοῦ ἢ θηλυκοῦ, ὁμοίωμα παντὸς κτήνους τῶν ὄντων ἐπὶ τῆς γῆς, ὁμοίωμα παντὸς ὀρνέου πτερωτοῦ ὃ πέταται ὑπὸ τὸν οὐρανόν, ὁμοίωμα παντὸς ἑρπετοῦ, ὃ ἕρπει ἐπὶ τῆς γῆς]" (Deut 4:16-18). Nonetheless, the apostate branch of Pauline Israel went right ahead and did so. They exchanged God for "the image and likeness of anthropomorphic, winged, four-footed, and belly-crawling creatures [ὁμοιώματι εἰκόνος φθαρτοῦ ἀνθρώπου καὶ πετεινῶν καὶ τετραπόδων καὶ ἑρπετῶν]" (Rom 1:23). The truth-suppressing people have consequently succumbed to the folly that befalls those who transgress God's will, as Jeremiah 2:4-5 and Psalm 93, in the Septuagint, indicate with more phrasing that Paul borrows. "They became senseless in their acts of reasoning [ἐματαιώθησαν ἐν τοῖς διαλογισμοῖς αὐτῶν]" (Rom 1:21), which in turn led them into polytheism and their other aberrant mores. Therefore the senseless folly (ἐματαιώθησαν) and apostasy that Jeremiah 2:4-5 carefully delimits to "the house of Jacob and the entire fatherland of the house of Israel" Paul transfers with breathtaking ease to polytheistic people in his Christian Israel.[9] The truth suppressors must thus be summoned back to Christian monotheism and its moral order, not persuaded to go there for the first time.

Given the nature of Paul's accusation, the precise identity of the alleged truth suppressors becomes a pressing question – whether they are humanity in its entirety or only some people, and if the latter, then who they are. This problem, however, remains an enigma in the text of Romans itself. As Origen astutely notes, Romans especially "uses phrases that are occasionally confused and not well explicated."[10] Romans 1:18 is an excellent case in point, for the truth suppressors are simply "people [ἀνθρώπων]" delimited by the participial phrase "who suppress the truth unjustly [τῶν τὴν ἀλήθειαν ἐν ἀδικίᾳ κατεχόντων]." Depending on the interpretive strategy one employs, the people's identity and the related scope of Paul's accusation vary considerably. Two alternatives – humanity or Gentiles as a whole – exhaust the repertoire of modern commentaries, though both interpretations are open to question.

By the broadest theological interpretation, Romans 1:18 delineates the human condition and ascribes rebellious sinfulness to everyone. This interpretation presupposes that Romans is Paul's tract on human sinfulness, which then allows one to infer from the phrase "every irreverence and injustice of people who suppress the truth unjustly" that all people suffer from sin and suppress the truth about God in this rather general sense.[11] This inference does not necessarily follow from Paul's wording. First, his concern is apostate idolatry, not generic sinfulness. Second, his statement that there are "people who suppress the truth unjustly [ἀνθρώπων τῶν τὴν ἀλήθειαν ἐν ἀδικίᾳ κατεχόντων]" does not commit him to the position that all people are truth-suppressors in the manner depicted in Romans 1:18-32. The universal interpretation is also tenuous on historical grounds given how openly polytheistic and icon-oriented the people are. Devout Jews and Christians in Paul's day do not fit this cultural description. If they are exempt from Paul's charge, as seems reasonable, then he did not direct his accusation at the entirety of humanity.

Alternatively, the truth suppressors are only the Gentile sector of humanity at large, who did use polytheistic icons in their acts of worship. Though this second interpretation of the people's identity shows a clearer historical grasp of Paul's Mediterranean social milieu, nothing in the wording of Romans 1:18 compels this conclusion either. Paul's statement signifies that all Gentiles who are truth suppressors have the cluster of deviant mores he ascribes to them, not necessarily that all Gentiles are such truth suppressors. These are two different propositions. Only the latter necessarily means that the people in question are Gentiles as a whole, yet Romans 1:18 commits only to the former. Hence, a significant third alternative remains viable – by "truth-suppressing people," Paul may be referring to some Gentiles, not all of them.

The third alternative, though invisible in modern commentaries, reflects the historically primary one offered in early Greek patristic exegesis: Romans 1:18-32 concerns Greeks either exclusively or in the main, along with their Hellenic culture of philosophy, other erudition, polytheistic icon worship and homoerotic sexual mores. This interpretation, though no more conclusive than the second reading, is an equal contender with it. The truth suppressors seemed obviously Greek to Paul's earliest exegetes for the following reasons. In Rom 1:14, Paul unambiguously distinguishes between "Greek and barbarian, wise and foolish" Gentiles. The Greeks are conceivably "the wise" as opposed to "the foolish" barbarian Gentiles. If true, as the first supporters of the Romans polemic believed, then it is redundant for Paul to belabor the obvious and explicitly name the Greeks again in his description of the so-called erudite culture in Romans 1:18-32. The stereotype mores Paul targets in this passage indicated clearly enough to them that he had the Greeks exclusively or chiefly in mind. No other culture besides the Greeks so well fits the cluster of traits toward which Paul directs his ire: polytheistic icons with a primary emphasis on anthropomorphism, the prominence of "wise men [σοφοί]" whose knowledge stems from dialectical reasoning, and openly homoerotic sexual practices. Thus at any rate Paul's earliest exegetes thought, regardless of whether anyone would agree with them today.[12]

One would be imprudent to dismiss the historically primary interpretation as impossible on the grounds that whenever Paul uses the term 'Greeks' he always means 'Gentiles' as a whole. No such synonymy holds for the crucial verse in question, Romans 1:14. There Paul directs his Gentile mission to "Greeks and barbarians, wise ones and foolish," which clearly differentiates Gentiles into two separate subgroups, Greek and barbarian Gentiles.[13] The remaining phrase in Romans 1:14, "wise ones and foolish," leaves Paul's patristic readers free to identify the Greeks as the wise ones, which they did. On that basis they then interpreted Romans 1:18-32 as Paul's stunning reversal and exposé about Hellenic wisdom and culture. Greek reasoning, far from being genuinely wise, provoked wrongful rebellion against God, remains egregiously misleading, and has led Hellenic culture into defiled perversions. Nonetheless, in the text of Romans itself the identity of Paul's "truth-suppressing people" remains undeniably open-ended, which likely precludes a modern consensus about the cultural identity of the people Paul had in mind. Be that as it may, the first trend in interpreting Romans 1:18-32 is the one that matters the most historically. Its effects on late antique religious values do not depend on whether it managed to get Paul's meaning right or would win acceptance today. Church fathers who support the Romans polemic first identify the apostate truth suppressors as Greeks exclusively or primarily among Gentiles and summon them back to God, as I will show below. Ancient Greek religion has not recovered since.[14]

Romans 1:18-32 offers a revolution in religious ideology because Christians who support it in principle must not tolerate the peoples assigned the truth-suppressing role. Polytheistic practices are absolutely forbidden to Israel by biblical law. Rebellious community members who worship gods other than or in addition to the Lord are brazenly in the wrong. Their practices defile the collective group and put the community at risk of suffering God's wrath. Such wrongdoers must be brought back to God in order to keep the community of believers safe and sound. Jeremiah 2:4-5 issues one such summons.[15] This strict religious code, however, applies only to members and to newcomers who convert and become members. Polytheistic outsiders, however, such as Greeks and other Gentiles, may be fools in terms of Hellenistic Jewish polemic, but they are religiously bearable fools, so long as they remain outside the covenant and do not impose polytheistic mores on the historical promised land and temple precinct. If some of the theologically blind Gentiles come to follow the ways of biblical monotheism, all the better. Yet, there is no religious justification or motive for compelling them to con-

010 Kathy L. Gaca

vert and become members. The polemical argument in Romans, however, offers precisely such a justification because it reclassifies such a vaguely designated group of Gentiles as egregiously aberrant insiders. To outlaw their deviant polytheism and return the people to God is the stance Paul's adherents must take in order to act on their conception of good faith. Romans 1:18-32 therefore presents nothing like a tame replica of the first polemic against polytheism, which criticizes Greeks and other Gentiles for being genuine religious aliens with little or no brain when it comes to thinking about God.[16]

The Persistence of the First Argument in Early Christianity

Paul's argument does not become influential immediately. It appears nowhere else in the New Testament, apostolic fathers, or the earliest Christian apologists. Apart from Romans 1:18-32, these Christian arguments against polytheism proceed with business as usual and wage the Hellenistic Jewish polemic in a Christian mode. Paul as a character in Acts preaches in Athens that "God set aside the times of ignorance by bringing the news [viz. the Christian gospel] to human beings." Residents of Athens had at most inchoate inklings about God. As shown by their altar to "the unknown God," the inhabitants of Athens "worship in ignorance" the god whose identity Paul knows and is trying to impart for the first time (Acts 17:30, 23).[17] In Eph 4:17-18, similarly, it is "ignorance" about God that leads "the Gentiles to go about foolish in their mind, darkened in their thoughts, alien to the life of God, and hardened in their hearts." While Ephesians deplores the unreceptivity of Gentiles, Ignatius celebrates the conversions gained so far. Thanks to Christ, "ignorance has been put to an end" within his religious community (*Eph* 19.3). The *Didache* likewise supports the theory of Gentile ignorance by alluding to Genesis. People who have not yet become Christian "do not know the one who created them" (5.2). Lastly, the *Epistle to Diognetus* contends that Gentiles and Jews alike did not know God prior to Christ's coming because Christ's intervention alone makes such knowledge attainable. "Who among human beings knew anything at all about what God is before he [the son of God] came?" All were in the dark hitherto (7.2, 8.1-11). The New Testament and apostolic writings thus explain Gentile polytheism by the same terms that the Hellenistic Jewish polemicists used. *Diognetus* further extends the ignorance into a broadly non-Christian human condition that encompasses Jew and Gentile alike.

The belief that religiously alien ignorance motivates polytheism remains in force among the early Christian apologists Aristides, Justin, Athenagoras, and Theophilus.[18] Aristides classifies Gentiles into three leading ethnic divisions of increasingly mindless theology (2.1). Chaldaeans do not know God, Greeks are even more vacuous, and Egyptians are the most mindless of the three (3.2, 8.1-2, 12.1).

Theophilus emphasizes the folly of the Greeks in particular. Greek writers "neither themselves knew the truth nor turned others to the truth" about God (3.3). "Let there be light" never illumined them, even though they were acquainted with Genesis, as indicated by their fumbling attempts to imitate it in Hesiod's *Theogony* and Plato's *Timaeus*. "Although they took their starting points from there [that is, Genesis] in dealing with the creation of the world . . ., they did not declare any chance spark worthy of the truth." Even though the poets and philosophers began their cosmologies by reading Genesis, the cosmologies they then produced show how poorly they understood and imitated Moses (2.12, 3.16). Their inability to understand Moses, though, is understandable, for Greeks in the time of Hesiod and Plato had emerged from illiteracy only in the recent past, unlike the Hebrews (3.30).[19] Since Hellenic culture was then somewhat new to the alphabet, their cosmogonies did not yet master the Alpha and the Omega.

Athenagoras gives the argument about Gentile ignorance its most succinct and lucid explanation. "The many [οἱ πολλοί] who accuse us [Christians] of atheism do not have the slightest inkling about what God is [οὐδ ὄναρ τί ἐστι θεὸν ἐγνωκότες]. They are without learning and do not see [ἀμαθεῖς καὶ ἀθεώρητοι] natural and theological reasoning. . . . They go to idols made from matter since they are unable to discern what matter is, what God is, and the extent of the difference between the two [διακρῖναι οὐ δυνάμενοι, τί μὲν ὕλη, τί δὲ θεός, πόσον δὲ τὸ διὰ μέσου αὐτῶν]" (*Presb* 13, 15). For Athenagoras, Plato is the glorious exception who alone among pagans saw the light of biblical monotheism (6). Athenagoras thus embraces Plato's pluralistic monotheism as though it were its biblical counterpart, just as Philo and Josephus do. Theophilus, instead, tries to correct this loose identification of deities in the Greek cosmogonies with the creator god in Genesis.

Justin likewise blames Gentiles for theological ignorance. Human beings have been created with the capacity to know the biblical God, as shown by the teleological argument. Gentiles have never exercised this ability and instead worship gods in the polytheistic manner of the Greeks, Egyptians, and others (*1 Apol* 28.2-3). Justin, however, finds the gods more culpable than the Gentiles themselves, for he thinks the gods are deceptive demons who have conspired to keep pagans in the dark. They foiled, for instance, Socrates' monotheistic insights. Socrates wisely tried "with true reason and due inquiry . . . to draw people" toward biblical monotheism and "away from their demon gods," only to have the demons brand him an atheist and condemn him to death (*1 Apol* 5.1-9). Except for God's enlightened messenger Socrates, pagans never saw the biblical truth. Failing to see beyond the deceptive demons, they killed the messenger instead. Justin, Aristides, Theophilus, and Athenagoras, therefore, adhere to the polemic against polytheism that was dominant through the mid-second century. Pagans

in the ancient Mediterranean are foolish religious aliens who never
knew about God in the past.[20] Socrates and Plato, however, are heroic
exceptions to this rule according to Justin and Athenagoras, just as they
are for Philo and Josephus as well. Ps.-Solomon and Theophilus allow
for no exceptions. Ps-Solomon places the philosophers one step away
from theological truth. Theophilus sees the cosmological poets and philosophers as Hellenic children trying too soon to imitate the sublimity
of Moses.

The Reception of the Pauline Argument
from Tatian through Chrysostom

Paul's argument in Romans 1:18-32 starts to come into its own in
Tatian's *Oratio ad Graecos*. The new polemic thereafter gains the support of church fathers who read Romans in Greek and wrote in Greek
themselves, such as Clement of Alexandria, Origen, Athanasius,
Gregory Nazianzen, and John Chrysostom. The Romans polemic also
receives the endorsement of Latin church fathers, such as Lactantius,
Augustine, and Ambrosiaster,[21] though my concern here is with the
patristic writers who wrote in Greek. The latter group, despite their
somewhat freeform explications of Romans 1:18-32, broadcast ideas
that are unparalleled in the first tradition: Apostates are in fact lurking
among the Gentiles; their identity is Hellenic exclusively or primarily;
and the Greeks' foolish wisdom reveals itself most damningly in the
philosophers who led the rebellion. Paul's mention of renegade σοφοί
in 1:22 is what incites the polemicists to travesty philosophers as the
leaders.

Tatian, unlike his former teacher Justin, ardently supports the polemic
in Romans 1:18-32. In his *Oratio ad Graecos*, he identifies the Greeks
as the truth suppressors and extends Paul's charge of apostasy to include
the Olympian gods as well. The teleological revelation in Romans 1:20
and its related accusation anchor Tatian's new faith in "the one sole
divine ruler of the universe." "We grasp the unseen nature of his [God's]
power through his works [τῆς δυνάμεως αὐτοῦ τὸ ἀόρατον τοῖς
ποιήμασι καταλαμβανόμεθα]."[22] His description of God's indirectly visible power refers succinctly to Romans 1:20: "His [God's] unseen
attributes are visible to the mind's eye through his works since the creation of the world, as well as his eternal power and divine nature, so
that they [the truth-suppressors] are without excuse [τὰ γὰρ ἀόρατα
αὐτοῦ ἀπὸ κτίσεως κόσμου τοῖς ποιήμασιν νοούμενα καθορᾶται, ἥ τε
ἀΐδιος αὐτοῦ δύναμις καὶ θειότης, εἰς τὸ εἶναι αὐτοὺς
ἀναπολογήτους]." Paul does not go so far as to charge that the Greek
gods too are apostates without excuse. Tatian does go this far, however,
because he reworks Justin's idea that the gods are deceptive demons. As
go the Greeks, so go their wicked gods as apostate demons, not as mere
deceivers. Once upon a time, demon angels, "their ringleader Zeus"

and "people [ἄνθρωποι]" committed high treason against God and were expelled from sharing in his presence (8.18-19, cf 7.17-29). Though Tatian uses Paul's vague term ἄνθρωποι to designate the truth-suppressors, the people he targets are worshippers of Zeus. Hence, he identifies the apostates as the Hellenic ancestors of his Greek contemporaries. Since that time the Greeks have led their religious lives as outrageously self-deluded dupes of the rebel Olympian angels, such as Aphrodite, Artemis, Poseidon, Athena, and, of course, Zeus (7.29-8.3, 8.18-9.23). Since the gods' "insurrection [ἐπανάστασις]" (13.26), God has fallen from the Greeks' historical memory and they seem not to know him (28.5-6, cf 14.12-13, 20-21). Tatian accordingly makes every effort to reawaken their memory. The Greeks and their gods are guilty of the religious practices they have been committing ever since the gods "threw off the reins [ἀφηνιάσαντες]" of God (13.22). Hellenes likewise "have plundered God and dishonor his creation" because they are accomplices of those "brigands of deity," the Olympians who stole biblical monotheism and parceled it out amongst themselves (11.13-14, 13.22). Therefore, Greeks and their gods are not ignorant outsiders according to Tatian, but blindly rebellious insiders who sacked their original heritage of Christian monotheism in order to fabricate the spurious polytheism they now wrongly follow.

The rebellion against God has tainted the Hellenic culture of philosophy and erudition throughout. As Paul states, the truth-suppressing σοφοί failed to give God thanks and instead exchanged his truth for their lie of renegade wisdom. Since the wise men are Greeks by Tatian's reading, he proudly denounces the condition of having once been a Greek by education himself.[23] Having been saved from Hellenic culture, he now divulges the real exposé about philosophy, the height of Greek wisdom. The philosophers who marveled at the sky and its formative principles did not make an incomplete or complete move in the right direction of biblical monotheism, as they do in the first polemical tradition. Rather, beginning with Thales they looked up only to fall into the pit of idolatry and other crazed products of philosophical thought.[24] Heraclitus fittingly died caking himself with his own excrement, a medical procedure on par with his philosophical ideas. Other philosophers are similarly vicious fools, including Plato, Aristotle, and Zeno the Stoic (2.17-4.19). Greek philosophers are Tatian's paragon rebels because Paul contends that falsely so-called wise men were the mad inventors of polytheistic icon worship. If Greeks are Paul's apostates, as Tatian believes, then Greek philosophical thought is at the root of the truth-suppressing evil. The sphere of Hellenic wisdom, however, extends beyond philosophy to all branches of their learning. Tatian accordingly condemns the culture of Greek erudition throughout. Poetry, drama, medicine, astrology, political theory, and tales about the Greek gods – the glory that was Greece is one big lie concocted by the gods in

league with their Hellenic followers. Hence the Greeks are unconditionally obligated to return to God, as Tatian, like a preacher, declares
to them in the collective first person voice. The search they must make
is an act of "looking again [ἀναζητεῖν]" for God, not looking for the
first time, because they search for "what we once had and lost, the holy
spirit and union with God" (16.4-6). Therefore the seething indignation
coursing throughout the *Oratio ad Graecos* is not, as it has often been
judged, an idiosyncratic fanaticism grounded in the first polemic that
Gentiles are theologically ignorant outsiders. Rather, Tatian's anger
breaks through the clouds because the Romans polemic elicits his light-
ning against the brazen Greeks.[25]

Clement of Alexandria, like Tatian, exhorts the Greeks in particular
to repent and be saved because he too identifies them as Paul's apostate
truth suppressors. In his *Protrepticus ad Graecos* Clement clearly
interprets Romans 1:18-32 to mean that Greeks must retrieve themselves from their apostate condition and go back to the Christian mode
of biblical monotheism.[26] "The holy apostle of the Lord accuses the
Greeks [τοὺς "Ελληνας] by saying that 'even though they know God,
they have refused to honor him as God or to give him thanks. Instead
they became senseless in their acts of reasoning and exchanged the glory
of God for an image of a human being, and they worshipped the created
world instead of the creator'" (*Protrept* 81.2, cf Rom 1:21, 23, 25).
Clement's "Ελληνες are the Greeks, with their Olympian gods, drama,
tales, and mystery religions – not Gentiles at large (1.1-2.2, 11.1-22.7).
Clement thus sees the icons of the Greek gods not as dumb wood,
marble, or bronze shaped by equally dumb makers, which is what the
polemicists in the first tradition saw when they viewed them. Rather, he
sees well-sculpted proof that the Greeks rebelliously hold God in egre-
gious disdain. "How are you [Greeks] not irreverent?" Clement presents this rhetorical question after he links Paul's accusation with
Genesis 1:1. Even though, as Paul states, the Greeks knew God, who "in
the beginning made heaven and earth" (81.3), they blatantly exchanged
their right reverence in favor of worshipping the created world. So of
course, they are outrageously irreverent.

Clement traces the Greeks' disobedient reverence for the material
world back to some Presocratic philosophers, such as Thales, whose
malady of "senseless wisdom [ἄσοφος σοφία]" led them to posit material first principles in place of the transcendent god of Genesis (64.1-3).
Clement diagnoses Thales and other Presocratics with senseless wisdom
because he identifies their ideas about the nature of the world and immanent deity with the false wisdom Paul condemns in Romans 1:22.
"Claiming to be wise, they [the truth suppressors] proved to be fools"
and worshipped the created world instead of God. Hence, as Clement
urges, the Greeks must "abandon the old way of life, which is wicked,
full of passion, and godless" (89.2). Since Presocratic ideas about mate-

rial first principles are wickedly forgetful rather than ignorant, leading as he thinks they did to polytheistic icons, the Greeks must undergo recovered memory and consign the Presocratics to oblivion. "Let us do away with, let us do away with our forgetfulness about the truth [τὴν λήθην τῆς ἀληθείας]!" (114.1). Similarly the Greeks must "run back [παλινδρομήσητε]" to God in heaven rather than run there for the first time (27.1), just as they must seek him anew according to Tatian, for "they abandoned the straight, right path" (27.4, *SibOr* fr. 1.23-5). These same allegations also appear in ps.-Justin.[27] To this notable extent, therefore, Clement advocates the innovative patristic view inspired by Romans, and when he advocates it, he becomes strident. As Paul divulges, there are apostates in the Gentile world, and the culprits are the Greeks. In light of Romans 1:22, Clement blames the Presocratics in particular for dragging Hellenic culture down into polytheistic mores. Tatian, by contrast, finds all Greek philosophers chiefly to blame for the foolish wisdom that has led the Greeks into religious deviance.

Clement nonetheless vacillates in the *Protrepticus* on the support he gives to the view that the Greeks once knew and have suppressed their knowledge about God. Both polemical traditions compete for his recognition and respect. Clement's fitful stance is historically valuable for two reasons. First, it reflects the mixed signals being brought to Christian polemics by the increasing authority of Paul's argument in Romans. Second, when Clement switches back and supports the first polemic, his disposition toward Greek philosophy improves markedly. This further indicates how the first polemic does not lead to hostility toward Greek philosophy, while that based on Romans does. In the *Protrepticus*, Clement occasionally reverts to the first argument that the Greeks are theologically foolish outsiders. He states, for instance, that "ignorance" is the underlying origin of Hellenic polytheism and other customs not in keeping with Mosaic law (99.2, 108.1-5, cf 23.1). Greeks unfamiliar with Christian monotheism thus have "ignorance" as their "pardon for the error" of their ancestral ways (100.2). Clement technically cannot have it both ways. The Greeks are motivated to be polytheistic either from ignorance or suppressed knowledge about God, not both. When Clement maintains the former, however, he adopts a more forgiving stance.

Clement in the *Protrepticus* similarly fluctuates about the religious status and worth of Hellenic wisdom. Learned Greeks such as the philosophers, he later states, had scintillating inklings about the word of God, but they never fully knew him. Much as they admirably tried to think like Moses, "they did not reach their goal" (74.7). This statement follows the first polemic as we have seen it in ps.-Solomon and Theophilus, not Clement's line about the Presocratics' egregiously ἄσοφος σοφία that he spins from Romans 1:22-23. When he supports the first polemic, further, then he makes the Greek philosophers as a whole earnest in their worthy quest for the biblical God – and recommended reading for Christians. This is the position Clement adopts in the *Stromateis*, which is frequently cited to show how enlightened the church fathers could be toward Greek philosophy. "The philosophical groups [and others] could be shown to have some share in the word of truth, some a considerable amount, others a small segment, as it happens" (1.57.1-6). Clement's *Protrepticus* therefore is of two conflicting minds about the religious status of the Greeks and the worth of philosophy. In light of Paul, the Hellenes are intolerably rebellious insiders who should repent and condemn their natural philosophers to oblivion. In light of the first polemical tradition, however, the Greeks are forgivably ignorant outsiders who should learn, emulate, and try to surpass the imperfect monotheism and first principles of their philosophers. Clement knows and tries to respect the first tradition, yet he also feels the need to honor "the holy apostle of the Lord" and the growing stature of Paul's divergent argument (81.2). He prefers to be of two minds in the *Protrepticus* rather than slight either authority. Clement later grows to favor the first polemic in the *Stromateis*. This is what saves him from adopting the unrelenting stance against Hellenism that Tatian takes.

Origen, unlike Clement, consistently endorses Paul's idea that there are Gentile truth suppressors.[28] Though he too identifies them as Greeks, he does not imagine that Hellenic culture as a whole is in rebellion, let alone humanity at large. Rather, as he states in *Contra Celsum* and his commentary on Romans, God's wrath in Rom 1:18 strikes only those who are genuinely qualified to be truth suppressors: "ira dei nunc revelari dicitur non . . . in omnes homines, sed in illos solos, qui veritatem dei in iniquitate detinent." The truth suppressors belong to the Greek intellectual elite, "those who are wise and learned about this world or philosophers" (*Comm in Rom* 16.134.17-20, 136.7-8). Like Tatian and Clement, Origen locates the rebellion in Greek philosophy. "Paul, who is a lover of the truth, says about some Greek sages, that they knew God wherein what they say is true . . . and he bears witness that they knew God" (*Cels* 3.47). The Greek sages, however, abandoned God, as Origen further testifies in light of Romans 1:19-23. "We bear true witness about some Greek philosophers, that they knew God 'since God revealed it to them' even though 'they did not glorify or give him thanks as God, but became senseless in their reasoning. Claiming to be wise, they proved to be fools, and they exchanged the glory of the incorruptible God for the image of a perishable human being, winged, four-footed, and belly-crawling creatures'" (*Cels* 4.30, cf 3.47). Since their transgression happened "not in ignorance, but with knowledge about the truth [non in ignorantia sed in scientia veritatis]" (*Comm in Rom* 16.138.17), "'they are without excuse,'" just as Paul states. "Though they knew God from his revelation, they did not honor or give him thanks as was fit, but through the vanity of their own thoughts they sought forms and images in God, wasted God's image on themselves, and fell into the deep dark depths of stupidity even though they seemed to boast that they were in the light of wisdom" (*Comm in Rom* 17.144.4-10). Therefore Paul's "accusation of impiety [crimen impietatis]" has rightly exposed them (*Comm in Rom* 16.140.11-17).

Origen screens the Greek philosophers to see which ones Paul rightly accuses of suppressing the truth. In his line-up of suspects are all the philosophers who have dealt with physics and metaphysics. They are the ones "whose discipline it is to engage in disputations about created things of the world and all things made in it, and then, through the visible things, to infer by reason those things that are unseen" (*Comm in Rom* 17.142.19-22). Origen dismisses many such philosophers as innocent because their thought disallows the intelligible world and a transcendent god in favor of the position that all things are physical, including immanent deity in pluralistic forms. For Origen, philosophers with no transcendent god never attained any truth to suppress, as indicated by their wild ideas that God is strictly immanent, physically grounded, and as such susceptible to mutability. Hence, their limited wisdom pertains only to "the cosmos [σοφία τοῦ κόσμου]" as opposed to "God [σοφία θεοῦ]" as he truly is beyond the phenomenal world. The Stoics are Origen's primary example of philosophers whose thought is too materialistic to be truth suppressing. As their physical logos shows, they shamelessly envisioned God as a material substance subject to change and to corruption (*Cels* 1.21, cf 3.47). Thus the Stoics "were unable to clearly perceive the natural idea about God, which is that God is imperishable, simple, uncompounded, and indivisible" (*Cels* 4.14, cf 6.71). By the same token, Origen would presumably reverse Tatian's and Clement's condemnation of Presocratics such as Thales, for their conceptions of deity are similarly immanent and physical. As far as Origen is concerned, Clement has identified the wrong philosophers as the truth-suppressing culprits and Tatian is far too indiscriminate in condemning all of them.

Though many Greek philosophers are called, Origen chooses few to know God. The chosen ones recognize the one supreme and transcendent God, such as Plato and the Platonic Socrates.[29] These two philosophers correctly teach that God exists in his kingdom of forms. Plato, when he elucidates the primary good, offers the same truth abstrusely as Matthew, John, Psalms, and Isaiah do more simply and accessibly in their insights into the light of the blessed (*Cels* 6.5). Further, God of Genesis in his ultimate being is "colorless, shapeless, impalpable," just as Socrates observes in the *Phaedrus* (*Cels* 6.19, *Phaedr* 247c6-7). Therefore philosophers such as Plato and Socrates have clearly attained the honor of knowing the one and only God beyond the phenomenal world (*Cels* 6.4). Origen here is expressing the same viewpoint as the one advocated in the first tradition by Philo, Josephus, Athenagoras, and Justin.

In light of Romans 1:22-23, however, Origen has grounds to suspect that Plato and Socrates are chief among the philosophers Paul condemns. Upon completing his investigation, he overturns the honor accorded to Plato, Socrates, and like-minded philosophers in the first tradition. By Origen's reading of Paul, God's chosen few philosophers stand accused of exchanging the truth about God for the lie of polytheism. To his dismay, as he combs Plato's dialogues to verify the charge, he catches Plato and Socrates in the act numerous times. Socrates in the *Phaedo* truly expounds the soul's trials in its ascent toward the biblical God. Then, however, he does just as Paul claims and abandons the truth at the end of the dialogue, where he drivels deceptively about sacrificing a cock to Asclepius (*Cels* 6.4). Even worse, the *Republic* begins with the descent to the Piraeus, where Socrates and Plato commit overt treason against God by attending an inaugural religious festival in honor of Artemis and praying to her.[30] Clearly, then, God's few enlightened philosophers are brazenly without excuse, for they knowingly promote religious falsehood to the Greeks rather than making their crooked ways straight (*Cels* 6.3-4). Their collusion even infects their metaphysical teachings. Plato lapses into idolatrous denial when he states in *Timaeus* 41a6-7 that God is the craftsman and father of the gods (*Cels* 6.10). Likewise the devil himself, "the prince of this realm," must have driven Plato to write in the *Phaedrus* that the souls of the purest departed philosophers "are with Zeus, while others are with other divinities [δαίμονες], some with one, others with another" (*Cels* 8.4, cf *Phaedr* 250b7-8). Through such dead giveaways Plato willfully "corrupted right reverence with idolatry and superstition" (*Cels* 6.17). Origen accordingly condemns the Greek philosophers who are honored for their theology in the first polemical tradition, Plato and Socrates foremost. They cease being heroic pagan visionaries with shining monotheistic insights and instead become glowing fallen angels destined for retribution. "We say that those who have both understood the true things about God and have not exercised a reverence of God worthy of the truth about him are subject to the punishment of sinners" (*Cels* 6.3). There is an element of Greek tragedy here, to see how the best of the Christian Platonists surrenders Plato and Socrates as religious traitors to Paul the lover of truth. There is also a touch of comedy that was no laughing matter for Origen, worthy as it would be of Aristophanes. Socrates goes down once more, condemned yet again, this time because of the chicken.

Athanasius follows and elaborates Romans 1:18-32 with unswerving loyalty in *Contra gentes*, and he takes it as a major statement about Hellenic and Mediterranean culture. He esteems Paul as the "holy interpreter of God's truth, . . . the holy servant of Christ," and as one of the eminent "men of theology" (*Gent* 26.8-9, 35.18-20).[31] Athanasius

accordingly supports the Romans polemic and interprets it as a historical document about how Mediterranean and primarily Hellenic culture
abandoned God long ago. The apostasy that Paul describes in Romans
is a second fall from God. Greeks and other Gentiles are the ones who
lapse into natural philosophy and polytheism, and the Greeks are primarily to blame for fomenting the rebellion and spreading it to other
Gentile peoples. In Athanasius's tale, once upon a time – sometime after the fall of Adam and Eve and before the coming of Christ, the
"people [ἄνθρωποι]" of Romans 1:18 regained enough ground in biblical theology that they once again inferred the invisible God from his
six-day work of creation. Romans provides all the crucial evidence
Athanasius needs. "I say this not on my own authority, but on the basis
of what I have learned from the men of theology, among whom is Paul,
who writes as follows to the Romans, 'God's invisible aspects are visible to the mind's eye through his works since the creation of the cosmos' [Rom 1:20]" (35.18-21). Theological progress came naturally to
humanity descended from Adam and Eve, for nature by design virtually
proclaims Genesis. "Knowledge about revering God and the truth of the
universe ... all but shouts every day in the [world's] works .... Creation
itself practically cries out and demonstrates its creator and maker, God
the ruler of all and father of our Lord Jesus Christ" (1.3-4, 27.16-19).

Despite nature's deafening clarity, the "people" once again fell away
from God, this time to contrive polytheistic idolatry and its deviant
sexual ways, just as Romans states. The first people are the Greeks.[32]
To underscore the enormity of their religious rebellion, Athanasius reinterprets ps.-Solomon's argument that "the discovery of idols is the corruption of life" (9.48, 11.1-3). Again, for ps.-Solomon, the discovery of
idols is rooted in religiously alien ignorance or κενοδοξία (11.2-23).
Athanasius recasts this discovery so that it becomes the second deliberate fall from God that Paul narrates in Romans (7.33-36). On this occasion, a particularly mad group of Gentiles, the Greeks, succumbed to
pleasure in their souls. As a result they once more "forgot the idea and
view about God," and then they contrived polytheistic corruption in
their collective soul (8.26-28). "The soul, teeming with every kind of
fleshly appetition . . ., finally fashioned in bodily and visible ways God
whom it had forgotten in its thought, attributing the name of God to
phenomena and glorifying these alone as it wishes and sees as pleasur-
able" (8.14-18). With their minds thus darkened,[33] the Greeks led other
Gentiles into polytheistic apostasy in precisely the manner Paul
describes. Their Gentile mind "leapt away from God" into the pitch-
dark depths of their own theological devices (9.1, 8.21-34). They are
thus without excuse for failing to remain biblical monotheists. Hellenic
culture is especially to blame among Gentiles because the Greeks
first "cut themselves off from the truth" and flagrantly "deny God"
(29.47-48, 26.25). Hence "the Greeks must not make any excuses [μὴ

προφατιζέσθωσαν ''Ελληνες] in defense of worshipping idols" (30.12-
13). They have only themselves to blame for their indefensible alliance
with Zeus, Aphrodite, and other Olympian gods. "If they had consulted
the mind of their soul, they would not have fallen entirely headfirst into
such practices and denied the true God, the father of Christ" (26.23-26),
which they manifestly did.

Athanasius chiefly blames philosophers with material first principles
for leading the Greeks and other Gentiles over the polytheistic edge. He
also finds room to blame Plato and Socrates as well in light of Origen's
argument. Athanasius groups the natural philosophers together as
"falsely so-called sages [δοκησίσοφοι]" because he identifies them as the
ones who "became senseless while claiming to be wise [φάσκοντες εἶναι
σοφοί, ἐμωράνθησαν]" in Paul's polemic in Rom 1:22. "The falsely so-
called sages reject God the father of Jesus Christ, yet they bow down to
and deify his creation" (27.19-21). The natural philosophers rejected
God by grounding deity strictly in the cosmos, as the Stoics do. "The
falsely so-called sages will say that the universe is God . . . [and] is
adequate and sufficient unto itself in all respects" (28.12-14). This
particular conception of deity and the phrasing used to describe it stems
from Chrysippus and other Stoics.[34] Athanasius finds it shocking even
to think, as they do, that God and the universe might be coextensive,
with neither need nor place for a transcendent god. "See what great
irreverence they utter against God by saying these things!" (28.21-22).
Greeks and other Gentiles follow fast on the heels of the natural philosophers, and they plummet even farther down than the foolish Greek
sages. Most drop like the stones they come to worship. Their increasingly corrupt sequence of gods reveals their relative states of theological decline. First comes the worship of the universe, with its stars,
planets, and related astral forces, and then gods depicted as ether and
air. Pagans at this level, such as the natural philosophers, revere creation and no longer hear nature's outcries about God's transcendence
(27.22-28.27). The majority of pagans plunge even deeper into poly-
morphous perversity: anthropomorphic icons of men, aniconic stones
and wood, crawling creatures, fantastic creatures, icons of sexual desire
and pleasure, emperor worship, boy worship by emperors, and lastly –
immediately before pagans descend into a coma about God the father
and son – anthropomorphic icons of women. "If only the madness for
idols had stopped with males and did not pitch downward to the point
of addressing the divine name to females! Yes, even women, who cannot be trusted even in public affairs, even women they honor and revere
with the glory due God!" (9.5-10.16). Athanasius thus finds the Piraeus
incident of religious treason especially shocking. When "Socrates and
Plato went down to the Piraeus," they were not merely leaders in
betraying God, as already shown by Origen. They were also helping
inaugurate a festival to honor the lowest of the low, one of those woman

gods (10.36-7).[35] Greeks and other Gentiles, since their second fall, are now all in the truth-suppressing condition that Paul delineates. They exchanged their inferential knowledge about God for the retributive condition of polytheism that they pass off as a bona fide religious heritage.[36] Formerly polytheistic Christians, Greek and barbarian alike, therefore must never again fall for Greek philosophical conceptions of deity. They need only look to Paul, as Athanasius does, to learn about the blight that struck them the first time they fell for such ideas and embraced immanent and pluralistic notions of God. Christians, instead, must always remember that "the Greeks tell mythology, not theology," just as we see in the web that Athanasius spins from Romans (19.34-35).[37]

John Chrysostom outstrips even Athanasius in ardently supporting Romans 1:18-32. In his *Homilies on the Letter to the Romans*,[38] Paul is his definitive theologian. "Let us open our eyes to the light of [Paul] the apostle's words so as not to proceed in the most impenetrable darkness, for indeed his tongue shone more brightly than the sun" (*Preface*, 1). By Chrysostom's reading, Rom 1:18-27 singles out the Greeks alone for being renegades against God. Only in Rom 1:28-32 does Paul broaden his cultural scope with the list of vices pertaining to all Gentiles. "Paul, it seems to me, is referring to Greeks ['Ελληνες]" as the recipients of God's punitive wrath in narrative starting at Rom 1:18 (*Hom* 3.1, 448e). The vice list in Rom 1:28-32 deals more generically with the sins of "other persons [ἕτερα πρόσωπα]," namely, "Gentiles [ἔθνη]" in addition to the Greeks (5.1, 460b). Therefore Chrysostom develops Romans 1:18-27 against "Ελληνες in no loose sense of the word.[39] He means Hellenic culture.

As Chrysostom clearly recognizes, apostasy is the formal charge being made in Romans 1:18-27. Paul accuses the Greeks of "the abandonment of God [ἡ τοῦ θεοῦ ἐγκατάλειψις]" (4.1, 455c). This is an accusation made with Septuagint phrasing and apostasy is the crime. In key passages of the Greek Bible, the verb ἐκαταλείπειν signifies that God's people have abandoned the covenant in order to worship other gods.[40] According to Chrysostom, this is the charge that Paul is bringing against the Greeks. He elucidates Paul's accusation by citing Jer 2:13 to explain Rom 1:21. To Paul's assertion, "'though they know God, they have refused to honor him or give him thanks as God' [Rom 1:21]," he adds Jeremiah's indictment: "They worshipped idols, just as Jeremiah said in this accusation: 'This people [ὁ λαὸς οὗτος] has done two wicked things. They abandoned [ἐγκατέλιπον] me, the fountain of living water, and they dug for themselves broken cisterns' [Jer 2:13]" (3.2, 450b). In Chrysostom's mind, however, ὁ λαὸς οὗτος in Jeremiah breaks from its historical grounding (Jews in the late seventh or early sixth century BCE) and incorporates the Greeks. He gains warrant for making the transfer given the cultural identity he gives to Paul's truth-suppressing people. Who are Paul's ἄνθρωποι? They are "this people," the Greeks. Hence, like Jeremiah's audience, so too have the Greeks shamelessly turned away from God the fountain in favor of polytheistic drought. Chrysostom astutely grasps that Paul is making "an enormous accusation [ἔγκλημα μέγιστον]" (3.2; 450b), not some tepid rendition of the Hellenistic Jewish polemic with which the apostle was familiar in the mid-first century. Chrysostom also commends Paul's verbal fire for being well placed under Hellenic culture and leaps ardently to fan the flames. The Greeks are guilty of "abandoning the fear of God" (4.3, 458d), and of "dismissing God" altogether (5.2, 461c). To understand the motives for his zeal, we need to explore his understanding of Paul's teleological revelation.

Chrysostom urgently endorses Paul's position that the teleological argument is a manifest revelation to Greeks and all Gentiles, not only to the Greeks. God of Genesis exists, as everyone undeniably knows from the world he designed in six days. All Gentiles know God, there-fore, but only the Greeks committed apostasy. Chrysostom highlights that the Greeks in particular were in on the revelation. "How is it clear, Paul, that God implanted knowledge [about himself] in the Greeks? Because, as Paul says, 'Knowledge of God is manifestly in them.'" Chrysostom then urges Paul to prove the assertion that the Greeks are apostates. "Paul, get ready and demonstrate that knowledge of God was clearly in them [viz. the Greeks] and that they willingly ran away. How was it clear to them?" (3.2, 449d). As ostensible proof Chrysostom simply restates Paul's teleological revelation in such a way as to make the Greeks more stupid than barbarians if they deny the veracity of Paul's assertion. "God set creation in their [the Gentiles'] midst, so that the wise and foolish, Scythian and barbarian alike learned how to infer God from the beauty of the visible world. And so Paul states, 'God's invisible characteristics became visible to the mind's eye through his works from the creation of the cosmos.'" Chrysostom thus gives the Greeks one of two choices. They either admit that they have known God all along, or else they shamefully lose face to the barbarians, who learned about God at the same time as the Greeks. "So then, what will the Greeks say on that day [of judgment], that 'we did not know you, God,' merely because you did not hear a voice from heaven" making the proper announcement? (3.2, 449d-e). Therefore, "God set forth the cosmos as a form of religious teaching in our midst," so that all Gen-tiles, Greeks and barbarians alike, know God and are obliged to fear him and follow his laws (3.3, 452b).

Though all Gentiles know God, only the Greeks had the intellectual audacity and innovative spirit to abandon God and become polytheistic truth suppressors. This crucial move in Chrysostom's interpretation turns on Paul's declaration that the truth suppressors "traded [ἤλλαξαν]" God for idols and thereby "traded in [μετήλλαξαν]" God's truth for a lie (Rom 1:23, 25). The Greeks "traded [ἤλλαξαν]" their knowledge of God

for polytheistic ways because of their penchant for intellectual innovation. "They wanted to discover something more, rather than remaining
within the ordained limits. In this way they fell away from the limits,
for they lusted after new ideas [καινοτομία] – all such traits are characteristically Greek ones" (3.3, 451a).[41] If only Hellenic culture were not
so trendy, the Greeks would never have invented polytheism and for-
saken the religious fountain of their ancestors, "the one God, the Lord
of all, the one who created them from nothing, God with providence
and mercy" (3.3, 451c).

The religious problem of the Greeks, however, runs far deeper than
setting new trends. The Greeks fell into rebellion because of their deep
trust in the power of reasoning and the discipline of the mind. "Paul
establishes the cause through which they fell into such great folly. They
trusted entirely in their acts of reason [τοῖς λογισμοῖς]" (3.2, 450c). As
Paul states, the truth suppressors "became senseless in their acts of reasoning [τοῖς διαλογισμοῖς] and their foolish heart was darkened" (Rom
1:21-23). Plato and Socrates, further, are the main philosophers to
blame for stimulating such trust in reason. Like Origen, Chrysostom
brandishes the Socratic chicken to silence the view that Greek philosophers are honorably inclined toward biblical monotheism. "This
Socrates of yours was the one who ordered that a cock be sacrificed to
Asclepius" (Hom 3.3, 451d).[42] According to Chrysostom, therefore, only
the Greeks, and their philosophers especially, could have invented polytheistic icon worship in flagrant disobedience to God, for only they
believed in and fostered human reason. Christians, accordingly, must
never again value rationality and its trends more than the recovery of
Christian doctrine from their suppressed memory. Reason on its own is
insubordinate and leads to many gods.

Chrysostom finds the apostasy of the Greeks written right into their
language. As Paul rightly detects, the Greeks have a distinctively Hellenic way of letting slip unawares that they know the biblical God.
Whenever they use the word θεός in the singular or plural, this surface
expression reveals their submerged memory of him. "As a sign that they
know God [εἰδέναι τὸν θεόν] and are not using this knowledge as they
should, Paul brings in this point, that they know gods [τὸ θεοὺς
ἐγνωκέναι]" (3.2, 450b-c). Hence whenever the Greeks use the holy
word θεός in the singular or plural, their choice of vocabulary itself
confesses that there is no God but God, which the Greeks knew long ago
and left unburied in their language, try as they may to pretend otherwise.

Chrysostom tells parables to drive home his invective against the
apostate Greeks. First, a royal treasurer takes the king's wealth entrusted to him and wastes it on thieves, whores, and magicians (3.2,
449b). Thus are the Greeks, who have squandered their knowledge of
God upon Olympians and other false gods. Second, a king's son dis-
honors his father and instead keeps company with thieves, murderers,

and tomb-robbers (3.3, 452c). Likewise the Greeks have dishonored God the father and creator through their truth-suppressing innovation of "'worshipping the created world' [Rom 1:25]" in place of the creator (3.4, 452d-e). Just as the king leaves his rebellious son in such bad company to teach him a hard lesson, God has abandoned his Greek children to the lawless and low-life gods of their own devising. The son, of course, must repent and return to his father. So too must the Greeks make a Hellenic exodus back to God the father from their Olympian penal colonies. Gregory Nazianzen similarly views Hellenic religion as a penal system brought about by God punishing the truth-suppressing Greeks for their rebellion.[43]

Conclusion

Romans 1:18-32 offers a highly unusual polemic against polytheistic and 'truth-suppressing' people. The exact identity of this people remains open-ended in Romans. The church fathers who wrote in Greek, however, identify the truth suppressors as exclusively or primarily Hellenic. This is historically the first of three conflicting ideas about the people's identity. Paul's argument is unusual because he recasts the Hellenistic Jewish teleological argument into an undeniable revelation from God and asserts that the revelation is known to the people in question. He also redefines humanity in general as the new Israel, which he takes as license to transfer Septuagint passages about rebellious Israel to the allegedly truth-suppressing people. Paul thereby radically reclassifies their polytheistic culture as an unbearably apostate one.

Before, during, and in the first century after Paul lived, the Hellenistic Jewish and early Christian polemicists continued to attribute polytheism to foolish ignorance. They classified Gentiles, including the Greeks, as religious outsiders who neither recognized nor had any affiliation with the biblical God, and never did. This argument is revisionist to the extent that it reclassifies natural law in Greek philosophy as God's Pentateuchal law and interprets the numerous projects of Greek philosophical monotheism as a search for biblical monotheism, with a few lucky hits by Plato, Socrates, and other philosophers. Its revisionism is smaller in scope than Paul's polemic. Proponents of this more original view include ps.-Solomon, Josephus, Philo, and the Sibyl, the authors of Acts, Ephesians, and Didache, as well as Aristides, Theophilus, Athenagoras, Justin, and Clement in the *Stromateis*.

Paul's argument in Romans remained uninfluential until the later second century. Beginning with Tatian's *Oratio ad Graecos* (ca 176), various patristic writers start to hoist Paul's argument through their exegesis and unfurl some of the most striking banners of revisionist history brought to us from antiquity.[44] The Greeks are transformed into apostate renegades who defile themselves through their punitive condition of philosophical reasoning, icon worship, and homoerotic sexual relations. They drag other Gentiles down along with them according to Athanasius and Lactantius. Hellenic or Gentile culture as a whole consequently needs to be summoned back to God and purified of such practices. Proponents of this argument include Tatian, Clement in sections of the *Protrepticus*, ps.-Justin, Origen with regard to particular Greek philosophers, Athanasius, Gregory Nazianzen, and John Chrysostom.

The different tenor of the two arguments against polytheism shows up especially well in the respective stature each accords to Greek philosophy. In the original polemical tradition, the outright vilification of philosophers and philosophy is absent. Instead, this tradition expresses admiration for philosophers having found the biblical God or reasonable disagreement with the Jewish and Christian admirers who assert that the Platonic or Stoic God is the same as the God of the Greek Bible. According to ps.-Solomon and Theophilus, Greek philosophers at least make an effort to attain biblical monotheism, though their handicap of Gentile ignorance proves insurmountable. According to Philo, Josephus, Athenagoras and Justin, philosophers of Plato's and Socrates' caliber heroically overcome their Gentile disadvantage and hobble all the way to the biblical God thanks partly to Moses' tutelage. Polemicists starting from Romans 1:18-32, by contrast, are incited and obliged by Paul's argument to attack Greek philosophers and their ideas, for they designate philosophers as the leaders in the outrageous cabal to suppress the truth about God. The philosophers they target for blame change like Proteus – all of them, the Presocratics, the Stoics, Plato, Socrates, or some combination thereof. The polemicists believe, in response to Romans 1:21-23, that Greek σοφοί fathered the religious rebellion Paul denounces, which is why Greek philosophers of some sort or other remain the constant opponent to wrestle and pin down. The most striking example of the difference between the two arguments is Origen's radical demotion of Plato's and Socrates' stature: They are biblical monotheists, as claimed by Philo and others in the original argument, but traitors to the cause in light of Romans. Plato and Socrates, even though they knew God, went down to the Piraeus to inaugurate more idolatry.

Romans 1:18-32 is but a page long in the New Testament and is anomalous regarding the status of Greek and other polytheistic religions. Nonetheless, unlike the polemical tradition that came before it, the Romans-inspired polemic produced a heady ideology conducive to helping reshape the Mediterranean region into a Christian society. Paul's argument prompts the forbidding and outlawing of whatever religions his supporters deem truth-suppressing and whatever customs they find integral to the apostasy. Hellenic culture is at the forefront of the patristic invective spearheaded by Romans, along with its customs of Greek philosophy and homoerotic sexual relations. The more Paul becomes Christ's theologian par excellence, Romans his definitive tract, and his supporters as prominent as Athanasius, Chrysostom, and

Augustine, the greater this potential for biblically motivated intolerance becomes. By contrast, the initial polemical tradition regarding ignorant religious outsiders allows Hellenistic Jews and early Christians to disapprove of, yet uneasily tolerate, the religious mores of their pagan neighbors. Mere theological fools and religious aliens may be left to their own rituals and other cultural practices, so long as they do not try to impose them on God's adherents. Pagans might see the light of pure monotheism one day, but the bearers of that light do not have a compelling biblical motive to pursue them and close down their temples, as they do in light of Romans 1:18-32.[45]

The increasing authority of the Romans polemic did not, in all likelihood, single-handedly motivate Christian intolerance toward pagan religion in the Roman Empire. Further study is consequently needed in order to grasp the complex historical relationship between the rise of this polemic and the social demise of the Greek and other pagan gods. What I have shown in this article is that the Romans polemic functions as an apostate conspiracy theory, wildly untrue and potent as such theories characteristically are. The further study to be done should concern precisely how the theory relates to the development of Christian intolerance in the late fourth century.

---

* This study was first published as an article in *Harvard Theological Review* 92 (1999), 165-98. Many thanks to the Editor of *Harvard Theological Review*, François Bovon, for permission to reprint it in this collection. This study is substantively the same as the article, aside from minor editorial changes. One editorial change worth mentioning is that this reprint has fewer notes, because many primary sources are cited parenthetically in the text, whereas the article cites all references in footnotes.

[1] The change in policy is reinforced by repressive social mechanisms, such as vandalism against temples and taking away their endowments. For some of the late-fourth century legal measures and social struggles over outlawing pagan religious practices, see, for example, A. H. M. Jones, *The Later Roman Empire 284-602*, (Oxford: Basil Blackwell 1964), 167-9, 938-43, R. MacMullen, *Christianity and Paganism in the Fourth to Eighth Centuries* (New Haven: Yale University Press 1997), 1-73, and A. H. Armstrong, "The Way and the Ways: Religious Tolerance and Intolerance in the Fourth Century A.D.," *VC* 38 (1984), 1-17.

[2] "Christian apology is the daughter of Jewish apology," J. Geffcken, cited with approval in A. J. Droge, *Homer or Moses?* (Tübingen: Mohr 1989), 8, and see Droge's n. 27 for more scholarly opinions to the same effect. So too E. Norden, "Es war althergebrachte Sitte schon vorchristlicher Zeit, den Kampf gegen den Polytheismus mit einer Polemik gegen die Idololatrie zu verbinden," *Agnostos Theos* (Leipzig 1913), 12. Similarly, for J. Daniélou, there is but one "Christian missionary proclamation to the pagan world" worked out in the early apologists, namely, condemnation of myths, philosophical teachings, pagan morals, and religion, *Gospel Message and Hellenistic Culture: A History of Early Christian Doctrine before the Council of Nicaea*, vol. 2, tr. J. A. Baker (Philadelphia: The Westminster Press 1973), 37, 16-24. Likewise J. Quasten, *Patrology* II, 8 and A. J. Festugière as cited by C. A. Forbes, *Firmicus Maternus*, *ACW* 37 (New York: Newman Press 1970), 29, n. 121. The misperception of common substance is most striking in direct comparisons made between Romans 1:18-32 and Hellenistic Jewish polemic, such as Wisdom of Solomon 13-14: B. Byrne (*Romans* [Collegeville,

Minn: Liturgical Press 1996], 65), "These parallels [between Romans and Wisdom of Solomon] show that in 1:18-32 Paul argues out of a defined tradition in Hellenistic Judaism . . . . [H]e . . . [uses] a conventional polemic against the Gentile world and its idolatry"; J. D. G. Dunn (*Romans 1-8* in *Word Biblical Commentary* series [Dallas: Word Books 1988], 61) states, "The argument [in Romans 1:23-27] now becomes almost wholly Jewish by drawing on the standard Jewish polemic against idolatry," and E. P. Sanders (*Paul, the Law, and the Jewish People* [Philadelphia: Fortress Press 1983], 123): "I think that in Rom 1:18-2:29 Paul takes over to an unusual degree homiletic material from Diaspora Judaism, [and] that he alters it in only unsubstantial ways."

[3]Joseph Ziegler, ed., *Sapientia Salomonis* (Göttingen: Vandenhoeck and Ruprecht 1962). This work is conventionally dated in the first century BCE, with Philo of Alexandria (ca 30 BCE-50 CE) providing Wisdom's terminus ante quem. D. Winston (*Wisdom of Solomon: A New Translation with Introduction and Commentary* [Garden City, New York: Doubleday and Company 1979], 20, 59-63) prefers to have ps.-Solomon depend on Philo rather than the reverse and thus is able to suggest that Wisdom dates as late as 37-41 CE. The consensus still stands, I think. Winston's argument would require one to believe that of all writers influenced by Philo (e.g. Clement and Origen), ps.-Solomon alone was able to use Philo's distinctive mix of Platonic and biblical elements without reflecting any of its Platonic aspects. This mix of elements in Philo's thought, however, is merged together and unmistakable, rather like an impressionist painting. Ps.-Solomon simply does not show this Philonic technique, while other writers influenced by Philo do.

[4]As here, 'ignorance' translates ἀγνωσία, ἄγνοια, or other cognate terms in all citations to follow from Hellenistic Jewish and c early Christian arguments against polytheism.

[5]Platonist philosophers make this observation themselves to contest the cogency of the second step in the Hellenistic Jewish and early Christian teleological argument. As Porphyry or a like-minded Platonist philosopher states, "Let us expressly investigate the question concerning the monarchy of the sole God and the manifold rule of the revered gods, because you do not even know how to explain the word 'monarchy'. A monarch is not one who exists alone, but is the only one ruling [others] . . . . [Similarly] God would not rightly be called a monarch unless he ruled gods. For this is fitting to the divine grandeur and great heavenly glory," *Apocriticus of Macarius Magnes*, 4.20, fr. 75 in A. Harnack, *Porphyrius "Gegen di Christen"* (Berlin: König. Akademie der Wissenschaften 1916). Hence "as far as the Platonists are concerned, the monarchy [viz. the supreme sole status] of God is not at all demonstrated," Theophilus, 2.4 and note as well Minucius Felix, *Octavius* 20.2, for popular pagan disbelief in the *unicus deus*. See further P. Courcelle, "Anti-Christian Arguments and Christian Platonism from Arnobius to St. Ambrose," in A. Momigliano, ed., *The Conflict Between Paganism and Christianity in the Fourth Century* (Oxford: Clarendon Press 1963), 158, and G. Fowden (*Empire to Commonwealth: Consequences of Monotheism in Late Antiquity* (Princeton: Princeton University Press 1993), 5. Consequently, the biblically grounded version of the teleological argument should not continue to be identified with its philosophical counterpart, as it is in the following instances. "The author of Wisdom has here reproduced the teleological and cosmological arguments for the existence of God which had already been elaborated by Plato, Aristotle, and the Stoa" Winston, *Wisdom*, 253; "On lisait le même idée [chez Paul et] . . . chez un Stoïcien péripatéticien du Ier siècle de notre ère dont l'oeuvre a été longtemps attribuée à Aristote [viz. *De mundo* 6]," M. J. Lagrange, *St. Paul Épitre aux romains* (Paris: Gabalda 1916), 24, Ambrosiaster provides a valuable corrective to such loose identifications. "God founded such beautiful stars so that he could be recognized [*ut possit agnosci*] and be worshipped alone [*et solus adorari*] as the very great and magnificent creator of them" (*Ad rom* 1.18). The second step, *ut possit solus adorari*, is entirely absent from the pluralistic monotheism of the philosophers, such as ps.-Aristotle, *De mundo* 6, ἀθεώρητος ἀπ' αὐτῶν τῶν ἔργων θεωρεῖται. Winston (*Wisdom*, 253) provides a valuable list of other Greek and Roman expressions of the teleological argument.

The first step of the Jewish teleological argument does not necessarily draw on the Greek philosophical tradition, for the same inchoate idea is in the Septuagint, such as LXX Ps 18:1 Οἱ οὐρανοὶ διηγοῦνται δόξαν θεοῦ, ποίησιν δὲ χειρῶν αὐτοῦ ἀναγγέλλει τὸ στερέωμα.

[6] For Josephus (ca 37 CE-100), nearly all philosophers had sound notions of God that they learned from Moses, but they wisely kept such biblical monotheism out of the populace's reach, *Ap* 2.168-9, 224, *Contra Apionem* in Josephus, LCL vol. 9 (tr. H. St. J. Thackeray 1956).

[7] L. Cohn, P. Wendland, *Philonis Alexandrini: Opera*, (Berlin: Reimer 1896-1930)

[8] J. Geffcken, ed., *Die Oracula Sibyllina* (Leipzig: J. Hinrichs 1902). The passages date to the second BCE, J. J. Collins, "Sibylline Oracles" in J. H. Charlesworth, ed., *The Old Testament Pseudepigrapha*, vol. 1 (Garden City, New York: Doubleday 1983-5), 354-5.

[9] Paul's phrase "They became senseless in their acts of reasoning [ἐματαιώθησαν ἐν τοῖς διαλογισμοῖς αὐτῶν]" echoes both Jer 2:4-5 and LXX Ps 93:11. Jeremiah says about apostate Israel, "Hear the word of the Lord, house of Jacob and the entire fatherland of the house of Israel. The Lord says, 'What fault did your fathers find with me, that they apostasized far from me, went after foolish things, and became senseless?' [ἀκούσατε λόγον κυρίου, οἶκος Ιακωβ καὶ πᾶσα πατριὰ οἴκου Ισραήλ, τάδε λέγει κύριος Τί εὕροσαν οἱ πατέρες ὑμῶν ἐν ἐμοὶ πλημμέλημα, ὅτι ἀπέστησαν μακρὰν ἀπ᾽ ἐμοῦ καὶ ἐπορεύθησαν ὀπίσω τῶν ματαίων καὶ ἐματαιώθησαν]." LXX Ps 93:11 concerns Israel's adversaries (κύριος γινώσκει τοὺς διαλογισμοὺς τῶν ἀνθρώπων ὅτι εἰσὶν μάταιοι). See E. Käsemann, *Commentary on Romans* (Grand Rapids, Michigan: W. B. Eerdmans 1980), 44; C. K. Barrett, *A Commentary on the Epistle to the Romans* 2nd ed. [London: A & C Black 1991), 37; H. Koester, *History and Literature of Early Christianity*, vol. 2 (New York: De Gruyter 1982), 140. Barrett and Koester recognize that Paul's accusation concerns rejected knowledge of God, not ignorance.

[10] *Comm in Rom*, Preface 62.3-4. This and later references to Origen on Romans are to the section, page, and line numbers of T. Heither's edition, *Origenes: Römerbriefkommentar*, vol. 1 (Freiburg: Herder 1990). Paul was active as a Christian missionary roughly from 35-60 or perhaps a little later. On the chronology, see H. Koester, *Early Christianity* 2nd ed., vol. 2 (2000), 105-13.

[11] For example, J. C. Walters, *Ethnic Issues in Paul's Letter to the Romans* (Valley Forge: Trinity Press International 1993), 70. Similarly, Dunn (*Romans 1-8*, 55-6) explicates ἀνθρώπων τῶν τὴν ἀλήθειαν ἐν ἀδικίᾳ κατεχόντων as Paul's statement about the universally sinful human condition. Käsemann and Barrett likewise refer Paul's argument to all humanity.

[12] The prevalence of anthropomorphism in Hellenic religion needs no proof, and zoomorphism also had its place, such as Athena as owl and Zeus as eagle. The Greeks were also well known for their subtle reasoning. "The dreadful thing about the Greeks was that they were so clever, thinking and talking twice as fast as any Roman who confronted them. Brainy Greeks, delighting in the exercise of proving a thesis and then, by clever argument, destroying it, were capable of proving that black was white," J. P. V. D. Balsdon, *Romans and Aliens* (Chapel Hill: The University of North Carolina Press 1979), 33, with primary evidence 30-54. Interestingly, Geffcken (*Zwei griechische Apologeten*, 59-60) briefly interprets Romans 1:22 just as the Greek patristic writers do, though he does not develop its implications for grasping the distinctive force of Paul's polemic. When discussing the trope of clever Greeks who prove to be theological fools, he includes Romans 1:22 as an example of the trope "which begins with Josephus and continues in the other apologists, who are dealing almost exclusively with Greek culture [das beginnt mit Josephus und setzt sich bei den anderen Apologeten weiter fort, *die ja fast nur mit der hellenischen Kultur zu tun haben*]" (italics mine). Some of Paul's patristic exegetes also presumed that what is gay must be Greek (e.g. Chrysostom), as we will see. On the norms behind this association, see K. J. Dover, *Greek Homosexuality*, 2nd ed. (Cambridge, Mass: Harvard University Press 1989)

and W. A. Percy, *Pederasty and Pedagogy in Archaic Greece* (Chicago: University of Illinois Press 1996).

[13] One wonders how Paul would have gotten around in his travels and readings if he followed modern-day exegesis and treated the two cultural designations 'Greeks' and 'Gentiles' as interchangeable, e.g. S. Stowers, "He [Paul] recognizes the dominance of Greek culture in the Roman East by interchanging 'Gentile' and 'Greek'," *A Rereading of Romans* (New Haven: Yale University Press 1994), 277, and see too *BAGD* and *TDNT* under "Ελλην. In Paul's era, "Ελληνες and ἔθνη were not interchangeable. If Paul on his missionary travels were to ask a ship captain to take him to the "Ελληνες, he would be dropped off in the Greek cities where he in fact went, such as Corinth and Thessalonica. Only if he asked to be brought to the ἔθνη would he find himself with a much broader range of places to disembark. The same basic distinction between "Ελληνες and ἔθνη holds true in the Septuagint. In a passage Paul must have known, Joel 4:2-6 foretells a gathering of a remnant of "Gentiles [ἔθνη]" before God, who are accountable for their injustice toward God's people of Israel. These Gentiles include peoples of Tyre, Sidon, Galilee, and "Greeks ["Ελληνες]." Paul knew this text, because in Romans 10:13 he quotes LXX Joel 3:5 to support his soteriological stance that "everyone who calls upon the name of the Lord will be saved." The LXX Joel 3:5 is but one verse removed from LXX Joel 4:2-6. Similarly, Isa 66:18-19 states that there will be a gathering of all "Gentiles and tongues [ἔθνη καὶ γλώσσας]" who will discover God's glory. Some from among this diverse gathering will be sent to "Greece" as well as to other nations besides Greece. Isa 9:11 and Ezek 27:13 likewise distinguish Greeks from other Gentiles. G. W. Bowersock (*Hellenism in Late Antiquity* [Ann Arbor, Mich: University of Michigan Press 1990, 9-10) further suggests that "the use of Hellenic or *Hellênikos* in the sense of 'pagan' seems to coincide with the beginning of late antiquity, if we understand that to be the Constantinian age." If his suggestion is right, which remains an open and interesting question, then the modern-day view that ἔθνη and "Ελληνες are interchangeable in Paul stems from late antique exegesis of Paul.

[14] Despite the persecution, aspects of Greek religion nonetheless persisted here and there (such as in rural areas and towns) much farther beyond the fourth century than previously thought, for, as R. MacMullen puts it, "progress toward the extirpation of religious error could only be slow." Other aspects of Greek religion were reshaped for Christian purposes, which helped make the church a more civically oriented religion than it was prior to becoming a social establishment, MacMullen, *Christianity and Paganism in the Fourth to Eighth Centuries* (New Haven: Yale University Press 1997), 1-73, esp. 24.

[15] Other such recalls with violent overtones include Num 25:1-9, 13, 4 Kgs 9:20-6, Isa 3:16-25, and Ezek 23:46-9.

[16] Scholars who have regarded Romans 1:18-32 as a thematic replica of Wisdom 13:1-14:31 have done so in one of two ways. Wisdom, despite what it says, really agrees with Romans and contends that Gentiles have renegade knowledge about God. Thus C. Larcher (*Le livre de la sagesse*, vol. 3 [Paris: J. Gabalda 1985], 752), "En revanche, *agnôsia* [dans *Le livre de la sagesse*] doit signifier une 'méconnaissance' délibérée et fautive." Alternatively Romans, despite what it says, really concurs with Wisdom and maintains that the truth suppressors are ignorant about God. So Lagrange (*Épitre aux Romains*, 25), "Encore n'est-il pas nécessaire de regarder cette connaissance [dans Rom 1:21] comme très explicite. Paul jusqu'ici a seulement prouvé que les païens auraient pu bien voir; ils ont vu assez pour que l'ignorance qu'il va leur reprocher ne puisse servir d'excuse."

[17] For the pre-Christian Greek significance of ἄγνωστος θεός in the singular and plural, see E. Norden, *Agnostos Theos* (Leipzig: Teubner 1913), 41-87.

[18] References to Aristides are to the original Greek fragments from his *Apology* in J. Geffcken, *Zwei griechische Apologeten* (Leipzig: Teubner 1907). Aristides' apology, the earliest one extant, dates to the reign of Hadrian (117-138). For Theophilus (fl ca 169-185), see R. M. Grant, *Theophilus of Antioch: Ad Autolycum* (Oxford: Clarendon Press 1970), ix-x. Athenagoras wrote *Legatio ad Graecos* between 176

and 180, and likely in 177. For his text consult Geffcken above. On Justin (ca 100-165), see A. Wartelle, *Saint Justin Apologies* (Paris: Études augustiniennes 1987).

[19] Josephus refers to the same idea: The Greeks "came to know the nature of writing late and with difficulty" *Ap* 1.10, unlike his Hebrew ancestors. Theophilus admires the profoundly ancient literacy of the Elohist creation account, which he explicates in day-by-day detail and praises to the firmament, 2.11-19, 1.6-7, 3.9.

[20] Aristides and Justin even adapt phrasing from Romans 1:21-3 in support of their argument about Greek and Gentile ignorance about God, "The Greeks, claiming to be wise, proved to be fools [οἱ οὖν Ἕλληνες σοφοὶ λέγοντες εἶναι, ἐμωράνθησαν]," Aristides 8.2. Gentiles have an ability to know God that they have not exercised, "so that there is no excuse [ὥστ᾽ ἀναπολόγητον εἶναι]," Justin, *1 Apol* 28.3.

[21] The bilingual Lactantius identifies the truth-suppressing people as primarily Greek and secondarily as Gentiles. Augustine and Ambrosiaster identify them more generically as Gentiles. Lactantius (ca 240-320) devotes the seven books of his lengthy *Divine Institutes* to the second argument that Greeks first committed apostasy from God, invented idolatry, and through this invention dragged Romans and other Gentiles down along with them [Quod malum a Graecis ortum est; quorum levitas instructa dicendi facultate et copia, incredible est quantas mendaciorum nebulas excitaverit. Itaque [Romani] admirati eos, et susceperunt primi sacra illorum, et universis gentibus tradiderunt]," *DivInst* 1.15.14-15. Gentiles could be pardoned their polytheistic mores, he adds, if only their religions were based on ignorance rather than, as he believes they are, on the unforgivably suppressed knowledge about God that the Greeks first started [Et tamen huic impietati hominum posset venia concedi si omnino ab ignorantia veniret hic error]" (2.1.6), S. Brandt and G. Laubman, eds., *Lactantii Opera omnia*, vol. 1 (Vienna: Tempsky 1890). Ambrosiaster (fl ca 363-384) interprets Romans 1:18-22 to mean that polytheistic peoples are guilty of treason for denying the truth they recognized and abandoning the law of nature and Moses. "To such an extent were they not ignorant [usque adeo non ignoraverunt] that they confessed there was one principle from which all things in the sky, land, and underground take their beginning . . . knowing even these things, they did not give thanks . . . . Rightly such people would be condemned for treason [rei maiestati]," 1.18-22, H. J. Vogels, *Ambrosiastri qui dicitur comentarius in epistulas Paulinas*, part 1, *In epistulam ad Romanos*, CSEL vol. 81 (Vienna: Hoelder, Pichler, Tempsky 1966). In the recently edited Mayence sermon 62, Augustine (354-430 CE) calls upon his brethren to accept Paul's argument that all pagans are criminals because of their apostasy. "Look, brothers, and understand how the apostle shows that all are criminals [reos] . . . Look, brothers, see how Paul does not say that the Gentiles do not have truth but does say, 'they suppress truth in iniquity'. . . Perhaps one of you would still ask, 'How can those who did not receive God's law have the truth?'. . . 'Because that which is known of God is obviously in them . . . . For the apostle did not say, 'They do not know God,' but 'Even though they know God, they have not honored him or given him thanks,'" Mayence sermon 62.690-7, 730-2, for which see F. Dolbeau, "Nouveaux sermons de saint Augustin pour la conversion des païens et donatistes (IV)," *RecAug* 26 (1992) 69-141. Augustine's zeal for this interpretation of Paul's argument resonates through his writings, G. Madec, "Connaissance de dieu et action de grâces: Essai sur les citations de l'Ép. aux Romains 1,18-25 dans l'oeuvre de Saint Augustin," *RecAug* 2 (1962), 273-309. My thanks to Peter Brown for informing me about sermon 62.

[22] 5.5-6, 30.11. I use the edition of M. Whittaker, *Tatian: Oratio ad Graecos* (Oxford: Clarendon 1982) and cite passages by the page and line numbers common to her edition and that of E. Schwartz, *Tatiani Oratio ad Graecos* (TU; Leipzig: Hinrichs 1888), 4.1.

[23] Though Syrian by birth, Tatian identifies himself as culturally Hellenic by education prior to abandoning things Greek through his conversion, *Orat* 2.9-10, 26.16-17, 43.9-12. He wrote *Oratio ad Graecos* ca 176. His proud stance that he – unlike the Greeks – would rather die than be an ungrateful liar (ψεύστης

ἀχάριστος, 4.28-9) alludes to Romans 1:21 and 1:25, where Paul states that the truth suppressors ungratefully failed to give God thanks and instead exchanged God's truth for the lie of polytheism. For Tatian's support of Pauline authority in his arguments, see R. M. Grant, "Tatian and the Bible," *Studia patristica* 1 (1955), 301-2.

[24] On Tatian's allusion to Thales at 27.19-20, see E. Schwartz, ed. ad loc. (*TU* [1888] 4.1), cited by M. Whittaker, 49 n. d, *Tatian Oratio ad Graecos* (Oxford: Clarendon Press 1982).

[25] Given the distinctive provocation of Tatian's polemic, it thus becomes eminently clear why "[t]he tone of [Tatian's *Oratio ad Graecos*] is very different from that of Justin, being a violent diatribe . . . [that] disparages the Greek philosophers [and mythology]," Daniélou, *Gospel Message*, 14. Similarly Quasten, *Patrology* I, 221. Tatian's anger intensifies in the face of Greeks responding with incredulity and mockery. When Greeks laugh at his thunderous declarations rather than running for cover, he warns that he is "the messenger of the truth [ὁ κῆρυξ τῆς ἀληθείας]," that the Greeks are suppressing. They, not he, are the irrational ones. The Greeks will be thrown into the fire of eternal punishment if they do not return to God, 18.18-23.

[26] Clement lived ca 150-215. *Protrepticus und Paedagogus*, 3rd ed. Otto Stählin and U. Treu, (Berlin: Akademie Verlag 1972); *Stromata*, 4th ed. O. Stählin, L. Früchtel, U. Treu, (Berlin: Akademie Verlag 1985).

[27] The anonymous third-century *Cohortatio ad Graecos* and *De monarchia* (both spuriously attributed to Justin) vividly support the second polemic about apostate Greeks. In the *Cohortatio* "Greeks [ὦ ἄνδρες "Ελληνες]" are urged to defect (ἀποστῆναι) from their ancestral religions and return to their primordial religion of Christianity, for Christ's coming and his word have "reminded us of the more ancient reverence practiced by our earlier ancestors, which their descendants abandoned" (35.1, 38.1). Similarly *De monarchia* contends that human nature once knew biblical monotheism – as proven by largely forged excerpts of Greek poetry and philosophy – only to abandon God for idolatry. Hence, Greeks and others must "run back [ἐπαναδραμεῖν]" to their former union with God (1, 6). For references see C. Otto, *Iustini philosophi et martyris opera quae feruntur omnia*, vol. 2, [Jena, 1879, repr. 1971]), and on the dates of the treatises, see M. Markovich, *Pseudo-Iustinus* (Berlin: De Gruyter 1990), 4, 82.

[28] Origen lived ca 185-253. References to *Contra Celsum* are to P. Koetschau, ed. *Gegen Celsus*, in *Origenes Werke*, GCS vols. 1 and 2 (Leipzig: J. Hinrichs 1899).

[29] Origen simply identified the Platonic Socrates with Socrates the historical figure. Origen's other truth-suppressing philosophers would include Greek thinkers in Numenius's now lost *On the good*, a section of which surveyed true Gentile ideas about the bodiless God. Origen approves of Numenius's survey, *Cels* 1.15. Heretics are also truth suppressors, *comm. in Rom.* 161.23-162.1.

[30] Origen identifies Glaucon as Plato, and he similarly identifies the Thracian goddess Bendis as Artemis, whose inaugural ceremony is mentioned in the opening of the *Republic*.

[31] Athanasius lived 295-373. For references see R. W. Thomson, *Athanasius: Contra gentes and De incarnatione* (Oxford: Clarendon Press 1971).

[32] Though Athanasius on occasion refers to the theological rebels as ἄνθρωποι (for example, 19.6), just as Romans 1:18 does, he means Greeks first and then other Gentiles, not humanity at large. The people are "crazed persons among human beings in the days of old [οἱ πάλαι τῶν ἀνθρώπων παράφρονες]," whose madness led them to contrive polytheistic mores, 8.26-8. The crazed people in question belong to the Gentile sector alone: "In the preceding part [that is, in *Contra gentes*] we have narrated sufficiently a few of the many things about the error and superstition of Gentiles [τῶν ἐθνῶν] about idols, such as their original invention of idols," *Incarn* 1.1-4. Finally, in this Gentile sector, the Greeks are the original inventors of polytheistic idolatry. "The Greeks cut themselves off from the truth" through devising the worship of numerous gods. Since then the Greeks have

become corrupted sexually and otherwise, and other Gentiles have followed suit, 29.47-8, cf 26.8-19, 29.37-40. According to Athanasius, therefore, the Greeks originally provoked the apostasy among themselves. Then the rebellion spread to other Gentiles. Thus Greeks are primarily to blame for the polytheistic alienation from God, as reported in Romans 1:18-32.

[33] Athanasius uses Pauline imagery about darkened thoughts, minds, and perception in *Gent* 7.18-23, 8.33-4, 9.5-6, 9.21-2. His phrase ἐσκοτίσθησαν τὸν νοῦν at 9.22 alludes to ἐσκοτίσθη ἡ ἀσύνετος αὐτῶν καρδία in Rom 1:21.

[34] For the Stoics, "God is physical spirit extending throughout matter." Chrysippus adds that "the cosmos alone is said to be sufficient because it alone has everything it needs within it. It is both nurtured and will grow from itself, with parts transferring into one another," *Stoicorum Veterum Fragmenta* 2.604, ed. H. von Arnim [4 vols.; Leipzig: Teubner 1905), see also DL 7.137-8.

[35] Athanasius refuses to envision God in the form of a woman partly because God the father and son faced such powerful competition from cults in honor of feminine deities, such as Demeter the mother and her daughter Persephone in the Eleusinian Mysteries. Among gods "on the female side," he explicitly mentions the Greek gods Demeter, Persephone, Athena, Artemis, Hera, Aphrodite, and the Hellenized Egyptian god Isis, 10.5, 10.15-16.

[36] Athanasius both paraphrases and quotes Paul on this point. "They have been abandoned through God's surrendering of them [παραδοθέντες ἐν τῷ ἀποστραφθῆναι τὸν θεὸν αὐτούς]." So too Paul, as directly quoted by Athanasius: "God handed them over to dishonoring passions [παρήδωκεν αὐτοὺς ὁ θεὸς εἰς πάθη ἀτιμίας]." (19.16-20, Rom 1:26).

[37] Hence P. Camelot (*Athanase d'Alexandrie, Contre les païens* [Paris: Cerf, 1947], 34, 136) is mistaken to regard Athanasius's argument as a boring replica of the standard Hellenistic Jewish and early Christian polemic against polytheism. "Il faut reconnaître qu'il [Athanase] n'a guère cherché à renouveler une matière cent fois traitée depuis des siècles, . . . dès longtemps traditionelle dans le judaïsme."

[38] References to Chrysostom (b. ca 349-354, d. 407) are to *Homiliae in epistulam ad Romanos*. My citation numbers indicate the homily and section number in the readily accessible *PG* 60, followed by the *PG* section number and more specific marginal letter in the far less accessible *Homiliae in epistulam ad Romanos* (Oxford: J. H. Parker 1849).

[39] Chrysostom further explicates his position that the accused in Romans 1:18-27 are Greeks rather than Gentiles at large. For example, God's revealed wrath in Romans 1:18 pertains to "the Greek" in Rom 1:18-27 and to "the unfaithful" at large in Rom 1:28-32, *Hom* 3.1, 448b. This phrasing distinguishes Greeks as a subset among the unfaithful Gentiles as a whole. In a more elaborate but substantively similar vein, Chrysostom states that Rom 1:18-32 as a whole pertains to "Scythian, barbarian, . . . and Greeks," 3.2, 449e. Here too the Greeks have to be Greeks and not Gentiles as a whole.

[40] In Deuteronomy, for instance, Moses as the voice of God states that the denizens of Israel "have provoked me with their religiously alien ways; they have embittered me with their abominations. They have sacrificed not to God but to demonic gods whom they did not know. Recent innovations have come, which their fathers did not know. You abandoned [ἐγκατέλιπες] God who gave birth to you and you forgot God who nurtures you," Deut 32:16-18. Jeremiah in the voice of God similarly states, "I will speak to them [the inhabitants of Judah] in condemnation of their wickedness, because they abandoned [ἐγκατέλιπον] me, made sacrifices to alien gods, and bowed low to the works of their own hands," Jer 1.16. Chrysostom's own phrase ἡ τοῦ θεοῦ ἐγκατάλειψις in *Hom* 4.1, 455c picks up and refers back to his quotation of Jeremiah 2.13 in *Hom* 3.2, 450b.

[41] Chrysostom here uses the stereotype of Greek intellectuals in Acts 17 to motivate why the Greeks exchanged God for false gods. "All the Athenians and foreigners dwelling in their city like nothing more than to say or to listen to something new

[τι καινότερον]," Acts 17:21. Homoeroticism as described in Romans 1:26-7 is central among the new ideas for which the Greeks yearned. "Legitimate pleasure is in accordance with nature. But when God abandoned [ἐγκαταλίπῃ] them [the rebellious Greeks], everything down became up, and up down [through homoerotic practices]," 4.1, 454d.

⁴² Chrysostom's strong disdain for Greek philosophy follows from his Pauline polemic against philosophers. He "attacks the philosophers for trying to subvert Christian doctrine," no philosopher more so than Plato, P. R. Coleman-Norton, "St. Chrysostom and the Greek Philosophers," CP 25 (1930), 305-6, 311.

⁴³ In Homily 39, which was delivered about 380, Gregory Nazianzen (ca 329-390) identifies the rebellious truth suppression mainly but not exclusively with Greek mysteries and other rituals, such as the Eleusinian mysteries and worship of Dionysus, Aphrodite, and Apollo at Delphi, 39.4-5. "Just as Paul states," Greek religious practices are "'the recompense their practitioners had to make for their error [πλάνη]' in their acts of reverence." Hence the practices are "wickedly possessed in all respects," for the participants "were taken down into the worship of idols" ever since "they fell away [ἀποπεσεῖν] from the glory of God." The people too "are an abomination [βδελυκτοί] because of their error." In fact, "they are even more of an abomination [βδελυκτότεροι] than the worthless nature of the objects they worship since they are even more insensible than the revered objects," 39.6. Βδέλυγμα is a technical Septuagint term referring to that which is repellent to God and prohibited to his people by law. Gregory is not merely attacking the outré side of Greek rituals, such as running wild with Dionysus, for seeming indecency is not what provokes him. Gregory is outraged at Greek religion for reasons that would baffle both the Pentheus-minded and the wearers of dappled fawn skins alike: Greek rituals one and all reflect the primordial rebellion and punitive condition of Christian Israel. The Greeks would need catechism in Romans to understand this charge out of the biblical blue, as Gregory's own homily shows. "Since we did not deem it worthy to keep the law [καθὼς οὐκ ἐδοκιμάσαμεν φυλάξαι τὴν ἐντολήν], we were handed over [παρεδόθημεν] to our self-regulated error [πλάνης]. Since we were led astray, we were dishonored through our objects of worship [ἠτιμάσθημεν ἐν οἷς ἐσεβάσθημεν]" (39.7). Gregory's collective confession of Hellenic guilt reflects point for point Paul's accusation in the third-person plural. "Since they [the truth-suppressors] did not deem it worthy to keep God in recognition [καὶ καθὼς οὐκ ἐδοκίμασαν τὸν θεὸν ἔχειν ἐν ἐπιγνώσει], God handed them over [παρέδωκεν αὐτούς] to a corrupted state of mind" (Rom 1:28), to punitive religious practices in penalty for their error (πλάνη), and to the attendant dishonor (ἀτιμάζεσθαι) that defiles the body through polytheistic reasoning and homoerotic sexual conduct (Rom 1:24, 26-27). C. Moreschini, ed. and P. Gallay tr., Grégoire de Nazianze Discours 38-41 (Paris: Cerf 1990), who discuss the homily's date at 16-22.

⁴⁴ As Bowersock vividly states (Fiction as History: Nero to Julian [Berkeley: University of California Press 1994], 1-2), "[T]he second century of our era, ... [was] a world in which the boundaries between creative imagination and willful mendacity, between fiction and lying, often proved impossible to determine .... The problem ... acquired a special urgency [in the second century] because apparent fictions about both past and present were proliferating at a rate that the classical world had scarcely seen before .... History was being invented all over again; even the mythic past was being rewritten." His comment concerns once local legends about heroes that undergo reshaping and broadening, yet it is eminently apropos for the method used by Paul and his patristic supporters to reinvent the culture of apostate Israel in Greek and Gentile lands.

⁴⁵ Justin's concluding appeal to the Roman senate exemplifies this more tolerant stance. "But if you publicize this treatise, we will make it available to all, so that, if possible, they may change their minds. For this was our sole purpose in composing these words .... We will not pursue the matter further, having done what was in our power, with our prayers, that all people everywhere may be found worthy of the truth," 2 Apol 15.2-9.

A Response: Reading Paul in a Frontier Context: Moral Criticism and Paul's Picture of "Gentiles"

Halvor Moxnes

———— ◆ ————

Kathy L. Gaca's "Paul's Uncommon Declaration in Roman 1:18-32 and Its Problematic Legacy for Pagan and Christian Relations" investigates two different strands of interpretation of Romans 1 among early Christian interpreters in the 2nd – 4th centuries. Her paper focuses on what meaning "pagans/heathens" in Paul's text may be given in the context under study, and particularly what function this (constructed) meaning has had in contemporary relations between Christians and pagans/heathens. Thus, the underlying question is that of the ethics of interpretation: what is the role of biblical texts and their interpretation in, to use modern terms, inter-faith, inter-ethnic or inter-racial relations where Christians are engaged? And what is the responsibility for the interpreter or the students of historical interpretations? I sense in this author a commitment to moral questions, and a willingness to evaluate the interpretations of 4th century Christian Greek authors from the perspective of their relevance to group relations and politics.

Moral Readings of Pauline Dichotomies

The paper represents a focus on one of the dichotomies of Galatians 3:28 that, strangely enough, has been least studied. I am thinking of "neither Jew nor Greek". I think it is right to say that the other two dichotomies of Galatians 3:28 have played an important role in recent New Testament studies. In fact, we may look upon the interest in them as indicative of developing trends of how the present context shapes questions addressed to biblical texts. Since the 1960s social issues and issues related to gender have been important concerns. The "neither slave nor free" is underlying the study of the social constructions of Early Christian groups. Was what

34

has often been perceived of as theological differences in fact based on conflicts between social groups? And the idea of "egalitarianism" has given way to a study of groups and internal social conflicts (e.g., John S. Kloppenborg, "Egalitarianism in the Myth and Rhetoric of Pauline Churches," in *Reimagining Christian Origins* (FS for B. Mack) ed. E. A. Castelli and H. Taussig, Valley Forge: Trinity: 1996, 247-63). Likewise, in the last decades the dominant interpretation of the "neither male nor female" has been an emphasis upon equality between the sexes (especially E. Schüssler Fiorenza). The Pauline statement has been taken to support egalitarian relations between men and women in the earliest Christian groups. Recently, however, critical – and feminist – voices have raised doubt about this consensus: rather than an emphasis upon equal rights, does Paul's position imply a swallowing up of the female in the male? Is it really creating a unity that is based on superiority of the male, as the model for the "new human being"? (e.g., L. Fatum, "Image of God and Glory of Man: Women in the Pauline Congregations," in K. Børresen (ed.) *Image of God and Gender Models in Judaeo-Christian Tradition*, Oslo: Solum 1991, (56-137).

When it comes to the third pair, "Jew and Greek", the focus of interest has been on Paul's construction of Jews, or rather, Paul's picture of the Jews as it has been constructed by Christian interpreters (e.g., E.P. Sanders, *Paul and Palestinian Judaism*, 1977). This, of course, is very much part of a hermeneutical issue: present-day Jews consider themselves as in some way heirs and related to the Jews at the time of Paul, just as Christians understand themselves as heirs and related to Pauline Christians. Therefore, the way in which Paul's picture of Jews is represented and understood in scholarship is directly relevant to present day relations and dialogues between Jews and Christians.

What is new to the contributions of Gaca is that she explicitly focuses on the other part in the "Jew and Greek" dichotomy, on Paul's construction of the Greek, as well as the hermeneutical implications of this picture. Probably one reason why this has not until now received so much attention, is that the Christian church and theologians understood themselves as "Greek" in contrast to the Jews. And since a "gentile/heathen" background was no longer a reality in the European and North-American cultures, that aspect of "Greek" receded into the background. It may be a sign of a growing awareness of the multicultural and multireligious context of Christianity and Christian theologians that Paul's discussion of "Greek/Gentile/pagan" now comes into view. And quite specifically it is a sign of a moving away from a European and Anglo-American context of doing Biblical studies.

Here the question of categories of representation and understanding of what was at stake in the first century is of great consequence. The categories that were coined in the 19th century were those of "nation" and "race", especially the last one with ominous consequences. This has led to a presentation of the conflicts involved in categories that were relevant to modern Europe. The present more widely used category is ethnicity (e.g., M.G. Brett (ed.), *Ethnicity and the Bible*. Leiden : E.J. Brill, 1996). From a Jewish perspective, it has been argued that Paul, exactly when he is including Jews, actually strips them of their identity. They are included, but at the cost of their own dearest concepts of identity: not the acts of observance of circumciscion and Torah themselves, but the central meaning attached to this observance (e.g., D. Boyarin, *A Radical Jew. Paul and the Politics of Identity. 1994*). This seems to be a parallel argument to the criticism that Paul includes the female by actually transforming it into the male.

We too easily use our own categories, when we make "Jews" into an essential entity. Gaca may do this, when she raises the question of "the precise identity of the alleged truth suppressers," and goes on to draw differences between "Gentiles" and "Greeks" (175). Her use of "Mediterranean" with religion, polytheism, and cultural identity (instead of "ethnic"?) indicates a modern perspective. That becomes visible also in an aside in a footnote, that "some of Paul's patristic exegetes also presumed that what is gay must be Greek (175 n.28)." Especially this last example, the use of "gay" or "homosexual" in discussions and even translations of Rom 1:26-27, shows how easily modern categories that come out of a totally different social and symbolic world can enter into studies of premodern periods (e.g., D.B. Martin, "Heterosexism and the Interpretation of Romans 1:18-32," *Biblical Interpetation* 3 (1995) 332-55). That is a problem in all historical studies, but particularly if the text is used as an authority in contemporary debates.

Thus, I suggest that interpretation is not only an attempt to clarify the meaning of Paul's statements (about Gentiles), but also to clarify the understanding and consequences in one's own time. Gaca rightly raises the question: Who are meant by the sinful Gentiles in Rom 1:18-32?

From an Imperial to a Frontier Context in the Reading of Paul's Letter to the Romans

The villain of Gaca's story is not Paul or his text in Romans 1:18-32 in itself, but rather its interpretation and use from the late 2nd century, and especially in the 3rd and 4th centuries. This spread of Paul's views has to do with his growing authority in the early Church. But it is combined with other elements: the social and political demise of the Greek and Roman gods, especially from the 4th century, and the growth of Christian polemics and intolerance toward pagan religion. Thus, Paul and his texts receive status as authorities, and Christians come into power, helped by imperial policy. We may say that this introduces a period (which has lasted until this day) when Romans has been read as being 'Paul's testament', his theological authority, his synthesis of Christian beliefs, and as being of general applicability to issues like the human condition, sin and salvation. With terminology borrowed from D. Chidester, *Savage Systems*, I suggest that this is to read Paul in an imperial context.

I suggest that the readings of Romans that Gaca presents, highlighting the contributions of Greek authors in 3rd and 4th centuries, represent an imperial reading. It does not necessarily imply that they had superior power in relation to pagans, but the frontiers were no longer a zone of contact, but closed borders and boundaries. Gaca points to the context of the interpretation of Romans 1 in Christian polemics against pagans, which grow stronger after Constantine. Then Romans 1 functions clearly against specific groups. But it strikes me also that the material Gaca presents, of the "double attitudes" that Origin, Clement and others have toward Greek philosophers, may be interpreted as an example of imperial reading in a specific context. Considering the importance of Greek culture, Greek paideia, and rhetoric for the Greek church fathers, is it possible to understand these two different attitudes as attempts to sort out for themselves what was valuable in Greek philosophy? They wanted to separate themselves from and delegitimise pagan cults and philosophical schools, at the same time as they employed Greek philosophy and rhetoric in their own expositions of Christian beliefs.

And after the 4th century the Christian interpretation of the Bible undisputedly gained hegemony. This perspective has characterised historical-critical scholarship, which came into its own in the modern period at the time of colonialism. Thus, it is fair to say that New Testament scholarship, with its European and North American domination, represents as paradigm of imperialism. For instance, in studies of the historical Jesus, Jesus was represented as progress, Judaism as backwardness. Likewise, Paul was read in the context of universalism, versus Jewish particularity. One example of this is the way in which "race" as a negative concept was brought in to characterise the Jews, and specifically of the sins of the Jews (e.g., C.J. Roetzel, "No 'Race of Israel' in Paul," *Putting Body and Soul Together. Essays in honor of Robin Scroggs*. Valley Forge: Trinity (1997) 230-44). "Race" was spoken from a position of power, so that it is not something that characterises "us", but always "the others", inferiors or savage people. Therefore, Paul is read as a universal, i.e., imperial theologian, speaking–in modern Western interpretations–from an imperial position of power. This is to read him from the perspective of his general, overall statements, e.g., salvation for all, God for all, and in emphasising the equality of all– Jews and Gentiles, i.e. of creating a unity, disregarding the differences.

Back to a Frontier Reading of Paul?

Can we move from a reading of Paul in an imperial setting to one in a frontier setting? This is a double question: Can modern readers who come from a hegemonic context in economy, power, culture, and ethnicity, accept or open up for readers from other contexts, with other perspectives of reading? And can we in this process construct a different scenario of Paul, not as an imperial theologian, but as a missionary in a frontier context?

What if we try to read Paul in a frontier setting, as one who tries to find a place for himself and the groups of Christ followers within the socio-cultural, religious and ethnic context? This implies that he does not have the full power to label, to identify. Gaca's conclusion that "in the text of Romans itself, the identity of Paul's 'truth-suppressing people' remains open-ended, which likely precludes a modern consensus about their cultural identity," points in this direction. I should include a caveat here, however. It may also be that the text is not meant to give information about cultural (or ethnic) identity, so that it will not respond to our culture-specific questions. Stanley Stowers has pointed to similarities between Rom 1:18-32 and Greco-Roman "decline of civilisation narratives" (*A Rereading of Romans*, New Haven: Yale (1994) 85-104). The purpose of such narratives is to describe "the other" in contrast to "self", so that they serve as arguments for organising society. Thus, the pictures are obviously stereotypes, clichés of "the other", part of a rhetoric, and may therefore not lend themselves to specific questions of identity. Therefore, when early Christian Greek writers raise such questions, they may be using the text for a different purpose than its first context.

But the observation that the text is "open-ended" is still valid and valuable, as it may point to the ambiguity of the "self" that Paul attempts to create as well. I still think that Paul in Romans wants to include (Christian) Jews and pagan Christians into some sort of unity by means of his argument about the impartial God. Thus, Paul is attempting to create a new understanding of identity, but it is something that cannot be taken for granted, or given a clear, conceptual expression, since it is not yet visible as a socio-religous entity. Since Paul never speaks of the Christian *ekklesia* in Rome, the most likely social setting presumed in Romans is that of Christians as subgroups that belonged within Jewish synagogues. That is, the separation had not yet taken place, and there was no defined "Christianity" in Rome (e.g., M. Nanos, *Mystery of Romans,* summarized in "The Jewish Context of the Gentile Audience Addressed in Paul's Letter to the Romans," *CBQ* 61 (1999) 283-304). Thus, both socially and conceptually Paul's addressees were in a frontier situation, without fixed boundaries, and Paul had an uncertain power base from which to enter into the relations.

I suggest that this frontier situation becomes visible in Romans 4, Paul's interpretation of Abraham (H. Moxnes, *Theology in Conflict. Studies in Paul's Understanding of God in Romans*, Leiden: Brill (1980) 117-282). Abraham as an ideal figure is in many ways the contrast to the negative picture of the Gentiles in Romans 1. His introduction as "ancestor" (4:1) makes him a positive identity figure for the audience. However, like Romans 1.18-32 this text is ambiguous and open-ended when it comes to the specific identification of those who may identify with Abraham.

Paul's interpretation of Abraham is an example of an inclusive use of a Jewish symbol. It was possible to read Abraham also as a symbol for pagans, as an idolater who converted and trusted in God (in contrast to the pagans in 1:20). Is this indicative of the frontier position – Abraham as a figure who can be read from two sides, who can be used as a figure of identification for pagans (or former pagans), but also (even more) for Jews? Paul attempts, for both groups, to reconfigure him, to make him primarily a figure of identification for Christians among Jews and pagans. But whereas it is clear that Abraham can only be a father figure for believing pagans, those who have turned away from idol worship, he remains a father for Jews regardless of whether they are Christian or non-Christian Jews! Thus, there is an ambiguity that remains, that shows how Paul speaks from within a frontier/dialogue context, not from an imperial context

We notice this ambiguity in Paul when he speaks of who the descendants of Abraham are in Romans 4. Paul here gives a reinterpretation of the narrative of Abraham. Instead of the focus on the obedience of Abraham, exemplified in his willingness to sacrifice Isaac (Gen 22), Paul puts the emphasis on Abraham receiving (and believing) the promise of land and descendants (Gen 12 and 15). The structuring element in Paul's midrashic interpretation of the Abraham story is a quotation from Gen 15:6, "Abraham believed in God and that was reckoned to him as righteousness" (Rom 4:3, cf. 4:5, 9, 22, 23). Although there is no mention of Jesus Christ in Romans 4 until v. 24, Paul's use of "faith", "believe" and "grace" clearly presupposes his understanding of God's act of salvation in Christ, and of the parallel between Abraham and those who now believe in Jesus. Thus, the logic of the argument would require that the descendants of Abraham were those Jews who believed in God "who raised Jesus our Lord from the dead" (4:24). But Paul does not say that, or at least not that it was only the Jews who believed in Jesus. Instead, in two instances in ch. 4, he seems to make a careful decision not to say that. "The purpose was to make him father of all who believe without being circumcised and who thus have righteousness reckoned to them, and likewise the father of the circumcised, of those who are not only of the circumcision, but also those who follow the example of faith which our father Abraham had before he was circumcised" (4:12, my translation). Paul speaks of τοῖς οὐκ ἐκ περιτομῆς μόνον ἀλλὰ καὶ τοῖς στοιχοῦσιν τοῖς ἴχνεσιν . . . . The problem of the two definite articles that indicate two different groups, is sometimes solved by correcting the second to αὐτοῖς, but there is no manuscript evidence for this (Moxnes 1980, 112). And the problem remains, since

4:16 is also ambiguous. Paul's draws the consequences of his argument
that the promise rests on grace and faith, only in that way can the
promise be guaranteed to all his descendants– "not only to the adherents of the law, but also to those who share the faith of Abraham."

How shall we understand the ambiguity of these expressions that in
their inclusiveness seems to go against the very thrust of Paul's
Christocentric argument? Paul's explicit use of Abraham, when he
turned circumcision and obedience to the law into "accompanying
signs" of the righteousness which he received though faith (4:11, 13),
served to make the signs relative as identity markers (Boyarin). This
was a position, which the church would elaborate explicitly to exclude
non Christian Jews from their place as heirs of Abraham. This is the
imperial position. But in the position in which Paul writes, this imperial
stand is not yet possible. He writes in a frontier situation, of Christ-
believing Jews and pagan Christians living as subgroups in the synagogues, or at least closely related to the synagogues. The attempt to
transform the identity of Abraham is a bold and central part of the main
structure of the text. But when Paul draws his conclusions, there is an
ambiguity that provides openings for an understanding that non-Christian Jews might hear as relataively unoffensive, as keeping open their
place as descendants of Abraham. Thus, there seems to be a correspon-
dence between the ambiguity of the identity of pagans/Gentiles in
Romans 1-2, and the ambiguity about the Jewish descendants of
Abraham in Romans 4.

Frontier and Morality

The study of Gaca has shown that readings of Paul from an "imperial
position" (be it by Christian Greek writers in the 4th century, or more
recently, are fraught with moral problems. But since such readings often
form part of the governing consensus and its hegemony of meaning,
these problems only become visible when they are confronted with readings from a frontier context. Historical studies have an important moral
function here. They can question the frames of interpretation, the cultural constructions and concepts that govern ongoing readings of
ancient texts. We know of the dangers and the fateful consequences of
pictures of the Jews, drawn (at least partly) on the basis of Paul and the
Gospels. Gaca has in a parallel way pointed to the danger of pictures of
"Gentiles" and "pagans" that can be and were constructed on the basis
of Romans 1. She has shown that the effect of a text, and the context
within which it is read, is an important part of the totality of a text as it
is handed down through history.

I have suggested that we make a distinction between an imperial
reading of Paul, and a reading of him in a frontier context. It think that
from a frontier context one may be better able to explain Paul's position

on Jews and pagans, his use of literary conventions and stereotypes, and even better understand the function of his views in his historical situation. I do not suggest, however, that this approach will solve all problems and make Paul's position on all issues morally acceptable. Nor can we put Paul above moral criticism. As long as his texts are used as authoritative and read with a view to their meaning for contemporary questions, we must engage in discussion with them and enter into moral arguments when needed.

– TWO –

Jewish Salvation in Romans according to Clement of Alexandria in *Stromateis* 2

Michael Joseph Brown

———— ◆ ————

Christianity and Judaism – A Strained Relationship

Since its inception Christianity has wrestled with the issue of the Jewish rejection of Jesus as the messiah. Although it began as a movement within Judaism, Christianity quickly became a predominantly Gentile religion. Christians attempted to address the problem of the Jewish rejection of the reputed messiah in a number of ways. Some Christians, notably the Gnostics and the Marcionites, rejected Judaism and its scriptures altogether. Others believed that God would find a way to redeem the Jews, regardless of their rejection of Jesus Christ. Still others continued a mission of evangelization, attempting to persuade Jews that Christianity represented the fulfillment of their messianic hopes. Paul's letter to the Romans 9-11 represents the first recorded "Christian" attempt to respond to a growing concern in the Christian community regarding Jewish unbelief.[1] The later patristic writers used Paul's argument in Romans, as well as others, as a basis upon which to construct their own arguments regarding the possibility of Jewish salvation. Clement of Alexandria was one of those authors.

In *Strom.* 2, especially 2. 6-9, Clement shares his understanding of the question of Jewish salvation with his readers, using Romans 10-11 as his basis. Clement's argument regarding the future of the Jews is intriguing because it runs counter the tendency in other early Christian writings to denigrate the Jews. He represents a strand of early Christian theology, predominantly Alexandrian, that sought to synthesize Hellenistic Judaism with Greco-Roman philosophy in a meaningful way. It displays the convergence of a number of intellectual and historical forces, and culminates in the belief that God in Christ has brought into being an institution (the ἐκκλησία) that seeks to overcome long-standing ethno-religious divisions. Clement of Alexandria's exposition on Judaism represents an interpretation of Paul's discussion in Romans that mitigates a growing Gentile Christian tendency towards supersessionism.

The Alexandrian Church

Roman Alexandria was a cosmopolitan city within the geographical, cultural, and economic confines of the province of Egypt. It was a distinctive city because it typified many of the syncretistic tendencies inherent in the Roman Empire of late antiquity; yet, it was a city with strong ethno-religious divisions. As the major Egyptian port city, it was the context for an enormous amount of intercultural interaction as compared to the rest of the province.

Alexandria was a hodgepodge of ethnicities and social groups. Romans, Greeks, Egyptians, and Jews, philosophers and sailors, indigenous and transplants, residents and pilgrims, military and civilian all interacted within its urban space. Yet, as in other ancient cities, Alexandria was basically a two-tiered social organism: a small group of upper-class individuals and a large number of lower-class persons.[2] The relationship between rich and poor in this urban environment was fundamentally symbiotic. The patronage system in the Roman Empire was such that the wealthy needed the support of the lower classes to maintain control and ancient sources indicate that Alexandria was a particularly difficult city to govern.[3] Such an analysis, however, may be an overstatement. A city with the size and diversity of Alexandria would pose a challenge to any governmental body, especially in the ancient world. The heterogeneity of the urban population called for a particular vigilance on the part of the imperial authorities.

The city's population was far greater than that of any other Egyptian city, and most other cities in the empire for that matter. Estimates of the population in this period are in the range of 500,000 to 600,000 people.[4] The united population of Alexandria and its hinterland would have comprised a significant portion of the overall Egyptian populace, possibly as much as a third. In a population of four to five million, this means nearly 1.7 million people lived in and around the metropolis of Alexandria.[5] The degree of urbanization in Roman Egypt was so high that it would not be rivaled again until modern times.[6] In this case, Alexandria was as different from the rest of Egypt as New York City is from the majority of the United States.

Socially, Roman Alexandria may be conceived as a sphere containing two concentric circles. The outer covering, or form of governance, was Roman. The inner circle, or day-to-day cultural activities were predominantly Greek, but the inner core was steadfastly Egyptian.[7] Under the Roman legal system, the highest citizenship status belonged to the citizens of Rome who resided in the province. Below them was a larger group of lesser-privileged citizens of the city. Below the Alexandrian citizenry was an even larger group with few privileges, the "Egyptians." The legal status, "Egyptian," however should not be understood to mean that all persons occupying that status were ethnic Egyptians. Many Greeks and Jews found themselves classified as "Egyptians" by Rome. Take, for example, the case of a woman named Dionysia who petitioned the prefect of Egypt against her father Chairemon (*P.Oxy.* II 237 coll. VI.4-VIII.7). In the petition, the laws to which the father and daughter appeal are called "Egyptian," but they are in reality appealing to Greek law. The legal situation in this period is muddled for the modern reader because of the idiosyncrasies of the Roman legal structure.

In addition to citizenship one must include a discussion of status as an important social indicator. Status was not always easily contained within the existing citizenship structure. The Roman citizenship structure did change, however, in 212 CE when the emperor Caracalla made Roman citizens of practically everyone living within the borders of the empire. Interestingly, this drastic change in the citizenship is an indicator of social status. Caracalla himself made a distinction between "true" Alexandrian citizens and others.[8] For example, in 215 CE Caracalla wrote of the apparent differences between Egyptians and others in the city:

> All Egyptians in Alexandria, especially country folk who have fled from other parts and can easily be detected, are by all manner of means to be expelled, with the exception, however, of pig-dealers and riverboatmen and the men who bring down reeds for heating the baths. But expel all others, as by the numbers of their kind and their uselessness they are disturbing the city . . . For genuine Egyptians can easily be recognized among the linen-weavers by their speech, which proves them to have assumed the appearance and dress of another class; moreover in their mode of life, their far from civilized manners reveal them to be Egyptian country folk (*Sel. Pap.* 2.215 [Edgar and Hunt, LCL]).

In short, second century Alexandria was a city with a diverse multiethnic population. Groups within the city were divided by citizenship status, social status, and ethno-religious allegiance. One group, however, that had been prosperous and powerful in Alexandria prior to the second century suffered a great setback during this period.

Jews had been in Egypt since the sixth century BCE, most likely as a result of the political troubles that marked the end of the Israelite monarchy.[9] A Jewish presence had existed in Alexandria from the reign of Ptolemy I onwards. Scholars believe that the primary reason for the rise in the Egyptian Jewish population during the Ptolemaic period result from the Ptolemies' extensive use of Jewish mercenaries. In addition, Jews may have been attracted to Ptolemaic Egypt because of the commercial possibilities available in the new capital, and as a means of escaping the policies of forced Hellenization instituted by the Seleucids.[10] Thus, by the first century CE, Alexandrian Jews could be found in a variety of occupations and social

positions. Like most ethno-religious groups past and present, the Jews could
be found in definable enclaves within the city. According to our sources,
one of the five districts in the city had been given to the Jews by their
Ptolemaic overlords. Christopher Haas has argued that this district was the
region situated beyond Lake Lochias, which would have placed them near
the governmental quarter of the city; although this thesis has not received
widespread scholarly approval.[11]

What appears to have bound this group together as an ethno-religious
unit were the city's synagogues. Foremost among them was the so-called
Great Synagogue, "a richly adorned basilica-like structure, which was so
immense that the hazzan had to wave a brightly colored scarf so that that
huge congregation, some too distant to hear, could respond with the Amen
after the benediction."[12] The Jewish *politeuma* was headed by an ethnarch
or hazzan, a synagogue official, who oversaw the day-to day administra-
tion of he community.[13] This appears to be the situation described in
Josephus, when he says, "There is also an ethnarch allowed [the
Alexandrian Jews], who governs the nation, and distributes justice to them,
and takes care of their contracts, and of the laws to them belonging, as if he
were the ruler of a free republic" (A.J. 14.7.2[Whiston]). The Jewish community also had various *collegia,* which met in the city's synagogues.
These associations were used as a means of voicing Jewish grievances,
expressing political sentiments, and taking collective action.

Although the Alexandrian Jewish community was large and diverse,
what is most notable about this community is the remarkable intellectual
contribution it made in the late Ptolemaic and early Roman periods. For
example, Alexandrian Jewish scholars were largely responsible for the
translation of the Jewish scriptures into Greek, the LXX. It would serve as
the authoritative text of the Old Testament for the later Christian religion
and served as a means of transmitting many Jewish elements into this developing community. In addition, the LXX is a good example of how some
segments of the Alexandrian Jewish community sought to integrate Judaism with Greco- Roman culture. Another example of this desire to integrate
the traditions of the Jews with that of their Greco-Roman rulers can be
found in the works of Philo.

Philo was a member of an affluent and powerful Alexandrian family.
His brother, Gaius Julius Alexander, was one of the most powerful people
in the metropolis. Alexander was chief of customs of the Eastern border of
Egypt and guardian of Tiberius' mother's properties in the province. His
name testifies to the fact that he was a Roman citizen, this having been
bestowed upon him by the emperor Augustus. Since we know that the be-
stowal of Alexandrian citizenship almost always preceded the grating of
Roman citizenship, it is safe to assume that he was at least a citizen of
Alexandria, and a Roman citizen himself. Alexander's wealth is exemplified by two acts: (1) his loan to King Agrippa I of Judea, and (2) his gra-

cious act of plating the gates of the Temple of Jerusalem in gold and silver. Philo's second brother, Lysimachos, was senior commercial partner of an import – export enterprise in the city. He married Princess Berenice, daughter of King Agrippa I. Philo's nephew, Tiberius Julius Alexander, had a public career that Alexander took him to the pinnacle of a Roman official in Egypt, prefect (66-70 CE). On July 1, 69, he had his solders and the Alexandrian populace swear allegiance to Vespasian, which became the official date of Vespasian's advent as emperor. Many call him an apostate because he was chief of staff under Titus during the siege of Jerusalem in 70 CE.[14] Although Tiberius was a member of a notable family and a citizen of Rome, the strong ethno-religious divisions that characterized the time can be seen in the writings of the Roman historian Tacitus, who called Tiberius "a native of the country [i.e., Egyptian]," a designation meant to denigrate him (*Hist.* 1.11[Mellor]).

Even though I shall say more about Philo below, two of his works highlight some of the problems faced by Alexandrian Jews in the first century. His *Legatio ad Gaium* and *Contra Flaccum* attest to the animosity harbored by ethno-religious groups in the city – an animosity that at times erupted into rioting and destruction. Riots erupted in 38 and 66, but they would pale in comparison to the revolt that began in 115 CE.

The emperor Trajan had just initiated his Parthian campaign. The attendant reduction in troop strength meant that the Legio III Cyrenaica, one of the two legions usually stationed in Alexandria's garrison suburb of Nicopolis, was off executing the war. Jews in Cyrenaica took this as an opportunity to rally behind a messianic king named Lucuas (Eusebius, *Hist. eccl.* 4.2.3-4). By 116 CE these Cyrenaican Jews were marching on Egypt. Trajan quickly recognized the gravity of the situation, and redeployed a portion of his forces, including the Legio III, to quell the revolt. In Alexandria, the Jews who revolted may have been motivated by the memory of the desecration of synagogues in the uprising of 38 CE. They destroyed roads and disrupted shipping along the Nile. According to our sources, the Jews attacked their Greek countrymen and destroyed portions of the city. The devastation was so extensive that the emperor Hadrian was later said to have "reconstructed Alexandria, demolished by the Jews" (Eusebius, *Chron.*; see also P. *Oxy.* 7.1045; BGU 1084; SB 7239, 7561). The revolt was eventually put down by the Legio III in a decisive battle, which ended the revolt in Alexandria, although it would take longer to quiet the revolt in the rest of the province. In the reprisals that followed, the Great Synagogue of Alexandria was destroyed (Eusebius, *Chron.* 2.223; see *Hist.* eccl. 4.2.3). Some Jews were forced to emigrate from Alexandria to Palestine. Others were forced by the prefect to relocate to a new settlement just outside the walls and to the east of the city. After this incident, Judaism in Alexandria ceased to exist as a strong ethno-religious force until the fourth century CE.

If scholars of this period are correct and the early Alexandrian Christian community was virtually indistinguishable from its Jewish predecessor, the turning point came with the revolt in 115 CE.[15] This is when Alexandrian Judaism faded and Christianity seized the initiative. One begins to hear from an Alexandrian church defining itself over against Judaism at this time.

The first Alexandrian follower of Jesus was Apollos, at least according to the Acts of the Apostles: "Now a Jew named Apollos, a native of Alexandria, came to Ephesus. He was an eloquent man, well versed in the scriptures. He had been instructed in the way of the Lord . . . and taught accurately the things concerning Jesus, though he knew only the baptism of John" (18.24-25 RSV). Scholars question whether this statement regarding Apollos means that Christianity had reached Alexandria by 50 CE.[16] What seems apparent, however, is that Luke regarded Christianity in Alexandria as having begun rather early.[17] In addition, this community appears to have been composed of Hellenized Jews. Eusebius credits Mark with bringing the gospel to Alexandria from Rome during the reign of Claudius (*Hist. eccl.* 2.16.1). He was a Jewish Christian missionary who assisted in various evangelization enterprises.[18] Today, Coptic Christians continue to revere St. Mark, who brought the gospel to Egypt. These traditions, although not decisive, indicate that the early church understood Alexandrian Christianity as having begun among Jews in the city. If the early community in Alexandria was virtually indistinguishable from its Jewish predecessor, at least to outsiders, then the radical changes that occurred in the wake of the revolt of 115 CE transformed the Alexandrian church into a Gentile community.

It is most likely that Alexandrian Christianity developed, if not within the Hellenistic Jewish community of Alexandria, at least in close intellectual proximity to it. This would help explain a number of issues involved in the historical reconstruction of this branch of the early church. First, the close relationship of Christianity to Hellenistic Judaism best explains the philosophical tendency encountered in the Alexandrian church. Philo maintained that Sabbaths should be devoted to philosophy (*Opif.* 43.128). This may indicate that at least a portion of the Jewish community in Alexandria was committed to interpreting scripture in light of Hellenistic philosophy.[19] Philo says in another place:

> [E]ven to this day, the Jews hold philosophical discussions on the seventh day, disputing about their national philosophy, and devoting that day to the knowledge and consideration of the subjects of natural philosophy; for as for their houses of prayer in the different cities, what are they but schools of wisdom, and courage, and temperance, and justice, and piety, and holiness, and every virtue, by which human and divine things are appreciated, and placed upon a proper footing? (*Mos.* 2.39.216 [Yonge]).

Although what Philo conceives of as a "school" sounds a lot like some sort of synagogue service, it is true that ancient synagogues were used as study houses.[20] Using synagogues as academies of learning would be in line with what we know of the activities of ethno-religious communities in Alexandria, who used these schools as a means of reinforcing ethno-religious identity.[21] In addition, the use of synagogues would assist in explaining Eusebius' claim that the Alexandrian Christian community had an "academy of sacred learning" (*Hist.* eccl. 5.10.1). The Christian academy may have been modeled after the Jewish one. If Christianity in the city originated with the model of the school as described by Philo, then it is conceivable that a number of teachers would have started their own schools devoted to the explicating of Christian philosophy. The schools would not have been "orthodox" in the traditional sense, given that orthodoxy and heresy did not exist.[22] Distinctions between orthodoxy and heresy did not arise until at least the third century. Prior to that time, the Alexandrian church sought its own voice in the context of its relationship to Judaism.

Second, the close relationship between Christianity and Judaism in Alexandria helps to explain the diverse manuscripts identified by Colin Roberts among others. Among the specifically Jewish manuscripts found in Egypt, almost all are from the Torah: Genesis, Exodus, and Deuteronomy.[23] Copies of the Psalms were also found, which might further validate the connection between Jews and Christians in the city.[24] The frequent use of diverse religious and philosophical texts by Clement and other Alexandrian Christian intellectuals may be attributed to a community attempting to define itself in contrast to its Jewish antecedents and other ethno-religious communities.[25] Most of Clement's polemics are aimed not at Jews but at Gnostics, especially those who would deny the validity of the Jewish scriptures to the Christian faith. In essence, this rejection of the Hebrew Bible amounted to a denial of the Jewish roots of Christianity. In response to this approach, Clement attempts to synthesize Judaism and Greco-Roman culture in a manner that would be palatable for thoughtful Christians. Thus, Clement of Alexandria stands as a pivotal figure in the development of orthodoxy in Alexandrian Christianity.

If it is true that Alexandrian Christianity owed a great debt to Hellenistic Judaism, it is even more plausible to believe that the type of Judaism manifested by Philo was predominant in this urban Egyptian church. It is not surprising to find that Clement used many concepts developed and discussed by Philo.[26] It is well known that Clement borrowed Philo's allegoric method and some of his elaborate allegories.[27] In addition, Clement co-opted Philo's doctrine of the Logos as the central concept in his presentation of Christianity.[28] Philo, linking the Hebrew phrase "the word of the Lord" with the Stoic doctrine of the *Spermatikos Logos* and Plato's doctrine of ideas, found in them a resulting conception of a divine, rational, and spiritual principle immanent in man and in the universe, and he also found a divine personality, or quasi-personality, to come between the Absolute and the world.[29] Philo's *Logos* mediates between humanity and God. Clement altars this doctrine of the *Logos* mediating between humanity and God.[30] Clement alters this doctrine of the *Logos* by equating Philo's Logos with the historic Jesus.[31]

Another Philonic idea found in Clement's writing is the repudiation of radical dualism. Philo's intermediaries are not the wicked and rebellious *archons* of Gnostic myth. And even though Philo disparages the sense-perceptible world, his ideas are far removed from the Gnostic myth of a premundane Fall that places the world and the demiurge in the realm of evil (see *Opif.* 3.15-4.17, 6.24).[32] Clement appears to hold the same doctrine, particularly when one views his soteriology. In short, it appears prudent to associate the early Alexandrian Christian community with Alexandrian Judaism, especially the type exhibited by thinkers such a Philo, when one considers the literary and historical evidence and the works of Clement of Alexandria.

Clement's Synthesis of Judaism and Paganism

Clement maintained that knowledge of God comes through the *Logos*, and is given in measure to a person's ability to understand (*Strom.* 7.1.2). The figure of the *Logos* plays a large role in Clement's theology. This most likely has to do with his emanationist doctrine of God, and his accompanying use of the Philonic and Stoic concepts of Logos. Unlike the Stoics and Philo, however, Clement's doctrine of the Logos is invested with a degree of personality (see 7.2.6). As T. B. Glover describes it, "[Clement's] Logos is indeed the Great High Priest . . . The great and characteristic feature of the Logos is that 'he took the mask (προσωπεῖον) of a man and molded it for himself in flesh and played a part in the drama of mankind's salvation'" (see 2.5.21.1-5).[33] Clement designates the *Logos* as the source of providence and a fundamental unity, "never divided, never dissevered, never passing from place to place" (*Strom.* 7.2.5 [Coxe, ANF]). It is not only ubiquitous; it is also the focal point of contemplation that brings disparate humanity into harmony:

> Let us who are many hasten to be gathered unto one according to the unity of the monadic essence (μοναδικῆς οὐσίας). Since we do good, let us in like manner pursue unity by seeking the good Monad. But the unity of many arising out of a multitude of separate voices takes on a divine harmony and becomes one concordant sound, following one director and teacher, the Logos, and coming to rest at the Truth itself saying, "Abba, Father" (*Protrept.* 7.2.7).

In *Strom.* 2.5.21.5, speaking of the *Logos*, Clement says, "[H]e gave the law by the mouth of the prophets, enjoining and teaching most distinctly what things are to be done, and what not" (see also *Paed.* 1.7.60). This statement highlights Clement's belief that the righteous life is properly the fulfillment of the purpose of the Logos. This purpose involves three areas: (1) habits and customs, (2) voluntary or conscious acts, and (3) doctrinal revelation. In short, the Logos acts in the role of παιδαγωγός or διδάσκαλος in order to bring about the divinization of the human being.[34] It is fundamentally a process of education. This educational process is necessary because the remedy for sin is education (cf. Plutarch, *Mor.* 439c-f; Plato, *Lysis* 208c, 223a). As Clement says, "Sinning arises from being unable to determine what ought to be done, or being unable to do it" (*Strom.* 2.15.62.3).

In *Strom.* 2 Clement draws his ideas concerning the necessity of education from Plato, particularly the *Laws.* It was Plato's contention that the lawgiver should supervise all the activities of the citizens, and should instruct them as to right and wrong. In short, the lawgiver had an educational role. Clement transforms this lawgiver into the *Logos* (1.5.21.5). Working through the church, the Logos serves an educational role in the life of the believer (see 7.2.6). This educational role is further illuminated through the application of moral norms to the believers' lives. According to Plato, education in this vein involves both persuasion and coercion.[35] As the divine lawgiver, the *Logos'* role is to instruct and educate the "children" in the church, possibly a reference to Christians without *gnosis* (cf. *Leg.* 857c-e). Such education is done by means of preambles, which use persuasion rather than threats, to produce the required behavior (cf. *Leg.* 722c-723d). Part of this training involves the "correct training of the emotions."[36] More than this, Plato believes "that only a limited number of citizens can come to a fully rational understanding."[37] These two ideas, the need for education and the limited number of persons who can obtain it, seem to correspond very well with how Clement conceives the role of the *Logos* and the attendant role of the church (see *Strom.* 7.1.3).

According to Plato, the divine aspect in the human being and its virtue is to be preferred above all human goods (see *Leg.* 631b-c, 697b, 726-728c). It is the immortal element of reason in the soul that is divine (*logos*), not the mortal elements, i.e. passions and desires (see *Leg.* 644c-645c, 713e; cf. *Tim.* 42c-44d, 69d-e). One honors the soul by resisting the blandishments of pleasure and by enduring pain and fear (*Leg.* 727c). Thus, the goal of the Platonic life is to struggle against pleasure in order to subordinate one's self to the dictates of reason (cf. *Tim.* 44c, 87a-b).[38]

According to Clement, everything that is contrary to sound reason (παρὰ τὸν λόγον τὸν ὀρθόν) is sin, and virtue is a disposition of persons sound in agreement with reason throughout the whole of life (see *Paed.* 1.13). Sin arises from the misuse of reason and the instability of the emotions (*Strom.* 2.15). The righteous life is defined by Clement as a system of rational behavior, the continuous fulfillment of the teaching of reason (see *Paed.*

21.13.102.3). Such education is a hallmark of the activity of the *Logos*. In short, the *logos* use various means to educate the believer: some listen to persuasion but others must be threatened. The disciplinary action of the Logos is not to be understood as discordant. God disciplines out of love not anger, argues Clement. God's apparent anger is really a sign of the divine, in actuality signs of God's concern for humanity, God's divine plan (see 1.8.70.1).

God has a definite agenda for the cosmos: to bring human beings into a state of salvation. God is intimately involved in this redemptive process. Clement quotes an old Pythagorean dictum to highlight God's activity in the cosmos:

> God is one and is not, as some suppose, outside creation but in it, existing wholly in the whole cycle, cause and guardian of all, the blending of the universe and fashioner of his own power in all his works, the giver of light in heaven, and father of the universe, mind and animating principle of the whole cycle, mover of all (*Protrept*. 6.72.4-5).

This is not to be taken to mean that God compels (or forces) persons to be saved. No, Clement is careful to avoid such an idea. Likewise, God does not display any favoritism with regard to persons or ethno-religious affiliation. As the source of all that exists, God's concern is for all, and thus God has established a plan of redemption equally accessible to all. Drawing upon the *Republic* (617e), he says "the conditions laid down by God are equal for all, and no blame can attach to him; but he who is able will choose, and he who wills prevails" (*Strom*. 7.3.20). God's power draws people to God's self, and through the use of persuasion God draws persons into a state of salvation (7.2.10). Persuasion is an important means of understanding God's influence on human beings, because it allows Clement to maintain two sometimes contradictory positions: the doctrine of an omnipotent deity and the doctrine of free will. Clement contends that it is God's constant purpose to save humanity, and if human beings would only believe and repent, all humans could be saved (*Protrept*. 11.116.1).[39]

Although scholars often overlook it, faith (πίστις) plays a prominent role in the soteriology of *Strom*. 2, just as it does in Romans 10-12. Clement lays down a number of arguments with respect to faith that expands upon his use of the term, but I will only deal with one: *Faith is based on choice, which is founded on desire, and is intellectual in natural* (*Strom*. 2.2.9.2). Here Clement's understanding of faith is grounded firmly in the doctrine of free will. According to the Alexandrian, to exercise faith is to be like God. Rational choice is the foundation for proper action, faith is discovered to be the beginning of action, being the foundation of rational choice in the case of any one who exhibits to himself the previous demonstration through faith (2.2.9.2).

The goal of the righteous life is to perform deeds conformable to reason. This idea is analogous to the later Christian concept of *fides caritate formata* as opposed to, say, *fides implicita,* which would be the type of faith characteristic of non-gnostic Christians. Moreover, since reasonable deeds can be found in all cultures, faith is inherent to the human condition (see 2.2.5.1; 2.3.11). This basic understanding of faith is analogous to what a contemporary theologian would call "the common faith or experience of all [persons] simply as such."[40] This would also be analogous to a statement made by Albert Camus, who said, "We choose to continue existing from the moment we do not let overselves die, and thus we recognize a value, at least, a relative one, in life."[41] For Clement, faith as inherent to the human condition (*fides humana*) must be joined with the *Logos* (*fides divina*) in order to become saving faith (*fides apprehensiva*). As later theologians would say, *Fides filios Dei facit.* The basis for this transformation from *fides humana* to *fides apprehensive* occurs in the act of choice, which is based on a deliberate preconception or anticipation (what the Stoics called πρόληψις ἑκούσιος).

What Clement is saying here is twofold. First, he is acknowledging that all human beings possess a common faith (ἡ κοινὴ πίστις), which underlies our most basic rational choices (*Strom.* 5.1). It is something so basic to existence that we make no initial choice for it, nor do we reflect much on it (see 2.4.16.1-3). This common faith exists all cultures. It is our initial contact with the grace of God (see 2.4: cf. Rom 1.18-20). Second, there is a saving faith based on common faith, along with instruction and the word of God. This is the type of faith to which Clement is referring when he says, "But we, who have heard from the Scriptures that self-determining choice and refusal have been given by the Lord to men, rest in the infallible criterion of faith, manifesting a willing spirit, since we have chosen life and believe God through his voice" (2.4.12.1). This type of faith is necessary because knowledge (ἐπιστήμη) can be submerged in ignorance (2.17.76.1). It is not until knowledge has been properly reconstituted by means of the *Logos* that a human being has the opportunity to experience the process of salvation. As Clement says, "[T]eaching is reliable when faith on the part of those who hear, being so to speak, a sort of natural art, contributes to the process of learning" (2.6.25.4). In other words, through the faith offered by the *Logos,* human beings have the opportunity to live a righteous life, a life in conformity with the commandments of God.

Righteous living, which is equivalent to service to God (θεραπεία θεοῦ), consists of two components: (1) self-discipline and (2) the cherishing of one's divine aspect (7.1.1). In Clement's thought, self-discipline appears to mean obedience to the commandments of God (7.3.16). Obedience, in turn, assists the Gnostic Christian in the cherishing of her divine aspect. It is the foundation for a higher revelatory experience that is entirely intellectual, being defined by Clement as "the habit of mind which preserves the fitting attitude toward God" (7.1.3). In short, the cherishing of one's divine aspect means intellectually grasping both the theory and practice of right living.

As I noted earlier, there is a universalist element in Clement's theology (7.2.6). Such universalism may have been developed in conversation with groups such as the Valentinians. By contrast to the Valentinians, Clement holds that all righteous persons are equal and perfected in the sight of God. As Casey states, "The notion of this perfection is one of Clement's subtlest thoughts, for in spite of the assertion that Christians share in the perfection of Christ, the meaning is not that Christ and Christians are exactly alike."[42] As understood by Clement, this perfection (τελείωσις) is relative and not absolute. His doctrine of salvation does not exclude important differences among believers themselves. Perfection and equality are posited solely in terms of God's providential purpose, which, according to Clement, may vary from case to case. The righteous are perfect, not because they all have the same measure of faith or *charismata*, but because in knowing God they have equally realized the divine will and can fulfill with equal acceptability God's purpose for them. [43] In short, universal salvation involves realizing God's providential purpose and does not involve adhering by necessity to a particular ethno-religious orientation.

The Seed of Abraham and the Law

Thus far, I have attempted to use the most wide-ranging language possible when discussing Clement's theology (e.g., "righteous" life instead of "Christian" life, or "saving" faith instead of "Christian faith). The rationale has been to use the most expansive language possible in outlining Clement's theology. At this point, the historical link between the Alexandrian Christian community and the Alexandrian Jewish community is important, because it forces one to reflect on the radically altered relationship between both groups during the second century CE.

It is quite apparent that Clement has little or no first-hand experience with Judaism.[44] The absence of a Jewish presence in Alexandria was the byproduct of the revolt of 115-117 CE. Anti-Jewish polemic was rife in Alexandria during Clement's time, and his portrayal of Judaism appears indebted more to a popular caricature of Jews than to actual contacts.[45] The context of the Alexandrian church at the time appears to be one of an educated and prosperous Gentile community with no meaningful connection to a once powerful Jewish community. Furthermore, this change in urban populace seems to have been accompanied by a change in the Christian community's attitude regarding Judaism. It may be analogous to the change that some scholars believe occurred in the attitude of the Roman church toward Judaism, and Clement may be transmitting some of this bias in his treatise.[46] For example, he tends to place the Jews in the same polemical category as he does the Gnostics, whose theology Clement attempts to invalidate: "For [the Jews] did not know and do the will of the law; but what they supposed, what they thought the law wished" (2.9.42.5). However, this should not be our final analysis of Clement's view of Judaism.

As noted previously, the intellectual connection between Alexandrian Christianity and Alexandrian Judaism is virtually without question. A historical, although tenuous, connection between the two groups in Alexandria appears reasonably valid. Yet, by the time of Clement there was little to no contact between Christians and Jews in the city.[47] Moreover, Clement reflects the popular anti-Jewish sentiment to be found in the city after the 115 revolt.

A great deal of *Strom.* 2 discusses the efficacy of the law as presented in the Hebrew Bible. Clement believed the law to have been given by the Logos. This makes it valid and worthy to be followed. As he says, "God deemed it advantageous that from the law and the prophets men should receive preparatory discipline by the Lord. The fear of the Lord was called the beginning of wisdom, being given by the Lord, through Moses, to the disobedient and hard of heart" (2.8.37.2). He calls the law our παιδαγωγός to Christ (2.7.35.2: cf. Gal 3.24). It is right reason, just, and the work of the Lord (see 2.4, 8, 12). The law "enjoins us to shun what are in reality bad things – adultery, uncleanness, pederasty, ignorance, wickedness, soul-disease, death (not that which severs the soul from the body, but that which severs the soul from the truth)" (2.7.34.2). In short, the law is the truth implanted by the *Logos* in Jewish culture, and, as such, is equal if not superior to the philosophy of the Greeks (see 2.18, 22).

Fear is an integral aspect of obedience to the law. The logic for this position proceeds from Clement's understanding of the divine educational project. As indicated above, it is necessary for God to coerce some to act properly: "For those whom reason convinces not, fear tames" (2.8.37.2). Yet, coercion "does not itself generate faith" (2.6.30.4). Fear is an instrument faith uses to lead one to salvation. In this respect, fear should not be seen as something bad – as "an irrational aberration, and perturbation of mind"– but as an entirely rational means to instruct one in righteousness (2.7.32.3). In fact, Clement says that if the philosophically minded desire to quibble about what he means by fear, "let the philosophers term the fear of the law, cautious fear (εὐλάβεια), which is a shunning agreeable to reason" (2.7.32.4).[48]

There is a definite connection in Clement's thought between faith and the law. As he says,

> Learning . . . is . . . obedience to the commandments, which is faith in God . . . . The highest demonstration, to which we alluded, produces intelligent faith by the adducing and opening up of the Scriptures to the souls of those who desire to learn; the result of which is knowledge (2.11.48.4).

Common faith is the foundation upon which saving faith is built. Saving faith is nourished through instruction by the *Logos*. The law, and the fear that accompanies it, is an acceptable divine instrument for leading one to salvation. In other words, the new covenant does not nullify the old. Clement makes this clear when he says, "Now the just shall live by faith," which is according to the covenant and the commandments; since these, which are two in name and time, given in accordance with the [divine] economy – being in power one – the old and the new, are disposed through the Son by one God" (2.6.29.2).

If the Jews have the law, and the law has not been nullified under the new covenant, then is it possible the Jews who possess faith – even if it is not faith in Christ – can be saved? This again raises the issue of the presentation of Jews in Clement's text. It cannot be denied that Clement gives some disparaging remarks about Jews. At the beginning of this treatise, he speaks of the possibility that a Jew may read this text and be converted: "[P]erchance the Jew also may listen and be able quietly to turn from what he has believed to him on whom he has not believed" (2.1.2.1). Furthermore, the central critique in this treatise regarding Jews comes directly from Clement's reading of Romans 10.2-3: "For [the Jews] did not know and do the will of the law; but what they supposed, what they thought the law wished" (3.9.42.5).

As mentioned earlier, this critique places the Jews in the same rhetorical category as the Gnostics and others, who also misunderstand the teaching of the *Logos*. Central to Clement's critique is the issue of scriptural interpretation. He says, "And [the Jews] did not believe the law as prophesying, but the bare word; and they followed through fear, not through disposition and faith" (2.9.42.5). Clement disparages the Jews for not reading the relevant scriptural texts in the same manner, as Christians like himself did. That is, Clement's method for reading the text places prophecy at the center of scriptural interpretation. Instead of the Jewish practice of reading the prophets as an interpretation of the law, Clement understands the prophets to be disclosing information that is to be understood in addition to he law. Moreover, Clement understands prophecy to be at work in texts not usually understood to be prophetic (e.g., the idea of the seed of Abraham). In this he follows a tradition laid down by Paul in Romans and Galatians.

The first quotation from Romans 10 comes in *Strom.* 2.6.25.1 when he echoes Paul: "Lord, who has believed our report?" (Rom 10.16; Isa 53.1). This is followed by a quotation of Rom 10.17: "For 'faith cometh by hearing, and hearing by the works of God,' saith the apostle." Subsequently, Clement quotes Rom 10.14, 15. That is, faith serves as the basis upon which one builds *gnosis*. Now it is not clear as to whether Clement is referring to common faith here or not. What is clear is that this faith serves as the foundation for further learning. Faith itself is not enough. Faith makes one receptive to the teaching of the *Logos*, but it is not sufficient in itself (2.6.26.1). Further, receptivity does not exclude the need for rational choice. The believer must still choose to follow: "[T]he divine work cries, calling all together; knowing perfectly well those who will not obey; whereas to obey or not is in our own power, provided we have not the excuse of ignorance to adduce" (2.6.26.3).

The implications of ignorance notwithstanding, Clement continues his argument by saying, "[The *Logos*] makes a just call, and demands of each according to his strength" (2.6.26.3). He is drawing on his doctrine of salvation here. He maintains that some are able, have the will or desire to improve. The linchpin is ignorance, and a person can progress only when she is not ignorant. However, the *Logos* accommodates itself to the abilities of the individual.

Drawing upon Rom 9.4, Clement says, "[The faithful servants] are entrusted with the utterances respecting God and the divine words, the commands with the execution of the injunctions" (2.6.27.2). Here he has clearly altered the Pauline text. In Romans, the Jews are the ones who possess the covenants and the divine commandments. The intent in *Strom.* appears to be a desire for greater inclusivity. This thesis, I believe, is confirmed when Clement says, "For we as seed of Abraham can be either Jews or Gentiles as long as their faith is founded upon hearing. Drawing upon John 9.4, Rom 9.4 and 10.12 (ὁ γὰρ αὐτός [ἐστιν] κύριος πάντων), he maintains that there is a need for inclusivity based on the inclusive nature of monotheism: "And if the same mansions are promised by prophecy to us and to the patriarchs, the God of both the covenants is shown to be one" (2.6.28).

Clement's next statement may be troubling to readers for two reasons. First, it does not appear in the Romans text. Second, it could suggest that Christians have supplanted Jews as the people of God. It reads: "Thou hast inherited the covenant of Israel" (2.6.29.1). Given the context of the statement, it appears that the best way to understand it is to say that Gentiles have inherited the covenant of Israel along with the Jews. This makes sense given that the next statement involves the inclusion of Gentiles into the plan of salvation, and is followed by the statement quoted that maintains that both covenants are in reality one in the divine economy. Quoting Rom 1.17, Clement then takes on a salvation history perspective when he says, "[T]he one salvation which from prophecy to the Gospel is perfected [is done] by one and the same Lord" (2.6.29.3). It appears reasonable to say that Clement's soteriology takes a salvation history perspective regarding the plan of salvation.

The crucial passage concerning Jews comes in *Strom.* 2.9. In this section, Clement quotes Paul's famous statement from Rom 10.2-3 regarding the zeal of the Jews. He then castigates them for their ignorance, again raising the issue of ignorance in the text. Earlier Clement argued that ignorance disables the individual in that the individual cannot know what is right.

Not knowing, and subsequently not doing, what is right is sin (2.15.62.3). The reason for this sin arises from a misinterpretation of scripture i.e., the Jews "did not believe the law as prophesying" (2.9.42.5).

For the argument in Rom 10.19-21, Clement maintains that the Jews are responsible for their own sin.[49] Their disobedience has cut them off from the truth. Yet, it is also their disobedience that opens up the possibility for the salvation of the Gentiles. This turn of events merits the Jews another opportunity for salvation. As he intimates, "Then the goodness of God is show also in this case"(2.9.43.3). Echoing Rom 11.11, the extension of salvation to the Gentiles is meant to provoke the Jews to jealousy and willingness to repent. What they need is education, given that repentance is "tardy knowledge" (2.6.26.50). This is made all the more intriguing when read in light of *Strom.* 6.14:

> So that when we hear, "Thy faith hath saved thee," we do not understand him to say absolutely that those who have believed in any way whatever shall be saved, unless also works follow. But it was to the Jews alone that he spoke this utterance, who kept the law and lived blamelessly, who wanted only faith in the Lord.

It appears that Clement holds out the strong conviction that Jews will be saved, when they accept the Lord. In this conviction he is clearly following the apostle Paul. As Ernst Käsemann says, "Paul seriously counts on it that the Gentile mission will make Israel jealous and lead to its conversion. This hope can be imagined only if the conversion itself stand beyond any doubt and only the way to it obscure."[50] This thesis is further validated by the passage that follows. Clement cannot speak on how the salvation of all the Jews will be effected in the future, but he can account for how those Jews preceding the Lord are saved. He says,

> And the Shepherd, speaking plainly of those who had fallen asleep, recognizes certain righteous among Gentiles and Jews, not only before the appearance of Christ, but before the law, in virtue of acceptance before God – as Abel, as Noah, as any other righteous man (2.9.43.5).[51]

God has prepared a means for the righteous dead to receive salvation. They are preached to *post mortem* and receive the "seal [of the preaching]" of Christ: "they fell asleep in righteousness and in great purity, but only wanted this seal" (2.9.44.3).

Clement believes that Christianity is the historical manifestation of God's plan for the inclusion of the Gentiles into the process of salvation. This means that God should not properly be viewed as the God of the Jews alone, but as the God of all. Clement argues that truth exists in all cultures and that God seeks the salvation of all. Jesus, the historical manifestation of the *Logos*, was Jewish because his coming was prophesied in the Jewish scriptures. Therefore, the incarnation was not meant to undermine Judaism but to demonstrate that its true purpose was to include all ethno-religious groups. As Clement says, "One righteous person is no different from another religious person, whether Jew or Greek. For God is not only the Lord of the Jews but of all humanity" (6.6).

What keeps the Jews from realizing this truth is the improper interpretation of scripture. Yet, Clement, like Paul, believes that Gentile inclusion will prompt Jewish repentance and, consequently, Jewish salvation. It is the *Logos* who guides proper scriptural interpretation, which in a practical sense means the acceptance of Jesus as messiah. When the Jew accepts Christ, she also realizes the proper fulfillment of God's purpose for Judaism. This is not the displacement of Judaism but the fulfillment of the providential plan of God: the overcoming of ethno-religious divisions. On a secondary level, the historical relationship between Judaism and Christianity is evident in the development of the Alexandrian church itself. Clement takes the Hellenistic Judaism to which the Alexandrian church is indebted and synthesizes it to Greco-Roman philosophy in a way that makes his theology the intellectual corollary of the Alexandrian historical paradigm. In Christianity, according to Clement, God's inclusive purpose for humanity is realized, and this inclusive purpose will eventually incorporate the Jews as an ethno-religious group – an attitude that initially grew out of the large-scale Christian frustration regarding the on-going Jewish rejection of Jesus Christ.

So what will become of the Jews? They will be saved, or at least a portion of them will be saved. Clement is not unambiguously clear on this matter. Still, what is apparent is that Christianity has not displaced Judaism, and that the rejection of the Jewish scriptures by certain Gnostic groups represents a misunderstanding of the providential process of salvation. *Strom.* 2 thus stands at a significant point in the history of Christian theology and scriptural interpretation. It represents a Christian attempt to define itself over against its Jewish predecessor, but in a way that acknowledges its dependence upon Jewish historical and intellectual roots. In Clement one finds the beginning of an argument that Christianity represents a divine attempt to overcome long established ethno-religious divisions – divisions that were often linked to particular cultures, customs, languages, and places. Paul's discussion of Jews in Romans 10-11 serves an advantageous purpose as a tool for the accomplishment of this aim.

---

[1] "Christian" as a substantive term is anachronistic when it comes to the apostle Paul, particularly when one considers that Paul never uses the term to describe himself or his religious practices.

[2] See Christopher Haas, *Alexandria in Late Antiquity: Topography and Social Conflict* (Ancient Society and History; Baltimore: John Hopkins University Press, 1997), 51.

[3] Ibid., 57

⁴See Roger Bagnall and Bruce Frier, *The Demography of Roman Egypt* (Cambridge Studies in Population, Economy and Society in Past Time 23; Cambridge and New York; Cambridge University Press, 1994), 54; cf. Haas, *Alexandria in Late Antiquity*, 46, and Alan Bowman, *Egypt after the Pharaohs 332 BC-AD 642*(Berkeley and Los Angeles: University of California Press, 1986), 17-18.

⁵See Bagnall and Frier, *Demography of Roman Egypt*, 56.

⁶Ibid., 56, and Roger Bagnall, *Egypt in Late Antiquity* (Princeton: Princeton University Press, 1993), 312.

⁷See Haas, *Alexandria in Late Antiquity*, 139.

⁸See Ibid., 60

⁹See Joseph Modrzejewski, *The Jews of Egypt: From Rameses II to Emperor Hadrian* (trans. Robert Cornman; Princeton: Princeton University Press, 1995), 21-26.

¹⁰Haas, *Alexandria in Late Antiquity*, 95

¹¹Ibid., 95.

¹²Ibid., 97

¹³Ibid., 96

¹⁴See Modrzejewski, *The Jews of Egypt*, 185-190, and Peder Borgen, "Philo of Alexandria," *ABD* 5:3333-342.

¹⁵See Colin Roberts, *Manuscript, Society and Belief in Early Christian Egypt* (The Schweich Lectures of the British Academy; London: Oxford University Press, 1979), 57-58.

¹⁶See L. C. Hurst, "Apollos," *ABD* 1:301; Ernst Haenchen, *The Acts of the Apostles: A Commentary* (trans. R. McL. Wilson; Philadelphia: Westminster, 1965), 549-551.

¹⁷See Gerd Lüdemann, *Early Christianity according to the Traditions in Acts: A Commentary* (trans. John Bowden; Minneapolis: Fortress, 1987), 207-209.

¹⁸See Clayton Jefford, "Mark, John," *ABD* 4:557-558.

¹⁹For a discussion of this in a larger context, consult Annewies van den Hoek, "The 'Catechetical' School of Early Christian Alexandria and Its Philonic Heritage," *HTR* 90 (1997), 59-87

²⁰See Shaye Cohen, *From the Macabees to the Mishnah* (ed. Wayne A. Meeks; LEC 1; Philadelphia: Westminster, 1989), 111-115, and Lee Levine, "The Nature and Origin of the Palestinian Synagogue Reconsidered," *JBL* 115 (1996), 425-448.

²¹See Haas, *Alexandria in Late Antiquity*, 62.

²²See Elaine Pagels, *The Gnostic Gospels* (New York: Vintage, 1981), 38.

²³Roberts, *Manuscript*, 10-14.

²⁴See Jakob Petuchowski, "The Liturgy of the Synagogue," in *The Lord's Prayer and Jewish Liturgy* (ed. Jakob Petuchowski and Michael Brocke; New York: Seabury, 1978), 55.

²⁵See Walter Bauer, *Orthodoxy and Heresy in Earliest Christianity* (trans. Philadelphia Seminar on Christian Origins; ed. Robert Kraft and Gerhard Krobel; Philadelphia: Fortress, 1971), 48, 53, and 59.

²⁶Clement quotes Philo approximately 125 times in his writings. See van den Hoek, "How Alexandrian was Clement of Alexandria?" *HeyJ*, 185.

²⁷R. Casey, "Clement of Alexandria and the Beginnings of Christian Platonism," in *Studies in Early Christianity: A Collection of Scholarly Essays* (ed. Everett Ferguson, David Scholer, and Paul Finney; The Early Church and Greco-Roman Thought 8; New York: Garland, 1993), 140.

²⁸T.B. Glover, *Conflict of Religions in the Early Roman Empire* (Boston, Beacon Hill, 1909), 271

[29] Glover, *Conflict of Religions*, 289; see also Casey, "Clement of Alexandria," 88; Ronald Williamson, *Jews in the Hellenistic World: Philo* (ed. P.R. Ackroyd, A.R.C. Leaney, J. W. Packer; Cambridge Commentaries on Writings of the Jewish and Christian World, 200 BC to AD 200; Cambridge: Cambridge University Press, 1989), 107.

[30] See Christopher Stead, *Philosophy in Christian Antiquity* (Cambridge: Cambridge University Press, 1994).

[31] Casey, "Clement of Alexandria," 107.

[32] See J. Dillon, *The Middle Platonists* (Ithaca: Cornell University Press, 1977), 158-159; M. Baltes, *Timaios Lokros. Über die Natur des Kosmos und der Seele* (Leiden: Brill, 1972), 105.

[33] Glover, *Conflict of Religions*, 297.

[34] See Van Den Hoek, "The 'Catechetical' School of Early Christian Alexandria," 64 n. 23, for a discussion of the terms παιδαγωγός and διδάσκαλος.

[35] See R. F. Stalley, *An Introduction to Plato's Laws* (Indianapolis: Hackett, 1983), 42.

[36] See Ibid., 67.

[37] Ibid., 43.

[38] See Ibid., 67.

[39] Robert Casey comments on God's friendly concern for man, his φιλανθρωπία in "Clement of Alexandria," 97.

[40] Schubert Ogden, *The Reality of God and Other Essays* (Dallas: Southern Methodist University Press, 1992), 124

[41] Albert Camus, "The Riddle," *Atlantic Monthly* (June 1963), 85.

[42] Casey, "Clement of Alexandria, 111.

[43] Ibid., 111.

[44] See van den Hoek, "The 'Catechetical' School of Early Christian Alexandria," 80, 82; idem, "How Alexandrian was Clement of Alexandria?" 185; cf. Haas, *Alexandria in Late Antiquity*, 105-106.

[45] Haas, *Alexandria in Late Antiquity*, 108; van den Hoek, "The 'Catechetical' School of Early Christian Alexandria," 80.

[46] See Daniel Patte, *Paul's Faith and the Power of the Gospel: A Structural Introduction to the Pauline Letters* (Philadelphia: Fortress, 1983), 247-248.

[47] van den Hoek, "How Alexandrian was Clement of Alexandria?", 185

[48] A Stoic term (see *SVF* 3.175.431; Cicero, *Tusc.* 4.6.13; Plutarch, *Mor.* 1037f).

[49] Except, of course, for the quotation of 10.4 immediately preceding this section.

[50] Ernst Käsemann, *Commentary on Romans* (ed. and trans. Geoffrey W. Bromiley; Grand Rapids: Eerdmans, 1980), 304. Daniel Patte makes a similar point in his exegesis of the passage. See Patte, *Paul's Faith and the Power of the Gospel*, 291-293.

[51] It is interesting that the image of the shepherd also appears in *Strom.* 6.14.

Bibliography

Bagnall, Roger, *Egypt in Late Antiquity*. Princeton: Princeton University Press, 1993.

Bagnall, Roger and Bruce Frier. *The Demography of Roman Egypt*. Cambridge Studies in Population, Economy and Society in Past Time 23. Cambridge and New York: Cambridge University Press, 1994.

Baltes, M. *Timaios Lokros. Über die Natur des Kosmos und der Seele*. Leiden: Brill, 1972.

Bauer, Walter. *Orthodoxy and Heresy in Earliest Christianity*. Edited by Robert Kraft and Gerhard Krobel. Translated by the Philadelphia Seminar on Christian Origins. Philadelphia: Fortress, 1971.

Borgen, Peder. "Philo of Alexandria." Pages 333-342 in vol. 5 of *The Anchor Bible Dictionary*. Edited by David N. Freedman. 6 vols. New York: Doubleday, 1992.

Bowman, Alan. *Egypt after the Pharoahs 332 BC-AD 642*. Berkeley and Los Angeles. University of California Press, 1986.

Camus, Albert. "The Riddle." *Atlantic Monthly* (June 1963).

Casey, Robert. "Clement of Alexandria and the Beginnings of Christian Platonism." In *Studies in Early Christianity: A Collection of Scholary Essays*. The Early Church and Greco-Roman Thought 8. Edited by Everett Ferguson, David Scholer, Paul Finney. New York: Garland, 1993.

Cohen, Shaye. *From the Maccabees to the Mishnah*. Library of Early Christianity 1. Edited by Wayne A. Meeks. Philadelphia: Westminster, 1989.

Dillon, John. *The Middle Platonists*. Ithaca: Cornell University Press, 1977.

Glover, T.B. *Conflict of Religions in the Early Roman Empire*. Boston: Beacon Hill, 1909.

Haenchen, Ernst. *The Acts of the Apostles: A Commentary*. Translated by R. McL. Wilson. Philadephia: Westminster, 1965.

Haas, Christopher. *Alexandria in late Antiquity: Topography and Social Conflict*. Ancient Society and History. Baltimore: John Hopkins University Press, 1997.

Hoek, Annewies, van den. "How Alexandrian was Clement of Alexandria?" *Heythrop Journal* 31(1990).

_____. "The 'Catechetical' School of Early Christian Alexandria and Its Philonic Heritage". *Harvard Theological Review* 90 (1997).

Hurst, L. D. "Apollos." Page 301 in vol. 1 of *The Anchor Bible Dictionary*. Edited by David N. Freedman. 6 vols. New York: Doubleday, 1992.

Jefford, Clayton. "Mark, John." Pages 557-558 in vol. 4 of *The Anchor Bible Dictionary*. Edited by David N. Freedman. 6 vols. New York: Doubleday, 1992.

Käsemann, Ernst. *Commentary on Romans*. Edited and translated by Geoffrey Bromiley. Grand Rapids: Eerdmans, 1980.

Levine, Lee. "The Nature and Origin of the Palestinian Synagogue Reconsidered." *Journal of Biblical Literature* 115 (1996).

Ludemann, Gerd. *Early Chrisianity according to the Traditions in Acts: A Commentary.* Translated by John Bowden. Minneapolis: Fortress, 1987.

Modrzejewski, Joseph. *The Jews of Egypt: From Rameses II to Emperor Hadrian.* Translated by Robert Cornman. Princeton University Press, 1995.

Ogden, Schubert. *The Reality of God and Other Essays.* Dallas: Southern Methodist University, 1992.

Pagels, Elaine. *The Gnostic Gospels.* New York: Vintage, 1981.

Patte, Daniel. *Paul's Faith and the Power of the Gospel: A Structural Introduction to the Pauline Letters.* Philadelphia: Fortress, 1983.

Petuchowski, Jakob. "The Liturgy of the Synagogue." In *The Lord's Prayer and Jewish Liturgy.* Edited by Jakob Petuchowski and Michael Brocke. New York: Seabury, 1978.

Roberts, Colin. *Manuscript, Society and Belief in Early Christian Egypt.* The Schweich Lectures of the British Academy. London: Oxford University Press, 1979.

Stalley, R.F. *An Introduction to Plato's Laws.* Indianapolis: Hackett, 1983.

Stead, Christopher. *Philosophy in Christian Antiquity.* Cambridge: Cambridge University Press, 1994.

Williamson, Ronald. *Jews in the Hellenistic World: Philo.* Cambridge Commentaries on Writings of the Jewish and Christian World, 200 BC to AD 200. vol. 1, part 2. Edited by P.R. Ackroyd, A.R.C. Leaney, J.W. Packer. Cambridge: Cambridge University Press, 1989.

A Response: Is Clement of Alexandria a Supersessionist?

Kathy L. Gaca

———— ◆ ————

Professor Michael Brown's paper, "Clement of Alexandria on Jewish Salvation in *Stromateis* 2," concerns Clement of Alexandria's interpretation of Romans 10-11 in *Stromateis* 2. Brown's paper extends his prior interest in Clement and patristic exegesis, which he shows in his dissertation on Clement's and Tertullian's readings of the Lord's Prayer.

The question of how Clement interprets Romans 10-11 is an important one given the hostile trend in patristic thought regarding the Jews' standing with God. Patristic advocates of this trend support the idea that Christians have displaced Jews as God's people because Jews dissent from central Christian tenets about Jesus, especially the position that Jesus is "Christ" or "Lord." The more such a trend prevails in the increasingly dominant Christian society of the patristic period (such as in the notorious homilies of John Chrysostom), the more Jews are likely to be socially stigmatized and victimized by Christian religious prejudice. As Brown points out, however, Paul in Romans 10-11 makes several comments that prima facie resist the view that Jews are outcasts. Paul contends that in the end both faithful Jews and Christians will belong to God's people, not that Christians have supplanted the Jews en bloc. According to Paul, "God has not rejected the people whom he acknowledged of old as his own." Indeed, a select group of Jews has already been saved by God's grace. In the future, further, "the whole of Israel will be saved" once "the Gentiles have been included in full strength" as Christians among God's people (Rom 10:2, 5-7, 25-26). How, then, do church fathers respond to comments such as these in Romans, especially if they elsewhere reveal doubt about the Jews' standing with God? Brown has chosen a valuable test case to explore in Clement, for Clement suggests that he harbors this doubt and yet tries to give a reasonably fair interpretation of Romans 10-11.

Brown explicitly addresses his important thesis in the last part of his paper, "The Seed of Abraham and the Law," where he questions

63

whether the Jews will be saved according to Clement. The extensive
first part of his paper aims to elucidate two points, first that the intellectual connection between Alexandrian Christianity and Alexandrian
Judaism is without question; and second, that a historical connection
between the two groups is reasonably clear.

I here restrict my comments to the last, and most pertinent, part of
Brown's paper. Brown concludes his main thesis by maintaining that
"Clement is not unambiguously clear on th[e] matter" concerning
whether the Jews "or at least a portion of them will be saved" according to Paul. Yet, Brown then adds, "what is apparent is that Christianity
has not displaced Judaism" in Clement's thought. By this, Brown means
that in light of Romans 10-11, "Clement's exposition on Judaism ...
mitigates a growing Gentile Christian tendency toward
supersessionism." I find these conclusions questionable. Clement seems
to me very clear about his stance on the question whether the Jews will
be saved. He favors the ideology that they will not be saved unless they
become Christian, which indicates that to Clement's mind Christians
have displaced Jews as God's people. Clement's exegetical argument
proceeds thus as I read it from Brown's quotations of Clement and from
Clement's text. A person needs what Clement calls "faith" to be saved.
"Faith" by his definition means "proper obedience to the commandments," which one acquires by learning the logos of Pentateuchal Law
(*Strom* 2.11). In order to acquire faith in this sense, further, one must do
what Clement refers to as "believing in the Law as prophecy, not the
bare word." By Clement's interpretation of Romans 10.2-3, however,
Jews follow the Law as bare word, not as prophecy; and they do so
through fear rather than faith (*Strom* 2.9). This means they are not
showing the "proper obedience to the commandments" that Clement
requires by his relevant definition of faith. Clement draws on Romans
10:2-3 to further support his view that Jews show improper obedience to
the Law. Paul here maintains that Israel, in ignorance of God's righteousness, sought to establish a righteousness of its own. As Clement
sees it, Paul's statement suffices to show that "[the Jews] did not know
and do the will of the Law [as prophecy]; but what they supposed, what
they thought the law wished" (*Strom* 2.9).

Clement finds it so critical to read Pentateuchal Law as prophecy
because, quite simply, the Law foretells that Jesus is Christ, or so he
believes. This is the cardinal prophecy from Moses that one must
believe in order to be saved. If one does not read the Law as prophecy,
then clearly one will not find this or any prophetic forecast latent in the
Pentateuch. Clement accordingly maintains that if a Jewish man were
to revamp his hermeneutic approach to the Law so as to uncover its
prophecies, which is what he should do, the man would find this central
prophecy about Jesus Christ in it. In so doing he would then rightly

"turn from what he has believed to him on whom he has not believed" (that is, Jesus Christ), gain faith (that is, proper obedience to the Law as prophecy), and thereby be saved. Clement in his exegesis consequently argues that only those Jews will be saved who, like Paul, believe that Jesus is Christ in light of the prophetic Law. It follows that in order for Jews to be saved according to Clement, they need to adopt the tenet that Jesus is Christ. This tenet was the formative point on which Christianity parted ways historically with Judaism. Clement therefore advocates the patristic ideology that Christians have displaced Jews, though he adds a kind of catch-22 qualifier: 'You are Jewish and wish to be saved? Become Christian and your wish is fulfilled.' Clement therefore does not support the inclusive vision that Jews and Christians are equally God's people, which Brown too generously tries to attribute to him.

Clement's ideology of displacement, moreover, is not far off the mark from Romans 10-11, even though it may initially seem to be. Granted, Paul contends that the whole of Israel will be saved, but he too attaches the following condition to this salvation, as Brown notes. The Jews, envious at Christianity's success among Gentiles, will eventually follow God's plan and hasten en masse to join the new religion. Thus, Paul's overall comments arguably play right into the patristic idea that Jews, like Gentiles, will not be saved unless they believe the Christian tenet that Jesus is Lord.

THREE

The Soteriology of Romans in Clement of Alexandria, *Stromateis* 2: Faith, Fear, and Assimilation to God

L.L. Welborn

———— ◆ ————

This essay suggests that Paul's Epistle to the Romans was one of the most important sources used by Clement of Alexandria in the composition of *Stromateis* 2, and that Romans probably suggested to Clement his larger rubrics of faith as the way to salvation and the fear of the law. Furthermore, this interaction with Romans shows that Clement played a key role in the development of a consistently epistemological interpretation of faith, an interpretation that charts a new direction in Pauline theology.

Since the work of E. de Faye,[1] it has belonged to the *communis opinio* that one seeks in vain for a principle of composition in the "Patchwork" of Clement of Alexandria. Although Eusebius names the *Stromateis* first in the catalogue of Clement's writings (*Hist. eccl.* 6.13.1), and reckons it, alongside the *Hypotyposeis*, as Clement's principal achievement (*Hist. eccl.* 6.13.4-8),[2] the eight preserved books, only seven of which are complete, give the impression of being improvisations of the moment, their principle of composition described by de Faye as "se laisser entraîner".[3] J. Munck also warns against seeking to impose an order upon the *Stromateis*: "Einem Stromateus gegenüber kann man nicht unrichtiger verfahren."[4] Naturally, interpreters have not been content with this situation, and remain determined to discover the design of the work. M. Pohlenz admonishes: "Es wäre gut, wenn die ganze Analyse der *Stromateis* nochmals von jemand aufgenommen würde, der nicht 'Quellen' und 'Abhängigkeit' feststellen will, sondern einfach geduldig den Gedankensprüngen und verschlungenen Pfaden von Klemens' Darstellung nachspürt."[5]

It was A. Méhat who finally succeeded in exposing the literary structure of the *Stromateis*: his painstaking investigation makes visible a design within the fabric of the text.[6] Méhat bases his understanding of the composition of the *Stromateis* not only on Clement's occasional statements of purpose, but also upon analysis of the text itself. Thus he delineates how Clement forms his paragraphs out of the raw material of quotations, excerpts, and summaries, how he constructs sequences of material, how the sequences are connected to one another, how sets of quotations are combined to form larger sections. Méhat's demonstration that Clement operates with certain compositional principles obliges interpreters to seek after the plan of the work. But how far interpreters are from comprehending the structure of individual books, not to speak of the composition of the *Stromateis* as a whole, is illustrated by Méhat's evaluation of previous literary analyses.

The prologue to the second book of the *Stromateis* exemplifies the problem. Clement begins by announcing his intention to demonstrate how the Greeks have pilfered the philosophy of Jews and Christians by plagiarizing and falsifying their sacred writings (1.1). Then, according to the sentence division proposed by Stählin and adopted by Méhat,[7] the second subject of Clement's prospectus is an exposition of "the virtues of truth," namely, πίστις, σοφία, γνῶσις, ἐπιστήμη, ἐλπίς, ἀγάπη, μετάνοια, ἐκράτεια, and φόβος θεοῦ (1.1). As a third theme, Clement promises an explication of what is "occult" in the philosophy of the Christians, that is, τό συμβολικὸν καὶ αἰνιγματῶδες εἶδος (1.2) Then, Clement proposes to add a sequel in which he defends those tenets, on account of which the Greeks have assailed Christians, hoping at the same time for the conversion of the Jews (2.1). Fifthly, Clement signals his intention to take up the most esteemed philosophers in a "friendly reproof" (ἔλεγχος ἀγαπητικός) both of their life and their teaching. The goal of the reproof, Clement assures his readers, is not retribution, but conversion. In this connection, once again, Clement threatens to point out the intellectual goods which the philosophers have stolen, in order to demolish their conceit (2.2-3). As a consequence, Clement expects to find it necessary to treat of what is called the "curriculum of study," and of astrology, mathematics, magic, and sorcery (2.4). Clement concludes the prologue with some observations on the literary style of his work, promising a truthful, rather than an artful, exposition (2.3).

When one turns to the second book, and seeks to verify the announcements of the prologue, one quickly discovers that the book contains little of what was promised. The demonstration of the theft by the Greeks of the truths of the barbarian philosophy, touched upon in initial fashion in book 2, is furnished at great length in books 5 and 6. The virtues, treated as characteristics of the wise man in book 2, are discussed thematically in book 3. The defence of the tenets of Christian faith against the Greeks is indeed contained in book 2. The symbolic and enigmatic form of Christian doctrine, on the other hand, is not dealt with until book 5. A refutation and reproof of the philosophers is found in book 2, just as Clement promised. But the curriculum of study is not discussed until book 6, and there only in the briefest manner. Thus it appears that what is presented in the proem is not a detailed disposition of the second book, but only a more or less vague plan of the work that follows.[8]

What one actually encounters in the second book of the *Stromateis* is an essay on Christian life more coherent and profound than the prospectus of the book would have led one to expect. Examination of the structure of the book makes clear that Clement aims at nothing less than a comprehensive picture of the Christian life: he begins with faith περὶ τῆς πίστεως, 4.1-77.6), and the knowledge which derives therefrom, proceeds then to expound the virtues (περὶ ἀρετων, 78.1-126.4), and ends with a discussion of the chief good (περὶ τέλους, 127-136), which is "assimilation to god" (ἐξομοίωσις τῷ θεῷ). In the midst of the discussion of faith are embedded excurses on the true wise man (18.2-22) and on the utility of fear, and the law (32.1-45.7), whose status and function remain to be determined. But that Clement aimed at a comprehensive account of Christian faith, and that he sought to inscribe this account within a coherent structure, is indicated by the arch which reaches from the ἀρχή in faith to the τέλος in God.

Is it possible to discern the purpose and motive of *Stromateis* book 2? Clement aims at the conversion (ἐπιστροφή) of the philosophically minded among the Greeks (2.1-2), and perhaps also, if they will listen, the Jews (2.1). The work would thus seem to have a protreptic function.[9] But this invitation to take up the Christian way of life is not motivated solely by a missionary impulse. Clement finds it necessary to defend (ἀπολογήσασθαι) Christian faith against the attacks of certain Greeks (2.1). Thus Clement's introduction and invitation to the Christian way of life also contains censure of the attitudes that have prevented Greeks and Jews from accepting the true philosophy.

This understanding of the goal and motivation of book 2 of the *Stromateis* is confirmed by both internal and external evidence. The internal evidence consists of explicit references by Clement to the objections of Greeks against the Christian gospel. Already in *Strom.* 1.88.5, Clement cites the opinion of the "seeming wise" (δοκησίσοφοι) among the Greeks that the Christian kerygma is μυθῶδες: "they consider it fabulous that God should have a Son, and especially that that Son should have suffered." But it is especially significant that Clement opens his discussion of faith in book 2 with a reference to Greeks who "disparage" the concept: πίστις δέ ἥν διαβάλλουσιν κενὴν καὶ βάρβαρον νομίζοντες Ἕλληνες... (8.4).

External indicators of an apologetic motivation are provided by the heightened polemic against the unphilosophical credulity of the Christians in the literature of Clement's pagan contemporaries. No longer content with the general reproach against Christians as "*odium humani generis*" (Tacitus *An.* 15.44.4; Suetonius *Nero* 16.2),[10] or the fantastic accusations of Thyestean feasts and Oedipodean intercourse (Athenagoras *Legatio* 3.1; Martyrs of Lyon 14)[11] pagan writers levelled criticism at the concept of "faith" itself. Galen openly criticized the inclination of Jews and Christians to believe in certain "undemonstrated laws" (νόμοι ἀναπόδεικτοι) and to accept everything on faith (*De pulsuum differentiis* 2.4).[12] Galen's critique of the credulity of Christians was surpassed in severity by Celsus, who made the groundlessness of "faith" the central object of his attack upon Christianity in his polemical treatise, the Ἀληθὴς Λόγος (fr. 1.9, 12, 27; 3.38-39, 42; 4.10; 6.7,8,10-14; etc.).[13] Indeed, it is possible that some of the apologetic statements in book 2 of the *Stromateis* are intended as implicit answers to the criticisms of Celsus.[14]

In general, one can say that Clement's defence of the life of faith in book 2 of the *Stromateis* is a response to the advanced stage of opposition by pagan intellectuals to the spread of Christianity. The point of issue between Clement and his pagan contemporaries is nicely defined by E.R. Dodds: "Had any cultivated pagan of the second century been asked to put in a few words the difference between his own view of life and the Christian one, he might reply that it was the difference between λογισμός and πίστις, between reasoned conviction and blind faith. To any one brought up on classical Greek philosophy, πίστις meant the lowest grade of cognition: it was the state of mind of the uneducated, who believe things on hearsay without being able to give reasons for their belief."[15] In the context of such criticism, "Clement seeks to relate the act of faith to the epistemological debates of the philosophical schools about the nature of proof and the ground of assent."[16] The result is a pioneering attempt to present Christian πίστις as the foundation of a wise and virtuous life. Karl Prümm accurately summarizes the achievement of book 2 of the *Stromateis* with the observation, "dass hier zum ersten Mal und sofort gründlich versucht wird, der geistigen Betätigung, die im christlichen Glaubensakt beschlossen wird, ihren besonderen Platz in dem Strom der verschiedenen Erkenntnisweisen anzuweisen, die der menschlichen Seele eigen sind. Es ist der erste Versuch einer Theorie der Erkenntnishaltung des Glaubens."[17]

Thus the purpose and function of book 2 of the *Stromateis* may be tentatively defined, despite the apparent discontinuity of Clement's train of thought. Recognition of the protreptic character of the *Stromateis* book 2 does much to explain the structure of Clement's argument. Protreptic writings invite readers to adopt a way of life, to accept a set of teachings as normative.[18] To this purpose, basic doctrines are frequently presented in a more comprehensive fashion, as in Clement's *Stromateis*. Protreptic works not only exhort their audiences to embrace a particular philosophy, but also seek to turn them away from an immoral, or futilely sensuous, way of life. Therefore censure or reproof may play a part in the protreptic work, if the author believes that the potential convert must overcome a misconception or a character problem before he or she can be initiated into a new way of life (cf. Epictetus *Dis.* 3.23). Most protreptic writings anticipate objections against the philosophy being recommended, and argue for its advantages or superiority. True to the principles of the protreptic genre, and in pursuit of its aims, Clement expounds the epistemology of the act of faith (4.1-77.6) as the very foundation of a virtuous life (78.1-126.4), and ends with a vision of perfect goodness as imitation of the divine (127-136). In order to make the invitation to the Christian life of faith more appealing to his audience, Clement presents the tenets of Christianity through quotations from Greek and Jewish philosophers, especially Plato and Philo. The point of this method of composition is to demonstrate that the life of the Christian, the true gnostic (97.1), is the realization of the ethic which the most esteemed philosophers taught.[19]

Yet, the appearance of disorderliness remains: thought seems to spring from topic to topic; the connections between source-materials are intricate and complex; the course of the argument is often tortuous and winding. Clement turns aside from the exposition to consider the vagaries of gnostic teachers, such as Basilides and Valentinus (36.1-40.3), or to explain the Scripture's puzzling ascription of human affections to God (72.1-75.3). Even after a hypothesis has been formulated regarding the form and function of Clement's *Miscellanies*, the principle of composition of the work continues to elude us.

The causes of the appearance of disorganization are principally three. First, the course of Clement's reflection is frequently determined by the sources to which he makes reference, or the literature upon which he is dependent.[20] Thus, at the beginning of the second book (4.1-4), a series of passages from Proverbs (3:5,6,7,12,23) are cited to recommend fear of God and submission to divine instruction as the attitude appropriate to the seeker after truth. When, as in this case, the source is explicitly mentioned, it is possible to follow the course of Clement's argument, to inspect his inferences, and even to identify the points of emphasis by careful examination of Clement's use of the source-material and a close comparison of tendencies. When, on the other hand, the source of Clement's citations is unacknowledged,[21] it is difficult to follow the course of his argument, and an appearance of disorganization arises.

Second, Clement makes use of philosophical commonplaces as principles of composition. That is to say, the raw materials of citations from disparate sources are selected, arranged, and sometimes recast in accordance with themes which had become established in the philosophical tradition.[22] Clement's intellectual contemporaries would have recognized the presence and operation of philosophical motifs, such as the doctrine of ὁμοίωσις θεῷ, "assimilation to God," first articulated by Plato in a famous passage in the *Theatetus*, and constantly echoed by the Platonists of Clement's day,[23] or the "*paradoxa Stoicorum*," that the wise man is the true king.[24] But even when modern interpreters are aware of the presence of such motifs,[25] their function as organizational principles is difficult to grasp. Thus it is only by means of a painstaking

analysis that Dietmar Wyrwa is able to show how Clement has used the
motifs of ὁμοίωσις θεῷ and *"paradoxa Stoicorum"* in sequence, like the
links of a chain, to organize disparate source materials in book 2 of the
Stromateis (80.5-6; 97.1-2; 100.3-104.3; 123.9-10.; 127-136).[26]

Finally, the excursuses on the true wise man (18.2-22), and on the
utility of fear and the role of the law (32.1-45.7), create an impression
of disorder. Nothing in the nature of those writings which fall broadly
into the tradition of the *protreptikoi logoi* explains the presence or function of these sections. Clement has obviously taken pains to embed the
excurses in their present contexts. One notes, for example, the repeated
use of the key-word σοφία in the excursus on the true wise man
(122.3,9,10,11; 123.1,5,9,17; 124.4,7,26; 125.3) following mention of
the ἀμαθής in 18.1. But to what purpose has Clement labored to integrate this excursus into his discussion of faith? The apology for fear and
the law in 32.1-40.3 is equally puzzling to interpreters. Prümm judges
that these chapters are "unwesentlich für den Gesamtablauf der
Erörterung über den Glauben."[27]

Perhaps the clue to the composition of book 2 of the *Stromateis* is to be
found in one of the principal causes of the appearance of disorder –
namely, in Clement's reliance upon literary sources for the presentation
of his argument. As Clement makes use of passages of Scripture and
citations from philosophers to organize his thoughts and to convey his
purpose from section to section, might he not have taken an unacknowledged source as the pattern for the composition of the book as a whole?
One may observe that the power of Clement's sources as compositional
principles seems greatest where his use of such works is unacknowledged.
For example, in *Strom.* 2.78-99 Clement sets himself to show that the
Mosaic law is the fountain of all ethics, and the source from which the
Greek philosophers drew the virtues on their lists. To do so, Clement
makes copious use of Philo's writing *De Virtutibus*.[28] The Old Testament
passages which Clement quotes follow the sequence established by Philo.
Clement borrows not only the substance of Philo's argument, but even the
wording. Yet the source of the extracts remains unacknowledged, "perhaps because Clement regarded them as merely references to Scripture to
which his attention has been called by Philo."[29] A little later (100.3),
when Clement quotes a non-scriptural maxim from the *Vita Mosis* (1.22),
he names "Philo the Pythagorean" as his authority.

Is the course of Clement's exposition in book 2 of the *Stromateis*
determined by use of an unacknowledged, scriptural source as a pattern,
or template? Yes, a pointer to the identity of this source is found in one of
Clement's compositional devices: the κύκλος.[30] In the construction of
arguments, Clement signals the completion of a theme by returning at the
close of a section to the word or motif he had used at the beginning. For
example, the conclusion of the excursus on the true wise man is marked
by the resumption of the key-word σοφία (σοφός) used at the beginning of

the digression: Πλάτων δὲ βασιλέα τὸν σοφὸν εἴρηκεν ἐν τῷ Πολιτικῷ, καὶ πρόκειται ἡ λέξις (22.8). With this resumptive reference, Clement recurs to his central discourse on faith: Τούτων δὴ ἐπιδεδειγμένων ἀναδράμωμεν αὖθις ἐπὶ τὸν περὶ τῆς πίστεως λόγον (23.1). The same device structures Clement's treatment of "assimilation to God" (ὁμοίωσις θεῷ) as the chief good and proper end of human beings: foreshadowed in 97.1 (οὗτός ἐστιν ὁ κατ' εἰκόνα καὶ ὁμοίωσιν), and explicitly anticipated in 100.3 (Πλάτων δὲ ὁ φιλόσοφος, εὐδαιμονίαν τέλος τιθέμενος, ὁμοίωσιν θεῷ φησιν αὐτὴν εἶναι κατὰ τὸ δυνατόν), the conclusion of the discussion is clearly marked by return to the language used at the opening: ἡμῖν δὲ αὐτοῖς εἰς τέλος ἀτελεύτητον ἀφικέσθαι πρόκειται πειθομένοις ταῖς ἐντολαῖς, τουτέστι τῷ θεῷ, καὶ κατ' αὐτὰς βιώσασιν ἀνεπιλήπτως καὶ ἐπιστημόνως διὰ τῆς τοῦ θείου θελήματος γνώσεως. ἥ τε τὸν ὀρθὸν λόγον ὡς οἷόν τε ἐξομοίωσις τέλος ἐστὶ καὶ εἰς τὴν τελείαν υἱοθεσίαν διὰ τοῦ υἱοῦ ἀποκατάστασις (134.1-2).[31]

If one applies this insight to the analysis of the second book of the *Stromateis* as a whole, then a hypothesis emerges as to the paradigm which Clement has followed in composing his invitation to the life of faith. After the prologue, Clement begins the exposition of "faith as the way" (4.2) to the hidden truth about God, "the professed aim of our philosophy" (5.2). A quotation provides the point of departure for the conception of faith that Clement will elaborate through all that follows: "Now my just one shall live by faith," the prophet said" (8.2).[32] On this basis, Clement proceeds to define faith as "a voluntary preconception" (πρόληψις ἑκούσιος), "the assent of piety" (θεοσεβείας συγκατάθεσις), a definition which relates the act of faith to the epistemological debates of the philosophical schools.[33] The prophet whom Clement quotes is, of course, Habakkuk. But Christian readers will more readily recall that Hab. 2:4 is the proof-text of the thesis statement of Paul's Epistle to the Romans (1:16-17), the first attempt to represent πίστις as the foundation of the redeemed life. In keeping with the ring-compositional device of *inclusio*, Clement returns to the quotation of Hab. 2:4 in 29.2 in order to signal the closure of the initial discussion περὶ τῆς πίστεως (8.4-31.3). On this occasion, Clement makes the reference to Romans explicit: "As the apostle also says in the Epistle to the Romans, 'For therein is the righteousness of God revealed from faith to faith,' teaching the one salvation which from prophecy to the Gospel is perfected by one and the same Lord." (29.3).

It is to the thesis statement of Romans that Clement recurs in 53.5 (πίστις δὲ ἰσχὺς εἰς σωτηρίαν), as he concludes discussion of the knowledge that derives from faith (48.1-55.6), and turns to examine voluntary actions and the life of virtue (56.1-3.). Clement concludes his discussion of the virtues in 126.3, by echoing, again, the Pauline formula, ἐκ πίστεως εἰς πίστιν, from Rom. 1:17: "Thus, then while we attempt piously to advance, we shall have put on us the mild yoke of the Lord from faith to faith." Finally, Clement closes his discussion of assimilation to God as the chief good of human beings (134-136) with a cluster of quotations from Paul's Epistle to the Romans (Rom. 8:17; 6:22; 5:4-5). These explicit citations are designed to demonstrate that Plato's opinion is in agreement with Scripture. But as the climax of the ascending spiral of Clement's thought, the Pauline citations form a fitting conclusion to the argument of the second book of the *Stromateis* as a whole: "But on us it is incumbent to reach the unaccomplished end, obeying the commands – that is, God – and living according to them, irreproachably and intelligently, through knowledge of the divine will, and assimilation as far as possible in accordance with right reason is the end, and restoration to perfect adoption by the Son, which ever glorifies the Father by the great High Priest who has deigned to call us brethren and fellow-heirs. And the apostle, succinctly describing the end, writes in the Epistle to the Romans: 'But now, being made free from sin, and become servants to God, you have your fruit unto holiness, and the end everlasting life'" (134.3).[34] Clement's consistent use of the *inclusio* device to signal opening and closure strongly suggests that the pattern employed in the composition of book 2 of the *Stromateis* is Paul's Epistle to the Romans.

At first glance, it hardly seems surprising that Clement should take Paul's Epistle to the Romans as the pattern for his invitation to the life of faith. Paul is an authority of the highest order for Clement. As "the holy apostles" Clement names "Peter, James, John, and Paul" (*Strom.* 1.11.3). But only the name of Paul is furnished with laudatory attributes: Paul is "the noble apostle" (2.136.1), "the good apostle" (5.15.3), "the divine apostle" (1.94.4), or simply "the apostle" (e.g. 1.41.2).[35] Moreover, at the end of book 2, Clement seems to acknowledge that it is Paul's example he has been following throughout in his invitation to the life of faith, insofar as Paul is the imitator of Christ: "And openly and expressly the apostle, in the First Epistle to the Corinthians, says, 'Be followers of me, as also I am of Christ,' in order that that may take place. If you are of me, and I am of Christ, then you are imitators of Christ, and Christ of God. He lays down as the aim of faith assimilation to God, then, so that as far as possible a man becomes righteous and holy with wisdom, and the end is that restitution of the promise which is effected by faith" (136.5-6).

The hypothesis that Romans is the paradigm for book 2 of the *Stromateis* is strengthened by observation of the similarity of situation and purpose of the two writings. Like the second book of Clement's *Miscellanies*, Paul's letter to the Romans is a protreptic writing in both form and function.[36] Paul introduces the Romans to his gospel of salvation by faith for both Jews and Greeks. Paul invites his Roman readers not only to embrace his teaching, but to become his partners in a new evangelical mission to Spain (15.24). In good protreptic fashion, Paul answers objections to his gospel made by an imaginary Jewish interlocutor (chs. 3-11). Also in a protreptic manner, Paul censures the attitude of arrogance that prevents Jews and Gentiles from accepting his gospel of reconciliation (2:1-6, 17-24; 3:1-9; 3:27-4:2; 9:19-21; 11:13-32; 14:1-15:13). Like Clement generations later, Paul has an apologetic motivation in writing. Paul finds it necessary to defend his gospel against the attacks of certain unnamed opponents who charge that he overthrows the law by his preaching of faith (3:31; 7:7), and that he promotes libertinism (3:8; 6:1,15). It is hardly surprising that, given the similarity of situation and purpose, Clement should discover in Paul's Epistle to the Romans a model to adopt. In his study of the dialogue of Paganism with Christianity, from the second to the fourth centuries, with regard to the difference between λογοσμός and πίστις, E. R. Dodds recalled that "St. Paul, following Jewish tradition, had represented *pistis* as the very foundation of the Christian life."[37] Is it not likely that Clement, seeking a way to defend Christian "faith" from the attacks of pagan intellectuals, such as Galen and Celsus, should have had the same recollection?

However plausible the hypothesis may be, interpreters have been slow to recognize a relationship between Clement and Paul, because Clement's understanding of Pauline theology is held to be superficial, and distorted by the influence of Greek philosophy.[38] Clement, it is alleged, had no understanding of the Pauline notion of the sinfulness of the "flesh" (Rom. 7:5, 13-20, 23-24), and thus failed to appreciate the necessity of the gift of the "spirit". For the Platonist Clement, as for Justin before him, every person is possessed of a divine spark, a spiritual principle, the *logos*, and requires only the teaching of Christ to bring the truth to life. A graver discrepancy between Paul and Clement is held to consist in their concepts of "faith". Clement's conception of the act of faith has a strongly intellectual component: faith is a "voluntary preconception" (πρόληψις ἑκούσιος), a "uniting assent" (ἐννοητικὴ συγκατάθεσις),[39] a choice (προαίρεσις), which is the beginning of action (*Strom.* 2.8.4-9.2). Faith is thus the foundation of virtuous deeds (9.1-4). Faith produces fear and hope, and so leads to a flight from sin, and to a life in obedience to the law of God (25.1-35.5). Clement is alleged to have completely misunderstood the Pauline conception of faith as the gift of God which saves apart from works of the law.[40] Clement's concept of faith is epistemological, its content determined by the goal of knowledge to which it leads. Lacking in Clement's notion of faith is the living relation to the person of Jesus, so crucial to Paul's understanding.[41]

Because the Paulinism of Clement of Alexandria is suspect, any investigation of the reception of Romans in the *Stromateis* must proceed with care. Four considerations belong to such an investigation: 1.) identification of the material from Romans, 2.) determination of the function of the ideas of Romans in the context of Clement's work, 3.) reconstruction of Clement's interpretation of Romans, and 4.) speculation about the motive and purpose of Clement's interpretation. Examination of each of these aspects will permit us to test our hypothesis about the role of Romans in the composition of the second book of the *Stromateis*.

With respect to the first point, the identification of material from Romans, the work has been accomplished, in large measure, by the editors of the text of the *Stromateis*, at least in terms of the citation of particular passages. Beginning with the Oxford edition of J. Potter (1715), continuing through the edition of W. Dindorf (1869) and the magisterial edition of O. Stählin (1906, ²1960), culmintating in the new Greek critical edition published in the *Sources chrétiennes*, allusions to Romans have been carefully noted.[42] To be sure, these identifications have not been reflected consistently in translations or in the secondary literature. Thus in the translation included in vol. 2 of *The Ante-Nicene Fathers*, references to Rom. 1:16-17 are missing in *Strom.* 2.8.2, 2.53.5, and 2.126.3, although these allusions are crucial to the structure of Clement's argument.[43] Similarly, the allusion to Rom. 7:14 in *Strom.* 2.22.5 (καὶ τὸ ἐπράθητε ταῖς ἁμαρτίαις ὑμῶν) goes undetected by the translators, as does the quotation of Rom. 8:17 in *Strom.* 2.134.2.[44] Because these allusions go unnoticed by Aleith, her evaluation of Clement's understanding of Paul is strongly negative.[45] Nevertheless, the task of identification of allusions and reminiscences, as well as explicit citations, has been largely completed by Stählin and his predecessors. What remains to be undertaken is an assessment of the influence of Romans upon the composition and structure of book 2 of the *Stromateis* as a whole.

With regard to points two and three, the function and interpretation of the theology of Romans in the *Stromateis*, a beginning has been made by Munck, Aleith, and Prümm, particularly with the concepts of πίστις and γνῶσις.[46] In considering the use that Clement makes of Paul's thought, it is important to bear in mind the possibility that Clement has transmuted Pauline concepts into a language that was more comprehensible to the intellectuals of Alexandria, without sacrificing the existential orientation of the concepts. Such may be the case with the term ἀποκατάστασις, used repeatedly by Clement in the final paragraphs of book 2 (134.2,4; 136.3, 6), but found nowhere in the Pauline corpus.[47] As the eschatological completion toward which the virtuous life reaches out in hope, ἀποκατάστασις seems to be a radical re-interpretation of the Pauline concept of "reconciliation" (καταλλαγή), so important in the Epistle to the Romans (5:10-11; 11:15).[48] Finally, with respect to the motivation of Clement's interpretation, one encounters only occasional statements in the literature, by those who profess to see an apologetic or propagandistic tendency.[49]

The hypothesis that Paul's Epistle to the Romans served as a model for the second book of the *Stromateis* may be evaluated, first, through analysis of the structure of Clement's argument.[50] Following the proem,

Clement offers the proposition that he will expound throughout the treatise: "faith is the way" (4.2) to perfection and truth (5.1) for the one who seeks wisdom. In location and function, Clement's proposition on faith corresponds to what is widely recognized to be the thesis statement of the Epistle to the Romans, 1:16-17.[51]

One might have expected that Clement would proceed directly to a definition of "faith," on the basis of which he would construct his proofs. This is the direction of Plato's argument in the protreptic discourse included in his *Euthydemus* (278e-282d): having proposed that "we all wish to do well in the world," (278e), Socrates proceeds to define the "good things," the possession of which make possible a good life (279a-280a). A similar plan is followed in Epicurus' protreptic letter to Menoeceus: after introductory exhortations, Epicurus goes on to articulate "the first principles of a good life."[52] But instead of proceeding directly to a definition of "faith," Clement dwells for several paragraphs (5.3-8.1) on the difficulty of knowing God, "the Ruler of all, a Being difficult to grasp and apprehend" (τὸν ἡγεμόνα τοῦ παντός, δυσάλωτόν τι χρῆμα καὶ δυσθήρατον). Clement insists that the truth has been hidden from those "taught by Greek laws, and by the other philosophers" (7.1), who do not possess the wisdom and instruction of Scriptures inspired by the Holy Spirit (7.3). Such persons do not truly understand the things that they have learned, a point that Clement seeks to confirm by appealing to Heraclitus (8.1).[53] In the conclusion of a section, following the proposition, which argues that "God is not to be known by human wisdom" (οὔποτε ἀνθρωπίνῃ σοφίᾳ γνωσθήσεσθαι τὸν θεόν, 6.1) and that "the truth has been hidden from us" (ἡμῖν ἐπικεκρύφθαι τὴν ἀλήθειαν, 6.4), Clement copies the pattern of the Epistle to the Romans, in which the proposition is followed by a discussion of how the Gentiles suppressed the truth of God (1:18-32): "for although they knew God, they did not honor him as God or give thanks to him, but they became futile in their thinking and their senseless minds were darkened" (1:21).

In the midst of Clement's exposition of the epistemology of faith (8.2-31.3) is found an excursus on the wise man as the true king (18.2-22.8).[54] The beginning and end of the excursus are clearly marked by the catchword σοφία (σοφός) in 18.2 and 22.8, and by quotations from Plato's *Politicus*. The excursus has three parts.[55] In the first (18.2-19.4), Clement presents a collection of citations from Plato, Pindar, and Speusippus which give expression to the Stoic paradox that the wise man is the true king. In the second part of the excursus (20.1-22.1), Clement claims a biblical origin for this teaching, appealing to Gen. 33:11, Ex. 3:16, and Gen. 32:29f., and Ex. 33:11, and adducing Abraham, Isaac, Jacob, and Moses as examples of the paradox. The third part (22.1-8) demonstrates that this doctrine is found in Plato, and that Plato's conception of the riches and freedom of the wise man agrees with the witness of Christian scriptures (Lk. 18:25; Lk. 6:20; Matt. 11:29; Rom. 7:14; John 8:32-36).

Interpreters have confessed their perplexity at the presence and function of this excursus within Clement's discussion of "faith".[56] Despite evidence of care in the construction of the excursus, nothing in the logic of Clement's argument about faith seems to require a discussion of the wise man as the true king. At the conclusion of the excursus, Clement explicitly recurs to his discourse on faith (23.1, Τούτων δὴ ἐπιδεδειγμένων ἀναδράμωμεν αὖθις ἐπὶ τὸν περὶ τῆς πίστεως λόγον), emphasizing the universality of the need of faith, and proceeding to argue that "faith is the greatest mother of the virtues" (23.5). The surviving examples of philosophical protreptic from the pre-Christian era, the pseudo-Platonic *Alcibiades I* and *Cleitophon*, and the excerpts from Aristotle's *Protrepticus* preserved in Iamblichus, provide no explanation of this element of Clement's text.[57]

We seem led to conclude that the section on the wise man is nothing more than a digression within Clement's discourse on faith – until we recall that in Paul's Epistle to the Romans the statement of the thesis and the rationale concerning the righteousness of faith (1:16-3:31) are confirmed by the example of Abraham (4:1-25), whose righteousness came through faith. In Paul's discussion of Abraham as "the example of faith," the emphasis falls upon the promise that Abraham and his descendants should "inherit the world" (4:13), and that Abraham should be "the father of many nations" (4:17, 18). It seems likely that Paul's description of Abraham as the heir and progenitor of the world and its nations led Clement to the association with the *paradoxa Stoicorum* of the wise man as the true king. This supposition appears to be confirmed by the fact that Abraham is the first of the wise men whose example is adduced by Clement in the excursus (20.2): Abraham is "the beloved of God," who is "expressly called 'friend'" (James 2:23).

At the close of the section περὶ τῆς πίστεως (23.1-31.3), having argued that faith is the foundation of the virtues, of repentance, of hope, and of love, Clement turns to answer the objections of those who "denounce fear" and "assail the law" (32.1ff.). The status and function of this portion of Clement's argument has likewise puzzled interpreters. Prümm finds the discussion of fear and the law "inessential to the course of Clement's exposition on faith."[58] Analysis of the structural components of the *logos protreptikos* provides a partial explanation of this section of Clement's exhortation. Evidence suggests that Aristotle's *Protrepticus* had a threefold structure, whose second section was *apelenktic*.[59] In this section, Aristotle answered objections attributed to fictional opponents.[60] Such is the function of this stage of Clement's argument. But the *content* of this section seems to be supplied by Paul's response to potential objections against his gospel in Romans 5-7. Having completed the argument for justification by faith in 1:18-4:25, Paul turns to consider the question of the role of the law, and the knowledge of sin which the law engenders.[61] That Clement's thought is guided by

Romans 5-7 throughout this section is demonstrated by the explicit reference to Rom. 5:13 (cf. Rom. 3:20) in 34.4-35.2. Clement asks: "How, then, is the law still said to be not good by certain heresies that clamorously appeal to the apostle, who says, 'For by the law is the knowledge of sin?' To whom we say, the law did not cause, but showed sin. For, enjoining what is to be done, it reprehended what ought not to be done. . . Now the apostle, whom they do not comprehend, said that by the law the knowledge of sin was manifested, not that from it it derived its existence."

The remaining stages of Clement's argument follow the outline of the Epistle to the Romans. Like Paul, (Rom. 5:1ff.) Clement proceeds to consider the consequences of faith (41.1ff.). The first named consequence in both cases is "hope" – for Paul, hope that "does not disappoint us, because God's love has been poured into our hearts" (5:5), for Clement, hope defined as "the expectation of good things, . . . which we have learned leads on to love" (41.1). Paul discusses freedom from sin as the result of justification by faith (5:6-7:25),[62] while Clement explores repentance in all of its dimensions, including desire and the exercise of the will (41.1; 45.1; 55.6-77.6). Where Paul discourses upon "life in the Spirit" (8:1-17),[63] Clement treats of the "virtues" that belong to the life of faith (78.1-126.4), summarizing his discussion with an explicit reference to Rom. 8:9 as the fitting characterization of the true gnostic: "Those who are superior to pleasure, who rise above the passions, who know what they do – the gnostics, who are greater than the world. 'I said, you are gods, and all sons of the Highest.' To whom speaks the Lord? To those who reject as far as possible all that is of man. And the apostle says, 'For you are not any longer in the flesh, but in the Spirit'." (125.4-6). Finally, as Paul concludes with reflections upon the hopeful suffering of the children of God, and the promise of "adoption" (8:18-30),[64] Clement points to "assimilation to God" and "restoration to perfect adoption" as the chief good and proper end of the life of faith (127-136), citing a cluster of passages from Romans (8:17; 6:22; 5:4f.) as the summation of his argument (134.2-3; 134.4).

Clement evidently regarded Paul's major argument about faith as complete within the first eight chapters of Romans. To be sure, there are citations of passages from the remaining sections of the letter, chs. 9-11 and 12:1-15:13. Thus, Rom. 12:2 is quoted in 41.1, Rom. 12:9-10, 18, 21 is cited in 42.3, Rom. 10:2-3 is rehearsed in 42.4, Rom. 10:4 is referenced in 42.5, and passages from Deut. 32:21 and Isa. 65:1-2 are quoted out of Rom. 10:19-21 in 43.1-2. In addition, Rom. 11:11 is cited in 43.4 and Rom. 2:14 in 44.4. All of these citations are found in a discussion of φιλοξενία and φιλανθρωπία as consequences of faith (41.3-44.4). It seems that Clement viewed Rom. 9-11 and 12:1-15:13 as providing examples and guidelines, negative as well as positive, of behavior which issues from faith. Clement's judgment on the Jews is clear: lacking faith, they fail to show hospitality and philanthropy; they have no "fellowship in life" (κοινωνία βίου, 41.2).

If it is established that the Epistle to the Romans served as the model for Clement in composing his invitation to the life of faith, then a more accurate assessment of the function and meaning of Paul's ideas in the second book of the *Stromateis* may be undertaken. In the first place, it is clear that major elements of the Pauline gospel have been subjected to an epistemological interpretation. That is, the meaning of concepts such as "faith," "sin," and "righteousness" is determined by the goal toward which the life of the Christian is directed – γνῶσις.[65] Thus "faith" is defined by terms (συγκατάθεσις, πρόληψις, προαίρεσις) borrowed from Stoics and Epicureans, which designate its position on the road toward knowledge.[66] Whereas Paul defined πίστις as the radical response of the whole person to God, a yes-saying like that which Jesus manifested in his death for sinners (Rom. 3:21-26),[67] Clement understands "faith" as a kind of immediate knowledge, a preconception that grasps at something evident, an assent to first principles incapable of demonstration (8.4-18.1).[68]

Clement's epistemological interpretation of Pauline concepts is forceful and consistent. Thus, Clement understands the difficulty in apprehending God to be a function of the natural limitation of human wisdom (5.3-8.3), whereas Paul explained the failure to perceive the eternal power and deity of God in creation (Rom. 1:20) as a result of the wickedness of human beings "who bind the truth under a spell through injustice" (Rom. 1:18b).[69] Similarly, "the faith that was reckoned to Abraham as righteousness" (Rom. 4:9) is understood by Clement to be a "regal wisdom" (18.2), in possession of which he is "beloved by God" (20.2).

A second characteristic of Clement's interpretation of Romans is an interest in the psychological dimension of commitment to the life of faith. At the place where Paul explores the role of sin in the divine economy of salvation (Rom. 5-7), Clement offers an analysis of "fear," whose utility is explained and defended (32.1-41.1). Clement carefully delineates the conception of "cautious fear" (εὐλάβεια), which is produced by the law, and which is receptive to instruction (32.4-33.4). He distinguishes "cautious fear" from "consternation" and "perturbation," misconceptions of the heretics (36.1-40.3). The same interest in the psychology of commitment comes to expression in Clement's analysis of the temporality of faith and repentance, which acquire a twofold nature as a result of their extension in time (53.1-59.6). Clement's repeated emphasis upon the "voluntary" character of faith, repentance, and virtuous actions (see esp. 60.1-77.6) reveals his preoccupation with the psychological mechanisms of commitment.

Finally, Clement interprets the eschatology of Romans in an ethical sense in the section περὶ τέλους (127-136). Paul had spoken of the longing of creation for freedom from bondage to decay and adoption as

children of God (Rom. 8:18-23). The transformation into the image of
God's Son is not yet seen, according to Paul, but we wait for redemption
with patience, in hope (Rom. 8:24-25). Clement's concept of "assimilation to God" involves "obeying the commands, and living according to
them, irreproachably and intelligently, through knowledge of the divine
will" (134.1).[70] "Assimilation to God" is thus perfection, insofar as possible, of the life of virtue. And yet, "assimilation to God" remains an
eschatological event for Clement, as expressed by the striking oxymo-
ron τέλος ἀτελεύτητον (134.1).[71] "Assimilation" is not solely an ethical
achievement of the virtuous philosopher, but necessitates the mediation
of God's Son, the great High Priest (134.2). As Clement's comments
on Rom. 8:17; 6:22; 5:4-5 make clear (134.2-4), he traces the connection between eschatology and ethics back to Paul. According to Clement, Paul taught a twofold ἐλπίς, which embraces not only the longing
for redemption to come, but also the present confidence that is the basis
of virtuous action (134.4; 136.3). In the confident hope of one who lives
virtuously, the eschatological completion is proleptically at work.

One cannot fail to notice in Clement's interpretation of Romans a
tendency to universalize the process of salvation. Clement's reading
transforms a message that was based upon apocalyptic premises into a
timeless quest for "assimilation to God". Paul's concern for the fate of
peoples at the end of the age emerges from the labyrinth of Clement's
reading as a search for the perfect goodness of the individual at the end
of life. Clement seeks beneath the Pauline concepts of "faith and "sin" a
universal sense of how every soul is constituted. The content of
Clement's interpretation is just as individualistic as that offered by various gnostic teachers. Clement warns, at the beginning of the Stromateis,
that his meaning will become clear only to the attentive reader. The
reader that Clement envisaged was the solitary individual.

Clement's reading will doubtless seem mistaken to the present generation of interpreters, who identify Paul's primary concern as the status of Jews and Gentiles before God, and who view Romans as an
attempt to elaborate a theological basis for a church out of Jews and
Gentiles.[72] But in defense of Clement's reading, one might observe that
a movement away from specific ethnic tensions toward abstract principles with general applicability is already apparent in the Epistle to
the Romans, and that this movement defines the genius of Romans, in
comparison with Paul's other epistles.[73] We would do well to heed the
warning of a historian who learned to read Paul through the eyes of the
third century: "If we want to understand what St. Paul taught to the
third century, I suspect we must stick to the old-fashioned notion that
the message of St. Paul was not founded on social premises, but on
universal expectations of immortality and salvation."[74]

[1] E. de Faye, *Clément d'Alexandrie* (Paris, 1906) 96-125.

[2] It is another reflection of the importance of the *Stromateis* that Clement is given the appellation ὁ Στρωματεύς by Julius Africanus and by Photius: see O. Stählin, *Clemens Alexandrinus, Die griechischen christlichen Schriftsteller der ersten drei Jarhhunderte*, Vol. 1 (Leipzig, 1936) ix, 7: xiv, 13.

[3] de Faye, *Clément d'Alexandrie*, 97.

[4] J. Munck, *Untersuchungen über Clemens von Alexandrien* (Stuttgart, 1933) 143; Munck continues: "Der Verfasser hat kraft seiner Wahl des Stils die Erlaubnis des Publikums erhalten, allerlei krumme Sprünge und Nebenbemerkungen zu machen. Er hat nichts versprochen, was ein wohl ausgearbeitetes Werk erwarten lassen könnte."

[5] M. Pohlenz, "Klemens von Alexandreia und sein hellenisches Christentum," *NGA*, phil.-hist. Kl. (1943) 151 n. 1.

[6] A. Méhat, *Étude sur les Stromates de Clément d'Alexandrie* (Paris, 1966) 96-279.

[7] Méhat, *Étude sur les Stromates*, 153 n.13, taking the section ἐν τε τοῖς πίστεως (113.9) through περιληφθήσεται (113.13) as a unit.

[8] Cf. Méhat, *Étude sur les Stromates*, 153.

[9] On protreptic in general, see P. Hartlich, *De Exhortationum a Graecis Romanisque Scriptarum Historia et Indole* (Leipzig, 1889); on the protreptic tradition in early Christianity, see G. Lazzati, *L'Aristote perduto e gli scrittori cristiani* (Milan, 1938); M. Pellegrino, *Studi sull' antica apologetica* (Rome, 1947).

[10] Cf. A. von Harnack, *Die Mission und Ausbreitung des Christentums*, Vol.1 (Leipzig, 1906) 281-89.

[11] See F.J. Dölger, "Sacramentum infanticidii," *AuC* 4 (1934) 188-288; J. Geffcken, *Zwei griechische Apologeten* (Leipzig, 1907) 167-69.

[12] *De Pulsuum Differentiis*, ed. C. Kühn, Vol. 8 (Lipsiae, 1824) p. 579.15. In the work *On Hippocrates' Anatomy*, preserved only in Arabic, Galen faulted Moses for being an unscientific lawgiver, whose "method in his books is to write without offering proofs, saying 'God commanded, God spoke'."; trans. by R. Walzer, *Galen on Jews and Christians* (Oxford, 1949) 10-11. In another work, Εἰς τὸ πρῶτον κινοῦν ἀκίνητον, which has survived only in Arabic, Galen denigrated the adherents of schools of medicine who rely on undemonstrated hypotheses, by comparing them with the followers of Moses and Christ: "If I had in mind people who taught their pupils in the same way as the followers of Moses and Christ teach theirs – for they order them to accept everything on faith – I should not have given you a definition,"; Walzer, *Galen on Jews and Christians*, 14-15.

[13] Fragments of Celsus, ed. by R. Bader, "Der Ἀληθὴς λόγος des Kelsos," *Tübinger Beiträge zur Altertumswissenschaft* 33 (Stuttgart, 1940); cf. C. Andresen, *Logos und Nomos* (Berlin, 1955) 167-74.

[14] D. Wyrwa, *Die christliche Platonaneignung in den Stromateis des Clemens von Alexandrien* (Berlin, 1983) 152.

[15] E.R. Dodds, *Pagan and Christian in an Age of Anxiety* (Cambridge, 1965) 120-21; cf. Walzer, *Galen on Jews and Christians*, 48-56.

[16] Thus the evaluation of Clement's discussion of faith in *Strom.* 2.8.4-31 by H. Chadwick, *Early Christian Thought and the Classical Tradition* (Oxford, 1966) 51-52.

[17] K. Prümm, "Glaube und Erkenntnis im zweiten Buch der Stromata des Klemens von Alexandrien," *Scholastik* 12 (1937) 22-23.

[18] See the general characterization of protreptic speeches and letters by S. Stowers, *Letter Writing in Greco-Roman Antiquity* (Philadelphia, 1986) 112-15, adducing as examples Aristotle's *Protrepticus* and Cicero's *Hortensius*, with the letters of Epicurus to Menoeceus, Anacharsis to Croesus, and Crates to Aper.

[19] Similarly, Wyrwa, *Die christliche Platonaneignung in den Stromateis*, 146.

[20] Rightly, Prümm, "Glaube und Erkenntnis in Strom. II," 18.

[21] As in *Strom*. 2.78.1-96.4, where Clement makes copious use of Philo's *De Virtutibus*, without acknowledging the source of the extracts.

[22] Wyrwa, *Die christliche Platonaneignung in den Stromateis*, 142-45.

[23] On the history of the motif, see the careful study by H. Merki, Ὁμοίωσις Θεῷ (Freiburg, in der Schweiz, 1952).

[24] On the Stoic paradox, see Zeno, *Fr.* 216, *SVF* I, p.53.10; Chrysippus, *Fr. mor.* 617-622, *SVF* III, p. 158.34-159.37; cf. E.R. Goodenough, "The Political Philosophy of Hellenistic Kingship," *YCIS* I (1928) 55-102.

[25] Munck, *Untersuchungen über Clemens von Alexandrien*, 52.

[26] Wyrwa, *Die christliche Platonaneignung in den Stromateis*, 142-89.

[27] Prümm, "Glaube und Erkenntnis in Strom. II," 35.

[28] As demonstrated by P. Wendland, "Philo und Clemens Alexandrinus," *Hermes* 31 (1896) 435-56; cf. Méhat, *Étude sur les 'Stromates'*, 238.

[29] F.H. Colson, *Philo*, Vol. 8, LCL (Cambridge, MA, 1968) xii note.

[30] On this rhetorical figure and its use in composition, see J.D. Denniston, *Greek Prose Style* (Oxford, 1952) 90. The term *inclusio* is sometimes used for this way of marking opening and closure; cf. G.A. Kennedy, *New Testament Interpretation through Rhetorical Criticism* (Chapel Hill, 1984) 34.

[31] On the compositional patterns at work in this section, see Wyrwa, *Die christliche Platonaneignung in den Stromateis*, 144-46.

[32] To this, Clement adds a citation from Isa. 7:9 in order to stress the connection between πίστις and γνῶσις.

[33] Cf. S.R.C. Lilla, *Clement of Alexandria. A Study in Christian Platonism and Gnosticism* (Oxford, 1971) 127-31.

[34] Clement follows this rhetorical climax with a clarification on the "twofold hope" (134.4), citing Rom. 5:4-5. On the Pauline citations as the climax of the section περὶ τέλους, see Wyrwa, *Die christliche Platonaneignung in den Stromateis*, 187-88.

[35] Cf. E. Aleith, *Paulusverständnis in der alten Kirche* (Berlin, 1937) 87.

[36] Stowers, *Letter Writing in Greco-Roman Antiquity*, 114; D. Aune, "Romans as Logos Protreptikos" in *The Romans Debate*, ed. K. Donfried (Peabody, MA, 1991) 278-96.

[37] Dodds, *Pagan and Christian in an Age of Anxiety*, 121.

[38] Aleith, *Paulusverständnis in der alten Kirche*, 87-98.

[39] On the Stoics' use of the term συγκατάθεσις, and on the Epicurean doctrine of πρόληψις see Lilla, *Clement of Alexandria*, 127-31.

[40] Aleith, *Paulusverständnis in der alten Kirche*, 90.

[41] *Ibid.*, 90-91.

[42] *Clementis Alexandrini Opera quae exstant omnia*, ed. J. Potter (Oxford, 1715); repr. in Migne, PG VIII, IX; *Clementis Alexandrini Opera*, ed. W. Dindorf (Oxford, 1869); *Clemens Alexandrinus. Zweiter Band: Stromata Buch I-VI*, ed. O. Stählin, GCS (Leipzig, 1906); *Clemens Alexandrinus. Zweiter Band: Stromata Buch I-VI*, ed. O. Stählin. 3rd ed. by L. Früchtel, GCS (Berlin, 1960).

[43] *The Ante-Nicene Fathers*, Vol. II: *Fathers of the Second Century: Hermas, Tatian, Athenagoras, Theophilus, and Clement of Alexandria (Entire)*, ed. A. Roberts and J. Donaldson (Grand Rapids, 1979).

[44] Note also the absence of a reference to Rom. 4:3, 9 in the *ANF* translation of *Strom*. 2.28.4 and 2.124.3, and the absence of reference to Rom. 10:17, 14-15 in *Strom*. 2.25.1-2.

⁴⁵ Aleith, *Paulusverständnis in der alten Kirche*, 87, 90-91, 93.

⁴⁶ See also the brief observations of Lilla, *Clement of Alexandria*, 139, 147; Wyrwa, *Die christliche Platonaneignung in den Sromateis*, 143-44.

⁴⁷ A. Méhat, "Apocatastase, Origène, Clément d'Alexandrie, Act. 3,21," *VigChr* 10 (1956) 196-214.

⁴⁸ C. Breytenbach, *Versöhnung. Eine Studie zur paulinischen Soteriologie*, WMANT 60 (Düsseldorf, 1989) 143-77.

⁴⁹ W. Völker, *Der wahre Gnostiker nach Clemens Alexandrinus*, TU 57 (Berlin, 1952) 94-95, 136, 145-46, 276-77, 323, 332-34.

⁵⁰ Compare the analysis of book 2 of the *Stromateis* by Méhat, *Étude sur les 'Stromates'*, 262ff., 276f.

⁵¹ Kennedy, *Rhetorical Criticism*, 153; R. Jewett, "Following the Argument of Romans" in *The Romans Debate*, ed. K. Donfried (Peabody, MA, 1991) 268-69; among others.

⁵² *Epicurus, the Extant Remains*, trans. C. Bailey (Oxford, 1926) 863-64.

⁵³ Fr. 17 Diels, I, 155.6-8; cf. T. Gomperz, *Sitzungsberichte der Akademie zur Wien* 113 (1886) 998.

⁵⁴ On the demarcation of the excursus, see Méhat, *Étude sur les 'Stromates'*, 262-63.

⁵⁵ See the analysis in Wyrwa, *Die christliche Platonaneignung in den Stromateis*, 143.

⁵⁶ E.g., Munck, *Untersuchungen über Klemens von Alexandria*, 52; Prümm, "Glaube und Erkenntnis in Strom. II," 31, who describes the section as an insert.

⁵⁷ S.R. Slings, *A Commentary on the Platonic Clitophon* (Amsterdam, 1981) 78-95; M.D. Jordan, "Ancient Philosophic Protreptic and the Problem of Persuasive Genres," *Rhetorica* 4 (1986) 314-27.

⁵⁸ Prümm, "Glaube und Erkenntnis in *Strom*. II," 35.

⁵⁹ G. Schneeweiss, *Der Protreptikos des Aristoteles* (Munich, 1912) 231-35.

⁶⁰ *Ibid.*, 233.

⁶¹ See the analysis of Jewett, "Following the Argument of Romans," 271.

⁶² Jewett, "Following the Argument of Romans," 273; Aune, "Romans as a *Logos Protreptikos*", 292-93.

⁶³ Jewett, "Following the Argument of Romans," 273; Aune, "Romans as a *Logos Protreptikos*," 293.

⁶⁴ Jewett, "Following the Argument of Romans," 273.

⁶⁵ Völker, *Der wahre Gnostiker*, 90-93.

⁶⁶ Lilla, *Clement of Alexandria*, 118-42.

⁶⁷ S. K. Williams, "Again *Pistis Christou*," CBQ 49 (1987) 321-42; S.K. Stowers, *A Rereading of Romans* (New Haven, 1994) 194-206.

⁶⁸ Lilla, *Clement of Alexandria*, 119-21, 132-35.

⁶⁹ Cf. E. Käsemann, *Commentary on Romans* (Grand Rapids, 1982) 36-38.

⁷⁰ On this passage, see Prümm, "Glaube und Erkenntnis in *Strom*. II," 53-55.

⁷¹ Cf. A. J. Festugière, *La Révélation d' Hermès Trismégiste*, Vol. 3 (Paris, 1953) 98-101.

⁷² E.g., K. Stendahl, *Paul Among Jews and Gentiles* (Philadelphia, 1976); F. Watson, *Paul, Judaism and the Gentiles. A Sociological Approach*, SNTSMS 56 (Cambridge, 1986); S.K. Stowers, *A Rereading of Romans: Justice, Jews and Gentiles* (New Haven, 1994).

⁷³ As argued by R. Jewett, *Christian Tolerance: Paul's Message to the Modern Church* (Philadelphia, 1982) 30-32.

⁷⁴ A. Momigliano, *On Pagans, Jews, and Christians* (Middletown, 1986) 164.

A Response: Elucidating Romans in *Stromateis* 2

Kathy L. Gaca

———— ◆ ————

In his paper, "The Soteriology of Romans in Clement of Alexandria, *Stromateis* 2: Faith, Fear, and Assimilation to God," Laurence Welborn argues that Clement in *Stromateis* book 2 analyzes the human soul by reinterpreting Paul's epistle to the Romans in Middle Platonist categories. Clement, through his exegesis of Romans, Welborn further maintains, transforms Paul's collectively apocalyptic message in Romans into a more individually oriented quest for salvation and immortality. Finally, Welborn argues, *Stromateis* 2 is a protreptic work and it depends on Romans for its hitherto unappreciated organizational basis. Here I will discuss Welborn's three major points, that Clement adapts Pauline concepts in Middle Platonist terms, that the *Stromateis* is a protreptic writing, and that Romans provides the pattern or model for *Stromateis* 2.

Welborn maintains that Clement reinterprets Paul's notions of sin, faith, and hope for the eschaton in Romans by assimilating them to Middle Platonist psychology. Middle Platonist psychology builds from a mix of Platonic, Stoic, and Pythagorean ideas. Where Paul advocates the importance of avoiding sin, Clement advocates the importance of showing cautious fear toward God in order to avoid sin. His conception of cautious fear is indebted to Stoic psychology, and especially to the Stoic position that cautious fear is a reasonable and beneficial emotion to have, unlike the damaging passion of excessive fear. 'Faith' in the Pauline sense means being righteous in the eyes of Christ by baptism, praying in Christ's name, and living a life of sincere obedience to him. Clement, by contrast, defines faith as the person's assent and choice to accept God and Christ. Clement likewise derives his ideas about assent and choice from Stoicism, which are central to the psychological dynamics of Stoic evaluative reasoning. Clement also transforms Paul's conviction that Christian salvation will occur at the impending end of time into the popular Platonic idea that human beings should strive to liken themselves to deity as much as possible, regardless of their time, place, or culture. Welborn's observations about the influence of Middle

84

Platonist psychology on Clement's thought are interesting, well-founded, and characteristic of Christian Platonist thought. What sets Welborn's argument apart and makes it new is that he links Clement's Christian Platonist psychology directly to Clement's interpretation of Romans in *Stromateis* 2.

Welborn also argues that Romans provides the organizational basis for *Stromateis* 2. Toward this end he maintains that both writings are protreptic, that is, that both expressly aim to win converts to Christianity. This means he has to demonstrate a rather novel thesis about *Stromateis* 2, for it is not usual to view the *Stromateis* as protreptic writing. Welborn seeks a protreptic purpose in *Stromateis* 2 because a genre link between this book and Romans strengthens his case that Romans strikes a deep responsive chord in Clement and inspires the organization and aim of *Stromateis* 2. For example, Clement cites verses from Romans in a ring composition at the beginning and end of the sections where *Stromateis* 2 shares common themes with Romans. Let us begin with Welborn's first argument.

Welborn infers a protreptic aim from the first two sections of *Stromateis* 2, in which Clement states that he works for the conversion of wise Greeks as well as Jews. "[Clement] aims at the conversion of the philosophically minded among the Greeks, and perhaps also . . . the Jews [as indicated in the first two sections of *Stromateis* 2]. The work [that is, *Stromateis* 2] thus has a protreptic function." This inference, however, does not follow from what Clement says. Yes, Clement wants to win as many converts as he can, but his comment about converting Greeks and Jews at the opening of *Stromateis* 2 concerns his driving purpose in life, not the manifest function of the book itself. The *Stromateis* contains myriad ideas that Clement can draw on and develop in order to win converts, but this does not make *Stromateis* 2 itself protreptic. While it would be safe to say that Clement's main goal in life is to convert intellectual Greeks, Jews, and others, Welborn applies this insight too narrowly as a way to classify *Stromateis* 2. His argument is not cogent for the following reasons. At the outset of the work Clement makes it very clear that the *Stromateis* is his treasure trove of notes or reminders. As he expressly states, he wants the *Stromateis* as his "potion against forgetfulness," so as to remember "the brilliant and lively arguments and the blessed and noteworthy men" who taught him the ideas that he records in his work (*Strom* 1.11.1). The contents of the *Stromateis* are rather deliberately "cloaked in erudition" and as such inaccessible to the uninitiated (*Strom* 1.20.4). Protreptic writing, by contrast, is an ancient counterpart to advertising, not advertising what to buy, but how to live. When Clement write in a protreptic mode, such as Clement's *Protrepticus ad Graecos*, he abides by the cardinal rule of this genre: Write in a very engaging and accessible style in order to attract new persons to the calling, which for Clem-

ent is Christianity. Unlike Clement's *Protrepticus*, *Stromateis* 2 is not
written in this mode, as Clement himself indicates. Hence it is not clear
why it is meaningful or useful to regard the book as protreptic.

Nonetheless, Welborn clearly explains what he means when he states
that Clement uses Romans as a pattern, model, or template for
Stromateis 2. Welborn uses the word "pattern" in three related senses.
First, "pattern" refers to Clement using key citations from Romans in a
ring composition, where he marks the beginning and end of certain
sections in *Stromateis* 2 by citing Romans on faith, hope, and so forth.
Second, in Welborn's paper, "pattern" also means that the content of
extensive sections of *Stromateis* 2 is modeled on substantive sections of
Romans (as opposed to Romans simply providing a framing device
through ring composition). Third, "pattern" also refers to Clement's
habitual tendency to adapt and transform ideas from Romans in a
Middle Platonist sense. Welborn persuasively shows that Romans has
thematic pride of place in *Stromateis* 2 in its treatment of faith, fear,
and hope. This interpretation makes two significant contributions. It
makes Clement's excursus on faith more coherent than has been appreciated hitherto; and it makes Clement's patristic understanding of
Romans more accessible and able to be appreciated on its own merits.

In conclusion, I think Welborn develops a number of interesting and
sound ideas about how Clement draws on Paul to develop a Middle
Platonist psychology of commitment to the Christian God. Clement, for
example, merges Pauline and Middle Platonist ideas in his understanding of faith, fear, and salvation. Romans provides an organizational
basis for *Stromateis* 2 that both elucidates book 2 and uncovers
Clement's pioneering engagement with Romans on concerns of key
interest today.

- FOUR -

Irenaeus as Reader of Romans 9-11: Olive Branches

Susan L. Graham

———— ◆ ————

Something of a "Copernican revolution" in the study of Irenaeus's use of Paul took place when Richard Norris began to investigate whether the Apostle contributed positively to his thought (Norris, 1990). Up to that time, the prevailing view, focused on the *Adversus haereses* (henceforth, *Haer.*), was that Irenaeus used Paul apologetically in order to legitimize the Apostle for the "universal church" (*Haer.* 1.10.1) – owing especially to Marcion's preference for Paul –, and mined his letters to support views that were not necessarily true to the Apostle's own. Against this line of thinking, Norris demonstrated Paul's influence on Irenaeus's theological vision in *Haer.*, particularly in the matter of Irenaeus's unified history of divine-human relations (Norris 1990, 84-95). That work has been corroborated by the subsequent studies of David Balás (1992) and Rolf Noormann (1994).

The present essay turns from *Haer.* to Irenaeus's other surviving work, the *Epideixis* (also known as the *Demonstration of the Apostolic Preaching*; henceforth, *Epid.*). It examines the potential for Irenaeus's use of Paul's Epistle to the Romans, and Rom 9-11 in particular, as he crafts his theological vision in the briefer, less polemically-interested treatise. In the *Epid.*, Irenaeus endeavors to "prove" that what the apostles preached about Christ was already foretold in the Law and the Prophets (Behr 2001, 112-13; cf. Graham 2001, 214-16). His proof is framed in a narrative of salvation history in a manner reminiscent of Luke 24:19-27, the great speeches of Acts, and Ignatius and Justin. One notable feature of Irenaeus's history is the attention it gives to the Noachic cycle (Gen 6:5-9:27). Irenaeus develops in particular the drama of Noah's three sons (Gen 9:18-27), their blessings and curse, and their role as progenitors of "three races, . . . one . . . under the curse, while two were under the blessing" (*Epid.* 23), to portray election and a soteriological scheme that takes account of Jews, Gentile believers and non-believers. The same three groups of people play on the stage of Romans, especially chapters 9-11, where Paul's drama describes the relations between Jews and Gentiles in salvation history (see Stendahl

1976, 3-4; Fitzmyer 1993, 543). His account of the three sons shares
a number of features with the history of divine election and salvation
that Paul presents in Rom 9-11, of which the olive tree metaphor in Rom
11:16-24 provides an illustration. Moreover, Paul is one of only two New
Testament authorities Irenaeus names in the *Epid.* Despite the very different imagery Irenaeus uses, this evidence suggests that, in the *Epid.*, his
interpretation of Noah's sons takes some of its inspiration from the
Apostle's arguments in Rom 9-11. To test this possibility, Irenaeus's text is
explored here in light of two further questions: first, whether Irenaeus's
theological notions expressed in his account of Noah's sons correlates with
Paul's in Rom 9-11, and, second, whether Irenaeus has borrowed from the
text of Rom 9-11 in discussing them. The affirmative answers to both questions, taken together, argue for an Irenaean use of Rom 9-11 in interpreting
the narrative of Noah's sons, and a use of Paul's epistle in the *Epid.* less
modest than it might appear.

Irenaeus's Treatment of the Three Sons of Noah.

Irenaeus gives the Noachic cycle (Gen 6:1-10:32) full and direct treatment in *Epid.* 19-22. The flood account does not detain him, in contrast
to nearly all of his Christian predecessors. Instead, he goes directly
from a list of those saved in the ark to the episode concerning Noah's
sons at the end of the biblical cycle (Gen 9:18-27; in *Epid.* 20-21), defer-
ring his treatment of the covenant to the conclusion of his account (Gen
9:1-17; *Epid.* 22). He ignores Noah's episode of drunkenness and expo-
sure (Gen 9:20-24) that demanded a show of filial piety from his sons,
and addresses instead the sons' actions and their results:

> But, on account of their deeds, one of these fell under a curse,
> while two inherited a blessing; since the youngest of them, called
> Cham, mocked their father, and, condemned for the sin of impiety
> because of hostility and offence to [their] father, received a
> curse . . . ; but Sem and Japheth, his brothers, because of their
> piety towards their father, obtained a blessing [cf. Gen 9:21-
> 27]. . . . (*Epid.* 20)

Noah's three sons, from whom the human race is to be "multiplied
again," overshadow the rest of the narrative. Each has a particular
relationship to God, and in turn they are forebears of peoples who share
those particular relationships to God (*Epid.* 23, quoted above).
Irenaeus's interest is the curse of Ham and the blessings on Shem and
Japheth. It is immediately clear that the blessings and curse, given at
the time when the world was re-created, provide him a vehicle to convey his notions concerning election, faith, righteousness and salvation
that will lead to his discussion of the end of the age in *Epid.* 86-97.

The first brother to note is Ham, progenitor of the sinners and the
"ungodly" (*Epid.* 20). Ham, having been described as impious, is prone to

wickedness, and subject to judgment for it. According to Irenaeus's compact description,

> . . . it happened that every generation after him, being cursed, increased and multiplied in sin; . . . Now the curse of Cham, with which his father Noah cursed him, was this: *Cursed be the child Cham, a slave shall he be to his brothers* [Gen 9:25]. On reaching adulthood, he had many descendants; they proliferated until about the fourteenth generation, when his race was cut down by God, being delivered to judgement – for the . . . offspring of Cham [cf. Gen 10:6-20] . . . all fell under the curse, the curse extending for a long time over the ungodly. (*Epid.* 20)

Ham and his descendants are sinners, and ultimately their sin is idolatry. This becomes clearer in a later reference to the Canaanites's worship of Baal (*Epid.* 95). Irenaeus may include among Ham's descendants the "apostates" in *Epid.* 85, when he speaks of Christ's role as judge of "his enemies." For their infidelity to the God of Noah, Shem, and Abraham, they are given speedy judgment: in the fourteenth generation, after the Exodus (*Epid.* 27), Ham's descendants, the seven tribes of Canaan, are conquered and destroyed by the descendants of Shem and Abraham (*Epid.* 28, cf. 24). Irenaeus does not develop the meaning of Ham's slavery to Shem, although he is firm about the fact that Ham is punished for his own misdeed. Ham, not Canaan, becomes the slave, in contrast to the account in the Septuagint and to his predecessor, Justin (*Dial.* 139). Placing the punishment on Ham himself keeps the matter of election within the one generation from which the world was repopulated. Irenaeus is concerned with the creation, and new creation, of humanity in the *Epid.*, and he locates faith in God, or lack of it, from the re-creation; the fruits of that faith come at the end of the created world.

Shem, by contrast, the pious eldest son, is "blessed with these words: *Blessed be the Lord God of Sem and let Ham be his servant*" [Gen 9:26] (*Epid.* 21). Irenaeus's interpretation of this passage, ambiguous in the Septuagint, is unambiguous:

> . . . The significance of the blessing is this, that the God and Lord of all became for Sem a peculiar object of worship. This blessing flourished when it reached Abraham, who, of the seed of Sem, [reckoned] by genealogy, was the tenth generation downwards [cf. Gen 11:10-26]; and for this reason the Father and God of all was pleased to be called *the God of Abraham, the God of Isaac and the God of Jacob* [cf. Exod 3:6; Matt 22:32], for the blessing of Sem extended to Abraham. . . . (*Epid.* 21)

Irenaeus turns the blessing of Shem into a gift. Shem is "given" the God of his father, Noah, and God becomes a possession, which can be passed on to his descendants. Irenaeus's language may play on the notion of

Abraham's inheritance (Rom 4:13-14). It also plays on the testamentary sense .of the Greek term for the covenant, διαθήκη, and his *jeu de mots* points toward the covenant account (Gen 9:1-17), which, in Irenaeus's narrative, immediately follows. More importantly, Irenaeus artfully stretches back to his ancestor Shem the traditions that call Abraham the father of faith (cf. Rom 4:16-17). In doing so, he establishes the origin of the Israelites – according to faith and to descent – in the first generation after the flood, at the very renewal of creation, i.e., with Shem, rather than with Abraham, though Irenaeus nowhere states it so baldly. Abraham will inherit this faith and manifest it in a superior manner (*Epid.* 24). After the connection is clarified, Shem disappears from Irenaeus's account, to be replaced by his more famous heir. Through Abraham, Shem's heirs, in the flesh and in the promises, are the Jews, descendants of Isaac and Jacob (*Epid.* 24). Irenaeus further extends the (paternal) line to Christ (*Epid.* 56, 59, 64), thus linking Christ, Abraham, and Shem in the history of salvation.

The third son, Japheth, is to share in Shem's blessing and dwell in Shem's house, at an unspecified future time:

> . . . While the blessing of Japheth was thus: *May God enlarge Japheth and let him dwell in the house of Sem, and let Cham be his servant* [Gen 9:27]. And this blossomed, at the close of the age, when the Lord was manifested, out of the calling of the Gentiles, when God enlarged the call to them, for *their voice has gone out to all the earth and their words to the ends of the world* [Ps 18:5 (LXX); Rom 10:18]. So, to *enlarge* is the calling of the Gentiles, that is, the Church; and he *dwells in the house of Sem*, that is, in the inheritance of the patriarchs, in Christ Jesus receiving the rights of the first-born. . . . (*Epid.* 21)

Genesis does not indicate any time when Japheth's blessing is to be fulfilled. Irenaeus seizes on this fact to give Japheth's blessing an eschatological perspective: his descendants are the Gentiles who enter into faith in God on the basis of the apostolic preaching at the end of the age: "So, in the order that each was blessed, in that same order, through their descendants, each receives the fruit of the blessing" (*Epid.* 21; cf. Gal 3:6-9). In addition to his eschatological perspective, Irenaeus appears to see the literal fulfillment of the blessing to Japheth in the evangelization of the Gentiles of Asia Minor and Gaul in his own day. Remarkably, for Irenaeus, Japheth does not displace Shem, as Justin has it (*Dial.* 139.4); he simply dwells in Shem's "house," possibly cohabiting it with Shem.

The primary narrative in *Epid.* 19-22 does not exhaust Irenaeus's discussion of Noah's sons. He returns to Shem in his treatment of Abraham, in whom Shem's blessing "flourishes" (*Epid.* 24). Ham's descendants, specified as "the seven tribes," reappear in the prophecy given to Abraham (*Epid.* 24) and its fulfillment in the Israelite conquest of Canaan (*Epid.* 29), and in references to unbelievers and idolaters (*Epid.* 91, 95). Further references to Japheth wait until *Epid.* 40-42a, where Irenaeus concludes part one of the *Epid.* with a comment on the apostolic preaching to the Gentiles, which he sees to be taking place in his own day:

> This is the fruit of the blessing of Japheth, made manifest, by means of the Church, in the calling of the Gentiles, [who were] waiting to receive the *dwelling in the house of Sem* according to the promise of God [cf. Gen 9:27]. (*Epid.* 42a)

The brief treatment of Japheth's blessing in *Epid.* 40-42a will be expanded in the parallel section that concludes the second part of the *Epid.* (*Epid.* 86-97). Japheth will not be named again, but there will be repeated references to "the calling of the Gentiles," a phrase connected with him in *Epid.* 21 and 42a. It will remind Irenaeus's reader that the preaching of the apostles in the latter days was promised at the beginning of time through this son of Noah, and allow Irenaeus to reinforce the notion that a single beneficent God has been acting in all of creation history: at the re-creation of humanity just as in the apostolic era (cf. *Epid.* 8, 97). The blessings and curse on Noah's sons in Gen 9:18-27, and their fulfillment in Abraham, the displacement of the Canaanites, and finally the inclusion of the Gentiles among the saved are all connected in the scheme of divine providence for humanity.

The content of Irenaeus's proof is organized in the body of the *Epid.* in what can be characterized as a diptych: a historical narrative from creation to the calling of the Gentiles at "the end of the age" (*Epid.* 8-42a), is repeated to frame the prophetic proof in the second part (*Epid.* 42b-97). The parallel structure is useful for expressing interconnected ideas. The reader will recognize that the interpretations of Japheth, for instance, early in the first part (*Epid.* 19-22) are recalled at the end of the first part (in *Epid.* 41-42a), explicitly tying the events of the early history of humanity to those of the Irenaean present. However, the meaning of Japheth's inheritance, only mentioned at the end of the first part, is fully developed at last in the corresponding place at the end of the second (*Epid.* 89-91, 94-95), a feature that ties together the two parts of the treatise. The work is also unified through extensive use of *inclusiones*. For instance, the culminating description of the divine plan in *Epid.* 97 strongly echoes its initial presentation in *Epid.* 8, forming a grand *inclusio* that unifies the entire work. References to Japheth at the several points in the *Epid.* already noticed reinforce this *inclusio*. Finally, the work is unified internally through the use of names or key phrases (*mots crochets*), among which we find terms associated with the sons of Noah. The interconnecting structure of the work supports Irenaeus's theological concern to link the "economies of God," or Divine Plan (*Epid.* 6), with prophecy, forming the premise on which the entire argument of the *Epid.* rests.

The story of Shem, Ham, and Japheth in the *Epid.* is made to convey a

good deal of information about those economies of God. Irenaeus's account
of Noah's sons provides him with a means to portray the election of
Israel, the inclusion of the Gentiles in the plan of election, and the exclusion
of non-believers from the divine promises, respectively. As such, Noah's
sons provide a means to describe the relationship between Gentile
Christians, Jews, and unbelievers in the divine scheme for humanity that is
reminiscent of Paul's summary in Rom 9-11. It is possible that Paul's line of
thought in Rom 9-11 has informed Irenaeus's interpretation of Noah's three
sons in the *Epid.* What would warrant this hypothesis? Two considerations
present themselves. First, a number of theological points made by Irenaeus
in his treatment of Noah's sons correspond to Paul's in Rom 9-11. They will
be considered in the following section. The second consideration is the
presence of a number of potential textual borrowings from Rom 9-11 in
passages where Irenaeus refers to Noah's sons in the *Epid.*: the primary
narrative in *Epid.* 19-22, later references in the history related in *Epid.*
24-25, 29, 40-42a, and in Irenaeus's concluding exposition of the apostolic
mission in *Epid.* 86-97.

Shared Theological Features.

Irenaeus's agenda in the *Epid.*, like Paul's in Rom 9-11, places the apostolic mission in the context of a larger historical and Christocentric
framework that includes both Jews and Gentiles in relation to the one
God (e.g., *Epid.* 8). In Rom 9-11, Paul addresses the respective places of
the Jews and Gentiles in the divine plan, possibly in response to the
failed mission to the Jews (Stendahl 1976, 3-4, 85; cf. Fitzmyer 1993,
541; Dunn 1988, 518-19). Within the framework of salvation history,
each author develops a series of points, a number of which they share.
The following summary of the most noticeable of these shared notions
cannot pretend to be exhaustive of this rich material, but it does raise
the likelihood that Irenaeus has incorporated some points expressed by
Paul in Rom 9-11 in his exposition and development of the implications
of Noah's sons in the *Epid.*

The gratuitous election of Israel (*Epid.* 21, 24; cf. Rom 9:6-13). The first
of these points is Israel's gratuitous election, which Paul locates in its
earliest ancestor, Abraham (Rom 9:6-13). Irenaeus does likewise (*Epid.*
24), but traces it to the blessing given to Shem ten generations earlier
(*Epid.* 21). He introduces a second notion, that of Abraham's "election" as
his "proper due," his inheritance from his ancestor (*Epid.* 24). Nevertheless, Irenaeus's use of the sons of Noah to describe divine election reflects in
essence, if not in example, Paul's treatment of the issue in Rom 9:6-13.
"Election" is the prerogative of Israel not named in Paul's list in Rom
9:1-5, though it is developed in Rom 9:6-13 and is at last named *per se* in
Rom 11:28 (Fitzmyer 1993, 543; cf. Cranfield 1983, 2:580-81). To look
forward briefly, the connection between Rom 9:6-13 and Rom 11:25-32
suggests that Irenaeus has Paul's culminating arguments in Rom 11 in mind

also, though textual borrowings from Rom 11 are hard to detect in the context of Noah's sons in the *Epid*. Irenaeus, like Paul, also considers those who are not elect: for Paul, they include Ishmael and Esau (Rom 9:8-13), while Irenaeus treats them under the head of the descendants of Ham (*Epid*. 20-21).

Election is a function of divine mercy (*Epid*. 24; also 41, 60, 96; cf. Rom 9:14-23). Twice in the narrative of the first half of the *Epid*., Irenaeus casts divine election in terms of mercy. The call of Abraham is merciful:

> Later, when time had passed, that is, in the tenth generation after the flood, we find Abraham seeking the God who was his proper due from the blessing of his forefather. And so, following the zeal of his soul, he wandered all around the world, seeking out the place where God was. And he was losing strength and falling away from the quest, when God, having mercy on him who, alone and in silence, sought Him, appeared to Abraham, revealing Himself through the Word, as through a ray of light. . . . (*Epid*. 24)

The same mercy characterizes God's disposition in sending the apostles to the Gentiles (*Epid*. 41, 97). The "calling of the Gentiles" is an extension of God's mercy beyond Israel – *Epid*. 41 includes a reminiscence of Rom 9:14-18. Dunn points out that Paul attempts to address the problems raised by his argument concerning divine mercy in Rom 9:6-13 by expanding its perspective, positively, to all of creation. He further points out that the discussion in Rom 9:18-23 points to the culmination of the argument in Rom 11:25-32 (Dunn 1988, 537). Irenaeus's treatment of the election in terms of Noah's sons likewise puts it in the context of all creation.

Righteousness is based on faith rather than on election or the Law (*Epid*. 19, 24, cf. 87; cf. Rom 9:30-10:4). Neither election by itself, nor observance of the Law, establishes righteousness. For Irenaeus, righteousness is based on faith in Christ (*Epid*. 41b, 87, 97), but there is room to argue that he also has in mind faith in God (cf. *Epid*. 3, 8). Like Paul, he associates "righteousness" with belief in and relationship with God. Noah was saved for his righteousness (*Epid*. 19), and the God in whom he believes – rather his faith in God – is given to Shem (*Epid*. 21). Abraham is made righteous by faith (Gen 15:6; *Epid*. 25, 93). Near the conclusion of the *Epid*., Irenaeus reinforces the idea that Gentile believers, too, depend for righteousness on the obedience that comes from faith in God: "So He [Christ] has increased, by means of our faith in Him, our love towards God and towards the neighbor, rendering us godly, righteous and good" (*Epid*. 87). Irenaeus refers to his audience who, presumably, are all Gentiles and hearers of the apostolic preaching mission through Irenaeus and others like him.

Irenaeus's development on the subject of faith with respect to the sons of Noah takes some peculiar turns. Shem and Japheth are portrayed as pious, and in this case piety involves respect for their father's nakedness. Irenaeus relates their act of filial respect to faith in God, though in the temporal order that faith is subsequent: Shem's reward is possession of this God (*Epid.* 21). Nevertheless, his faith will be handed down to Abraham, and from him to the chosen people (*Epid.* 25). By faith, too, the Gentiles receive "the promise [made to] the patriarchs," which consists of the following: "that, to those who believed and loved the Lord, and who lived in holiness and righteousness and in patience, the God of all would offer eternal life" (*Epid.* 41). Later, reiterating the idea, Irenaeus states that salvation comes "not by the prolixity of the Law, but according to the brevity of faith and love" (*Epid.* 87; cf. Rom 9:28; Isa 10:22-23).

A providential "hardening," or disbelief, of Israel makes possible the inheritance of the promises by the Gentiles (*Epid.* 91-95; cf. Rom 11:11-24). For Irenaeus as for Paul (Rom 11:11-24), the disbelief of Israel makes possible the inheritance of the promises by the Gentiles (*Epid.* 91). Irenaeus itemizes the points demonstrating that disbelief in *Epid.* 95, where the forsaking of God, the killing of the prophets, the denial of "the Eternal King," and scorn of the son, provide reason for God to give the inheritance to "the foolish Gentiles." Irenaeus's understanding that Israel's disbelief offers an opening for the Gentiles corresponds to, and may best be understood in terms of, Paul's reference to Israel's "stumbling" (παράπτωμα) in Rom 11:11 that may come about on account of its failure to understand the Law and respond in faith (so Dunn 1988, 667).

Irenaeus also associates the Gentiles' inheritance with the prophecy of Jeremiah. In place of the old covenant, in which "their fathers . . . did not remain," a new covenant would be established (*Epid.* 90, quoting Jer 38:31-34 [LXX]; cf. Heb 8:8-12), and its promises inherited by the Gentiles (*Epid.* 91). Irenaeus describes that inheritance as the entry of Japheth into the house of Shem, to share the inheritance of God with him, and refers to it as the "calling of the Gentiles." The "calling of the Gentiles" is the principal feature of Irenaeus's treatment of the apostolic preaching, and the point of *Epid.* 41b-42a and 86-97. He points out that it was proclaimed in former days by the prophets, "according to the mercy of God" (cf. Rom 9:12-16) (*Epid.* 41). In turn, it was manifested to "us" (*Epid.* 92), so that the people who were not God's people before are now God's people (*Epid.* 93, quoting Rom 9:25-26; cf. Hos 2:25, 1 [LXX]). The "new calling" brings about a change of heart in the Gentiles (*Epid.* 94), who are included on the grounds of faith (cf. Rom 9:30) and receive life in consequence. For Irenaeus, then, Abraham's faith is summed up in the faith of the Gentile believers (*Epid.* 95).

The election of the Gentiles is connected to the promises made to Israel (*Epid.* 86-87, 95-96; cf. Rom 10:1-4; 11:1-32). For Paul, "the calling of the Gentiles" depends on Israel's promises and does not exist except in relation to Israel (see Fitzmyer 1993, 622 on Rom 11:25). Irenaeus also clearly indicates that what the Gentiles receive is "the promise made to the patriarchs" (*Epid.* 41b). Although Irenaeus contrasts the church to "the former synagogue," and points out that now it bears God more children than the synagogue (*Epid.* 94), it does not exist except in relation to the "synagogue" (*Epid.* 90-91). Irenaeus's contrast between church and synagogue concerns the observances of the Mosaic Law (*Epid.* 89-97), not the promises, the patriarchs and the covenants.

The Mosaic Law is related to the "new Law" (Rom 9:30-33; *Epid.* 86-87, 97). Like Paul, Irenaeus is eager to establish a solid relationship between the Mosaic Law and the "new Law" in the *Epid.* (cf. *Haer.* 4.9-16). In this vein, he quotes Jer 38:31-34 (LXX) in *Epid.* 90-91. However, there are differences: the old Law is "prolix" and the new one a "short word" (Rom 9:28; cf. Isa 10:22-23) – Irenaeus has in mind the summing up of the Decalogue in the two great commandments (Matt 22:37-40) (*Epid.* 87; cf. *Epid.* 95) – and the law of Christ is more strict (*Epid.* 96, quoting from Matt 5:17-48). Irenaeus also takes care to point out that the word (the new Law) goes from Zion (Jerusalem), as prophesied (*Epid.* 86). The origin of the New Law in Jerusalem supports his overall agenda in the *Epid.* to show that the apostolic preaching is grounded in the Law and the prophets who came before it. Earlier in the text, he points out that Christ was proclaimed by the Law (*Epid.* 40). He reiterates the Pauline statement that love fulfills the Law (Rom 13:10), perhaps alluding also to Rom 10:4 (*Epid.* 87). Nevertheless, his attitude is not ambivalent: the preaching of Christ is a "new way," and the faithful are not to turn back to Mosaic Law (*Epid.* 89). The "letter" is replaced by the "spirit," and the new law is written in their hearts (*Epid.* 90; cf. Rom 9:30-33).

Human freedom, as well as divine authority, is involved in the "election" (Rom 9:30-10:21; *Epid.* 20, 95). Both Irenaeus and Paul underscore the divine authority in making the "election" (Rom 9:6-13; cf. *Epid.* 8). Nevertheless, freedom is a concern in Irenaeus's teaching about grace: *Haer.* 4.37-39 is devoted to the discussion of human freedom (see Bacq 1978, 253-69, 363-88). In *Epid.* 20, Shem, Ham, and Japheth receive blessings and a curse as a direct result of their freely chosen actions, expressed in the primary narrative as respect toward their father, Noah. Like later believers, Shem and Japheth are saved by their faith, and Ham is cursed for his lack of faith (disrespect). Irenaeus has turned the three sons into exemplars of idolaters, Israelites, and Gentiles who come to believe. He will use the negative example of Ham again as an ethical warning in *Haer.* 4.31.1. Because the three sons are exemplars, the boundaries between the three groups of their descendants are porous. Those who were not faithful can become so, and some of those who are "faithful" might abandon their fidelity (*Epid.* 95; cf. 8). There is a tension between divine sovereignty in the matter of election, and human freedom in the matter of faith. Irenaeus does not resolve it any more than Paul does (Fitzmyer 1993, 576).

To remain "elect," Gentiles must continue to fulfill the obligations of faith (*Epid.* 41b-42a, 96; cf. Rom 11:22). Paul's treatment of the subject requires the Gentile believers who have been "grafted in" to "continue in [God's] kindness; otherwise [they] will be cut off" (Rom 11:22). Irenaeus also is clear about the ethical implications of belief in Christ. The apostles turn converts away from idolatry, fornication, avarice —the peculiar sins of Ham (*Epid.* 41a; cf. Acts 21:25; *Epid.* 20). If the Gentiles live "in holiness and righteousness and in patience," the Lord offers eternal life, but the "faithful" must keep their bodies "stainless" and souls "uncorrupted" so as not to lose the indwelling Holy Spirit (*Epid.* 41b-42a; cf. 96, 97). Irenaeus recognizes that a hedge has been cultivated around the Spirit dwelling in the believer: the demands of the law of faith, which preserve the Spirit, are more strict than the Mosaic law, and the latter is not needed for those who follow the former (*Epid.* 96, quoting Matt 5:17-48).

Despite appearances, the divine mind has not changed about the election of Israel (*Epid.* 40b-42a; cf. Rom 9:1-5; 11:11-24). If Israel is the elect people of God, then does its rejection mean God has changed, and that the covenants are revoked (cf. Rom 9:1-5)? Paul links the history of Israel with the history of the Gentile believers (see Fitzmyer 1993, 608-10) in an argument that shows God's constancy (cf. Rom 1:16; 2:9-10). Irenaeus does likewise in arguing for the veracity of the apostolic preaching. He opens the body of his treatise with a statement that God is "merciful, compassionate, good, righteous, the God of all – both of the Jews and of the Gentiles and of the faithful" (*Epid.* 8). This image of God is repeated at the end (*Epid.* 86-97, especially 97) in a grand *inclusio* that uses this notion to reinforce the underlying point that God is manifested in a continuous salvation history both before and after the appearance of Christ. Here is a clue to the value of Rom 9-11 in the *Epid.* Paul provides an authoritative precedent for Irenaeus's connection between "the adoption, the glory, the covenants, the giving of the Law, the worship, and the promises, . . . the patriarchs, and . . . the Messiah" (Rom 9:4-5). The Gentile believers, who will inherit these promises (*Epid.* 41, 91), stand in a line of descent that goes back to Shem, and to his father, Noah.

Irenaeus seems to lend more nuance to Paul's concept, developed in Romans and culminating in Rom 9-11, that salvation is for Jew and Greek alike, the Jew first (Rom 1:16-17; cf. 2:9-10; 3:9). The patriarchs are the forerunners of those Gentiles who believe, love the Lord, and live "in holiness and righteousness and patience" (*Epid.* 41b). Irenaeus's language recalls his description of Abraham in particular (*Epid.* 24). Elsewhere, Irenaeus clearly allows for the salvation of the patriarchs and other faithful who came before Christ.

> . . . For those who died before the manifestation of Christ there is hope, when raised at the judgement, to obtain salvation, whoever feared God and died in righteousness, and had the Spirit of God within them, such as the patriarchs, the prophets and the righteous. . . . (*Epid.* 56)

Irenaeus clearly understands that the righteous both before and after Christ will be saved, like Abraham, on account of their faith (cf. Rom 4:16-18). This appears to be the way he understands "the Jew first." However, after the "manifestation of Christ," it will be necessary to turn to Christ: "But for those who, after the manifestation of Christ, did not believe in Him, there is, in the judgement, inexorable vengeance" (*Epid.* 56). This is one possible understanding of Paul's statement in, e.g., Rom 11:23. Elsewhere in the *Epid.* this position is not so clear (e.g., *Epid.* 8).

"Israel" is taken to refer, at least in part, to an eschatological Israel rather than an ethnic one (*Epid.* 97; cf. Rom 11:1-24). Paul, on the other hand, argues strenuously that there is a remnant in Israel (Rom 11:1-10), and that Israel's failure is partial and temporary (Rom 11:23-24). Does this mean that Jews will be saved independently of faith in Christ? This section of Romans, and its olive tree metaphor, make most sense when "Israel" is taken to refer to an eschatological Israel rather than an ethnic one, that is, a group composed of Gentile believers and a remnant of Jews who believe in Christ (Fitzmyer 1993, 610). The Jews will be shown mercy too (Rom 11:29-31), when Israel's idolatry is finally removed (cf. Rom 11:26), and it recognizes "the final or true form of [its] own religion" (Davies 1977-78, 27; cited in Fitzmyer 1993, 625).

Irenaeus's treatment of the narratives of Shem, Ham, and Japheth indeed conveys the notion that at the end of the age a "spiritual Israel" will be saved, which is comprised of both Jews and Gentiles who have believed the Gospel. In fact, he articulates that notion in *Haer.* 4.2.7, where he quotes Rom 11:26 (see Fitzmyer 1993, 624; cf. Noormann 1994, 171-73). In the *Epid.*, his statement, "This is the *fruit* of the blessing of Japheth" (*Epid.* 41-42a), refers to the inheritance of the kingdom of God. The blessing of Japheth is *manifested* by the calling of the Gentiles. The calling of the Gentiles does not mean the completion of the blessing on Japheth: the blessing has eschatological import. Those who believe in Christ will share in the resurrection of the just. Such a suggestion fits Irenaeus's larger agenda to show the continuity of God's graciousness through all of human history up to its eschatological *dénouement*, and to show that the legislation given to the Jews before Christ is not really a provision separate from the one given to the Gentile believers after the Incarnation. At the end, all will be judged by the ascended Christ (*Epid.* 85). Irenaeus does not seem to picture an Israel *displaced* by the Gentiles who believe in Christ before that judgment. In this he parts company with Justin. His picture of Shem, Ham and Japheth allows him to treat the Gentile church as an entity distinct from both pagans and Jews.

A "spiritual Israel" so described may be reflected in the closing summary of his teaching about salvation history in *Epid.* 97, which reiterates the key ideas articulated in *Epid.* 8, and largely consists of a quotation from Baruch 3:20-4:1 (attributed to Jeremiah). In this passage,

Irenaeus lets the prophet state the permanent value of the Mosaic Law in salvation history:

> *. . . He found out the whole way by understanding, and gave her [the law] to Jacob, his servant, and to Israel, His beloved. After which she appeared on earth and conversed with men. This is the book of the commandments of God, and of the law, which is for ever. All who keep her [are] unto life; but they who forsake her, will die. . . .* [Bar 3:36-4:1]. (*Epid.* 97)

His interpretation turns the passage into a statement of the activity of the Logos in creation, but even that interpretation does not mitigate the statements found here about giving the Law: it can be presumed that the Wisdom of God gave it.

The foregoing summary indicates a number of theological notions that Irenaeus expresses in his treatment of Noah's sons which he shares with Rom 9-11. Those shared opinons, however, do not constitute an incontrovertible case for a dependence on Rom 9-11 in his treatment of Noah's sons. Paul does not use the Noachic cycle, nor does Irenaeus, in the *Epid.*, employ the image of the olive tree, or the comparison between Jacob and Esau (Rom 9:11-13). However, a second observation about Irenaeus's interpretation of the sons of Noah contributes evidence to support the suggestion that Irenaeus had Rom 9-11 in mind. Irenaeus borrows from the text of Rom 9-11 a number of times as he develops his account of Shem, Ham, and Japheth.

Irenaeus's Use of Rom 9-11 in His Interpretation of Noah's Sons.

Owing to the purpose of the work, the *Epid.*'s explicit use of the New Testament is modest – knowledge of the content of the apostolic preaching is presumed – and thus, material for direct comparison with the text of Romans is limited. Nevertheless, the book contains many reminiscences of the Gospels, Acts and Pauline epistles, as well as borrowings from the Septuagint that probably came by way of the Gospels and Paul. Moreover, Irenaeus invokes Paul's authority in the *Epid.* as he does in the *Haer.*, naming him three times, twice as the "Apostle Paul" (*Epid.* 5 and 87), and once as "the blessed Apostle" (*Epid.* 8). In all three instances, the reference accompanies a quotation – two of them come from Romans, though neither is from Rom 9-11. The *Epid.* includes at least 90 other possible borrowings from the Pauline and deuteropauline epistles (Irenaeus does not distinguish them). Thirty-five of these come from Romans, of which thirteen are associated with Rom 9-11. These facts signal the importance of Paul, and possibly of Romans in particular, in the *Epid.*, and reinforce the likelihood of Irenaeus's dependence on Rom 9-11 in treating Noah's sons.

Therefore, we will next consider Irenaeus's likely borrowings from Rom

9-11 in the *Epid.*, in the restricted case of passages where Irenaeus invokes the sons of Noah. The term "borrowing" will be used here as a comprehensive term to include all quotations, paraphrases and reminiscences of the biblical texts (Hoek 1988, 20-22; and 1996, 228-29). The borrowings to be considered here will be treated in the following order: quotations, reminiscences, and a special category of reminiscences connected with the phrase "the calling of the Gentiles," which, as we will see, refers to Rom 10:18.

Direct quotations of Rom 9-11. Eight direct quotations in *Epid.* have potential dependence on Rom 9-11. All eight quotations also depend on a text from the Septuagint. Irenaeus attributes six of them to a Septuagint author, in one case specifying an author where Paul does not, and two of them are not attributed to any particular author by either Paul or Irenaeus. Two of these eight quotations are associated with Irenaeus's treatment of the Noachic cycle: the potential quotations of Ps 18:5 (LXX) (Rom 10:18) in *Epid.* 21 and of Deut 32:21 (Rom 10:19) in *Epid.* 95. It must be borne in mind that close textual comparisons cannot be undertaken in this case, since the original Greek *Epid.* does not survive, and the Armenian translation is subject to interpolations from the Armenian Bible.

The first potential quotation from Paul to be considered here appears in the initial narrative of Japheth's blessing in *Epid.* 21. This blessing ". . . blossomed, at the close of the age, when the Lord was manifested, out of the calling of the Gentiles, when God enlarged the call to them, *for their voice has gone out to all the earth and their words to the ends of the world.*" As the text reads, Irenaeus could have borrowed his text either from Ps 18:5 (LXX) or from Rom 10:18. Irenaeus does not attribute the passage to any author – it is one of the two without attribution –, and Paul himself in Rom 10:18 quotes verbatim from Ps 18:5, also without attribution. Irenaeus's text could have been derived from either source. No other identifiable quotation from Paul appears in this passage to suggest that Irenaeus has the Apostle in mind.

However, the context lends some probability that the quotation derives from Rom 10:18. The passage is introduced in a discussion of Japheth, who is associated in *Epid.* 21 with the apostolic mission to the Gentiles that takes place at the "close of the age" – the association will be confirmed in *Epid.* 42a. Paul speaks of the apostolic mission in Rom 10:14-18. Thematically, Irenaeus's use of the verse is like Paul's. Psalm 18:5, on the other hand, describes a creation glorifying its God. The function of the text in *Epid.* increases the probability that Irenaeus has borrowed it from Paul, not the Psalms. Moreover, Irenaeus explicitly connects the verse to Japheth, the apostolic preaching mission and a phrase, "the calling (out) of the Gentiles," that he will use repeatedly as the *Epid.* progresses. Despite the lingering possibility that Irenaeus borrows from the Psalm in this case, these contextual considerations give some weight to the probability that he here depends upon Rom 10:18.

The second quotation connected to the Noachic cycle in the *Epid.* appears near the end of the treatise, in *Epid.* 95, where Irenaeus again appears to connect the history of Noah's sons with Rom 9-11. Here, a reference to the idolatry of Canaan recalls his father Ham (*Epid.* 20), and a reference to the "calling" again recalls Japheth. Irenaeus aims to show the immediate cause of the apostolic mission to the Gentiles and to connect the promises of Israel to the salvation of the Gentiles. He supports his argument with a quotation that he credits to Moses (Deut 32:21), as does Paul when he quotes it (Rom 10:19):

> But Moses also says, in Deuteronomy, that the Gentiles are to be *at the head* and the disbelieving people *at the tail* [cf. Deut 28:44]. And again he says, *You have stirred me to jealousy with what were no gods, and have angered me with your idols; and I will stir you to be jealous with those who are no people, and anger you with a foolish people* [Deut 32:21; Rom 10:19]. For they forsook the God who is, and served the gods who were not; and they killed the prophets of God, and prophesied by Baal [cf. Jer 2:8; 23:13], who was the idol of the Chanaanites; and He who is, the Son of God, they scorned, but chose Barabbas, a robber caught in murder; and they denied the Eternal King, and acknowledged a temporal Caesar as their king: – [therefore] God was pleased to bestow His inheritance on the *foolish Gentiles* who were neither of the citizenship of God nor knew who God is. Since, then, by this calling, life has been given and God has recapitulated in us the faith of Abraham, we should no longer turn back, that is, I mean, to the former legislation. . . . (*Epid.* 95)

Irenaeus quotes Deut 32:21 fully; Paul quotes only the second half of the verse. Certainly Paul is not Irenaeus's only source; Justin is a possible source, as is Deuteronomy itself. However, Paul changes the personal pronoun from "they" (Deut 32:32 [LXX]) to "you," and Irenaeus follows Paul's lead throughout the quotation, even changing that part of the verse not used by Paul. The quotation thus is a good indicator of interpretive dependence on Rom 10:19. Irenaeus probably took the verse and its attribution from Rom 10:19 and supplemented it.

Context strengthens the theory that Rom 10:19-20 inspired Irenaeus's quotation of Deut 32:21 in *Epid.* 95. The chapter also speaks of the "calling" of the Gentiles: the reappearance of the term, which is connected to Rom 10:18 in *Epid.* 21 (see below) increases the probability that Irenaeus depends on Rom 10:19 for his use of Deut 32:21 (cf. Skarsaune 1987, 446-47). Other elements in *Epid.* 95 point to Rom 10:14-21. Irenaeus contrasts the "Gentiles," who receive "the calling" (Japheth) to the "unbelieving people." To whom is this condemnation directed? Ham is the most logical possibility. The Canaanites, descendants of Ham, despise the true God (*Epid.* 20) and reject God: they "have an idol" (*Epid.* 95). Irenaeus has already spoken of "apostates" (*Epid.* 83; cf. Behr 1997, 117 n. 210). However, Irenaeus's language reflects Paul's, concerning the "disobedient and contrary people" (Rom 10:21, quoting Isa 65:2): they are those Jews, descendants of Shem and Abraham, who have rejected the true God by now rejecting the Son. They are therefore placed "at the tail" and their inheritance offered to Gentile believers (cf. Rom 10:19, possibly Rom 11:11-12). Irenaeus, like Paul, turns the distinction between Israel and not-Israel, not on an ethnic difference, but on one of faith (see Fitzmyer 1993, 558-59), which consists in the "possession" of the God of Shem and Abraham. Irenaeus may go further, hinting possibly at Rom 10:4: by receiving the Lord of the Law, the τέλος of the Law, the believer has no more need of the "former legislation." Finally, in *Epid.* 95, the rejection of the Jews brings about the possibility for the "foolish Gentiles" to be granted God's inheritance (cf. Rom 10:19-20; cf. 11:28-32). Irenaeus's conformity to Paul's version of the quotation of Deut 32:21 and its context in an assemblage of reminiscences from Romans 10:14-21, renders it probable that he has depended on Rom 10:19 to some degree for his quotation, even though he has had to go beyond Paul to complete it.

The two quotations just examined, which appear in passages in which Irenaeus brings up Noah's sons again, appear to depend upon Rom 9-11. To the degree that this is so, they add to the evidence suggesting that at least some of Irenaeus's teachings about God, election and salvation history, conveyed in his interpretation of the narrative concerning Noah's sons, could derive from Rom 9-11. Elsewhere in the *Epid.*, in contexts where he does not treat Shem, Ham, or Japheth, Irenaeus also quotes Scripture in apparent dependence on Rom 9-11. A full analysis of these quotations goes beyond the scope of this paper. The results must be used advisedly, as Irenaeus's potential borrowings from Paul's text are briefer and less securely identified than Clement's from Philo, and the comparison is rendered difficult owing to the Armenian text of the *Epid.* Both of the quotations just considered have been tentatively placed in category "B." Other potential borrowings from Rom 9-11 outside the context of discussions of the sons of Noah range from clear dependence to nondependence. The other apparent borrowings from Rom 9-11 support the more slender evidence derived simply from the passages where Irenaeus treats the sons of Noah.

One might then wonder that Irenaeus does not often claim to quote Paul directly in the *Epid.*, and attributes none of his borrowings from Rom 9-11 to Paul. His knowledge and use of the Gospels and apostolic writings betrays itself in the number of quotations ostensibly from the Septuagint that appear in their New Testament form, and the number of his potential borrowings from the Gospels is equaled by the number that can be attributed to Paul. In any case, he has already signaled the importance of the Apostle (*Epid.* 5, 8). The peculiarity may be explained by the nature of *Epid.*'s argument, which focuses on what was foretold by the patriarchs and the prophets. Indeed, the tissue of his argument is Scripture, which recounts those prophecies, just as the tissue of Paul's argument that attempts to relate the Gospel and the Law in Rom 9-10 is Scripture also (cf. Rom 3:31; Fitzmyer 1993, 539). However, it would suit Irenaeus's purpose to borrow passages from Scripture which the Apostle himself used. To the degree that his readers could identify his proofs with the preaching ministry of the Apostle, his use of Paul's writings could help drive home, implicitly, the argument of the *Epid*.

Reminiscences and paraphrases from Rom 9-11. In addition to the quotations that show some degree of dependence on Rom 9-11, there is evidence of a different kind of dependence in the form of reminiscences. Reminiscences of Irenaeus's authoritative texts are important to the organization of his arguments. His units of thought center on a passage, usually quoted (sometimes paraphrased), followed by a commentary that introduces related texts and concludes with a repetition of the central passage, often in the form of a paraphrase or reminiscence. He uses the paraphrases and reminiscences to link his arguments and ideas. This organizational pattern has been shown for the *Haer.* (Bacq 1978, 20 and 41-47), and it is equally true of the *Epid*. This feature of Irenaeus's writing means that his use of supporting reminiscences and paraphrases is at least as important to understanding his use of a biblical text as his use of direct quotations. A number of such reminiscences from Rom 9-11 reintroduce Ham and Japheth at different points in the *Epid*. In a number of such passages, other borrowings from Rom 9-11 appear also.

The first consideration goes to the simple reminiscences appearing in *Epid*. 24, 41, and 95. *Epid*. 24 elaborates on Abraham, quoting from Rom 4 as well as Gen 12-25, linking the Patriarch with his forebear, Shem, by tracing Abraham's faith in God, and that of his heirs, back to the blessing on Shem:

> And so, in this way, the original blessing [given to] Sem passed to Abraham, and from Abraham to Isaac [cf. Gen 21:12], and from Isaac to Jacob [cf. Gen 25:23; 27:27-30; Mal 1:2], the Spirit assigning the inheritance to them [cf. Rom 9:6-8], for He was called *the God of Abraham and the God of Isaac and the God of Jacob* [cf. Exod 3:6; Matt 22:32]. And to Jacob there were born twelve sons, from whom the twelve tribes of Israel are named [cf. Gen 35:22; Acts 7:8]. (*Epid*. 24)

Irenaeus's summary of the patriarchal history could well be an elaboration of Rom 9:6-8 (so Behr 1997, 56) – possibly the longer passage Rom 9:6-13 – including Paul's reference to the "children of the promise [who] are counted as descendants" (Rom 9:8). In this case, the reminiscence is secured more firmly by the fact that Irenaeus's question is the same as Paul's: to whom belongs Abraham's inheritance? It belongs to Isaac, Jacob, and Jacob's descendants. However, Irenaeus extends its origins farther back than Paul does: to Shem's blessing in the "possession" of the one God (cf. *Epid.* 21).

In *Epid.* 41, Irenaeus refers to Japheth obliquely by invoking the phrase "the call of the Gentiles" – the connection is made explicit in *Epid.* 42a (cf. *Epid.* 21). (The phrase itself, reminiscent of Rom 10:18, will be considered in its own right momentarily.) Irenaeus combines in this passage reminiscences of Rom 9:16, Rom 9:4-5 and what appears to be a paraphrase of Rom 10:14-18:

> . . . His [Christ's] disciples and witnesses . . . are the apostles, who being sent by Him, with the power of the Holy Spirit, into the whole world, realized *the call of the Gentiles*, showing mankind [sic] the way of life, turning them away from idols and from fornication and from avarice [cf. Acts 21:25], cleansing their souls and bodies by the baptism of water and the Holy Spirit [cf. John 3:5], distributing and dispensing the holy Spirit, which they received from the Lord, to the faithful – and in this way they established the churches.
>
> With faith and love and hope they established *the calling*, previously proclaimed by the prophets, *of the Gentiles*, according *to the mercy of God which was upon them*, making *their calling* known through their ministry and receiving them into the *promise made to the patriarchs*; thus they promised that, to those who believed and loved the Lord, and who lived in holiness and righteousness and in patience, the God of all would offer eternal life by means of the resurrection from the dead, through Him who died and rose, Jesus Christ. . . . (*Epid.* 41; author's italics)

Irenaeus, like Paul, connects "the promise made to the patriarchs" (cf. Rom 9:4-5) to the free "call" of the Gentiles according to "the mercy of God," as noticed earlier (cf. Rom 9:16; perhaps Rom 9:12-16; cf. Rom 9:23-24; Rom 11:29-32 expresses the same idea). *Epid.* 24 had already identified divine mercy with the promise given to Abraham. Irenaeus associates these reminiscences from Rom 9, which describe the divine promises and divine mercy, with an extended reminiscence of Rom 10:14-18 that summarizes the apostolic mission to the Gentiles, which will make "'their calling' known through their ministry." In short, Irenaeus's use of these reminiscences from Rom 9:12-24 and 10:14-18 integrates into his discussion large parts of the salvation history Paul has articulated in Rom 9-11.

Epid. 95, considered before for its likely borrowing from Rom 10:19, contains other reminiscences from Rom 9-11. Besides reiterating the reference to a "foolish nation," Irenaeus hints at Rom 11:11-12 by his reference to the "disbelieving people" that have rejected God and have thereby allowed a "foolish people" into the arena of divine mercy. The passage includes yet another reminiscence from Rom 10:18 in its reference to "the calling" of the Gentiles. The clustering of reminiscences from Rom 10 and possibly Rom 11, along with the quotation discussed earlier, reinforces the probability of a substantial borrowing from Paul in this section. That probability gains further strength from the appearance of other likely borrowings from Rom 9-11, not directly connected to the narrative of Noah's sons, in *Epid.* 92, 93, 96, and 97.

Passages referring to "the calling of the Gentiles." A number of the reminiscences considered already take the form of the phrase, "the calling from out of the Gentiles," ἡ ἐξ ἐθνῶν κλῆσις (*Epid.* 21, 41, 42a, 89, 91, 95). The phrase first appears, three times, in *Epid.* 21. There, Irenaeus uses it to describe the "enlarging" of Japheth (Gen 9:27) and connects it explicitly to the apostolic preaching mission that Paul describes in Rom 10:14-18. When the phrase next appears, it is associated again with the apostolic preaching (*Epid.* 41), and with "the fruit of the blessing on Japheth" (*Epid.* 42a). Irenaeus thus uses the phrase to draw together the idea of Japheth's blessing, which includes the Gentiles in the divine plan of salvation from the very beginning, with its accomplishment in Irenaeus's present, and with the apostolic mission that is the means by which to accomplish it. Japheth will not be named again in the *Epid.*, but variations on the phrase "the calling of the Gentiles" reappear three more times when Irenaeus turns again to his proof that the apostolic mission to the Gentiles was prophesied (*Epid.* 86).

This use of the phrase, "the calling of the Gentiles," is a striking example of a typical Irenaean procedure in using biblical texts. Abbreviated reminiscences of previously quoted texts, or texts soon to be quoted, function as mnemonics that link and unite his arguments. By establishing and employing it in *Epid.* 21 (three times), *Epid.* 41 (twice), and *Epid.* 42a, he ties the blessing on Japheth at the re-creation in the days of Noah to its fulfillment in the ingathering of the Gentiles at the end of the age. By reiterating it in *Epid.* 89, 91, and 95, Irenaeus creates a literary link between the two parts of the *Epid.*'s body, and a theological link between his proof that the sending of the apostles to the Gentiles fulfilled what the patriarchs and prophets foretold, at the end of the *Epid.*, and his historical summary in the first part (*Epid.* 41-42a).

As a linking phrase, "the calling of the Gentiles" provides a particularly strong case for the association of Rom 9-11 with Irenaeus's treatment of the sons of Noah. It is established in the context of a quotation from Rom 10:18 in *Epid.* 21, and serves as a reminiscence of that verse, and possibly of Rom 10:14-18, in the remainder of the text. Further confirmation for the phrase's association with Rom 10:14-18 comes in *Epid.* 41, quoted above, where Irenaeus invokes it together with a paraphrase of the passage. *Epid.* 42a repeats the association and specifies its connection with Japheth, whose blessing is fulfilled in the mission of the apostles:

> This is the fruit of the blessing of Japheth, made manifest, by means of the Church, in the calling of the Gentiles, who were

> waiting to receive *the dwelling in the house of Sem* according to the promise of God. (*Epid.* 42a)

For Irenaeus, it appears that the phrase, "the calling of the Gentiles," functions as a kind of shorthand to refer to the Gentile preaching mission and to the earlier discussion of Japheth's blessing, and to summarize Rom 10:14-18.

In the conclusion of the treatise, Irenaeus uses the phrase several times as he develops the implications of the Gentile mission. In *Epid.* 89, he describes "the calling of the Gentiles" as a "new thing," a way in the wilderness and the desert (cf. Isa 43:18-21), and clearly warns Gentile believers not to "turn back" to the Mosaic Law (cf. Gal 3:23-29!), because the Gospel message is a new way to salvation. Irenaeus also associates "the calling of the Gentiles" in *Epid.* 91 with the "new covenant" prophesied in Jer 38:31-34 (LXX). *Epid.* 94 speaks of "the new calling," which brings "a change of heart . . . in the Gentiles, through the Word of God," and *Epid.* 95 expands on the new life that comes through this calling. Irenaeus's concern to point out that the Gospel represents a new way of salvation independent of the Law in this section of the *Epid.* seems to reflect the argument of Rom 9-11. *Epid.* 95 shows that Irenaeus clearly has in mind the "stumbling" of Israel that allows the mission to the Gentiles, which is entirely consistent with Paul's argument in Rom 9-11, especially Rom 9:30-10:4 and 11:1-10.

The considerations of quotations, reminiscences, and the key phrase, "the calling of the Gentiles," make it very probable that Irenaeus used Rom 9-11 in his interpretation of the Noachic cycle in the *Epid.* First, all of Irenaeus's potential quotations from Rom 9-11, even those not connected with the account of Noah's sons, appear in the same sections of the *Epid.* in which Irenaeus deploys the story of Noah's sons (*Epid.* 21 and 24, 41-42a, and *Epid.* 86-97). A large half (15) of the other reminiscences of Rom 9-11 examined above (27) are also connected with the Noachic material. Even omitting three quotations that probably were not borrowed from Romans (in *Epid.* 87, 92, and 96), the strong correlation suggests that Rom 9-11 influenced Irenaeus's deployment of the account.

Second, the borrowings from Rom 9-11 relating to Irenaeus's treatment of Noah's sons are extensive. Quotations and reminiscences generally come from Rom 9 and 10, and there is a possible reminiscence of Rom 11:11-12 in *Epid.* 95. Other lines of thought corresponding to Paul's argument in Rom 11 have been noted. In particular, Irenaeus in his account of Shem, Ham, and Japheth, privileges Romans 9:6-28 which concerns the election and the extension of the divine provision to the Gentiles, and Rom 10:13-20, which addresses the preaching of the Gospel, and the "calling of the Gentiles" by God (Rom 10:18).

Finally, although there is no special ordering in Irenaeus's borrowings from Rom 9-11, in the *Epid.*, his Pauline references cluster tightly. All of the quotations can be associated with Rom 9:6-30 and Rom 10:13-20. On the other hand, the Septuagint texts Paul quotes in those passages range widely through the Law, Prophets, and Writings. This fact strengthens the probability that Irenaeus has used Rom 9-11 for at least some of his references to the Septuagint. The reminiscences extend somewhat further into Paul's text, some coming from Rom 9:4 (in *Epid.* 41), and possibly Rom 11:11-12 (*Epid.* 95) and Rom 10:6-7 (*Epid.* 97). In sum, several passages in which Irenaeus brings up Noah's sons again, especially Japheth, contain scriptural borrowings that can reasonably be considered to have taken their source in Rom 9-11. To the degree that this is so, these passages confirm the earlier contention that many of Irenaeus's teachings about God, election and salvation history are shared with Paul and derive from Rom 9-11.

Conclusions.

Irenaeus's development of Shem, Ham, and Japheth shares Paul's concerns about divine election, faith, righteousness, and the history of salvation that are articulated in Rom 9-11, as we have seen. In particular, he shares with the Apostle the concept of a powerful and benevolent God, in charge of all things, who is not capricious, but rather is faithful, merciful, and who rewards those who believe. For this reason, if no other, Paul is useful as a guide and as an authoritative source for Irenaeus. Paul's magisterial view of divine power is articulated in Rom 9:1-24 and again in Rom 11:33-36. Irenaeus's view is articulated in the programmatic chapter of the first part of the *Epid.*, which includes, indeed, a paraphrase of Rom 9:22:

> ... God, ... is the Maker of heaven and earth and the whole world, ... by whom all things exist, and from whom all things are nourished – merciful, compassionate, good, righteous, the God of all – both of the Jews and of the Gentiles and of the faithful. However, to the faithful He is as a Father, since in the last times He opened the covenant of the adoption as sons; while to the Jews He is as Lord and Lawgiver, since in the intervening period, when humans had forgotten, abandoned and rebelled against God, He brought them into slavery by means of the Law, that they might learn that they have [as] Lord the Maker and Fashioner, who also bestows the breath of life, ... and to the Gentiles He is as Creator and Almighty. But for absolutely everyone He is the Nourisher and King and Judge, for no one shall escape His judgement, neither a Jew nor a Gentile, neither a sinful believer nor an angel; but those who, at this time, do not believe in His goodness, will know *His power* [cf. Rom 9:22] in the judgement, as the blessed Apostle says. ... (*Epid.* 8)

God is God of all, and all answer to God in the judgment. There is a place for the Jews and for the Gentiles. Here, the Law is an enslavement (recalling Gal 4:22-31), though it is also a means of human education and growth. *Epid.* 8 suggests that Irenaeus views the "faithful" as coming from both Jews and Gentiles. The goal for all is to be faithful, and for all the faithful to know God "as a Father." His statement envisions a scenario in which all will be incorporated into the "covenant of the adoption." This corresponds to the notion that Paul articulates in Rom 11:23, 27-29 and 10:12-13. *Epid.* 8 is consistent also with Irenaeus's programmatic statement of salvation history in *Haer.* 1.10.3, a passage in which, it happens, he quotes the doxology of Rom 11:33.

Norris proposed that investigations concerning Irenaeus's use of Paul will find their richest ground in the terrain of his theology of history and human salvation (Norris 1990, 98). Romans 9-11 concerns that history, and Paul's picture of continuous divine providence affirms the place of Israel and the Gentiles in it: the metaphor of grafted olive branches is one way he describes it (Rom 11:16-24). Irenaeus's vision also includes a unified history of divine-human relations, with continuity among the covenants, including the Law and the Gospel (Norris 1990, 84-95). The *Epid.*, in its very organization, intends to show that continuity from creation to the Irenaean present. Its agenda compares well with Rom 9-11. The finding of a number of textual borrowings from Rom 9-11 in it, especially from Rom 9 and 10, secures the relationship.

Irenaeus's treatment of the history of Noah's sons is essentially typological. However, he does not describe the curse and blessings given to Noah's sons explicitly as "typological" or "prefiguring." He does speak of their fulfillment, or "blossoming" (*Epid.* 21), in prophetic terms. The promise given Japheth in the course of ancient historical events (as he sees them) is fulfilled in the preaching of the Gospel in the Irenaean present (*Epid.* 20-21), and the analogies he draws between them, especially in the last section of the work, are plain enough. Further, by characterizing the curse and blessings of Shem, Ham, and Japheth as inheritances (*Epid.* 20), Irenaeus establishes continuity between the three sons and their heirs.

At the time of their inheritances, the heirs of Noah's sons will be characterized by their belief in God (or lack thereof), or by their acceptance of the apostolic preaching. As noted earlier, under the head of human freedom in accepting God's promises, Irenaeus makes the three sons exemplars of pagans (and non-believers), Israelites, and Gentile believers (*Epid.* 20, 95). In so doing, he creates an ambiguity between faith and historical lineage as the proper basis for claiming to inherit Shem's blessing. Ambiguity also characterizes Paul's identification of "Israel" and even of "the law" in Rom 9-11 (Rom 11:26; cf. 11:17, 23). Although Irenaeus does not, in *Epid.*, use Paul's image of the olive tree (Rom 11:16-24), his use of the material concerning Noah's sons in *Epid.* 94-95 in many ways is reminiscent of Paul's ambiguity on the point. In any case, there is no surety about remaining "on the tree": one must first believe, then continue to be faithful to God.

However, despite the similarity to Paul manifested in his programmatic statements, Irenaeus's interests are not identical to Paul's. Irenaeus is not pastorally concerned with the relationship between Jews and Gentiles. There is no reason to think he actually knew any Jews. The earliest evidence for any Jewish presence in Roman Lugdunum is later than Irenaeus. Passages in *Epid.* 89 and 95, which warn against turning back to the Mosaic Law, could be leveled against Jews. However, we cannot rule out the possibility of a Judaizing faction in Lugdunum, or that Irenaeus was writing the *Epid.* in part for Christians in Asia Minor, where, e.g., Melito and Ignatius had already taught against Judaizing elements influencing their communities. Certainly, Irenaeus was familiar enough with controversies surrounding Judaizing factions to be able to mediate in the Quartodeciman controversy (Eusebius, *Hist. eccl.* 5.24.12-17).

Irenaeus's situation may account for some features Paul develops that are absent from Irenaeus's portrayal. For instance, Irenaeus does not concern himself with Paul's "remnant" among the Jews (Rom 11:22), although it does not appear that he cuts them off from the possibility of salvation, at least not so firmly as Justin does in *Dial.* 139-140 (Skarsaune 1987, 341-44). Even in *Haer.*, where there is the possibility of discussing this remnant – in the context of the olive tree image (Rom 11:16-24), for instance –, Irenaeus is concerned instead about the "wild olive branches" who have been "grafted on," that is, the Gentiles who have, by faith, been made participants in salvation. His focus is the evangelization of the Gentiles, including the barbarian Celts among whom he lives (*Haer.* 1.Pr.3; cf. *Haer.* 5.33.4 and 3.4.2).

In any case, Irenaeus's understanding of the place of the Jews in light of the preaching of the Gospel is no less problematic than Paul's. Paul's statements in Rom 11:12, 26-32, leave some ambiguity. A Christological interpretation of Rom 11:27 argues for a Pauline view that Jews could be saved now only through faith in the Gospel; *Epid.* 86-97 can be interpreted in the same way. However, Irenaeus, in *Epid.* 8, also leaves room for something of a *Sonderweg* for non-Christian Jews – Stendahl and Gager, for instance, argue for such a reading of Rom 11:17-32 – but this text seems to be contradicted by Irenaeus's later statements. In *Epid.* 94, Irenaeus identifies the "former Synagogue" with the Jews, and follows in *Epid.* 95, with a reference to the "disbelieving people" of Deut 28:44 and an exhortation not to turn back "to the former legislation." All this is framed by a rather Pauline discussion of righteousness by faith in *Epid.* 93. Irenaeus's real issue with "disbelievers" might be with those who "turn back" once they have heard the apostolic message, i.e., the apostates and possibly the heretics. Such a possibility might account for how little he speaks about the Jews.

Irenaeus's interpretation of the narrative of Noah's sons in the *Epid.* is corroborated in part by the theology articulated in *Haer.*, where Irenaeus does quote Rom 11:16-24. Like Paul, he is concerned that the Gentiles recognize the mercy that has been shown to them (*Haer.* 4.20.12), and that they do not fail to continue in God's kindness, lest they be cut off from the tree again (*Haer.* 5.10.1-2, using Paul's language in Rom 11:22; cf. the teaching of the Presbyter in *Haer.* 4.27.2). Irenaeus expresses a rather harsh view of the continuing value of Israel and Jerusalem – with the image of a fruit-bearing vine –, to point out that it has already borne its fruit by producing Christ according to the flesh (*Haer.* 4.4.1), and has no further use for believers. This view is softened, however, by his comments in *Haer.* 4.2.6-7, where he points out that Christ's teaching did not abrogate or even blame the Law. Its purpose was to lead people to Christ (he quotes Gal 3:24), and Christ came to fulfill it. Those denounced were the ones who transgressed the Law, who despised God: in short, the scribes, Pharisees, and money-lenders in the Temple. By contrast, those who were "anxious about his law" also came to believe in Christ, and were saved. For the rest, "the Law never hindered them from believing in the Son of God" (*Haer.* 4.2.7 [Roberts]). Irenaeus's comments do not foreclose the salvation of the Jews; indeed Irenaeus quotes Rom 11:26, "And so all Israel shall be saved" (*Haer.* 4.2.7). His "Israel," evidently like Paul's, is eschatological. The same is true in the *Epid.*

Even though Irenaeus does not follow Paul on every point, the evidence of the *Epid.* suggests strongly that he uses Rom 9-11 in his interpretation of the story of Shem, Ham, and Japheth. This is a good deal to say for a work that does not base the content of the apostolic preaching on the Gospels and apostolic writings – in contrast to the *Haer.* – and quotes from them so little. Yet, even in the very restricted case considered here, the evidence reveals that Paul's notions about grace, election, and the relation of Jews and Gentiles in the divine plan lie just beneath the surface of the *Epid.* The number of theological points he shares with the Apostle as he treats Shem, Ham, and Japheth suggest that he has appreciated Paul's argument in Rom 9-11 and incorporated it in a non-Pauline image that suits his own purposes better. Even some of his quotations from the Scriptures are Pauline in form. While Irenaeus could be using Rom 9-11 simply as a source for scriptural prooftexts, the many other reminiscences of Rom 9-11 that appear in those parts of the text concerning Noah's sons suggests a more thoroughgoing use of these chapters. Nevertheless, while Irenaeus demonstrably uses Rom 9-11, he does not use Paul's arguments slavishly or exclusively. He is a creative reader of Paul, and is quite capable of interpreting Romans through other texts. The fact that here he has interpreted other texts through Romans argues for his respect for Paul's thought as he articulates his own notions about salvation history. We can say, in conclusion, that in the *Epid.*, Irenaeus shares many of Paul's views on divine election, mercy, and God's constancy in human history, even in "the calling of the Gentiles," and that he appears to have used Rom 9-11 when developing his exposition of that history in his account of the three sons of Noah.

References

Aland, B., K. Aland, J. Karavidopoulos, et al., eds. 1998. *Novum Testamentum Graece*. 27th ed. Stuttgart: Deutsche Bibelgesellschaft.

Allenbach, J., A. Benoît, D. A. Bertrand, et al., eds. 1975. *Biblia patristica: Index des citations et allusions bibliques dans la littérature patristique 1. Des origines à Clément d'Alexandrie et à Tertullien*. 5 vols. Paris: Éditions du Centre national de la recherche scientifique.

Bacq, P. 1978. *De l'ancienne à la nouvelle Alliance selon S. Irénée: Unité du Livre 4 de l'Adversus Haereses*. Collection «Le Sycomore», Série Horizon; Bibliothèque de la Faculté de philosophie et lettres de Notre-Dame de la Paix (Namur) 58. Paris: Lethielleux.

Balás, D. L. 1992. "The Use and Interpretation of Paul in Irenaeus' Five Books *Adversus Haereses*." *Second Century* 9:27-39.

Behr, J., ed. 1997. *St. Irenaeus of Lyons: On the Apostolic Preaching*. Crestwood, New York: St. Vladimir's Seminary Press.

———. 2001. *The Way to Nicaea*. The Formation of Christian Theology 1. Crestwood, New York: St Vladimir's Seminary Press.

Campenhausen, H. F. von. 1972. *The Formation of the Christian Bible*. Translated by J. A. Baker. Philadelphia: Fortress.

Cohick, L. H. 2000. *The* Peri Pascha *Attributed to Melito of Sardis: Setting, Purpose, and Sources*. Brown Judaic Studies 327. Providence: Brown Judaic Studies.

Cranfield, C. E. B. 1983. *A Critical and Exegetical Commentary on the Epistle to the Romans*. International Critical Commentary. 6th ed. 2 vols. Edinburgh: T. & T. Clark.

Dassmann, E. 1979. *Der Stachel im Fleisch: Paulus in der Frühchristlichen Literatur bis Irenäus*. Münster (Westfalen): Aschendorff.

Davies, W. D. 1977-78. "Paul and the People of Israel." *New Testament Studies* 24:4-39.

Dimant, D. 1988. "Use and Interpretation of Mikra in the Apocrypha and Pseudepigrapha." Pages 379-419 in *Mikra: Text, Translation, Reading and Interpretation of the Hebrew Bible in Ancient Judaism and Early Christianity*. Edited by M. J. Mulder. Compendia Rerum Iudaicarum ad Novum Testamentum 2.1. Assen/Maastricht: Van Gorcum; Philadelphia: Fortress.

Daniélou, J. 1950. *Sacramentum Futuri: Études sur les origines de la typologie biblique*. Études de théologie historique. Paris: Beauchesne.

Dunn, J. D. G. 1988. *Romans 9-16*. Word Biblical Commentary 38b. Dallas: Word Books.

Farkasfalvy, D. 1968. "Theology of Scripture in St. Irenaeus." *Revue bénédictine* 78:319-33.

Fitzmyer, J. A. 1960-61. "The Use of Explicit Old Testament Quotations in Qumran Literature and in the New Testament." *New Testament Studies* 7:297-333.

———. 1993. *Romans.* Anchor Bible Commentary 33. New York: Doubleday.

Froidevaux, L.-M., ed. 1959. *Irénée de Lyon, Démonstration de la prédication apostolique: Nouvelle traduction de l'arménien avec introduction et notes.* Sources chrétiennes 62. Paris: Cerf.

Gager, J. G. 1983. *The Origins of Anti-Semitism: Attitudes toward Judaism in Pagan and Christian Antiquity.* New York & Oxford: Oxford University Press.

Graham, S. L. 2001. "Structure and Purpose of Irenaeus' *Epideixis.*" *Studia Patristica* 36:210-21.

———. 2002 [forthcoming]. *'Zealous for the Covenant': Irenaeus and the Covenants of Israel.* Traditio Exegetica Graeca. Leuven: Peeters.

Hoek, A. van den. 1988. *Clement of Alexandria and His Use of Philo in the Stromateis: An Early Christian Reshaping of a Jewish Model.* Supplements to Vigiliae Christianae 3. Leiden: Brill.

———. 1996. "Techniques of Quotation in Clement of Alexandria: A View of Ancient Literary Working Methods." *Vigiliae Christianae* 50:223–43.

Hoh, J. 1919. *Die Lehre des Hl. Irenäus über das Neue Testament.* Neutestamentliche Abhandlungen Bd. 7, Heft 4.5. Münster (Westfalen): Aschendorff.

Lampe, G. W. H., and K. J. Woolcombe. 1957. *Essays on Typology.* Studies in Biblical Theology 22. Naperville, Ill.: Alec R. Allenson.

Lewis, J. P. 1968. *A Study of the Interpretation of Noah and the Flood in Jewish and Christian Literature.* Leiden: E. J. Brill.

Lubac, H. de. 1998. *Medieval Exegesis.* Vol. 1. Translated by M. Sebanc. 2 vols. Grand Rapids, Michigan: Eerdman's; Edinburgh: T&T Clark.

MacLennan, R. S. 1990. *Early Christian Texts on Jews and Judaism.* Brown Judaic Studies 194. Atlanta, Ga.: Scholars Press.

Metzger, B. 1987. *The Canon of the New Testament: Its Origin, Development, and Significance.* Oxford: Oxford University Press.

Noormann, R. 1994. *Irenäus als Paulusinterpret: Zur Rezeption and Wirkung der paulinischen und deuteropaulinischen Briefe im Werk des Irenäus von Lyon.* Wissenschaftliche Untersuchungen zum Neuen Testament 2.66. Tübingen: Mohr [Siebeck].

Norris, R. A. 1990. "Irenaeus' Use of Paul in His Polemic Against the Gnostics." Pp. 79-98 in *Paul and the Legacies of Paul,* ed. W. Babcock. Dallas: Southern Methodist University Press.

Olson, M. J. 1992. *Irenaeus, the Valentinian Gnostics and the Kingdom of God (A.H. Book V): The Debate About I Corinthians 15:50*. Lewiston, New York: Edwin Mellen.

Painchaud, L. 1996. "Use of Scripture in Gnostic Literature." *Journal of Early Christian Studies* 4:129-47.

Peretto, E. 1971. *La lettera ai Romani, cc. 1-8, nell' 'Adversus Haereses' d'Ireneo*. Bari: Istituto di Litteratura Cristiana Antica.

Reynders, B. 1958. *Vocabulaire de la «Démonstration» et les fragments de Saint Irénée*. Chevetogne: Éditions de Chevetogne.

Roberts, A., W. H. Rambaut, trans. 1867–1872. *The Writings of Irenaeus*. 2 vols. Ante-Nicene Christian Library 5, 9. Edited by A. Roberts and J. Donaldson. Edinburgh: T&T Clark. Repr. in *The Apostolic Fathers with Justin Martyr and Irenaeus*. Vol. 1 of The Ante-Nicene Fathers. Edited by A. Cleveland Coxe. American ed. 11 vols. New York: Scribner's, 1885-1887; repr. Grand Rapids: Eerdmans, 1987.

Robinson, J. A., ed. 1920. *St. Irenaeus, The Demonstration of the Apostolic Preaching. Translated from the Armenian with Introduction and Notes*. Translations of Christian Literature: Series IV, Oriental Texts. London: S.P.C.K.; New York: The Macmillan Co.

Rousseau, A., ed. 1995. *Irénée de Lyon, Démonstration de la prédication apostolique*. Sources chrétiennes 406. Paris: Cerf.

Rousseau, A., L. Doutreleau, B. Hemmerdinger, et al., eds. 1965-82. *Irénée de Lyon: Contre les hérésies*. 10 vols. Sources chrétiennes 100, 100.2, 152, 153, 210, 211, 263, 264, 293, 294. Paris: Cerf.

Sanders, E. 1969. "The Hamitic Hypothesis: Its Origins and Functions in Time Perspective." *Journal of African History* 10:521-32.

Simon, M. 1978. "Judaïsme et christianisme – Gaule." Pp. 257-66 in *Les Martyrs de Lyon (177): Actes du Colloque International de Lyon, 20-23 septembre 1977*, ed. J. Rougé and R. Turcan. Col. intern. du C.N.R.S. 575. Paris: Éditions du C.N.R.S.

Skarsaune, O. 1987. *The Proof from Prophecy: A Study in Justin Martyr's Proof-text Tradition: Text-Type, Provenance, Theological Profile*. New Testament Studies 22. Leiden: E. J. Brill.

Smith, J. P., ed. 1952. *St. Irenaeus: Proof of the Apostolic Preaching*. Ancient Christian Writers 16. London: Longmans, Green and Co.; Westminster, MD: Newman.

Stendahl, K. 1976. *Paul Among Jews and Gentiles*. Philadelphia: Fortress.

Ter-Mekerttschian, H. L., E. Ter-Minassiantz, and A. v. Harnack, eds. 1907. *Des Heiligen Irenäus Schrift zum erweise der apostolischen Verkündigung in armenischer Version entdeckt, herausgegeben und in Deutsche übersetzt mit einem Nachwort und Anmerkungen von Adolf Harnack*. Texte und

Untersuchungen zur Geschichte der altchristlichen Literatur 31.1. Leipzig: J. C. Hinrichs.

Ter-Mekerttschian, H. L., and S. G. Wilson, eds. 1919. ΕΙΣ ΕΠΙΔΕΙΞΙΝ ΤΟΥ ΑΠΟΣΤΟΛΙΚΟΥ ΚΗΡΥΓΜΑΤΟΣ. *The Proof of the Apostolic Preaching with Seven Fragments*. Patrologia Orientalis 12.5. Paris: Firmin Didot.

Unger, D. J., and J. J. Dillon, eds. 1992. *St. Irenaeus of Lyons Against the Heresies, Book 1*. Ancient Christian Writers 55. New York: Paulist.

Warren, D. H. 2001. "The Text of the Apostle in the Second Century: A Contribution to the History of Its Reception." Th.D. Diss., Harvard University.

Werner, J. 1889. *Der Paulinismus des Irenaeus: Eine kirchen- und dogmengeschichtliche Untersuchung über des Verhältnis des Irenaeus zu der paulinishen Briefsammlung und Theologie*. Texte und Untersuchungen zur Geschichte der Altchristlichen Literatur 6.2. Leipzig: J. C. Hinrichs.

Westermann, C. 1984. *Genesis 1-11: A Commentary*. Translated by J. J. Scullion. Minneapolis: Augsburg.

Wevers, J. W., ed. 1974. *Genesis*. Septuaginta: Vetus Testamentum Graecum 1. Ed. Academia Scientiarum Gottingensis. Göttingen: Vandenhoeck & Ruprecht.

FIVE

Irenaeus Reads Romans 8: Resurrection and Renovation

D. Jeffrey Bingham

———— ◆ ————

The second half of the twentieth century witnessed a trend in positive appraisals of Irenaeus's use of Paul. This couldn't necessarily be said about studies published at the end of the nineteenth or during the first three decades of the twentieth centuries. In them Irenaeus's use of Paul was assessed as reluctant and distorted.[1] The recent works of R. Noormann, D. L. Balás, and R. A. Norris have contributed greatly to a more favorable and accurate evaluation of Paul in Irenaeus.[2] E. Peretto helpfully treated, in particular, Romans 1–8 in Irenaeus.[3] This present essay has profited from their labor. It attempts, however, to focus specifically on Romans 8 and to provide an understanding of how Irenaeus read that chapter in a unified manner for his anti-gnostic polemic. And polemic it was. He studied Paul's material within the context of an exegetical controversy. That context, he believed, necessitated his rescuing Romans 8 and other sacred words from misuse.

In what is traditionally recognized as his description of the tenets of the Ophites, Irenaeus lists a belief which this sect understood the disciples of Jesus to have embraced in error (*Adv. Haer.* 1.30.13 [SC 264:382.249–53]):[4]

> In this way, they claim, the disciples fell into the enormous error of imagining that Jesus was raised in his worldly body (*corpore mundiali*), because they were ignorant that "flesh and blood do not inherit the kingdom of God (1 Cor. 15:50)."

The unspoken implication, of course, as with all of Irenaeus's discussions of his opponents' exegesis, is that the Ophites have misunderstood the Pauline text of 1 Corinthians 15:50 and that the disciples imagined correctly. That is, for the bishop of Lyon, Jesus *was* raised in his worldly body. Irenaeus will make further comments upon his adversaries' exegesis of 1 Corinthians 15:50 in the final volume of *Adversus Haereses*, but it is important to see it linked so early in his polemical program to one of the gnostic sects.

According to Irenaeus (*Adv. Haer.* 5.9.1 [SC 153:106.3–5]), this passage is cited "by all the heretics in their folly and from it they strive to prove that there is no salvation for the creation of God (*plasmationem Dei*)." And furthermore, through their failure to grasp the apostle's meaning, they destroy "the entire economy of God (*universam dispositionem Dei*; *Adv. Haer.* 5.13.1 [SC 153:168.37–43])." That is, they "repudiate the salvation of the flesh, scorning its regeneration by insisting that it is incapable of receiving incorruption" (*Adv. Haer.* 5.2.2 [SC 153:30.18–21]). Their reading of 1 Corinthians 15:50, "Flesh and blood cannot inherit the kingdom of God," according to Irenaeus, suggests that Paul contradicts himself, for the apostle in many other passages declares without obscurity "the resurrection and incorruptibility of the flesh (*Adv. Haer.* 5.13.5 [SC 153:180.126–182.128])."[6] The interpretation of the heretics puts false interpretations upon several other texts because they pervert the meaning of the one (*Adv. Haer.* 5.13.5 [SC 153:182.128–29]).

According to Tertullian, 1 Corinthians 15:50 is the pre-eminent text within the systems of those who would deny the resurrection of the flesh. They fortify their line of battle with it in first place (*Resurr.* 48.1).[7] Tertullian, on the other hand, first builds an interpretive context from it and then treats it. And this is, as we shall see, in parallel with the approach of Irenaeus. 1 Corinthians 15:50, for the orthodox, must be read within an intricately composed network of other biblical texts. Such a network is needed because the heretics, it is thought, employ the one phrase in disconnection from the proper interpretive model.

Outside of Irenaeus's reference to the Ophite interpretation of 1 Corinthians 15:50, the *Gospel According to Philip* (second half of third century?) provides a glimpse of a Christian Gnostic, perhaps Valentinian, reading of the Pauline passage. *Gospel According to Philip* 56.26–57.19 (Schenke, *Say.* 23) is notoriously difficult to interpret.[8] Its apparent contradictions have frustrated more than one student, leading to conclusions of inconsistency and absence of a synthetical idea.[9] Some, however, have pushed through the conflict to resolution. In addition, some of the language seems to call into question Irenaeus's (and Tertullian's) blanket statements concerning gnostic interpretations of 1 Corinthians 15:50. Here is the text:

> Some are afraid lest they rise naked. Because of this they wish to rise in the flesh, and [they] do not know that it is those who wear the [flesh] who are naked. [It is] those who [. . .] to unclothe themselves who are not naked [2 Cor. 5:1–4]. "Flesh [and blood shall] not inherit the kingdom [of God]" (1 Cor. 15:50). What is this which will not inherit? This which is on us. But what is this, too, which will inherit? It is that which belongs to Jesus and his blood. Because of this he said, "He who shall not eat my flesh and

drink my blood has not life in him" (John 6:53). What is it? His
flesh is the word, and his blood is the holy spirit. He who has
received these has food and he has drink and clothing. I find fault
with the others who say that it will not rise. Then both of them are
at fault. You (sg.) say that the flesh will not rise. But tell me what
will rise, that we may honor you (sg). You (sg.) say the spirit in the
flesh, and it is also this light in the flesh. (But) this too is a matter
which is in the flesh, for whatever you (sg.) shall say, you (sg.) say
nothing outside the flesh. It is necessary to rise in this flesh, since
everything exists in it.[10]

Immediately the reader senses a contradiction: the flesh is not raised,
yet it is; the author faults the claim of the resurrection of the flesh and
then asserts its necessity. The teaching revolves around three New
Testament texts: 2 Corinthians 5:1–4; 1 Corinthians 15:50; John 6:53.
The problem seems framed by the two Pauline passages. What is it to be
naked? What is it to be clothed? What inherits the kingdom? The solution is offered in the Johannine passage. The one who has partaken of
Jesus inherits and is clothed.

M. L. Turner emphasizes the rhetorical force and the Valentinian
flavor of the passage's duality (1996, 230–34). She explains that the
opposites are positioned in such a way as to teach that they dissolve
into an unexpected middle. The author rejects three positions: (1) the
resurrection of the flesh; (2) the denial of the resurrection of the flesh,
and, (3) the resurrection of the spirit alone. Rather than affirming any
of these notions the passage argues that it is *Jesus' flesh* that will arise,
that is, Word and Holy Spirit. Anyone who has received, been clothed
in, these (by baptism and Eucharist) will arise. John 6:53 receives a
spiritualized, non-sacramental reading. Thus the author is not interested in the experience of the human body, but in Jesus' flesh. He or she
is interested in the mystical awareness which brings the salvation of the
spirit which has received Word and Holy Spirit. For the *Gospel According to Philip*, it is not the body that is raised, nor the spirit alone, but
the spirit with Jesus' flesh or the spirit with Word and Holy Spirit.

A. H. C. Van Eijk has a similar, but expanded reading (1971). The
author of the *Gospel According to Philip* denies the resurrection of the
flesh in the sense that flesh is not the body, but "the sphere marked by
human weakness and sin. *This* flesh has to be stripped off, *this* nakedness we have not to be afraid of (95)." But on the other hand, there will
be resurrection of the flesh, since the flesh of Jesus, the Word and Spirit,
will be raised. Van Eijk notes that in this text "it is only the flesh of
Christ that rises; in this flesh the individuality of the gnostic's flesh
seems to disappear completely; having Christ's flesh and blood as food,
drink, and clothing, it loses its own identity (98)." This resurrection is a
present experience in this world by means of the sacraments (100).

Through the Eucharist one "becomes the Logos, the Pneuma, the Perfect Man," that is, one who realizes his or her true identity and destiny in unity with the Pleroma (103–05).

For both Turner and van Eijk, then, the passage teaches Valentinian soteriology: the gnostic comes to self-realization. Van Eijk, however, sees a more sacramental realism than Turner does.

Williams, although maintaining the Valentinian model, brings some different perspectives to the passage's interpretation (1971, 16). For him, that which inherits the kingdom is the spirit of the gnostic which is born at baptism and chrism. It is born or raised, however, in the flesh of its worldly habitation. But this flesh is not that which is immortalized, although the gnostic wears it from baptism to death, when it is finally stripped off. Resurrection, then, happens presently through the sacraments, when the "living man" begins immortal existence. In this way the text teaches "that the flesh does have a definite part in the resurrection and also that it is not the flesh which provides the true clothing of the 'living man' (16)." Thus, the passage knows nothing of "the resurrection of a person whose physical body has died. Resurrection means the birth of the soul and spirit within a spiritually dead (100, 11) individual at initiation [through baptism and chrism] (16)."

My purpose in recounting these three prominent interpretations is not, finally, to provide warrant for one over the other. Rather, I mean only to show that contemporary scholars have given common readings to elements within this text, which has Valentinian associations. Each of our commentators, even with the passage's language of the necessity of rising in the flesh, ultimately concludes that the passage does not teach the resurrection of that flesh (body) which has died. *The Gospel According to Philip* does not provide an interpretation of 1 Corinthians 15:50 which should cause us to question Irenaeus's or Tertullian's characterization of gnostic readings of this Pauline text.

It has been necessary for us to endure this examination of 1 Corinthians 15:50 in the second (and third) century, because it is in answer to his opponent's exegesis of this passage that Irenaeus offers a key aspect of his exegesis of Romans 8. He eventually cites the Pauline text in *Adversus Haereses* 5.9.1, although he has been anticipating it since 5.1.3:

> Vain therefore are the disciples of Valentinus, who teach this doctrine [of docetic Christology] in order to exclude the flesh from life[11] and to dismiss the creation of God (*Adv. Haer.* 5.1.3 [SC 153:24.58–60]).
>
> It is also this which has been spoken elsewhere by the Apostle: "Flesh and blood cannot inherit the kingdom of God [1 Cor. 15:50]." This is the text which all the heretics cite in their folly and from it they strive to prove that there is no salvation for the creation of God (*Adv. Haer.* 5.9.1 [SC 153:106.1–5]).

In partial response to these concerns (exclusion of the flesh and creation from salvation) Irenaeus develops elements of Romans 8 in three locations. The first two are concerned with anthropological issues treated under the rubric of resurrection. The third concerns cosmological interests treated under the concept of renovation.

Resurrection: The Body Spiritually Changed

Irenaeus centers his citation of 1 Corinthians 15:50 between two major discussions involving Romans 8:5, 8, 9, 10–11, 13–15. The first discussion takes place in *Adv. Haer.* 5.7.1–8.2 (SC 153:84.82–98.51) while the second occurs in 5.10.2–11.1 (SC 153:126.35–136.38).

In the first discussion Irenaeus pivots his comments around Paul's phrase "He . . . shall also quicken your mortal bodies (*Vivificabit et mortalia corpora vestra*) in Romans 8:11. Irenaeus then complements that focus with insights gained from Romans 8:9 and 8:15:

> For you are not in the flesh, but in the Spirit if in fact the Spirit of
> God dwells in you
> [We have received the Spirit of God] by which we cry, Abba,
> Father

In the first discussion within *Adversus Haereses* 5.7.1–8.2 and from other scattered locations in which Irenaeus discusses these texts, he develops the notion of resurrection as transformation within time. There is continuity yet change of substance there is future consummation, but present inauguration of blessing.

Body: Continuity and Change

Informed by 1 Corinthians 15:53 ("It is necessary that this mortal nature [*mortalis*] put on immortality [*immortalitas*] and that this corruptible [*corruptibilis*] nature put on incorruptibility [*incorruptela*])"[12] since *Adversus Haereses* 5.2.3, Irenaeus emphasizes the need for the human creature to be transformed by the Creator. The creature is not immortal by nature, he insists, but must receive this excellence from the intervention of God.[13] Such a state of corruptibility and the dependence of the creature upon the Creator for incorruptibility breeds humility rather than pride. Through the process of transformation from mortal to immortal the redeemed human learns the utter distinction between the natures of the infirm creature and powerful Creator. God's act of vivifying the mortal and bringing incorruptibility to the corruptible manifests that he is powerful and that the human's proper response is to love the Creator. Irenaeus reasons that since God created the mortal it is thoroughly conceivable that God would transform it.

In support of this thesis he uses the language of Romans 8:11 in a unique manner. "Shall also quicken (*vivificabit*; ζωοποιήσει) your mortal bodies" becomes "the Creator does even here quicken our mortal bodies (*Demiurgo enim et hic vivificante mortalia corpora nostra*; *Adv. Haer.* 5.4.1 [SC 153: 56.11–12])."[14] Irenaeus views Paul's language as timeless. It applies to the original creation and the eschatological recreation. For the bishop of Lyon, God, of course, will give the body eschatological life, for he has given it temporal life; of course flesh can bear eschatological life, for God gave it temporal life. He provides warrant for the future force of "he shall also quicken" in Romans 8:11 (a force he has yet to discuss) by first developing the obvious empirical accuracy of its present force. This argumentation discloses an abiding bias in Irenaeus's exegesis and theological construction: the variance between the different economies of creation and salvation or old covenant and new covenant is one of degree *not* substance. These economies are different stages of the one united agenda of the one God. They are not opposite or contradictory but common in property.[15] Irenaeus can also read Romans 8:18 in this manner. Although the main force for him is futuristic, as will be seen below, there is also a present sense to it. Matched with Romans 8:28–30, the bishop understands that those who love God are already being prepared to advance into the future glory (*Adv. Haer.* 4.20.8 [SC 100.2:193–96]). The orthodox have this view of God's progressive, successive, gradual workmanship: "For there is only one salvation and only one God, but there are many precepts for forming humanity and the stages which lead to God and not few (*Adv. Haer.* 4.9.3 [SC 100.2:486.76–79])." What is true of the present, is true of the future, there is only difference in degree. For Irenaeus, then, if God is already *now* imparting life to bodies he will in *the future* impart life to them everlastingly. It is improper for the heretics to hold that mortal bodies cannot receive life. They already have life. Bodies receive life as the Creator determines. If he did not raise them he would be seen as impotent.[16]

It is significant that the language of Romans 8:11 is used in this discussion of the present, empirical basis for resurrection which culminates in an apology for God's power. Romans 8 has its own concerns for issues of God's power as it gives life to Christians through the Spirit. This is ultimately clear in Romans 8:31–39.[17] Also present in Romans 8 is the instruction that the present sets the pattern for the future (vv. 11, 13, 17, 23–25, 29–30). Irenaeus has extended the line of continuity further into the past. For Paul the present ministry of the Spirit in redemption determines the eschaton. For the bishop of Lyon the universal act of God in original creation and in providence begins the paragon culminated in resurrection.

When Irenaeus reaches *Adversus Haereses* 5.7.1, however, he concentrates on the future force of Romans 8:11 as written by Paul. In addition he highlights the phrase "mortal bodies" in an attempt to define specifically what it is that is raised. In the same way in which Christ was raised in "the substance of flesh," he argues, so shall the redeemed be raised by his power (1 Cor. 6:14). He unites 1 Corinthians 3:16, 17; 6:13, 14 and John 2:19–21 in order to prove that the redeemed have their bodies raised (they are the Spirit's and Christ's temples/members) just as Christ was raised in flesh (his wounds demonstrate this).

This parallel between the resurrection of Christ and that of the redeemed is present also in Romans 8:11 (*Adv. Haer.* 5.7.1 [SC 153:84.6–8]):

> If the Spirit of him who raised Jesus from the dead dwells in you,
> he who raised Christ from the dead will also give life to your
> mortal bodies (*mortalia corpora*).

Irenaeus begins his exposition of this passage with the question he intends to answer: "What, then, are mortal bodies (*mortalia corpora*)? (*Adv. Haer.* 5.7.1 [SC 153:84.9]). His response comes in stages throughout the rest of 5.7.1 and into 5.7.2 (SC 153:84.9–92.59). "Mortal bodies" (*mortalium corporum*) are not incorporeal souls, the breath of life (Gen. 2:7), immortal substance. Neither is the "mortal body (*mortale corpus*)" the spirit. Instead, the "mortal body (*corpus mortale*)" is the flesh, that which dies, decomposes, becomes breathless, and inanimate. "This, then [the flesh], is what is mortal (*mortalia*). And it is this of which he also says, "He shall also quicken (*vivificabit*) your mortal bodies (*mortalia corpora*)." In support he connects Romans 8:11 to 1 Corinthians 15:36 by means of the linking term "quicken (*vivificatur*)": "That which you sow cannot be quickened unless it first dies." Here are two important elements to his definition. The mortal is sown because it dies. The language of 1 Corinthians 15:42–44 also lends support by means of the term "sow." The body is sown in corruption, dishonour, weakness, and physicality. Mortal bodies, then, are bodies of flesh which succumb to death, but through the Spirit's power they are raised.

Irenaeus takes the reader from "mortal" to "flesh," with all its humble characteristics because the problematic term in 1 Corinthians 15:50 is *flesh*. This argument comes forth again in *Adversus Haereses* 5.13.3–5 where he challenges his opponents' understanding of the term. He rallies for his offensive the Pauline texts of Philippians 3:11, 20–21; 2 Corinthians 3:3, 4:10, 11, 5:4; 1 Corinthians 6:20, 15:13–21, 32, 50, 53–55. All together they teach the resurrection of that which is *mortal* (*mortalis*), the flesh which dies.[18] Two passages carry particularly pointed language:

> It is necessary that this corruptible nature put on incorruptibility
> and that this *mortal* nature put on immortality. When this *mortal*

nature puts on immortality, then this word of Scripture will be fulfilled: "*Death* has been swallowed up in victory. O *death*, where is your sting? O *death*, where is your victory?" (1 Cor. 15:53–55; *Adv. Haer.* 5.13.3 [SC 153:170.48–53]).[19]

... always carrying with us in our bodies the death of Jesus so that the life of Jesus Christ might also be manifested in our *bodies*: for if we, the living, are delivered to death because of Jesus, it is so that the life of Jesus might also be manifested in our *mortal flesh* (2 Cor. 4:10–11; *Adv. Haer.* 5.13.4 [SC 153:176.84–88]).[20]

The terms which call these texts into relationship with the teaching of Romans 8:11, of course, are "death," "mortal," "bodies," and very helpfully, the phrase "mortal flesh (*carne mortali*)." So, Irenaeus's first interest is to bring to relief Paul's concept of mortal. His second interest, however, has to do with Paul's concept of "quicken." The flesh is not only that which encounters death; it is also that which is raised. This interest runs quite deep, for it counters the belief of the Valentinians. They hold that:

God himself is a slave of this necessity so that he is unable to impart immortality to that which is mortal or to confer incorruptibility to that which is corruptible [Cf. 1 Cor. 15:53–54], but that each being returns to the substance corresponding to its nature (*Adv. Haer.* 2.14.4 [SC 294:136: 76–80]).

For the Valentinians, according to Irenaeus, God does not transform natures. Mortal remains mortal, it does not become spiritual. Dead flesh remains dead. Likewise, those who are by nature immortal or spiritual remain immortal and are saved.[21] The orthodox believe otherwise, and it is a fundamental issue of theological reflection for Irenaeus.[22] For the creature, immortality is a matter of modification not nature, for God "resuscitates (*resuscitans*) our mortal bodies (*mortalia corpora*)" because he is more powerful than nature (*Adv. Haer.* 2.29.2 [SC 294:296.39–298.42]). Already in *Adversus Haereses* 2 Irenaeus is anticipating his exegesis of Romans 8:11 in book 5.[23] For him, that Pauline text addresses the issues of God's freedom and power, the nature of the substance of creatures, and the destiny of that substance. Romans 8:11, in connection with a host of other texts which together form an interpretive network, sets forth the idea "that material continuity accounts for identity," that "what falls must rise," or that, in resurrection, it is 'flesh which undergoes fundamental organic change.'"[24] For Irenaeus, Romans 8:11 contributes to the orthodox confession that salvation is not by nature of original substance, but by transformation of that original substance through the power of God. According to the Rule of Faith in *Adversus Haereses* 1.10.1 (SC 264:158.23) "God bestows incorruptibility," it is not an endowment of nature.

Change: Future Yet Present

Having treated the issue of the transformation of the mortal flesh by
means of Romans 8:11, Irenaeus turns to the topic of the present
inaugural experience of that quickening or resuscitation of the mortal.
In the same way that he argued that general creation is in continuity
with resurrection, now he argues that already in the mortality of their
flesh, believers participate in immortality. The argument comes in
Adversus Haereses 5.8.1–2 (SC 153:92.1–98.51). Romans 8:9, 15
provide material conducive to a realized eschatology of incorruption.

At the end of *Adversus Haereses* 5.7.2 (SC 153:90.53–92.59) Irenaeus
cites 1 Corinthians 13:9, 12; 1 Peter 1:8 in order to introduce the idea
that, although fullness of joy in the vision of God comes only in the
future, there is "now" (*nunc*) a partial entrance into that delight. He
complements this introduction with a citation of Ephesians 1:13, which
teaches the good news of the present earnest or deposit (*pignus*) of the
Holy Spirit. This leads to a citation of Romans 8:9:

> "For you," he says, "are not in the flesh, but in the Spirit if it is
> true that the Spirit of God dwells in you."

Also, he presents a citation of a phrase from Romans 8:15, three times,
which speaks of a response true of those who have now, in the present
time, received the Spirit of God:

> "[by this Spirit of God] we cry, Abba, Father."

From these two passages of present force ("are not," "[are] in," "is
true," "we cry") he develops the thesis that the present earnest of
the Spirit "renders us already spiritual and the mortal [is already]
swallowed up by immortality (2 Cor. 5:4)." This present state, however,
does not take place outside the flesh, as if it were cast away, for those to
whom Paul wrote were still in their flesh. Rather, the present realization
of immortality means the reception of God's Spirit which enables us
now, in part, prior to the eschatological vision of glory, to cry to him in
joyful triumph. Earlier in *Adversus Haereses* 4.9.2 (SC 100.2:484.62),
he also refers to the Spirit's present cry of "Abba Father" (perhaps this
time from Gal. 4:6).[25] Again he connects it to the eschatological joy and
vision of 1 Peter 1:8 and 1 Corinthians 13:12, but qualifies that focus
with the good news of the believer's current cry of joy and progress
towards the final consummation.

Nevertheless, for Irenaeus, the cry of those indwelt by the Spirit (or
the Spirit's cry from within those indwelt by him) is a meager one compared to the eschatological exclamation. He reads the present utterance
of "Abba, Father," almost as if it were a whisper awaiting the clamor
associated with the full vision of the Father. This is why he connects it
to 1 Peter 1:8. There Peter speaks of an eschatological "joy unspeak-

able (*inenarrabilis*)" and in his own mind this conjures up visions of the redeemed who will "burst forth into a hymn of exultation" (*Adv. Haer.* 5.8.1 [SC 153:94.18–20]). The believer's "Abba, Father" is only a slight foretaste consistent with the earnest of the Spirit. The lesson is this: although the redeemed are presently spiritual in their flesh, do not mistake the present blessing of the Spirit's earnest for the eschatological transformation of the flesh. The future resurrection is in no way marginalized by the presence of the eschaton.

Apparently, the current state of being God's children by possession of his Spirit (Rom. 8:15–17) is, for Irenaeus, a state entered into now only *in part* (cf. 1 Cor. 13:12). Believer's, as God's children, are in their current position connected more closely with their inheritance of Christ's suffering (Rom. 8:17), rather than his glory (Rom. 8:17). He reads Romans 8:15 and its "Abba, Father" in light of Romans 8:18 and Romans 8:22–23:

> I consider that the sufferings of this present time are not worth comparing with the glory that is to be revealed to us.
> We know that the whole creation has been groaning in travail together until now; and not only the creation, but we ourselves, who have the first fruits of the Spirit, groan inwardly as we wait for adoption as sons, the redemption of our bodies.

The believer's "Abba, Father" is as a prayerful groan of the one who in the midst of suffering awaits incomparable adoption and bodily redemption. Exultation in the present is tempered by the fullness of the future.

In continuity with this bodily hope, then, we find him explaining the "adoption" of Romans 8:15–17, 23 in terms of 1 Corinthians 15:53–54; 2 Corinthians 5:4. To be adopted as God's children is to be transformed progressively from a corruptible and mortal state to our incorruptible and immortal one by means of the Son of God's own complete union with flesh, a union that after Romans 8:3 was "in the likeness of sinful flesh."[26] He who is immortal by nature imparts immortality to humanity through his union with humanity. Only those adopted in body on the foundation of the incarnation (on the basis of the Son's healing of humanity by imparting to it the divine attribute of incorruptibility) and through reception of the grace of the Holy Spirit (Rom. 8:15) can therefore be recognized as deified.[27] He understands this adoption, informed as he is by Romans 8:29, to be the fashioning of the whole human after the image of the Son of God (*Adv. Haer.* 4:37.7 (SC 100.2:942.175); 5.6.1 [SC 153:72.2]).

Spiritually Natural: Flesh and Spirit

In his second major discussion of the material in Romans 8, Irenaeus shifts to the issue of distinguishing the substance of flesh from the works of the flesh, in order to define what is spiritual and natural. In *Adversus Haereses* 5.10.2–11.1 (SC 153:126.35–136.38) his texts are Romans 8:4, 8–11, 13–14. Again, we will see how important canonical networks of texts are to his exegesis. In this context, Romans 11:17, 24 provide the paradigm for his reading of the language of Romans 8. Paul's metaphor of the olive tree becomes a picture of Irenaeus's anthropology.[28] By virtue of the Spirit, fleshly humans are grafted into spiritual humanity, that which was created after the image and likeness of God. Rather than teaching the loss and gain of Israel and the Gentiles in redemptive history, the metaphor describes how unrighteous humans attain to a nature which may inherit God's kingdom: "Admirably, then, does the apostle demonstrate our nature (*naturam ostendit*) and the whole economy of God when he speaks of flesh and blood as well as the wild olive (*Adv. Haer.* 5.10.1 [SC 153:124.17–19]).

Irenaeus's reading of Romans 8 in relation to Romans 11:17, 24 must be understood against the background of the Valentinian exegesis of the olive tree metaphor. For Irenaeus Romans 8 enables an orthodox interpretation of Paul's metaphor, which negates that of his opponents. Early in *Adversus Haereses* 1.8.3 (SC 264:122.81–124.95), he notes that Romans 11:16 is used by the Valentinians to distinguish the spiritual class of people (who are spiritual by nature [*naturaliter spiritales*])[29] from those of the church, the ensouled or "psychic" ones. The members of the church are capable of a meager salvation in the intermediate place only by virtue of being gathered in through the nature of the spiritual ones. The "psychic" class is made "holy" through the Valentinian spiritual class.

Clement of Alexandria's *Excerpta ex Theodoto* 56.3–57 provides further insight into Valentinian exegesis of Romans 11.[30] There are three races: the spiritual one is saved by nature (πνευματιὸν φύσει σω=ζόμενον); the psychic (ensouled) one has freewill; and the material one is corrupt and perishable by nature. Being grafted into the spiritual olive tree saves the psychic. From Paul's teaching, the Valentinians gather that "Israel" refers to the spiritual ones who will see God and are associated with the free-woman rather than the slave-woman of Egypt (Gal. 4:23). On the other hand the psychic are the Gentiles, those who "according to the flesh" are children of the slave-woman. For the spiritual, there is a "formation" of the element natural to them which gives them a salvation superior to that of the psychic. For the psychic, there is a "freedom" of a measure of salvation in the Ogdoad, but not a "formation" which leads to the Pleroma. The "fatness of the olive tree" is incorruptibility, which the spiritual have by nature, but into which the psychic may be grafted by choice of faith. This is not incorruptibility of flesh or body, however, but of the psychic element, which the spiritual shed for their final abode in the End. Even here with Theodotus, we find that salvation is by nature of spirit or incorruption of soul, not by transformation of the substance of flesh into spiritual flesh.

Against this interpretation Irenaeus places his own, informed by Paul's words in Romans 8 (*Adv. Haer.* 5.10:1–2 [SC 153:122.1–132.71]). Humans by their own fault become unfruitful in righteousness because of their lusts of the flesh. This unfruitfulness is like unto the deadness of the untended wild olive. They are in the flesh, producing works of the flesh. Such persons must receive the Holy Spirit by faith and be grafted into the good olive tree, that is, into the "pristine nature of humanity (*pristinam hominis naturam*) that which was created in the image and likeness of God (*Adv. Haer.* 5.10.1 [SC 153:126.32–34])." Such engrafting certainly does not alter the former substance of that which is engrafted. The wild olive does not lose "the substance of its wood (*substantiam ligni*)." The human remains flesh; he or she does not lose the substance of flesh (*substantiam carnis*). The engrafting changes the quality of the fruit and gives the previously called wild olive a new name: good or fruit-bearing olive. In the same way, the unfruitful, "fleshly," unrighteous human of mere flesh and blood produces the fruit of righteousness and is given a new name: spiritual human. Thus, to be flesh and blood, after the manner of 1 Corinthians 15:50, is to be without the Spirit, without faith, without righteousness, and with the lusts, works of the flesh. Such persons are disconnected from the incorruptible, pristine human nature created by God.

Here is how Irenaeus uses the language of Romans 8 to his benefit. Romans 8:8, "Those who are in the flesh cannot please God," speaks not in repudiation of the substance of flesh, but in repudiation of the flesh's lusts, a Spirit-less flesh. Humans are corrupt not because of the flesh, but because of the works of the flesh. Ignatius has something similar: "But even those things which you do in the flesh are spiritual (*Eph.* 8.2 [Lindemann, 184.6]).[31] The verse which then follows in Irenaeus, Romans 8:9, solidifies this interpretation. It addresses those mortal and corruptible ones who through the Spirit have put on immortality and incorruptibility (1 Cor. 15:53): "But you are not in the flesh, but in the Spirit, if it is true that the Spirit of God dwells in you." Those who by faith have received the Spirit have been engrafted into the humanity of the Spirit and are no longer ultimately associated with the humanity of flesh, mortality, and corruption. Righteousness and life, not sin, death, and the works of the flesh, marks the new association.

He continues his argument by citing Romans 8:10–11, 13. His point? The body of flesh dies because of sin, the works and life of the flesh. But, the Spirit who indwells and works righteousness (the same Spirit of the God who raised Jesus) gives life and will raise the mortal body of flesh which dies. It is not life in bodily, mortal flesh which is the enemy of the Spirit, but life lived in the lusts or works of the flesh. If God quickens the mortal body, flesh in Romans 8 and 1 Corinthians 15 cannot mean body.

Romans 8:13–14, then, gains this interpretation: if you put to death the works of the flesh (unrighteousness, the Spiritless humanity outside of the image and likeness of God) by receiving the Spirit, you will *live incorruptibly, immortally, in your body of flesh*. This is the case, because those who are led by the Spirit, that is, those who engrafted into the incorruptible humanity, bring forth the fruit of the Spirit, are God's children in the flesh. This connection between righteousness and the resurrection in Romans 8:11 (cf. 2 Cor. 4:14) is strongly anticipated in terms of Jesus' teaching by Polycarp (*Phil.* 2.2).[32] For Irenaeus, the particulars of the lusts of the flesh which prevent access to the kingdom and the fruits of the Spirit which are consistent with life in the Spirit, are declared in Galatians 5:19–23 (*Adv. Haer.* 5.11.1–2 [SC 153:132:1–140.59]). The *Epistle to Diognetus* seems to have captured Irenaeus's idea in its own pithy statement of the meaning of Romans 8:12–13. Speaking of Christians it says: "They are "in the flesh" but they do not live "after the flesh" (5.8).[33]

Against the Valentinians, the bishop of Lyon develops the thesis that the spiritual is not natural, but it is flesh. On the other hand, the flesh is natural and not spiritual. Yet, the natural is the original creation of God, the image and likeness of God which is spiritual. To this the redeemed are returned, but it is theirs by engrafting, not by nature. Romans 8, with its language of body, flesh, life, and Spirit, allows the bishop to substantiate his interpretation of Romans 11 and to navigate skillfully two meanings of flesh and nature, while producing one meaning of spiritual. Romans 8 in his second discussion is all about the semantics of flesh and spirit. In his first discussion of the chapter, he was concerned with the semantics of "body." For Irenaeus, Paul's thought is thick with information on the nature of humanity, redeemed and unredeemed.

Renovation: The Creation Renewed

But our bishop does not find Paul speaking merely of anthropology in Romans 8. For Irenaeus, the apostle's thought encompasses the nature of the whole creation. Not only does he envision from Romans 8 the restoration of human nature to its pristine condition, but also the restoration of "creation (*conditio*) itself" to its "pristine (*pristinus*) state" (*Adv. Haer.* 5.32.1 [SC 153:398.17]). In *Adversus Haereses* 5.32.1 (SC 153:396.1–398.24) he has been arguing the renovation of this creation (*conditio*) as the proper eschatological environment of the righteous. The creation (*conditio*) in which they endured suffering (Rom. 8:17, 18), the creation (*conditio*) in which they were martyred, and the creation (*conditio*) in which they were in bondage (*servitus*; Rom. 8:21) should be the location of their blessed destiny. This eschatological, earthly kingdom will be the inauguration of incorruption (*incorruptela*) as the righteous begin to comprehend God. He supports his eschatological vision from Romans 8:19–21:

> The creation (*creatura*) waits with firm expectation for the revelation of the children of God. For the creation (*creatura*) has been subjected to vanity, not of its own will, but because of the one who has subjected it in hope: because the creature (*creatura*) itself will be delivered from the bondage (*servitus*) of corruption (*corruptela*) into the liberty (*libertas*) of the glory of the children of God.

Conditio and *creatura* are used in parallel throughout *Adversus Haereses* 5 to represent κτίσις in Irenaeus's Greek. In regard to the issues of Romans 8, he develops four points.[34] First, the creation (*conditio*), formed by God, is for the benefit of humanity, for it was made for humanity, not humanity for it (*Adv. Haer.* 5.29.1 [SC 153:362.7–9]). Second, the eschatological blessing of God includes the renovation and restoration of this creation (*creatura*; *conditio*) as well as its liberation (*libero*; Rom. 8:21) with God's children and its subjection to them (*Adv. Haer.* 5.33.3–4 [SC 153:414.63–65; 420.172–14]). Third, this renovation of the creation (*creatura*) to be enjoyed by God's children will involve great fruitfulness and result in great feasting (*Adv. Haer.* 5.34.2–3 [SC 153:424.28–30; 432:86–88]). Finally, such a restoration of the creation (*conditio*) is in keeping with the faithfulness of its Creator (*Adv. Haer.* 5.36.1 [SC 153:452.3–6]).

All of these points contribute to the main orthodox thesis that "neither the substance nor the matter of the creation (*conditio*) will be annihilated," but instead there will be "the new heaven and new earth in which the new humanity shall remain always conversing with God in a new manner (*Adv. Haer.* 5.36.1 [SC 153:452.4–6; 454.14–16])." In the final chapter and paragraph of his five-book work, he alludes to Romans 8:19–21 in summary of his thesis:

> It is this that the apostle Paul confesses when he says that the creation (*creatura*) will be liberated from the bondage of corruption in order to have part in the glorious liberty of the children of God (*Adv. Haer.* 5.36.3 [SC 153:464.56–58]).

A host of other biblical passages are gathered into an intertextual network in which Romans 8:19–21 finds its meaning. Texts which speak eschatologically or in promise concerning the earth, land, fruitful harvests and lavish banquets are particularly important (e.g., Gen. 13:14–17; 15:19–21; 23:3–20; 27:27–29; Ps. 103:30; Isa. 6:12; 11:6–9; 26:19; 30:25–26; 31:9–32; 54:11–14; 58:14; 65:17–25; 66:22;

Jer. 16:14–15; 23:7–8; 31 [38]:10–14; Baruch 4:36–5.9; Ezek. 28:25–26; 37:12–14; Matt. 5:5; 12:5; 26:27–29; Luke 14:12–13; 1 Cor. 7:31; Rev. 20:11–14; 21:1–6). But also in these texts and in Romans 8, one finds emphasized the exalted state of the human who is served and bountifully nourished by the creation. Redeemed humanity will have dominion over the new earth and it is the liberty of humanity in which the earth will share.[35] In other words, the renewal of humanity ushers in the renewal of the rest of creation. This second century notion of humanity's return to its natural state and dominion as the foundation for creation's renewal is made explicit in the *Epistle of Barnabas* and Theophilus of Antioch.[36] The latter also seems to be informed by Romans 8:19–21.[37]

Conclusion

Anthropology (Rom. 8:5–17) provides the foundation for understanding cosmology (Rom. 8:18–25). Irenaeus reads Romans 8 as telling us something about our own nature: it reveals to us at least in part what we are. It speaks to us anthropologically, informing us about what it is to be human. Flesh is an essential component of humanity whether in original creation or in resurrection, whether in realized or consummative eschatology, whether in corruption or incorruption, whether with or without the Spirit of God. Romans 8 also speaks cosmologically. The creation is essentially and substantially worthy of renovation. Its bondage is linked to the bondage of its master, the human. So, too, its restoration is linked to the liberty of humanity. The creation has entered corruption only through humanity. It will receive its incorruption only in the glory of the human.

Against his opponents, the bishop of Lyon delves beneath the soteriology, pneumatology, and eschatology of Romans 8. These issues are not ignored, of course; but it is the anthropology and cosmology underlying Paul's discussion that consumes his interest. He draws Paul's implicit principles forth and makes them explicit, in concert with a network of biblical passages drawn widely from the canon. The immediate literary context is *a* context for understanding the thought of the apostle, but by no means is it the only or even necessarily the primary context. The mind of the apostle is in continuity with the mind of the Spirit displayed harmoniously throughout the biblical canon. Within his polemical environment, Irenaeus could take nothing for granted. The web of anthropology and cosmology needed to be elucidated. Romans 8 provided the material around which to center and unify that explanation.

Yet Romans 8, and the networks associated with its interpretation, contribute to a larger network aimed at providing an orthodox reading of 1 Corinthians 15:50. The heretics' interest in this text determined

Irenaeus's fixation. So he employs Romans 8 with its networks as a component in that battle, and thereby demonstrates a polemical technique common to orthodox and heretic alike. 1 Corinthians 15:50, for Irenaeus and Tertullian, could only be properly read within a carefully constructed canonical network. As we saw in the *Gospel of Philip,* the same was true of their opponents. Neither was ignoring the problematic text. The issue was the interpretive network. Within the second century exegesis and theology are issues of canonical connection. And as Irenaeus has shown through Romans 8, exegesis and theology are informed by assumptions implicit in certain key texts. So, Irenaeus, for instance, sees implicit in Romans 8 anthropological and cosmological truths. Without those truths firmly in hand, one cannot understand Romans 8, or ultimately 1 Corinthians 15:50. Moreover one cannot construct the network.

---

[1] See the survey in E. Dassmann, 1979, 305-07.

[2] Noormann, 1994, *Irenaeus als Paulus Interpret*; Balás, 1992, "The Use and Interpretation of Paul in Irenaeus's Five Books *Adversus Haereses*"; Norris, 1990, "Irenaeus' Use of Paul in His Polemic Against the Gnostics."

[3] E. Peretto, 1971. *La lettera ai Romani cc. 1-8 nell' Adversus Haereses d' Ireneo.*

[4] The critical editions used for Irenaeus, *Adv. Haer.*, are: *Irénée de Lyon: Contre les hérésies, Livres l, 2, 3, 4, 5,* ed. A. Rousseau, L. Doutrelau, et al., Sources chr,tiennes (SC), nos. 263, 264, 293, 294, 210, 211, 100.1, 2, 152, 153 (Paris: Cerf, 1979, 1982, 1974, 1965, 1969). They are referenced as SC no.

[5] See SC 152:201. The language emphasizes God's action in forming, fashioning by his own hands the human body. Such personal attention (based upon Gen. 2:7) confers majesterial dignity upon God's humble creature, creation, our human flesh, our gender that which is corporeal and passible, that which can enter into sacred marital, sexual union, that which Christ took upon himself, and that which is saved. Cf. Adv. Haer. 1.22.2 (SC 264:310.26); 1.28.1 (SC 264:354.10); 3.16.6 (SC211:312.214); 3.17.1 (SC 211:330.21); 4. Pref. 4 (SC 100.2:390.71); 4.40.3 (SC 100.2:980.45); 5.1.1 (SC 153:20.32); 5.1.2 (SC 153:24.60); 5.12.3 (SC 153:150.55-56).

[6] For the charges of contradiction see *Adv. Haer* 5.13.3 [SC 153.170.44-47]; 5.13.5 [SC 153:180.116-121].

[7] Tertullian, 1954, 987.1-5.

[8] *Gospel According to Philip,* 1989, 152; *Das Evangelium nach Philippus,* 1960, 42.

[9] Schenke, 123-24; Wilson, 1962, 87.

[10] *Gospel According to Philip,* 1989.

[11] After the Armenian and the Greek we read "life" rather than "salvation." Cf. SC 152:202.

[12] Cited in *Adv. Haer.* 5.10.2 (SC 153:130.54-56).

[13] Cf. Peretto, 1971, 209.

[14] See the phrase again in *Adv. Haer.* 5.3.3 (SC 153:52.80-81).

[15] Cf. *Adv. Haer.* 4.9.2 (SC 100.2:480.29-486.70).

[16] *Adv. Haer.* 5.4.2 (SC 153:58.28-60.39).

130   *D. Jeffrey Bingham*

[17] Cf. for the theme of power by means of God's Spirit in Rom. 8: Käsemann, 1980, 212-52.

[18] Note the repetitive occurrence of *mortalis: Adv. Haer.* 5.2.3 (SC 153:38.60); 5.3.1, 2, 3 (SC 153:42.16; 44.33; 52.81); 5.4.1 (SC 153:56.12); 5.7.1 (SC 153:84.8, 11; 86.14, 17, 18; 88.31, 32); 5.8.1 (SC 153:94.10); 5.10.2 (SC 153:130.55, 63); 5.13.3 (SC 153:170.49, 50, 53; 172.67, 70; 174.75, 76); 5.13.4, 5 (SC 153:176.88; 180.124, 125); 5.14.4 (SC 153:192.84).

[19] CF. *Adv. Haer.* 5.13.5 (SC 153:180.123-25).

[20] Cf. *Adv. Haer.* 5.13.5 (SC 153:180.125-26).

[21] Cf. *Adv. Haer.* 1.6.2 (SC 264:92.24-94.42).

[22] Cf. *Adv. Haer.* 1.10.3 (SC 264:164.74-76); van Unnik, 1977.

[23] Cf. SC 293:326-27.

[24] Bynum, 1995, 34, 38.

[25] This time the Spirit cries. Cf. SC 100.2:484, n.k.

[26] *Adv. Haer.* 3.19.1 (SC 211:374.20-28); 4.11.1 (SC 100.2:498.11-20); 3.20.2 (SC 211:107.10); 4.2.7 (SC 100.2:412.111).

[27] *Adv. Haer.* 3.6.1 (SC 211:66.24-36; 4. Pref. 4 (SC 100.2:390.68-75). Cf. Fantino, 1994, 214. Salvation, for Irenaeus, is ministered within a Trinitarian schema.

[28] Cf. Noormann, 1994, 303.

[29] *Adv. Haer.* 1.6.2 (SC 264:94.31).

[30] *Clement of Alexandria*, 1970, 172-73; cf. 174, 175, nn. 1-5; *Exc. ex Theod.* 63-65; *Clement of Alexandria*, 1934, 22-25; Orbe, 1985, 465-66; Sagnard, 1947, 530-37.

[31] Cf. Peretto, 1971, 211.

[32] *Die Apostolischen Vater: Griechisch-deutsche Parallelausgabe*, 1992, 246.5-14.

[33] *A Diognete*, 1997, 62.

[34] Cf. *Adv. Haer.* 5.36.3 (SC 153:452.4) where we have Irenaeus's Greek (κτίσεως) fr. gr. 29.1); Reynders, 1954, 2:61, 73.

[35] Cf. Noormann, 1994, 368.

[36] *Ep. Barn.* 6.18-19; *Ad Auto.* 2.17.

[37] *Biblia Patristica*, 1986, 437.

References

Die Apostolischen Väter: Griechische - deutsche Parallelausgabe. 1992. Ed. and trans. A. Lindemann and H. Paulsen. Tübingen: J. C. B. Mohr (Paul Siebeck).

Balás, D. L. 1992. "The Use and Interpretation of Paul in Irenaeus's Five Books *Adversus Haereses.*" *Second Century* 9:27-39.

Biblia Patristica: Index des Citations et Allusions Bibliques dans la Litterature Patristique, vol. 1, *Des origines à Clement d'Alexandrie et Tertullien.* 1986. Ed. Centre de'Analyse et de Documentation Patristiques. Paris: ECNRS.

Bynum, C. Walker, 1995. *The Resurrection of the Body in Western Christianity, 200-1336.* New York: Columbia University.

Clement of Alexandria. 1934. *The Excerpta ex Theodoto of Clement of Alexandria.* Ed. and trans. R. P. C. Casey. London: Christophers.

Clement of Alexander. 1970. *Clement d'Alexandrie Extraits de Théodote*. Ed. and trans. F. Sagnard. Sources chrétiennes. no. 23. Paris: Cerf.

Dassmann, E. 1979. *Der Stachel im Fleisch: Paulus in der früh christlichen Literatur bis Irenäus*. Munster: Aschendorff.

A Diognète. 1997. Ed. and trans. H. I. Marrou. Sources chrétiennes, no. 33. Paris: Cerf.

Eijk, A. H. C. van. 1971. "The Gospel of Philip and Clement of Alexandria." *Vigiliae Christianae* 25: 94-120.

Das Evangelium nach Philippus. 1960. Ed. H.-M. Schenke. Pp. 31-65, 81-82 in *Koptische - gnostische Schriften aus den Papyrus - Codices von Nag Hamadi*. Ed. J. Leipoldt and H.-M. Schenke. Hamburg: Herbert Reich.

Fantino, J. 1994. *La théologie d'Irénée*. Paris: Cerf.

Gospel According to Philip. 1989. Ed. B. Layton and trans. W. W. Isenberg. Pp. 129-215 in *Nag Hammadi Codices* 2.2-7, vol. 1. *Nag Hammadi Studies* no. 20. Ed. B. Layton. Leiden: E. J. Brill.

Irenaeus of Lyon. 1979, 1982, 1974, 1965, 1969. *Irénée de Lyon: Contre les heresies, Livres 1, 2, 3, 4, 5*. Ed. A. Rousseau, L. Doutrelau, et al. Sources chr,tiennes, nos. 263, 264, 293, 294, 210, 211, 100.1, 2, 152, 153. Paris: Cerf. Referenced as SC no.

Käsemann, E. 1980. *Commentary on Romans*. Grand Rapids: Eerdmans.

Nag Hammadi Texts and the Bible: A Synopsis and Index. 1993. Ed. C. A. Evans, R. L. Webb, and R. A. Wiebe. Leiden: E. J. Brill.

Noormann, R. 1994. *Irenäus als Paulusinterpret*. WUNT 2.66. Tübingen: J. C. B. Mohr (Paul Siebeck).

Norris, R. A. 1990. "Irenaeus' Use of Paul in His Polemic against the Gnostics." Pp. 79-98 in *Paul and the Legacies of Paul*. Ed. W. S. Babcock. Dallas: SMU.

Orbe, A. 1985. *Teología de San Ireneo*, vol. 1. Madrid: La Editorial Catolica.

Peretto, E. 1971. *La Lettera ai Romani cc. 1-8 nell' Adversus Haereses d'Ireneo*. Bari: Istitutio di Letteratura Cristiano Antica.

Reynders, B. 1954. *Lexique comparé, du texte grec et des versions latine, arménienne et syriaque de l'Adversus haereses' de saint Irénée*, 2 vols. Louvain: Imprimerie Orientaliste L. Durberq.

Sagnard, F. 1947. *La Gnose valentinienne et le témoignage de saint Irénée*. Paris: Librairie philosophique J. Vrin.

Schenke, H.-M. 1968. "Auferstehungsglaube und Gnosis." *Zeitschrift für die Neutestamentliche Wissenschaft* 59: 123-26.

Tertullian. 1954. *De Resurrectione Mortuorum*. Ed. J. G. Ph. Borleffs. Pp. 919-1012 in *Tertulliani Opera*, Part 2, *Opera Montanistica*. Corpus Christianorum Series Latina, no. 2.2. Turnholt: Brepols.

Turner, M. L. 1996. *The Gospel According to Philip*. Leiden: E. J. Brill.

Williams, M. A. 1971. "Realized Eschatology in the Gospel of Philip." *Restoration Quarterly* 14: 1-17.

Wilson, R. McL. 1962. *The Gospel of Philip*. New York: Harper and Row.

Unnik, W. C. van. 1977. "An Interesting Document of Second Century Theological Discussion (Irenaeus, *Adv. Haer.* 1.10.3)." *Vigiliae Christianae* 31:196-228.

A Response to
Jeffrey Bingham
and Susan Graham:
Networks and Noah's Sons

Jouette M. Bassler

———— ◆ ————

My assignment is to respond to Prof. Jeffrey Bingham's and Prof. Susan Graham's respective analyses of Irenaeus's interpretations of Romans 8 and 9-11 and in doing so to contribute to the dialogue of scriptural criticism, itself a multi-layered discipline. With so many layers of authors, texts, and disciplines the task is daunting, but I have been greatly informed by the earlier work of this seminar[1] and so I welcome the offer – and the challenge – of joining the conversation. I come to this conversation as someone immersed most recently not in Romans but in the Pastoral Letters. Yet that is not bad preparation for reading Irenaeus, who quotes 1 Tim 1:4 in the first sentence of his *Adversus Haereses*. The techniques of the two ancient writers are different – the Pastor puts words in Paul's mouth while Irenaeus (at least in *A.H.*) puts an interpretative network around Paul's words – but their mindsets are similar. And they share the same goals: to reclaim the apostle for one side of a controversy when his words often give apparent support to the other (as in *A.H.*) or to rethink the apostle's ideas within a different context (as in the *Epideixis*). The similarities between the Pastor and the Bishop triggered a measure of hermeneutical wariness, for I have learned from the former that in a polemical situation reconstructing the background of an argument requires taking the author's explanation with a grain of salt.

I also come to this conversation having taught a seminar on Romans recently, one that I have come fondly to refer to as The Course From Hell. Last spring, for the first time in many semesters, I found it difficult to get students engaged with the text, excited about it, urgent to claim – or challenge – its relevance for their lives. The fault, I fear, was at least partly my own, and so I come eager to learn, for my students' sake, how to engage more effectively in scriptural criticism. And finally, I come to the writing of this response shortly after September 11 (and with a daughter who works in lower Manhattan). The events of that day – visual and visceral in their impact – and the ongoing repercussions of those events are now inescapable aspects of my encounter with this or any other text. The significance of identifying these elements of my own context should become clear in the response that follows. I begin with Prof. Bingham's paper.

Irenaeus's Reading of Romans 8

I would summarize Prof. Bingham's analysis of Irenaeus's reading of Romans 8 in the following way, using the three poles of scriptural criticism. A single pragmatic consideration dominates Irenaeus's reading of the text – the real and present threat of Gnosticism. He reads Romans 8, and all other scriptural texts, from a fixed and inviolate theological perspective – the rule of faith. And his exegetical method is a sophisticated version of proof-texting[2] – he constructs a "canonical network" within which problematic texts were properly (that is, orthodoxly) to be read. What follows is not presented as a critique of this analysis. In fact, it seems to me to be sound, interesting, and informative. Rather, I offer some observations generated by the particulars of my own circumstances.

Beneath and Beyond the Polemic:
Contextual Considerations

Irenaeus clearly states that his reason for composing *A.H.* was to expose and refute the teachings of various Gnostic groups, especially the Valentinians. Though written over the course of several years, under occasionally difficult circumstances,[3] the work adheres to a careful plan. After describing the beliefs of various Gnostic groups (Book I) and refuting the principle theses of the Valentinians regarding the nature of God and creation (Book II), he then sets forth the unified teaching of the church on these issues (Book III) and confirms this teaching with the words of Christ found in the Gospels (Book IV). In the first part of Book V he sets out to correct Gnostic interpretation of Paul and to show that Paul's message is in complete accord with the message of truth. At the center of Irenaeus's concern here is Gnostic appropriation of 1 Cor 15:50 to support their rejection of the material world and denial of a resurrection of the flesh. The verse seems to offer them excellent support: "Flesh and blood cannot inherit the kingdom of God, nor does the perishable inherit the imperishable." But Irenaeus sets out to reclaim the verse, and the apostle, for the orthodox doctrine of redemption of the flesh.[4]

In the context of this exegetical controversy Irenaeus develops a network of texts to support his counter interpretation of 1 Cor 15:50. Bingham lends concreteness to the controversy by providing ancient

examples (and modern interpretations) of Gnostic exegesis of this verse;
then he focuses on two portions of Irenaeus's argument where
Romans 8 figures strongly in his counter-exegesis, *A.H.* 5.7.1–8.2 and
5.10.2–11.1.[5] Overall Bingham describes Irenaeus's response as an
intellectual *tour de force*. He shows how Irenaeus went ideologically
and exegetically head to head with his opponents and countered their
doctrines and interpretations with arguments grounded in tradition,
scripture, and reason.

What struck me was the absence of experience from this calculus.
This is particularly striking, because the experience of the Bishop's own
flock – the intense persecution and martyrdom of Christians in Lyons
only a few short years before the composition of this work – seems very
germane to the topic of resurrection of the flesh. The Letter of the
Martyrs of Gaul, written soon after the tragic events, even notes that
the persecutors burned the bodies of the martyrs and threw them into
the Rhone River so "that they might not even have hope of resurrection" (*E.H.* 5.1.60-61). Clearly the persecutors' understanding of Christian belief was that resurrection was not conceivable without the
participation of the fleshly body. It has been noted that the Letter of
the Martyrs "does not show any theological concern about the loss
of the martyr's remains" and seems to assume that they obtained life at
the very moment of their death.[6] Resurrection of the flesh – or not;
instantaneous life after death – or later resurrection with the body. These
issues that surface in the Letter of the Martyrs are the very issues that
Irenaeus addresses in Book V![7] Is it possible that Irenaeus's view of the
resurrection and his reflections on the scriptural texts relevant to that
doctrine were forged exclusively in anti-gnostic dispute, with no pastoral roots in the experience of the members of his own church?[8]

Irenaeus does not often refer to the martyrs, but he does occasionally,
and I found one of these references in the section of *A.H.* framed by the
two passages that Bingham treats:[9]

> On the other hand, as many as fear God and trust in His Son's
> advent, and who through faith do establish the Spirit of God in
> their hearts, – such men as these shall be properly called both
> "pure," and "spiritual," and "those living to God," because they
> possess the Spirit of the Father, who purifies man, and raises him
> up to the life of God. For as the Lord has testified that "the flesh is
> weak," so [does He also say] that "the spirit is willing." . . . If,
> therefore, any one admix the ready inclination of the Spirit to be,
> as it were, a stimulus to the infirmity of the flesh, it inevitably
> follows that what is strong will prevail over the weak, so that
> the weaknesses of the flesh will be absorbed by the strength of the
> Spirit; . . . Thus it is, therefore, that the martyrs bear their witness,
> and despise death, not after the infirmity of the flesh, but because
> of the readiness of the Spirit. For when the infirmity of the flesh is

> absorbed, it exhibits the Spirit as powerful; and again, when the
> Spirit absorbs the weakness [of the flesh], it possesses the flesh as
> an inheritance in itself, and from both of these is formed a living
> man,– living indeed, therefore, when destitute of the Spirit of God,
> is dead, not having life, and cannot posses the kingdom of God . . .
> but where the Spirit of the Father is, there is a living man; [there is]
> the rational blood preserved by God for the avenging [of those
> that shed it]; [there is] the flesh possessed by the Spirit, forgetful
> indeed of what belongs to it, and adopting the quality of the Spirit,
> being made conformable to the Word of God. (*A.H.* 5.9.2-3)

There are, to be sure, no direct quotations of Romans 8 in this passage,
so it is understandable that Bingham did not treat it; but it is filled with
reflections on the overcoming of the flesh by the Spirit, a concern that
dominates that chapter of Paul's letter. If Irenaeus thought of the martyrs when writing these words in chapter 9, did he also have them in
mind when he wrote in chapter 7 that those who do not now see the face
of God shall see it and shall rejoice with unspeakable joy?[10] And since
he regards the martyrs as examples of the Spirit overcoming the flesh,
did he also have them in mind when he wrote on the same topic in
chapter 8, where Romans 8 is explicitly cited? Thus I wonder: How
would it change the perception and analysis of Irenaeus's reading of
Romans, if it were framed, not simply in the words of the Gnostic
exegetes as Bingham has done, but also in the words of and about the
Christians of Lyons who died for their faith in firm expectation of resurrection from the dead? It might highlight a different set of verses in
Romans and track a different line through Irenaeus's argument.

It might also raise another set of questions that are important to ask,
even if they prove to be ultimately unanswerable. Did the martyrs share
Irenaeus's concern about the resurrection of the flesh? The Letter
suggests that they did not. It was their sense of the abiding presence of
the Lord that sustained them in their trials, not church doctrine on the
resurrection of the flesh.[11] Had they perhaps come to disdain the flesh in
ways that approached Gnostic perceptions?[12] Were there competing
bases for the authoritative revelation?[13] The martyrs and those influenced by them clearly located authoritative revelation in their experience. Irenaeus locates it in scripture (interpreted by the rule of faith).
Was a struggle within the orthodox church occurring in the shadow of
the Gnostic controversy? The voices of the martyrs are important in this
dialogue, for they show how Irenaeus's interpretation of Romans 8
touched (or could have touched) and informed (or was informed by) real
lives and deaths. To ignore this possibility deprives Irenaeus's text of
religious relevance and restricts its significance to doctrinal debate.

These suggestions and comments are, I realize, highly speculative,
and I admit that they have been informed by the catastrophic destruc-

tion of the World Trade Center, by the obscene sight of burning flesh and falling bodies, and by the indomitable spirits of the rescuers. Out of this came a need to acknowledge the martyrs' voices, to inject somehow their mutilated flesh and bodies and indomitable spirits, their heteronomous experience into Irenaeus's coolly analytical arguments.[14]

Contemporary exegetes face similar questions about the relevant context (or contexts) for interpreting Romans. Is it Paul's theological conflict – real or anticipated – with the Jerusalem church that guides his choice of topics and arguments, or is it his awareness of (and sympathy for) the experience of the weak in the church in Rome (whoever they are)? Has his anticipated mission trip to Spain led him to recapitulate the theological core of his universal gospel, or did his experience in Corinth and Galatia leave a residue of polemical or pastoral urgency on his words to Rome?[15] The text of Romans chapter 8 also invites attention to the spiritual experiences of the readers (vv. 9-11, 14-16, 23, 26), but who were those readers? Were they Jewish Christians or Gentile Christians, or both? And if both, did they experience the Spirit in the same way? Exegetes struggle to identify the experiences that served as the context for the writing and the reading of the letter. Some reconstructions highlight the ideological dimension of the letter; others the pastoral or religious dimensions. Only sometimes do we seem aware that our own experiences incline us toward certain understandings of Paul's.[16] And then we work out our interpretations in the *agon* of scholarship, where again ideas prevail, rarely concerned with the experiences of the text that our students and readers have had. The tripolar paradigm presses us to give more serious attention to experience, at all levels of our interpretation.

Locating the Audience:
Some Hermeneutical Presuppositions.

Though Prof. Bingham defines the polemical context of *A.H.* in significant detail, he does not describe the intended (authorial) audience of the work. I understand the difficulties involved. Nowhere does Irenaeus identify the "dear friend" who asked him to write the work (5. praef.). He anticipates that this friend will present and interpret the work to others (1.praef.3), and he envisions a different group of "others" reading and pondering his work themselves (5.praef.). Who these others were and where they might have lived is the source of some speculation, but no certainty,[17] and Bingham does not offer any concrete suggestions. So while the work has a known author and a fixed point of origin, the authorial audience remains shadowy, both in the text of *A.H.* and in Bingham's analysis of it, enhancing the timeless quality that Irenaeus assumes for Paul's words. This enhanced timelessness come home to roost in the conclusion of Bingham's paper when "we" are identified with the intended audience: "Irenaeus reads Romans 8 as telling us something about our own nature. It reveals to us at least in part what we are. It speaks to us anthropologically, informing us about what is to be human." After these comments the confessional "we" disappears again beneath Bingham's historical analysis. But what does its brief appearance imply? Let me offer an observation and invite Prof. Bingham's response.

Bingham reads Irenaeus's reading of Paul with obvious appreciation, setting himself at the outset within a "trend in positive appraisals of Irenaeus's use of Paul." Thus his conclusion is framed very positively: "He [Irenaeus] draws Paul's implicit principles forth and makes them explicit." The web that Bingham has detected and defined does not distort; it clarifies and focuses. Because Irenaeus is so attuned (in Bingham's view) to the apostle's thought, the Bishop assumes, for a moment at least, Paul's mantle of canonical authority. His words transcend his historical context and situational polemic and speak directly to "us," and by implication to all humanity. Thus Bingham reinforces the authority of Irenaeus's interpretation, an authority which Irenaeus himself, with due rhetorical modesty, implicitly claims.[18] Bingham's appreciative reading has gone far in elucidating the power and purpose of Irenaeus's canonical network. A resistant reading could complement his work by identifying with equal clarity its problems.

The Irenaeus in Each of Us: Observations About Method.

Bingham notes that, in the end, there is no substantive difference in method or technique between Irenaeus and his Gnostic opponents: "For Irenaeus and Tertullian, [1 Cor 15:50] could only be properly read within a carefully constructed canonical network . . . . [T]he same was true of their opponents." We can go one step farther and note that the charges Irenaeus brings against his opponents' use of scripture are in many ways valid criticism of his own work:

- They gather their views from sources other than the scripture (1.8.1) – so does Irenaeus, whose starting point of interpretation was the unwritten rule of faith.
- They disregard the order and connection of the scriptures and transfer passages and rearrange them (1.8.1) – so does Irenaeus, who recontextualizes the texts as a canonical web.
- They gather together sayings and names from scattered places and transfer them from a natural meaning to an unnatural (1.9.4) – so does Irenaeus.
- "Obviously," says Grant in response to Irenaeus's charges, "what appealed to Gnostic converts was the theological synthesis of diverse scriptural passages, along with a secret pattern [Gnostic cosmology

or anthropology] to hold them together"[19] – the same is true of Irenaeus. Except, of course, his pattern was not secret; it was the rule of faith.

By its very nature, the web of scriptural texts that Irenaeus created had the potential of generating dialogue among the many perspectives represented by these varied texts and enhanced by their various intertextual associations. But Irenaeus invokes the rule of faith to level out the differences, to remove ambiguities, and thus to control the dialogue. The rule determines which Pauline texts are given voice (Rom 8:3 is notably absent!) and then tunes the selected texts to a single orthodox key. Though Irenaeus speaks repeatedly of the authority of scripture (e.g., *A.H.* 2.28.2; 3.21.4),[20] this is always subordinated to the higher authority of the rule of faith, exercised through the teaching magisterium of the church.[21]

Thus for Irenaeus it is not a matter of good versus bad exegetical practices, but the validity of the pattern that controls the exegesis, whether Gnostic cosmology or the orthodox rule of faith, whether (in Irenaeus's polemical terms) myth or truth. At an even deeper level, I think, what is also important is the issue of the one versus the many. Irenaeus develops this contrast in many ways – the oneness of God (versus Gnostic separation of the Gods of the OT and NT or the plurality of the Aeons), the oneness of Christ (versus the Gnostic separation of Jesus and the Christ), the unity of the body (versus Gnostic separation of spirit and flesh). He also contrasts the unity of the message produced by orthodox exegesis (no great surprise, since the exegesis is controlled by the rule of faith!) and the diversity of interpretations (the "contradictions," as he calls them; 5.praef.) offered by Gnostic exegetes. Indeed, he says, by their diversity of interpretations they convict themselves of falsehood (4.35.4; see also 5.20.1-2), for truth is singular by definition. This then reveals the power and purpose of Irenaeus's web – it eliminates the possibility of different interpretations, for if that were permitted the orthodox position would be no more secure than the Gnostics'. Irenaeus sees clearly that a multiplicity of interpretations undermines the very concept of orthodoxy, which rests on the claim of the singularity of truth.

It is exceedingly ironic, then, that this seminar, with its presupposition of the legitimacy and plausibility of divergent interpretations,[22] should focus attention on Irenaeus. To be sure, he represents one interpretation of Romans, but it is an interpretation that would, on principle, exclude all others, for to admit to an alternative reading would be to step on the slippery slope that leads to contradictions and falsehood. What can biblical scholars committed to "the legitimacy and plausibility of divergent interpretations" learn from such an intractable dialogue partner as Irenaeus?

As it turns out, Irenaeus holds up a mirror to us that reveals our own practices of web creation and web-maintenance and warns us against absolutist claims for our interpretations. A few familiar examples must suffice to illustrate how commentators have created interpretive webs to bring a level of coherence to Paul's notoriously ambiguous anthropological terminology. It is not a point that needs to be belabored.

In his commentary on Romans, Ernst Käsemann worked essentially within the web of existentialist assumptions developed by his teacher and mentor Rudolf Bultmann. To this he added a greater emphasis on the eschatological and cosmological dimensions of Paul's thought and a concern over Christian enthusiasm, which, he said, not only disturbed Paul's churches but those of his day as well.[23] He defines "flesh" in Bultmannian terms as the sphere of subjection to the world, which, even in its piety, is unholy (188-91). Because of his anti-enthusiast concerns, however, the concept of spirit seems to interest him more. Indeed, he reads chapter 8 as Paul's manifesto against enthusiasm (212f.), and that provides him with its interpretive key. Thus he identifies Paul's frequent references to the indwelling spirit as the language of enthusiasm, but language transformed by the apostle into an ethical category meaning "standing under the present Lord" (223). The groanings of the church (v.23) he heard as a reference to the ecstatic cries of the enthusiasts, redefined by Paul into a sign of weakness (240f.). "The apostle's intention is clear," says Käsemann, "even if his mode of expression is difficult to understand" (224). Such is the power of Käsemann's interpretive web. Yet if Käsemann claims to penetrate the apostle's intent, he acknowledges the provisional nature of his insight and welcomes critical testing and open discussion of his conclusions (viii).

James D. G. Dunn reads the letter through a different but equally distinctive grid, that of the new perspective on Paul that he has helped to articulate and popularize.[24] According to this perspective, Paul rejected justification by works of law not because it was a legalistic system of earning merit, but because it expressed a sense of national privilege restricting God's grace to ethnic Israel. This perspective provides Dunn with the hermeneutical key to crucial passages like 2:12-29; 3:27-31; 7:14-25; 9:30-10:4; and 12:1-15:6. It does not dominate his interpretation of chapter 8 to quite the same degree, but the presence of this grid is evident when Dunn clarifies the meaning of flesh. "Flesh," he claims, is basically an apocalyptic category denoting "an unavoidable attachment and tie to this age" (1.391). As such it has both individual and corporate dimensions, encompassing both the weakness and corruptibility of the creature and also – and most distinctively for Dunn – the central failing of Paul's own people, who "regard the national badge of circumcision 'in the flesh' as that which marks them off from Gentiles as God's chosen people" (1.363). This perspective colors his exegesis in subtle ways throughout the chapter. No less than Käsemann, Dunn reads this chapter polemically; he just defines the opposing position differently and thus locates the polemical thrust in different verses. It is mildly ironic that Dunn introduces his new perspective by decrying the way "that Protestant exegesis has for too long allowed a typically Lutheran emphasis on justification by faith to impose a hermeneutical grid on the text of Romans" (1.lxv). His new perspective replaces that grid with another, "which binds the whole letter into a cohesive whole" (1.lxxii), but this one, Dunn maintains, derives from the apostle's own context.[25]

Stanley Stowers also wants to establish an interpretive grid from Paul's own context, but for him the ruling schema is Gentile struggle for self-mastery over passions. In light of this schema, Stowers interprets "flesh" exclusively as a moral category (and emphatically not as a theological or apocalyptic one) – the place where passions and desires reside. Romans 8 then relates the reversal of the divine curse on gentiles (Stowers refuses to universalize the message to refer to humankind) that made the flesh weak and particularly vulnerable to sin.[26] Empowered by the spirit, gentiles can resist the flesh and gain the self-mastery and divine approval that they seek. Few interpreters are as sensitive as Stowers to the power of an interpretive grid to control the readings of a text (1-16). He respects the inevitability, and the validity, of multiple readings (esp. pp. 4, 16), yet he urges the advantages of his own unipolar reading. It provides, he says, as others do not, a coherent understanding of Paul's discourse.

Daniel Boyarin reads Romans 8 from the perspective of yet another master narrative – Gal 3:28-29, which he takes to announce the erasure of human difference and hierarchy.[27] This perspective determines the meaning of "flesh," which Boyarin views as the site of difference, whether it is understood as the penis, which defines sexual difference, or physical kinship, which creates ethnic difference. He reads Romans 7-8 as the description of bondage to and release from sexuality, with 8:13 providing the climax:

> So then, brethren, we are debtors, not to the flesh (that is, not to the obligation to procreate), to live according to the flesh – for if you live according to the flesh you will die, but if by the Spirit you put to death the deeds of the body (sex and procreation) you will live – bearing spiritual fruit for God.

Boyarin makes no absolutist claims for his interpretation. It derives, he recognizes, from his choice of Gal 3:28 as his starting point; other starting points and other interpretations have equal validity (5).

All these different and plausible valuations of Paul's anthropological language in Romans 8 derive from the application of different master narratives or interpretive grids to the text. Where Irenaeus used the rule of faith, others use different construals of the story behind the letter or of the central concepts of Paul's theology to shape and level Paul's thought and thus to achieve coherence and consistency in his message. To assert this, however, is to assert the obvious. Some construal is necessary to interpret the text of this complex, convoluted letter. Yet the path of Pauline interpretation is littered with the textual debris of this drive toward theological consistency. Thus the mirror Irenaeus holds up reveals an Irenaeus in each of us. We grant interpretive authority to a master narrative or grid; on the basis of this we prioritize certain verses in our interpretation; we strive toward an ideal of consistency. The crucial point is the degree of openness to alternative readings. Irenaeus rejects them, but the text itself pushes us toward openness. There is a resilient level of indeterminacy to Paul's language, especially his anthropological language.[28] It resists definitive packaging. And so with each interpretation there are verses that refuse to fit smoothly, arguments that refuse to convince utterly. The context of our interpretation shifts and the door opens to yet another reading of this text, another master narrative, another attempt to engage in dialogue with this most protean of theologians.

Irenaeus as Reader of Romans 9-11

Professor Graham shows us in the *Epideixis* another side of Irenaeus's reception of Paul – quite different from the explicit appropriation of the apostle's words in *A.H.* to create an interpretive network around a problematic verse. She maintains that Irenaeus had Romans 9-11 "in mind" when he wrote this survey of salvation history. More specifically: though Irenaeus did not use the imagery of Romans and though he did not cite Paul's words, nevertheless, she maintains, when he wrote about the events of Genesis 6-10 he incorporated a great deal of the apostle's theology of election and salvation history into his depiction of Noah and his three sons. To prove such a subtle thesis requires a subtle methodology, and Professor Graham has given us one. She notes shared theological features, similar patterns of Old Testament quotations, and what appear to be reminiscences of (or allusions to) specific portions of Romans 9-11. There is no smoking gun, but the circumstantial evidence that she presents is impressive, and my initial skepticism gave way to admiring assent.

That said, the thesis poses an interesting challenge to the practitioner (or evaluator) of scriptural criticism. In this tractate Irenaeus does not explicitly cite, analyze, or even acknowledge the text of Romans, nor does he reflect on his operative hermeneutical assumptions. And if it is clear that Irenaeus had Romans 9-11 "in mind," it is equally clear that he had other texts "in mind" as well. Thus, for example, a passage that Graham describes as a combination of reminiscences of Romans 9:12-18 and 9:4 with a précis of Romans 10:14-18 (*Epid.* 41, cited on p. 14) is laced with allusions to Acts, John, and 1 Corinthians as well. And a text that she presents as a paraphrase of Romans 9:22 (*Epid.* 8, cited on p. 18) could, I think, be described with equal justification as a paraphrase of Acts 17.[29] It is not just Romans 9-11 that is consciously or unconsciously influencing the bishop's thought but a broad amalgam of texts which tempers the impact of the individual components. It would be informative, I think, to complement Graham's analysis of the similarities between Romans 9-11 and the *Epideixis* with a brief consideration of distinctive features of Romans 9-11, that have been suppressed in the interplay of the various texts in Irenaeus's mind. Then we can reconsider the question, addressed in Graham's concluding observations, about the likely reasons for this particular reception of Romans 9-11. And finally, a few words about some hermeneutical implications of this reception of Romans. First, though, which of the distinctive features of Romans 9-11 are lost in Irenaeus's reading of Genesis 6-10?

Like Yet Unlike: Interpretation by Omission

Graham mentions a number of shared theological features, identifying as most significant the gratuitous (merciful) election of Israel and the consistency of God. Mercy defines God's actions in both Romans 9-11 and the *Epideixis*, but absent from Irenaeus's discussion is the radical edge of Paul's understanding of election. Instead of the willful, almost capricious, deity depicted in Rom 9:15 ("I will have mercy on whom I have mercy"), instead of the apostle's emphatic insistence that God "has mercy on whomever he chooses and hardens the heart of whomever he chooses" (9:18), the picture that emerges in Irenaeus's tractate is of a God whose merciful actions are an appropriate response to diligent human endeavor. This is particularly clear in the way that key figures in the narrative are depicted.

Irenaeus remains true to the text of Genesis when he asserts that Noah was chosen because of his righteousness (justice). His description of Shem and Japheth's behavior, however, expands the terse text of Genesis to include the explanation that theirs was an act of filial "dutifulness" or "piety," thereby justifying the blessings they received. The offensiveness of Ham's behavior – not altogether clear from the Hebrew text, which states simply that he "told" his brothers of his father's nakedness outside the tent where Noah lay – is given even more thorough elaboration. It is represented as an act of mockery and impiety, justly evoking the curse he received.[30] Even more dramatic are the alterations to the story of Abraham. There is in Irenaeus's retelling no unprovoked divine call to an unremarkable Chaldean. Instead Irenaeus gives us an Abraham who was actively "seeking the God who was his rightful due by the blessing of his progenitor," "going about all the earth" in his quest for God and growing faint with effort. God's call comes in response to this diligence, evidence of divine "pity"[31] says Irenaeus, not gratuitous election.[32] Like Paul, Irenaeus regards God's actions as rooted in a form of mercy, but the Bishop does not push the concept in the direction of Paul's thoughts in Romans 9-11. It is, as Graham notes, "a vision of a benevolent God ... who rewards those who are faithful." Irenaeus eliminates the arbitrary side of mercy suggested by Romans 9,[33] but – see below – he also eliminates the radically inclusive side of mercy that is proclaimed in Romans 11 ("God has imprisoned all in disobedience so that he may be merciful to all").

Similarly, Paul's concern for divine faithfulness – given poignant expression in Paul's explicit (11:1) and implicit (9:6) questions, "Has God rejected his people?" and "Has the Word of God failed?"– is significantly diluted when it emerges in the guise of Irenaeus's concern for the coherence of all salvation history. Gone entirely is the concept of the remnant (used by Paul to document God's fidelity to Israel). Gone also is the mystery surrounding the salvation of "all Israel," replaced by Irenaeus's certitude concerning the necessity of faith in Christ (*Epid.* 51) and, in *A.H.*, by the chilling view that Israel has already borne its fruit in producing the Christ and is of no further value (or interest) in salvation history.

Of course, much of this can be explained by changed circumstances. As Graham notes, "Irenaeus is not pastorally concerned with the relationship between Jews and Gentiles." There were no Jews in Lyons, no Jewish Christians in the Bishop's churches. But does that account for all the shifts of emphasis? Why would Irenaeus be concerned to dilute so drastically the concept of election? Why would he focus on God's reward for faithful behavior rather than on God's unmerited grace? Why this particular modulation of Romans 9-11?

Graham observes at the beginning of her paper that the *Epideixis* is less burdened with polemical interests than Irenaeus's principle work, *Adversus Haereses*. Yet "less burdened" does not mean unburdened, and there are enough explicit references to heretics to suggest that Irenaeus had them at least occasionally in mind when he composed his later work.[34] If this is so, it offers a ready explanation for some of the shifts of emphasis we have seen, for they occur at points where Paul's distinctive emphasis was overly congenial to Gnostic appropriation.

Paul's radical doctrine of election was a particular favorite of the Gnostics, since it expressed a primary feature of their beliefs; and Romans 9:10-18 was a *locus classicus* of the church's exegetical controversy with them. The concept of the remnant readily lent itself to the

Gnostic distinctions among various classes of persons, and the apostle's emphasis on grace apart from works nicely supported their deterministic claims about salvation.[35] Read against the ever present backdrop of the Gnostic controversy, however muted it might be in the *Epideixis*, Irenaeus's subtle and not-so-subtle modulations of the message of Romans 9-11 make good sense. The Bishop has eliminated not only those aspects of Paul's message "that are not germane to his pastoral concerns" – those concerning the relationship of Jews and Gentiles – but also, it seems, those aspects that are counter-productive with regard to his polemical concerns. With Romans 9-11 only in mind and not here in debate, there was no reason for Irenaeus to reproduce the more problematic aspects of Paul's argument. He did not need to wrestle with difficult verses or formulate any exegetical principles more complicated than simply keeping in mind the more agreeable portions of Paul's argument. This made it easier for Irenaeus's intended audience to follow the path of truth, but how are we to respond to his reading of Romans?

A Residue of Ambiguity: Hermeneutical Reflections

Irenaeus is driven by the conviction that the truth is unambiguous and singular, "a single upward path, lit by heavenly light" (*Epid.* 1). Under the influence of Romans 9-11, he refocuses the story of the patriarchal blessing to make it relevant to his gentile audience, immune to Gnostic misreadings, and unambiguous in its unfolding. Instead of tracking the blessing through the Isaac-Ishmael or the Jacob-Esau splits, which demonstrates that "not all of Abraham's children are his true descendants," but require torturous exegesis to be made relevant to gentile concerns, Irenaeus highlights the earlier blessing to Noah's sons and see in *its* unfolding the sequence and goal of salvation history – destruction of the ungodly (Ham), temporary flourishing of Israel (Shem), and final fulfillment in the mission to the Gentiles (Japheth). Irenaeus turns the ambiguities of the Genesis text against Shem and his descendants: they do not receive a direct blessing[36] (Why not?) and their "tents" (that is, their heritage) are ultimately inhabited by (Or shared with?) others. Irenaeus sees this worked out when Israel is made the "tail" to the gentiles' "head" (*Epid.* 95). With his Noachic typology Irenaeus is able to maintain Israel as an entity distinct from the gentiles, thus avoiding Paul's cooptation of the title "Israel" for all people of faith. Israel's salvation, however, is made entirely and explicitly dependent on their coming to faith in Christ (*Epid.* 56). Thus the ambiguities of Romans 9-11 have been resolved as well – and again not in Israel's favor. However, though Irenaeus's intent is clear – to produce an unambiguous story and a singular path to salvation – he does not succeed in eliminating all the tensions that can allow creative space to develop alternative theological potentialities.[37] I mention only two examples.

The description of the unbelieving people who are to become the tail when the descendants of Japheth become the head is, as Graham notes, ambiguous (*Epid.* 95). They are described in terms reminiscent of *both* Ham and Shem. But those to whom the inheritance is now given – the offspring of Japheth – are also described in terms reminiscent of Ham. Ham's descendants, says Irenaeus, are the "ungodly" (*Epid.* 20), and he defines the ungodly at the opening of the tractate as "the peoples that know not God. . . who do not worship Him who IS" (*Epid.* 2). But this is also how he defines those who are to become the head: "God was pleased to grant His inheritance to . . . those who were not God's citizens, and *know not who God is*" (*Epid.* 95). The categories are not simply porous; they are muddled and overlapping and the tail, it seems, has become the head again.[38]

Irenaeus seems, however, entirely unambiguous about the means of Israel's salvation: before Christ, "whoever feared God and died in justice and had the Spirit of God within them" had hope of attaining salvation in the judgment of the risen Christ. For those who come after the manifestation of Christ and "have not believed in Him, there is in the judgment inexorable vengeance" (*Epid.* 56). One must believe in the Son or face inexorable vengeance, but does that comport with the nature of the Father whose Son his is?[39] Early in the *Epideixis* Irenaeus gives what appears to be a definitive statement of the nature of God (*Epid.* 8) that undermines the harsh eschatological vengeance that he later depicts. What is stressed in the earlier passage is God's universal rule and overwhelming compassion:

> And the Father is called by the Spirit *Most High,* and *Almighty,* and *Lord of Hosts,* that we may learn that God is indeed such, that is, creator of heaven and earth and the whole world, and maker of angels and men, and Lord of all, who upholds all things, and by whom everything is sustained; merciful, compassionate and most tender, good, just, God of all, both of Jews and of Gentiles and of the faithful.

To be sure, the various groups experience God differently:

> But to the faithful He is as a Father, for in the end of times He has opened the testament of adoption of sons. But to the Jews He was as Lord and Lawgiver, for when in the mean time mankind had forgotten and fallen away and rebelled against God, He brought them into subjection through the Law, that they might learn that they had a Lord who was author and maker, who grants the breath of life, and to Him we must return homage by day and by night. But to the Gentiles He is as Maker and Creator and Almighty. But for all alike he is sustainer and nourisher and king and judge.

Even for the Jews and Gentiles the experience of God has a positive goal. And for all alike God is sustainer and nourisher as well as, and before, God is king and judge. To be sure, Irenaeus concludes by saying that "none shall escape immune from His judgment, neither Jew nor Gentile nor sinner among the faithful, nor angel"; but he defines that judgment in the words of "the blessed apostle" as rendering to each according to their works, not according to their Christian faith. Every subsequent claim that Irenaeus makes needs to be tested again this depiction of the unchanging, merciful, compassionate, most tender – and just – God. If the categories of persons are not simply porous but overlapping and transparent to each other, the fixity of Irenaeus's scheme of salvation history becomes dislodged. And if the God of All is first and foremost the compassionate sustainer and nourisher of all, Irenaeus's certainty about the fate of those who have not believed becomes suspect.

Epilogue

At the opening of this essay I referred to changing contexts that evoke new interpretations. Those words formed the platitudinous ending of a draft of this response written before September 11. Now they have real import. We must acknowledge that the context of our lives and therefore of our interpretations has changed far more dramatically and far more suddenly than anyone could have anticipated. The first round of essays to emerge from the work of this seminar focused – appropriately – on reading Romans 9-11 in a post-Holocaust context. The terrorist attacks on September 11 do not diminish the importance if that task, but they add another task, or another dimension to that task.

Daniel Patte has noted that meditating "before the Holocaust," that is, meditating on the practice of biblical criticism in the shadow of the Holocaust, reveals our status as outsiders. In so doing it transforms our awareness of others – whether they be the Other of Israel, for whose suffering in the Holocaust our discipline shares accountability; or the Other of the Reader-believer, whose views and religious experiences we have dismissed as childish and naïve; or even the Other of the Other Scholar, whose interpretations we seek to discount and supplant. These are all, in one way or another, proximate Others, Others whom we share a canon, a faith, or an academic context. Now I think we are called to consider a more distant Other, a different level of Otherness. I am not alluding here to the perpetrators of the attacks on September 11, but to the Muslim world and Islamic faith, whose sense of alienation from our world and faith and whose perception of our attitude toward them to be one of disregard and disrespect seem to have created the climate in which these extremist acts were possible. These are

Others who are essentially nameless and faceless in Romans 8, at worst
a part of "them"– those who do not have the spirit of Christ and who
therefore do not belong to God (Rom 8:9); at best a part of "creation,"
which eagerly awaits the revealing of the children of God (8:19) – as
outsiders. Irenaeus exacerbates the problem when he creates a web of
texts that allows him to gloss Paul's claim that creation will share in the
glorious liberty of the children of God (8:21) with the contradictory
assertion that it will do so *in subjection to* these children (*A.H.*
5.33.3-4). The Bishop takes creation to refer exclusively to the material
world, but even if he recognized the possibility that it included the non-
Christian human world as well,[40] I do not think he would have altered
his conclusion.

In Romans 9-11 Paul wraps Israel's place in salvation history in a
mystery that permits interpretive choices.[41] This mystery spills over
onto the non-Christian, non-Jewish world with the climactic affirmation, "God has imprisoned all in disobedience *that he may have mercy
on all.* O the depth of the riches and wisdom and knowledge of God!
How unsearchable are his judgments and how inscrutable his way"
(Rom 11:31-32). Irenaeus's typology eliminates the mystery in favor of
judgment. Ham's offspring, which included "the Arabs . . . all the
Egyptians and the Lydians" (*Epid.* 20; the last group may refer to
Libyans[42]), stand under a curse unless they turn in faith to Christ. This
does not foster respectful interfaith dialogue! Rather it contributes to the
ignorance and fear that leads to the hatred and violence that has been
revealed to us on September 11 and in the days and weeks following.
Patte has said – correctly! – that we cannot proceed with biblical
interpretation solely from a stance of scientific detachment,[43] not in a
post-Holocaust world and not in a post-September 11 world. We need to
facilitate the creation of bridges of understanding to this more distant
Other. Irenaeus does not show us the way here, except by a *via
negativa.* But even his carefully constructed version of salvation history
shows a crackle of ambiguity that allows space to explore alternative
theological possibilities.

---

[1] Especially as published in *Reading Israel In Romans: Legitimacy and Plausibility
of Divergent Interpretations* (ed, C. Grenholm and D. Patte; Harrisburg: Trinity
Press International, 2000).

[2] In using this term I do not meant to denigrate Irenaeus's method or insights. As
Bingham notes, for Irenaeus "the immeidate literary context [of a text] is a
contect for understanding the thought of the apostle," and the Bishop is snesitive
to many aspects of Paul's thought. Yet indisuptably his primary concern is to
prove the orthodox interpretation of some peoblematic verses by linking together
citations of biblical texts.

[3] In addition to the obvious pressure of the gnostic threat that motivzates the work,
some historians believe that at least Book II was written during atime of persecution
(see Dominic J. Unger, *St. Irenaeus of Lyons: Against the Heresies* [ACW 55; New
York: Paulist, 1992] 4).

⁴ Echoes of this exegetical controversy can still be heard in contemporary scholarship. Some maintain that Paul's comment is not a rejection of the reserrection of the dead at all, but a reference to those who are alive – real "flesh-and-blood" people as opposed to corpses (see e.g., Joachim Jeremias, "Flesh and Blood Cannot Inherit the Kingdom of God (I Cor. xv.50)," *NTS* 2 [1955/56] 151-59; Gordon D. Fee, *The First Epistle to the Corinthians* [Grand Rapids: Eerdmans, 1987] 799). Others insist that the words accurately reflect Paul's conviction (shared by many in his world) that a resurrection of a flesh-and-blood body is not possible; what is reurrected is "a 'pneumatic body' – that is, a body composed only of pneuma with sarx and psyche having been sloughed off along the way" (Dale B. Martin, *The Corinthian Body* [New Haven: Yale University Press, 1995] 104-36, esp. p. 126). For a survey of the shift from the biblical concept of resurrection of the dead (e.g., Mt 22:31, Lk 22:35; Rom 1:4; 1 Cor 15:12-57) to the creedal affirmation of the resurrection of the flesh, see H. B. Swete, "The Resurrection of the Flesh," *JTS* 18 (1917) 135-41.

⁵ Bingham gives less attention to a third section (at the end of book V) where Irenaeus again invokes Romans 8; my response, like his paper, focuses primarily on the earlier passages.

⁶ Denis Farkasfalvy, "Christological Content and Its Biblical Basis in the Letter of the Martyrs of Gaul," *Second Century* 9 (1992) 5-25 esp. p. 13.

⁷ Though not highlighted in Bingham's paper, one aspect of Irenaeus's polemic with the gnostics was whether souls separated immediately from the body at death to ascend into heaven, or awaited "in the invisible place allotted to them; later resurrection with their bodies (*Adv. Haer.* 5.32.2).

⁸ Compare, e.g., the assessment of H. B. Swete, who, like Bingham, links the church's insistence on the resurrection of the flesh to the second century anti-gnostic polemic ("Resurrection of the Flesh," 137) with that of Caroline Walker Bynum, who claims that in the treatises on the resurrection from the late second century (including Irenaeus's work) "the palpable, vulnerable, corruptible body Christ redeems and raises was quintessentially the mutilated cadaver of the martyr: (*The Resurrection of the Body in Western Christianity, 200-1336* [New York: Columbia University Press, 1995] 43, see also pp. 38-39).

⁹ Bingham notes that Irenaeus alludes to the martyrs in section devoted to the renewal of creation. My question is whether their experience affected his earlier reflection on the resurrection of the flesh.

¹⁰ *Adv. Haer.* 5.7.2. the text cited is 1 Pet 1:8, but the expectation of *future* rejoicing is new, perhaps an echo of Rom 8:18, a verse that was important to the martyrs (see Farkasfalvy, "Martyrs of Gaul," 10).

¹¹ Martin draws a similar conclusion: "my guess is that [ordinary Christians] seldom thought about the resurrection systematically" (*Corinthian Body*, 124).

¹² We do not have evidence from the Gallic martyrs, but a few years later in the city of Carthage, the young martyr Perpetua recorded among her own visions that of Saturus, one of her fellow prisoners (or a later compiler included Saturus's vision with hers). His vision included the observation, "We had died and had put off the flesh," and Perpetua's comment (she was present in the vision) was, "I am happier here now than I was in the flesh" (cited in Joyce E. Salisbury, *Perpetua's Passion: The Death and Memory of a Young Roman Woman* [New York: Routledge, 1997] 112-113).

¹³ See, e.g. Maureen A. Tilley, "Scripture as an Element of Social Control: Two Martyr Stories of Christian North Africa," *HTR* 83/4 (1990) 223-97; Fannie J. LeMoine, "Apocalyptic Experience and the Conversion of Women in Early Christianity," *Fearful Hope: Approaching the New Millennium* (ed. C. Kleinhenz and F. J. LeMoine; Madison, WI: University of Wisconsin Press, 1999) 201-6).

¹⁴ I am indebted here also to the reflection of Cristina Grenholm and Daniel Patte ("Receptions, Critical Interpretations, and Scriptural Criticism" and "A Post-Holocaust Biblical Critic Responds," pp. 1-54 and 225-45 in *Reading Israel*).

[15] For a survey of the various proposals, see A. J. M. Wedderburn, *The Reasons for Romans* (Edinburgh: T. & T. Clark, 1988).

[16] This situation is, of course, changing with the growing influence of cultural studies on biblical interpretation; see, e.g., Daniel Boyarin, *A Radical Jew: Paul and the Politics of Identity* (Berkeley: University of California Press, 1994) esp. pp. 1-6.

[17] Cf., e.g., Unger, *St. Irenaeus*, 4-6 (who favors Rome) and Robert M. Grant, *Irenaeus of Lyons* (Early Church Fathers; London and New York; Routledge, 1997) 6 (who favors Asia and Phrygia).

[18] See, e.g., *Adv. Haer.* 1.praef.2: "I have deemed it my duty . . . to unfold to thee, my friend, these portentous and profound mysteries, which do not fall within the range of every intellect, because all have not sufficiently purged their brains (or, have not sufficient brains). . . . Not that I am practised either in composition or eloquence; but my feeling of affection prompts me to make known to thee and all thy companions thoses doctrines which have been kept in concealment until now, but which are at last, through the goodness of God, brought to light."

[19] Grant, *Irenaeus*, 25.

[20] See also Unger, *St. Irenaeus*, 8-11.

[21] Irenaeus even warns against reading scripture alone. It should be done in the company of the presbyters of the church, "among whom is the apostolic doctrine" (4.32.1).

[22] In the words of the opening essay of the first volume to come from the work of this seminar, "claiming a single criterion of truth is . . . scandalous" (Grenholm and Patte, "Receptions," 7).

[23] Ernst Käsemann, *Commentary on Romans* (trans. G. W. Bromiley; Grand Rapids: Eerdmans, 1980) 212.

[24] James D. G. Dunn, *Romans* (Word Biblical Commentary 38; 2 vols.; Dallas: Word, 1988) 1.xvi.

[25] But see now the critique of the claim by John M. G. Barclay in "Neither Jew Nor Greek": Multiculturalism and the New Perspective on Paul," *Ethnicity and the Bible* (ed. Mark G. Brett; Biblical Interpretation Series 19; Leiden; Brill, 1996) 197-214.

[26] Stanley K. Stowers, *A Rereading of Romans: Justice, Jews, and Gentiles* (New Haven: Yale University Press, 1994) 279-84.

[27] Boyarin, *Radical Jew*, 22. Others interpret the implications of Gal 3:28 differently; see, e.g., Lone Fatum "Image of God and Glory of Man: Woman in the Pauline Congregations," in *Image of God and Gender Models in Judaeo-Christian Tradition* (ed. K. E. Borresen; Oslo: Solum, 1991) 56-137, esp. pp. 62-70; Martin, *Corinthian Body*, 230-32.

[28] See, e.g., Robert Jewett, *Paul's Anthropological Terms: A Study of Their Use in Conflict Settings* (AGAJU 19; Leiden: Brill, 1971) 1; also Dunn, *Romans*, 1.445.

[29] Correspondences with Acts 17 include the depiction of God as Maker of heaven and earth (v. 24), the One who bestows life and breath (v. 25), who upholds and sustains all things (v. 28), and who will render final judgment after a period of kindness (vv. 30-31).

[30] The targums move in this direction by translating the Hebrew "outside" (as "in the streets" or "in the marketplace" – that is, in a public place where everyone could hear him.

[31] So translated by Joseph P. Smith (*St. Irenaeus: Proof of the Apostolic Preaching* [ACW 16; London: Longmans, Green and Co., 1952] 62); John Behn, cited by Graham, uses the word "mercy" in his transalation. I do not know the Armenian original.

[32] Irenaeus deletes Ishmael and Esau from the record, obviating any need to justify the choice of Isaac and Jacob.

³³ Dunn calls Paul's conclusion in 9:18 "severe" but he celebrates the fact that the words "on whomever he chooses" show that the apostle looks beyond the narrow election-conscious framework of the elect (*Romans*, 2.563). Gordon Kaufman, on the other hand, sees "serious problems" with the verse, for in depicting God as an authoritarian tyrant it encourages and enables domineering patterns of human behavior (*In Face of Mystery: A Constructive Theology* [Cambridge, MA: Harvard University Press, 1993] 270).

³⁴ In fact, references to these opponents frame the body of the tractate; see *Epid.* 2, 99, 100.

³⁵ See Elaine Heisey Pagels, *The Gnostic Paul; Gnostic Exegesis of the Pauline Letters* (Philadelphia: Fortress, 1975) 37-42.

³⁶ The text of the Hebrew Bible and of the Septuagint does not have the expected blessing of Shem ("Blessed by the Lord God be Shem") but a surprising blessing of God ("Blessed be the Lord the God of Shem"). This is usually understood positively within the framework of Genesis as a foreshadowing of God's election blessing to the Patriarchs.

³⁷ See Greenholm, "A Theologian and Feminist Responds," in *Reading Israel*, 105-23, esp. p. 115.

³⁸ Scholars note the same destabilizing potential in Paul's description of God as the one "who justifies the ungodly" (Rom 4:5). As Andrew Lincoln observes, "the formulation of 4:5 also by implication places Abraham among the ungodly (cf. 1:18), who deserve only God's wrath and therefore have to receive justification as a gift . . . [This] opens up for Jewish Christians a perception of Abrahamn, their forefather according to the flesh, and, by extenion, themselves as being in exactly the same position as Gentile Christians in regard to receiving justification" ("From Wrath to Justification," in *Pauline Theology, Vol. III: Romans* [ed. D. M. Hay and E. E. Johnson; Minneapolis: Fortress, 1995] 151). Or, in the words of Brendan Byrne, "in painting Abraham in these colors Paul is taking the provocative step of making the 'Gentile' stance before God somehow the norm" (*Reckoning with Romans* [Wilmington: Glazier, 1986] 97). The same observations apply, *mutatis mutandis*, to the impact of Irenaeus's comments about Japheth on the position of the offspring of Ham.

³⁹ See Grenholm's perceptive comments on "construing a father" in "A Feminist Responds," esp. pp. 118-20.

⁴⁰ The intended referent of κτίσις is highly debated; cf. Dunn, *Romans*, 1.469-70; Käsemann, *Romans*, 232-33.

⁴¹ Patte, "Post-Holocaust Biblical Critic," 231-32, 241-42.

⁴² See Smith, *St. Irenaeus*, 60, also 158 n. 106.

⁴³ Patte, "Post-Holocaust Biblical Critic," 232-35.

A Response to
Jeffrey Bingham
and Susan Graham

Christoph Markschies

———— ◆ ————

It seems reasonable to respond to Jeffrey Bingham first and then to
Susan Graham. But first of all one general remark: as both contributions are close accounts of Irenaeus's argumentation, it is difficult for
me to find specific points in the very full papers I absolutely must
contradict. Therefore I will concentrate on a few general remarks on
the history of tradition underlying Irenaeus's argumentation and on the
characteristic outline of the argumentation.

Jeffrey Bingham opens his sensitive and close account of Irenaeus's
argumentation with the reconstruction of the Gnostic argumentation
regarding the resurrection of the flesh in the *Gospel according to Philip.*
This exciting and highly disputed passage indeed would be worth an
extra lecture – something which, of course, I will not give now; it would
not contribute a lot to our current section, anyway. Nevertheless, one
observation regarding the passage from the Gospel seems relevant to
me, because it implies *a first critical point* I intend to make in my
response to Jeffrey Bingham. Therefore I start with an observation concerning the Nag Hammadi text.

In his new commentary on the *Gospel according to Philip,* which was
published only recently in the series "Texte und Untersuchungen" (TU)[1],
Hans-Martin Schenke states that first of all one must interpret Logion
23 of the Gospel with regard to its three separate passages: The first
paragraph begins with the words "Some are afraid lest they raise
naked," and this is polemics against people who desire to rise in their
worldly flesh. The second paragraph begins with a quotation taken from
the New Testament: "Flesh and blood shall not inherit the kingdom of
God" and it disputes the opinion that the worldly flesh should inherit
the kingdom of God: only the flesh and blood of Jesus, that is to say, his
Word and his Spirit, shall inherit the kingdom. The third paragraph
begins with "I strongly criticize" (the translation "I find fault with" is

not strong enough) those who claim that the flesh cannot be raised, and it holds the conciliatory position which allows to say that those are wrong who completely deny the resurrection of the flesh, as well as those who simply maintain the resurrection of the flesh without any proviso. Schenke is absolutely right here: all three paragraphs of this passage are very different in what concerns style and content and they are linked in a grammatically more than difficult way: "The linking of the paragraphs somehow is 'not right'"[2]. Of course, the individual paragraphs can be harmonized – more or less clever instances can be found in secondary literature –[3] but, taken individually, the position taken up in the first paragraph, on the contrary, criticizes those who distance themselves from the resurrection of the flesh. The best way of explaining this sequence difficult in both content and grammar, is to assume that the text of the *Gospel according to Philip* we have in hands today underwent a process of growth in three stages. This is what Hans-Martin Schenke assumed[4]. Of course, I am aware of the fact that with questions of literary criticism one never reaches full consensus, but this is not what I am aiming at now anyway. What I am saying is that the passage taken from the Gospel according to Philip stresses the point that there was *not one single* Gnostic position as to what regards resurrection, but that there were debates within one and the same school and that, therefore, there was quite a range of "Gnostic" positions[5]. The fact that some Gnostic *also* taught the resurrection of the flesh is shown by the so-called "Treatise on Resurrection", also known as "Epistle to Rheginus": "Why should it be that you do not regain your flesh when you ascend to the aion?" (p.47,7). Of course, this refers to Paul's σῶμα πνευματικόν (1 Cor 15:44-45.), but the identity of the worldly and the heavenly flesh is claimed[6]. Now, is the range of Gnostic positions on the resurrection reflected in one way or the other in Irenaeus's texts? There is a negative answer to this question: Irenaeus and Tertullian both drew a very schematic picture of the Gnostic position. This can be seen clearly from the passage quoted by Jeffrey Bingham (Irenaeus, *Adv. Haer.* I 30,13): *hunc maximum errorem inter discipulos eius fuisse dicunt, quoniam putarent eum (sc. Iesum) in corpore mundiali resurrexisse*, "the Gnostics claim, the disciples fell into the enormous error of imagining that Jesus was raised in his worldly body". But even this polemical wording shows that the Gnostics mentioned also referred to Paul: *Corpus mundialis*, σῶμα πνευματικόν[7] of course is not more than the pointed translation of the Pauline σῶμα ψυχικόν found in the First Epistle to the Corinthians (1 Cor 15:44). The *first point* I want to make in my response to Jeffrey Bingham is to point to the haeresiological construct of the position of his opponents that Irenaeus provides. To put it another way: Instead of drawing a colorful picture of "Gnostic" positions like the one in the passage of the *Gospel according to Philip*, Irenaeus comes up with a clearly profiled black and white drawing. To put it again another way: Irenaeus makes it easy for himself, when, in the fifth book of his work, he argues against the position that the body, the *plasmatio Dei*, πλάσις τοῦ θεοῦ, could not be saved (*Adv. Haer.* V 9,1)[8]. Surely this is what some Gnostics claimed; but other Gnostics, following Pauline tradition, as we have seen, taught the transformation of the body[9]. Besides this, the Gnostic opponents also used as an⁻ argument passages from the Epistles of the Apostle Paul[10]: ὁ Παῦλος ἀνατάσεως Ἀπόστολος γέγονεν wrote the Valentinian Theodotus[11].

I come to my *second point*. As we have just seen, Irenaeus simplified the positions of his opponents, the Gnostics, with a rhetorical and a polemical aim. But did he contribute to this complex, topical debate of his times by his position on the transformation of the body, which was presented by Jeffrey Bingham? I mean the debate the question, in how far the raised body as a σῶμα πνευματικόν was different from the worldly body as a σῶμα ψυχικόν or κοσμικόν. In my opinion, Irenaeus's argumentation on the "Continuity and Change" of the human body in the fifth book (also presented by Jeffrey Bingham in a very sensitive manner) must be interpreted in the context of this topical debate. The latter observation is the second point of my response to Jeffrey Bingham's paper.

I will give reasons for my point. A quotation taken from Methodius shows that Justin already maintained an anti-Gnostic exegesis of 1 Cor 15:50b ("flesh and blood do not inherit the kingdom of God"). Unfortunately, this fragment is too short to help us reconstruct exactly the pre-history of Irenaeus's passages (this means that Friedrich Loof's speculation on Theophilus as an intermediate link[12] must be ruled out). But there are reasons enough to assume that Irenaeus's position that "flesh" indeed did not inherit anything, but was taken into possession by the inheritance (*hereditate autem acquiritur caro[13]*), was taken from Justin, who, according to Methodius, said "that whatever dies (that is: the flesh) is taken into possession"[14]. In order to position Irenaeus's argumentation correctly in the debate of his times over the relation between the worldly and heavenly body, I will choose two more definite references, a clearly earlier one and a later one: Origen and Pseudo-Justin.

In his work "On the resurrection" (*De resurrectione*: CPG I, 1481), which has come down to us only in fragments and which was written some thirty years after Irenaeus's anti-Gnostic work, Origen tried to describe precisely which parts were transformed and which parts remained the same in the process of resurrection: the *substantialis ratio*, the λόγος τῆς οὐσίας, "the formular of being" of the body will be kept after death[15] and therefore will be able to form a new spiritual body[16]. This new body is a "most fine, pure and shining body"[17], so, as far as its material being is concerned, it even surpasses the ethereal body of fire of the angels. Thus, for his precise answer to a heavily disputed question, Origen uses a well-known philosophical term, which is also often found e.g. with Aristotle[18] (λόγος τῆς οὐσίας). At the same time he always brings in Pauline passages for his explanations, mainly passages taken from the eighth chapter of the Epistle to the Romans and the fifteenth chapter of the Epistle to the Corinthians. So much for Origen, who to a larger extend than Irenaeus took into consideration the "scientific" argumentation of his times. (Though it must be noted that Irenaeus did allude to Stoic positions on 'matter' (ὕλη) and on the 'forming logos' in his own position on the spirit forming and giving life to the matter of flesh[19].) Thus, according to Irenaeus, the worldly and the heavenly body – in Aristotle's words – are not different in substance, but in quality[20].

Unfortunately, large parts of Christian literature of the second century are lost and therefore it is difficult to reconstruct the state of the debate in the eighties of the second century, when Irenaeus was writing. There is the work *De resurrectione* by Pseudo-Justin – which has come down to us in fragments mainly in John of Damascus's writings – which can be taken into consideration. It can be deduced from clearly definable quotations in Theophilus of Antioch that *De resurrectione* must have been written before 180. The arguments against a resurrection of the flesh which Pseudo-Justin decribes as wide-spread ones, also form the background of the passages in the fifth book by Irenaeus. It is said that the flesh decayed due to death and dissolved into its finest components[21]. Against this position, Pseudo-Justin[22] and Irenaeus maintained the transformation of the worldly body as described by Paul in the Epistle to the Corinthians: δεῖ λὰρ τὸ φθαρτὸν τοῦτο ἐνδύσασθαι ἀφθαρσίαν (1 Cor 15:53a[23]). Pseudo-Justin, as well as Irenaeus, argued against the polemical objection that the entirely restored body again would carry its corporeal defects and desires[24]. Pseudo-Justin assumed that the desires and the respective parts of the body which cause those desires "would be set out of function"[25] and that the freedom from harm of the flesh would be guaranteed marvelously[26]. Irenaeus shares the same opinion[27]. So, the *second point* I want to make in my response to Jeffrey Bingham's paper is to point to the heated dispute about the topic among Christian theologians of the late second century[28]. Of course, it was not my intention to dispute the originality of the artful intertextual network of biblical passages which Jeffrey Bingham has demonstrated in such an impressive manner – but the threads Irenaeus was weaving and the models he had for his orientation had long been prepared. Besides, one must not underestimate the importance of philosophical theorems. This is what Winfried Overbeck showed in great detail some time ago[29].

I now come to Susan L Graham and her contribution to "Irenaeus as Reader of Romans 9-11". Susan Graham has shown that Pauline theology has had a formative influence on the argumentation of the ἐπιδεξις on the three sons Sem, Ham and Japheth. Even more instances could be given, for example details in the portrait of Abraham (*Epid.* 24). The wording: "He believed the voice from heaven" (*Epid.* 24) sounds like a variation of the verse ἐπίστευσεν δὲ Ἀβραὰμ τῷ θεῷ, which Paul (Romans 4:3) had taken from the first book of his Bible (Gen 15:6). This reference is made explicit elsewhere[30]. My *third point*, an addition to Susan Graham's explications, again only refers to the history of tradition and the immediate context of Irenaeus's argumentation. It is true that in *Lugdunum*/Lyon there was no considerable Jewish community at the time of Irenaeus's episcopate[31], and yet, were proud and theologically self-confident synagogue communities not known to him from Asia Minor? Is it not the case that Irenaeus – as can be seen in the fourth book of *Adversus Haereses* – strictly thought in terms of two covenants, both prefigured in Abraham (IV 25,1)[32]? Did he not accept Paul's naming of the epoch of the Sinaitic law as "servitude": *servitus* (δουλεία) or *servitus iugum* (δουλείας ζυλόν)[33]? And did Irenaeus not change dramatically the original sense of the parable of the olive tree in his only existing detailed reference to the Israel-chapters in Paul's Epistle to the Romans in the fifth book of the *Adversus Haereses*? Whereas in Paul's text, contrary to a common gardener's practice, a *wild* shoot is grafted into a *cultivated* trunk (Romans 11,17), Irenaeus mentions a "*wild* olive tree which received engrafting"[34]. Therefore I would prefer to interpret Irenaeus more along the lines of the classical theory of substitution than Susan Graham did. At any rate, with his passages on the three sons in the Ἐπίδεξις is a brilliant example of the point that before Tertullian, there was no fixed terminology or theology if the thought that Christians were *tertium genus*/τρίτον γένος[35].

To sum up my thoughts on both papers in conclusion: it is astonishing to a modern observer, to what extent Pauline texts are established in the argumentation of the second and third century. For Irenaeus, the incomparable effectiveness of the divine power is the crucial factor for the resurrection of the flesh[36], and this is a central theologumenon of Pauline theology taken from the Second Epistle to the Corinthians[37]. Susan Graham calls it a "Copernican revolution" that scholars have become increasingly aware of this leading influence of Paul on the theology of Irenaeus, and that this has been shown in the texts since the research of Richard Norris[38]. Susan Graham is absolutely right here.

[1] *Das Philippus-Evangelium* (Nag Hammadi Codex II, 3), revised edition, with translation and commentary by H.-M. Schenke, TU 143 (Berlin, 1997) 229-37.
[2] Schenke, *Philippus-Evangelium*, 235.

³Some of them are named in J. Bingham's paper; for other examples, see Schenke, *Philippus-Evangelium*, 236-37.

⁴Schenke, *Philippus-Evangelium*, 236 (with reference to earlier works).

⁵On the theme in general, see Ch. Markschies, *Gnosis* (Munich, 2001).

⁶In favor of a pneumatic nature of the flesh, see, among others, M. Lee Peel, *Gnosis und Auferstehung. Der Brief an Rheginus von Nag Hammadi* (Neukirchen-Vlugn, 1971) = idem, *The Epistle to Rheginos*, trans. W. Funk (Philidelphia, 1969) 154-57; in favor of a material nature, see, for example, Zandee, van Unnik and Danie′lou (bibliography in *The Epistle to Rheginos*, 155 n. 140). The philosophical background of the passage has been illuminated by B. Layton, *The Gnostic Treatise on Resurrection from Nag Hammadi*, HDR 12 (Missoula, Montana, 1979) 77-78.

⁷B. Reynders, *Lexique compare′ du texte Grec et des versions Latine, Arme′nienne et Syriaque de 1′ "Adversus Haereses" de Saint Ire′ne′e*, Vol. 2, *Index de mots Latins*, CSCO 142 Sub.6 (Louvain, 1956) 203, *s.v.*

⁸On the understanding of this concept, see already Overbeck, *Menschwerdung*, 596, and, even earlier, G. Joppich, *Salus Carnis. Eine Untersuchung in der Theologie des hlg. Irenäus von Lyon*, MüSt 1 (Münsterschwarzach, 1965) 27-38. The saying "There is no salvation for the flesh" may be derived from *Adv. haer.* V. 2, 2-3; 3, 3; 4, 1; 9, 1 and 12, 6 (cited in Overbeck, *Menschwerdung*, 117). Whether the saying was formulated in this very pointed way by the Valentinians themselves, or is not rather a conscious simplification of the dialectical position of the Valentinians for the sake of argument, is a matter that requires further discussion. Overbeck explains the very crass stylization of the opponents in *Adv. haer.* V. 1-14 (in debate with A. Orbe) on the hypothesis that in addition to the gnostic denial of the bodily resurrection a similar theology held by some *within the church* is also in view (*Menschwerdung*, 122). Cf. also Ps.-Justin *Res.* 8, 7: "For where God proclaims to save the human person, God also proclaims this with respect to the flesh,"ἔνθα γὰρ τὸν ἄνθρωπον εὐαγγελίζεται σῶσαι καὶ τῇ σάρκι εὐαγγελίζεται (p. 120, 13-14, Heimgartner).

⁹Moreover, the claim of Irenaeus that God does not transform the natures (cf. Bingham, p. 6, with references) is obviously an extremely polemical statement.

¹⁰One could also illustrate this highly selective evaluation of Gnostic hermeneutics by reference to the anti-Valentinian interpretation of the parable of the olive tree in *Haer.* V. 10, 1-2., which Bingham has already reconstructed (p. 8f.): Is there a strict anthropological "doctrine of three classes" in the sense that Irenaeus (and many modern interpreters) assume? (Cf. B. Aland, "Erwählungstheologie und Menschenklassenlehre. Die Theologie des Herakleon als Schlüssel zum Verständnis der christlichen Gnosis?" in *Gnosis and Gnosticism. Papers read at the Seventh International Conference on Patristic Studies*, NHS 8 (Leiden, 1977) 148-81. The literature on this question has now been collected by R. Noormann, *Irenäus als Paulusinterpret*, 495.

¹¹Clemens Alexandrinus, *exc. Thdt.* 23.2 (SC 23, 106 Sagnard).

¹²F. Loofs, *Theophilus von Antiochien adversus Marcionem und die anderen theologischen Quellen bei Irenaeus*, TU 46/2 (Leipzig, 1930) 230-31.

¹³Irenaeus, *Adv. Haer.* V. 9, 4 (FChr 8/5, 82, 4 Rousseau/Doutreleau); for interpretation, see Overbeck, *Menschwerdung*, 202-209 and R. Noormann, *Irenäus als Paulusinterpret. Zur Rezeption und Wirkung der paulinischen und deuteropaulinischen Briefe im Werk des Irenäus von Lyon*, WUNT 66 (Tübingen, 1994) 486-92. Noormann speaks with Bengsch of a "Tauschtheologie" and its "Tauschformeln."

¹⁴Methodius *Res.* II, 18, 9 (also with translation and commentary by Heimgartner, 54-55; there also p. 61 linguistic observations on the authenticity of the fragment).

¹⁵Origen, frag. *apud* Pamphilius, *Apol.* 7 (PG 17, 594-95). The identity of the earthly body and the resurrection body is emphasized by Origen also in *De prin.* II. 10, 1 (GCS Origenes V. 173, 14-174,10 Koetschau).

[16] Origen *De prin.* II. 10, 3 (176, 6 Koetschau): *ratio* (logos) *ea, quae substantiam continet corporalem.*

[17] Origen *De prin.* III. 6, 4 (286, 1-2 Koetschau).

[18] H. Bonitz, *Index Aristotelicus,* Aristotelis Opera, Vol. V (Berlin, 1870) *s.v.,* p. 434.

[19] Irenaeus, *Adv. Haer.* V. 9, 1 (FChr 8/5, 74, 14 Rousseau/Doutreleau) in the Jena papyrus, for *formatur* probably μορφουμε μενου (SC 153, 106 App.)

[20] Overbeck, *Menschwerdung,* 220-21.

[21] Frag. 2, 2 in John of Damascus, now newly edited in *Pseudojustin - Über die Auferstehung. Text und Studie* by M. Heimgartner, PTS 54 (Berlin/New York, 2001) 106, 2.

[22] Ibid., Frag. 10, 10 (p. 128, 16 Heimgartner): . . . τὴν φθορὰν ἀφωαρσίαν ποιεῖν; cf. 4, 5 (p. 110, 9).

[23] Irenaeus *Adv. Haer.* V. 2, 3 (FChr 8/5, 36, 10-12 Rousseau/Doutreleau).

[24] Ibid., Frag. 3, 1-2 (p. 108, 1-7 Heimgartner).

[25] Ibid., Frag. 3, 18 (p. 110, 33-34, καταργεῖν).

[26] Ibid., Frag. 4, 5 (p. 110, 10-11 Heimgartner).

[27] With Heimgartner, *Pseudojustin,* 77-82, I assume a use of the writing by Irenaeus; differently Overbeck, *Menschwerdung,* 102-104, and more cautiously, 160-64 (in both passages one also finds presentations of the history of research on our problem).

[28] For the pre-history of the debate in Judaism, cf. G. Kretschmar, "Auferstehung des Fleisches. Zur Frühgeschichte einer theologischen Lehrformel" in *Leben angesichts des Todes. Beiträge zum theologischen Problem des Todes.* Helmut Thielicke zum 60. Geburtstag (Tübingen, 1968) 101-37, esp. 106-37.

[29] W. Overbeck, *Menschwerdung. Eine Untersuchung zur literarischen und theologischen Einheit des fünften Buches* 'Adversus Haereses' *des Irenäus von Lyon,* BSHST 61 (Bern, 1995) 589-600. Cf. especially p. 102: "Wenn sich Irenäus hier im ersten Hauptteil von *AH V* dem Thema der *salus carnis* widmet, kann er also bereits auf einen reichen Schatz an argumentativen Hilfen zurückgreifen."

[30] Irenaeus, *Adv. Haer.* IV. 5, 4 (FChr 4, 42, 1-11 Rousseau/Doutreleau).

[31] Graham, "Olive Branches," n. 61, with reference to Simon.

[32] Noormann, *Irenäus als Paulusinterpret,* 388-89.

[33] Irenaeus, *Adv. Haer.* IV. 15, 1; cf. on this point the observations in Noormann, *Irenäus als Paulusinterpret,* 396.

[34] Irenaeus, *Adv. Haer.* V. 10, 1, following the translation of Overbeck, *Menschwerdung,* 214 (Ibid., in n. 2 a detailed justification of the translation).

[35] Thus, with evidence, W. Kinzig, *Novitas Christiana. Die Idee des Fortschritts in der Alten Kirche bis Eusebius,* FKDG 58 (Göttingen, 1994) 162-63.

[36] Noormann, *Irenäus als Paulusinterpret,* 486.

[37] Cf. Irenaeus, *Adv. Haer.* V. 3, 1 and the citation from 2 Cor. 12:7-9.

[38] Graham, "Olive Branches," p. 87.

– SIX –

Origen's Readings of Romans in
Peri Archon: (Re)Constructing Paul

Ruth Clements

———— ◆ ————

I. Introduction

The title of this paper aligns my presentation with recent approaches in Pauline studies which make clear the fact that the Paul whom we have inherited is the product of centuries of synthesis and theological reflection.[1] In Origen's writings, and quite clearly in *Peri Archon*, we can see the synthesizing process at work, as well as the consequences of that synthesis for subsequent theologies and praxes of Christian biblical interpretation.

The starting point for this investigation is a prior inquiry into Origen's use of Jewish interpretation in his exegetical procedure. Origen invokes two opposing rhetorical constructions of Jewish interpretation. On the one hand, he utilizes the exegesis of Philo, readings of Greek biblical versions other than the Septuagint, and contemporary rabbinic traditions, as authoritative supporting materials for his own explications of the "literal" sense of the biblical text, which then becomes the basis for "spiritual" (allegorical) exegesis. On the other hand, at the level of "spiritual" explanation Origen caricatures and castigates Jewish interpretation as impossibly literalist, using "examples" drawn from Christian anti-Jewish polemical exegesis to create a foil for the beauty and fitness of his own approach.[2]

The theoretical foundations for this exegetical "rhetorics of Jewish interpretation" are laid already in *Peri Archon*. Here, Origen's reading of Paul plays a crucial role in shaping his construction of proper Christian biblical interpretation and its relationship to Jewish interpretation. Crucial texts in this task are: Romans 2:28–29; 9:6, 8; 1 Cor 10:11, 18; Hebrews 8:5, 10:1; and 2 Cor 3:14–17. Origen's reading of Romans in this project is interesting as much for what he does not draw on as for what he does use and how he construes it.

In this paper, I illustrate how, in *Peri Archon*, Origen constructs his theological opposition between "fleshly Jews"/"Jewish literalism" and "spiritual Christians"/Christian "spiritual" interpretation by transformative readings of its Pauline building blocks, with particular attention to texts from Romans. I end with a discussion of Origen's use of key Romans texts in several sermons, to illustrate the complex interaction between rhetorical context and exegetical emphasis in Origen's writings.

Origen was born in ca. 185 CE in Alexandria. He seems to have begun his work as a writer of biblical commentary some time after 220 CE, following a trip to Rome during which he may have encountered Marcionite text criticism and Valentinian commentary, as well as the work of Hippolytus.[3] In about 234 CE, as a consequence of increasing conflict with the Alexandrian bishop, Demetrius, Origen moved to Caesarea in Palestine, where he organized a school of advanced biblical studies with the blessing of the bishops of Caesarea and Jerusalem. Origen remained active in Caesarea until the outbreak of the Decian persecution. He died some time after 250 as a result of imprisonment during the persecution, though not as an actual martyr. The bulk of Origen's extant exegetical works, including, it seems, most of his sermons, date from his Caesarean sojourn.[4]

Two related Pauls appear in Origen's collective works. One, the exegeted Paul, is the complex writer who stands forth in Origen's commentary on Romans and in fragments on other Pauline letters. The other Paul, the constructed or exegetical Paul, to some extent precedes and informs the exegeted Paul. This is the authoritative Apostle to whom Origen appeals constantly in *Peri Archon*. This Apostle emerges through Origen's reading across the Pauline corpus, which in *Peri Archon* includes the deutero-Paulines, the Pastoral Epistles and the Letter to the Hebrews, as well as the letters accepted as authentically Pauline by modern scholars.[5] This Paul appears frequently in Origen's exegesis of non-Pauline material, as the source and grounding for Origen's own exegetical insights and in contradistinction to the Paul of Valentinus and Marcion. The Paul in view in this paper is primarily Origen's exegetical Paul.

II. Peri Archon (On First Principles): The Theory of a Praxis

Peri Archon was written ca. 229 CE in Alexandria. It presents a systematic exposition of the basic tenets of the Christian faith, in an essentially neo-Platonic framework, the first real Christian systematic theology. By the time of its composition, Origen had been established as a Christian teacher, connected with the Alexandrian church, for perhaps ten years. One precipitating cause of the writing of *Peri Archon* seems to have been worsening relations with Origen's bishop, Demetrius. This worsening of relations appears to have arisen through a combination of factors: Demetrius' bid to centralize the teaching authority of the

Alexandrian church;[6] Origen's growing reputation as a teacher; his use of non-literal interpretation of biblical texts.[7] Unfortunately, *Peri Archon* itself seems merely to have crystallized opposition to Origen within the Alexandrian church; following its publication he made his first trip to Palestine, which later became his permanent home.[8]

Peri Archon defends an intellectual approach to matters of faith, while at the same time arguing against Marcionite and Valentinian exegesis and assertions. Its climax in Book IV is an articulation of the theory behind Origen's allegorical method of exegesis. Book IV has been substantially preserved to us in the original Greek as well as in Rufinus' Latin translation.[9] *Peri Archon* represents a mid-point in the shaping of Origen's exegetical practice. It follows the completion of commentaries on Psalms 1–25, Lamentations, and Genesis, and precedes the *Commentary on John*, the first five books of which were completed in Alexandria. It precedes as well Origen's move to Caesarea and first substantial encounters with contemporary Judaism.[10] The theology of interpretation which crystallizes in *Peri Archon* becomes formative for the later period, but the move to Caesarea prompts other developments as well, particularly in terms of the way Origen begins to value and use rabbinic interpretation.

Paul appears in the very first paragraph of *Peri Archon*'s Preface.[11] Origen begins the treatise as a whole by setting forth the theological foundation of his hermeneutical method. He asserts that the "words and teaching of Christ" are the only source for the knowledge (*scientia*) which leads human beings towards a "good and blessed life." However, says Origen, these words encompass not only Christ's earthly teachings, but also the "words and deeds" of Moses and the prophets, who prophesied about him. As proof that the spirit of Christ spoke through Moses, Origen quotes "this one testimony of Paul, taken from the letter which he writes to the Hebrews," Hebr. 11:24–26.[12] He then quotes a second Pauline passage, 2 Cor 13:3, to show that Christ continued to speak with his apostles even after he ascended into heaven.[13] From the very beginning, then, it is Paul's apostolic authority that underwrites Origen's fundamental principle of the unity of the scriptures: Moses, the prophets, the Gospels (the historical record of Jesus' own teaching), and the other apostolic writings (produced after Jesus left the scene) all equally record the "words and teachings of Christ." This construal stands in direct opposition to the Marcionite use of Paul to set Law against Gospel.[14]

The remainder of the Preface sets forth in brief what Origen calls the "apostolic teaching" on the nature of God, Christ, the Holy Spirit and the other several topics to which Origen will apply reasoned scrutiny in the ensuing books. In paragraph eight, he returns again to the subject of scripture. Church teaching, says Origen, includes the doctrine that the scriptures, composed via the Spirit of God, have both an obvious meaning and a meaning that is hidden from most readers. Without naming Paul, Origen alludes to Rom 7:14 to assert the *unanimity* of the whole church on the point that though the "whole law is spiritual," the spiritual meaning is grasped only by a few, who are especially gifted by the Spirit with wisdom and knowledge. Thus, Origen uses Rom 7:14 to cast his assumption of multiple levels of scriptural meaning, a cornerstone of his own controversial method, as a universally acknowledged truth.[15] In the process he both positions himself as spokesman for the whole church, and robs Valentinian interpretation of its claim, based on its own reading of Paul, to be the mediators of the true spiritual meaning of the Law.[16]

A. Origen's Exegetical Procedure: From the Literal Meaning to the Spiritual

Book IV of *Peri Archon* lays out a tripartite schema of scriptural meaning. Origen designates these levels the "bodily," "soulish" (psychic), and "spiritual" senses of scripture. The designations correspond to Origen's descriptions of the modes of human existence. The soul is the primal "estate" of a rational being. The body encloses the soul as punishment for the original rebellion against God and fall from his presence (*Peri Archon* I.8), and every soul possesses at least the potential to raise itself back to a spiritual state (*Peri Archon* II.8). As applied to scripture, these terms denote that "scripture meets the needs of rational creatures at different levels of progress":[17] the "simple man" is helped by the body of scripture; those who have made some spiritual progress are enlightened by its soul; and one who is "perfect" in the sense of 1 Cor 2:6–7 may be taught by the spiritual sense. Neither in their anthropological sense nor in their spiritual sense do these terms represent static modes of being.[18] The possibility of movement between more "bodily" and more "spiritual" states of being contrasts with the static and predetermined divisions between psychic and spiritual Christians in Valentinian thought.

In *Peri Archon* IV.2, Origen develops a contrast between the spiritual meaning of scripture and the "fleshly" or "bodily" meaning (ἡ σάρξ τῆς γραφῆς, 2.4; τὸ σωματικόν, 2.5, *passim*). The designation of the literal meaning as the bodily sense of scripture denotes its theological distance from the spiritual meaning; the appellation "fleshly," drawn from Paul, increases the rhetorically negative casting thus given to the literal sense.[19] It is true that the "bare letter" (τὸ ψιλὸν γράμμα; IV.2.4) contains much in itself to edify the multitude (2.8); however, the proper task of Christians is to try to penetrate at least to the "soul" of scripture (roughly speaking, in this exposition, the moral or doctrinal level), and for those who are able, to pursue the yet higher spiritual meaning (2.6).

Scripture contains deliberate "stumbling blocks" (σκάνδαλα), "hindrances and impossibilities," in its bodily sense, to ensure that the perceptive reader is not lulled by the usefulness of much of the narrative sense into forgetting to seek the higher, truer meanings toward which all the words of scripture point (2.9). Thus, if it is held in too high a regard, the bodily sense in itself becomes a stumbling block, because it prevents the reader from pursuing this more essential quest.

In Origen's sermons and commentaries, the literal meaning takes on different terminology and a more positive cast. Karen Jo Torjesen has described Origen's *de facto* exegetical method as a series of steps that Origen employs consistently across the variety of biblical literary genres.[20] The first step is to establish the "grammatical" reading and sense of the text; the second is to describe the "concrete and/or historical reality to which the grammatical sense refers." Origen associates both of these steps with the "literal" meaning of the text, denoted in exegetical contexts by the grammatically technical term, πρὸς τὸ ῥητόν;[21] I designate this the "philologically literal" sense of the text. The third exegetical step explicates the meaning(s) beyond this historical or literary sense, which the Logos wishes to convey (ἡ ἀναγωγή, τὸ βούλημα, ὁ σκοπος).[22] The fourth and final step applies these universal spiritual meanings to the reader (the "contemporary" sense, in Torjesen's words, described by such terms as [πνευματική] διδασκαλία, νόημα, δόγμα, τὰ πνευματικά).[23] In practice, then, the philologically literal sense has only positive connotations, providing as it does the basis for the hermeneutical movement to discover the spiritual meaning of the text and its contemporary application. The proper activity of the exegete is to read through this philological or "historical" meaning of the text to activate its spiritual sense, the teaching activity of the Logos in the soul of the contemporary reader/hearer.[24]

However, even though the literal sense has a positive hermeneutical function in Origen's exegetical practice, within the theological context of *Peri Archon*, literal reading remains nearly synonymous with literalism, that is, with reading practices which muffle the voice of the Logos speaking through the text.

B. Literalism on the Spiritual Plane: Peri Archon IV.2–3

At the beginning of *Peri Archon* IV.2, which opens his discussion of the proper interpretation of scripture, Origen describes three groups of erring, 'literalist' readers: Jews, "heretics," and many simple Christians. The Jews have missed the fact of the coming of Christ, because Jesus' actions and the historical circumstances of his life did not fulfill historically and in literal detail the words of the prophets. The errors of heretics and simple Christians spring from a different fault of literalism which they hold in common with each other: taking at face value every word that the scriptures say about the divine. The heretics deal with scripture's incongruous statements by postulating an inferior creator god who is the source of all unsavory traits; simple Christians believe notions about God and/or Christ which are unworthy of the holy (IV.2.1). Furthermore, says Origen, even some sophisticated Christians understand that the words of Scripture clothe mysteries and point through types toward higher realities; but they either fail to understand how to derive the mystical meaning, or they apply the notion of typology unsystematically, and in *this* way fail to derive scripture's true meanings (2.2). These "true meanings" are pre-eminently "the doctrines about God and his only-begotten Son" (2.7).[25] If one fails to discover these doctrines, no matter what one's intention or method, one is reading only the "bare letter."

"The Hebrews" have previously achieved a negative spotlight in *Peri Archon* IV.1.3–4, where Origen sets out proofs for the divinity of scripture.[26] At IV.1.3, he reads Gen 49:10 as a prediction linking the contemporary destruction of the Temple, cult and political entity of Israel to the advent of Christ.[27] IV.1.4 brings together Rom 10:19 (Deut 32:21) and 1 Cor 1:26–29 with 1 Cor 10:18, to show that "God's former people," "Israel according to the flesh," have been replaced by a "foolish nation," chosen through the advent of Christ. Paul's opposition between the "foolish things of the world" (1 Cor 1:27) and the "wise according to the flesh" (1 Cor 1:26) is transformed into an opposition between the new and former people. Origen concludes the section: "So let not 'Israel according to the flesh,' which is called by the Apostle, 'flesh' 'glory before God.'"[28]

This replacement of fleshly Israel by the "foolish nation" sets the stage for a discussion (IV.1.4) of specific prophecies. In IV.1.6, Origen restates in part his opening argument, that the coherence between the scriptures and the life of Jesus demonstrate both his divinity and the divine inspiration of the scriptures themselves. However, he says, it is only since the advent of Christ that these scriptures can be clearly seen to be divine. The section closes with a composite allusion to 2 Cor 3:15–16 and Hebr 10:1. Until the coming of Jesus, the light contained in the law of Moses was hidden under a veil, but with its removal came the knowledge of those good things of which the law held a shadow.[29] Chapter 1 closes (IV.1.7) with an exhortation not to be fooled into disbelief by the obscurity of the scriptures. A concatenation of Pauline passages, drawn primarily from the Corinthian literature, justifies the "earthen vessels" in which the divine teaching is contained, and urges the reader to "leave behind the first principles of Christ" and "press on to perfection" so that the wisdom of the scriptures "may be spoken also to us."

Origen's use of the writings of Paul in the remainder of *Peri Archon* IV.2 and 3, to illustrate the contrast between spiritual interpretation and literalist reading, serves to make the reading practices of "those of the circumcision" (as distinct from the gnostics or the simple Christians) synonymous with improper, literalist reading. At IV.2.6, after allowing that one may be edified by the bodily meaning of scripture, Origen cites 1 Cor 9:9–10 as an example of an explanation "which penetrates as it were to the soul." In this passage, Paul interprets Deut 25:4 not as applying to oxen but as meant metaphorically "for our sake."

Origen then continues:

> But it is a spiritual explanation when one is able to show of what *heavenly things* the *Jews according to the flesh served* (ἐλάτρευον) *a copy and a shadow*, and of what *good things to come the law has a shadow*.[30]

The language of this sentence is drawn from Heb 8:5, Heb 10:1, and 1 Cor 10:18. "Spiritual explanation," is posed here not strictly in opposition to the "bodily sense" in itself, but rather in opposition to the cultic observance (λατρεία) of the "Jews according to the flesh," that is, in opposition to the cultic practices resulting from their reading of scripture. These two verses from Hebrews appear at least twelve times in *Peri Archon*, occasionally together; at times, as in this context, they are used not only to make a statement about how to understand scripture, but also to assert that the worship offered by the Jews was neither true nor spiritual.[31]

A series of examples follows, to illustrate what "the Apostle" means by spiritual interpretation. First Origen quotes 1 Cor 10:11 and 10:4 as "the Apostle's" statement of the hermeneutical principle that the biblical narratives were written "for our sake," and were to be interpreted figuratively (τυπικως). He briefly cites Hebr 8:5, which itself quotes Exod 25:40 and its allusion to the "figure" (τύπος) shown to Moses on the mount. He then discusses Gal 4:21–24, in which Paul uses the technical term ἀλληγορέω; Origen reads the passage as Paul's assertion that observance of the law is *not* synonymous with "understanding and knowing" (νοεῖν καὶ γινώσκειν) the law. It is those who *desire* to be under the law, not those who *are* under the law, who should be able to comprehend (ἀκούειν) the meaning of the law, "the allegories in the scriptures" (ἀλληγορίας . . . ἐν τοῖς γεγραμμένοις). Next comes Colossians 2:16–17, which speaks of food laws, holidays and the Sabbath as a "shadow of the things to come." The "shadow" language of Col 2:17 reminds Origen once more of the beginning of Hebrews 8:5, which he now quotes more fully, thereby extending the sense of "serving a copy and a shadow" to encompass not merely the temple cult, but Jewish religious observance in general. These examples reinforce the

section's opening definition of spiritual interpretation as understanding
the meaning of the biblical text in opposition to the way that Jews read
scripture.[32]

Peri Archon IV.3 provides exegetical demonstrations of the theoretical statements about interpretation outlined in IV.2, and develops a
general framework of biblical typology from which to proceed to the
analysis of specific biblical texts. The chapter begins with a broadside
against persons who take literally certain types of ridiculous or unworthy statements in the creation accounts and likewise in the gospels, as
referring to the actual nature of God and Christ.[33] The discussion then
moves (3.2) to the "Mosaic legislation," concerning which Origen
brings forth several examples that are "irrational" (τὸ ἄλογον) or "impossible" (τὸ ἀδύνατον) to obey literally.[34] It is not coincidental that the
examples are drawn from the areas of circumcision, dietary laws, and
Sabbath observance, the three realms of distinctive behavior for which
Jews had long been widely known to non-Jews in the Hellenistic world,
and which are already controversial topics in the New Testament
writings.

In his references to circumcision and dietary laws, Origen contents
himself with pointing out inconsistencies or "impossibilities" in the
reading of the biblical text; he faults "those of the circumcision" for
ignoring these difficulties when they prove too difficult to explain away.
In referring to Sabbath observance, however, Origen brings forth two
instances of derived halakhic rules for behavior,[35] as examples of the
"copious babbling" (φλυαροῦσιν εὑρησιλογοῦντες) and "ceaseless
talking" (ἀπεραντολογία) of the "teachers of the Jews," who bring forth
"frigid traditions" (ψυχρὰς παραδόσεις) to try to turn literal impossibilities into practice.[36] This caricatured portrait of voluble contemporary Jewish misinterpretation proves to be the climactic example of
literalist reading of the (Old Testament) scriptures.[37]

Chapter 3.3 proceeds with more brevity to list some instances in the
"gospel" and the "apostle" which are likewise impossible, says Origen,
to understand literally.[38] The next section reiterates the argument that
scripture contains both problematic and obviously edifying or historically true statements. Section 5 discusses how the careful reader can
distinguish between the literally true and untrue elements of scripture,
and makes the transition to delineating the method of its interpretation.

This method begins with the observation that the historical narrative
of the scriptures contains the story of a nation chosen by God and the
country God gave to them (IV.3.6). The key to the spiritual meaning of
this historical narrative is found in the words of the Apostle, "Behold
Israel according to the flesh" (1 Cor 10:18), "as though there is an Israel
according to the spirit" (ὡς ὄντος τινὸς κατὰ πνεῦμα). Origen then
adduces a string of further Pauline verses (notably Rom 9:8, 9:6, and
2:28–29) to demonstrate that it is "not the children of the flesh [the

Jews] who are the children of God" (Rom 9:8), but rather those who are "Jews inwardly," whose circumcision is of the spirit, not the letter (Rom. 2:28–29). It is this Israel, "a race of souls," to whom belong the promises of scripture, which are spiritual, albeit clothed in material imagery. Thus (IV.3.8), even the promises of the New Testament addressed to "Israel" (Origen's example is Mt 15:24) refer to spiritual Israel, i.e. the church, not "fleshly" Israel.[39]

Origen closes the section by first quoting "the Apostle" (Gal 4:26) to show that references to Jerusalem indicate a heavenly city, and then by saying that, in order to understand these biblical references, we must "listen to Paul's words as the words of God and the utterances of Wisdom."[40] It is pre-eminently Paul who tells the Christian 1) to read the scriptures spiritually; and 2) that the true, spiritual promises of scripture point not to contemporary Jews and contemporary Jerusalem, but to "Israel according to the Spirit" and the "Jerusalem above."

Origen's deployment of 1 Cor 10:18 as the hermeneutical key to the reading of scripture is a unique exegetical move in relation both to his predecessors and to his immediate contemporaries; however, the opposition between "Israel according to the flesh" and "Israel according to the spirit," drawn somewhat tentatively in *Peri Archon*, becomes a taken-for-granted assumption in Origen's later exegetical writings. This revolutionary reading of 1 Cor 10:18 emerges from the way Origen has read across the Pauline corpus. Because he brings together diverse texts which pose differently nuanced oppositions – flesh/spirit, letter/spirit, shadow/heavenly things, above/below, life/death, "outward"/"inward" Jews, circumcision of the flesh/circumcision of the heart, within the law/without the law, slavery/freedom – all these oppositions come to stand for one another. In Origen's reading, "flesh" must always exist in opposition to "spirit," so that "Israel according to the flesh," by whom Paul means the biblical Israelites, must exist in opposition to "Israel according to the spirit," a phrase Paul himself never uses.

The combination in *Peri Archon* IV.3.6–8 of 1 Cor 10:18 with Romans 9:8, 6, and 2:28–29, rhetorically echoes and extends the contrast between spiritual interpretation and Jewish literalist interpretation posed in 2.6. By the authority of "the Apostle" himself, *Peri Archon* IV.2 and 3 establish not merely that Jewish biblical interpreters are wrongheaded because they fail to recognize the Christ/Logos, but that in fact the true promises of scripture have *always* been intended for the followers of Christ, and have *never* applied to "those of the circumcision."[41]

The Paul who disinherits the "Jews according to the flesh" is the Paul most frequently seen in *Peri Archon*. Citations from Romans and elsewhere that indicate the priority of Israel in Paul's thinking (e.g., Rom

11:1–2, 26) are conspicuous mainly by their absence. Romans 3:2, which on the surface would seem to indicate the priority and privilege of the Jews as those who first received the "oracles of God," comes in the course of Origen's discussion of the "race of souls" in sections nine to twelve. It follows close upon another citation of Romans 9:6 ("they are not all Israel who are of Israel" [IV.3.11]), to illustrate that it is only spiritual Israel, through whom all other souls are to be enlightened, who possesses the oracles of God and whose name means "to see God" (IV.3.12).[42] The etymology is drawn from Philo, who uses it as a foundation for his own reading of the biblical "history" as an allegory for the journey of the soul in which gentiles as well as Jews may participate, but in Origen's context of Pauline oppositions the etymology comes to *exclude* Jews.

Significantly, the "positive" cluster that appears most prominently is Rom 7:12–14, on the goodness of the law. In *Peri Archon* II.4–5, Origen presents a sustained argument against Marcionite criticisms of the Jewish scriptures. In chapter four, after enlisting various sayings of Jesus which indicate that the God of Jesus is the God of Abraham, Isaac, and Jacob (e.g., Mt 22:31–32), Origen invokes the words of the Apostle himself, citing in this order 2 Tim 1:3, 2 Cor 11:22, Rom 1:1–4, 1 Cor 9:9–10, Eph 6:2–3, and Col 1:15. Chapter five refutes the Marcionite distinction between the just and the good. The culminating paragraph, Section 4, enlists Romans 7:12–13 to show that Paul himself aligned the just with the good and called the law "holy and just and good." We have already noted the critical junctures at which Rom 7:14 itself takes on the role of a hermeneutical principle. However, as we have already seen, anti-Marcionite appreciation for the "spiritual" law does not extend to the contemporary practitioners thereof.

This 'disinheriting' trend seems to be an intentional rhetorical strategy. John McGuckin has documented that Origen most often cites Pauline passages that are critical or condemning of Jews and Judaism, and censors "Paul's doctrine of the priority of Israel."[43] McGuckin relates this tactic to contemporary *Caesarean* Christian polemic against Jews. Our exploration of *Peri Archon* suggests, however, that this "censored" Paul preceded Origen's move to Caesarea.

In fact, the constructed Paul of *Peri Archon* resurfaces almost immediately in Alexandrian exegetical dress. The Preface to the *Commentary on John* (*CJn* I.1–89) begins with the hermeneutical statement that just as "the people once referred to as 'of God'" (Num 27:17) were divided into tribes, so "the whole people of Christ, entitled Jewish in secret and circumcised in spirit [Rom 2:28–29], has, in a very mysterious way, the properties of the tribes."[44] Much of the preface is devoted to explaining the name "Gospel" and exploring the connection between the gospels and the rest of the Scriptures. In *CJn* I.32–43,

Origen tries to clarify further the relationship between the law and the prophets and the gospel, drawing on the Pauline complex we have already seen at work. From 2 Cor 3:15 to Hebr 8:5 to 1 Cor 10:11 (with John 4:24), we see that only Christ at his coming showed the truth of what was veiled, of what was previously only hinted at in copies and shadows and figures. Hos 10:12 combines with Rom 7:6 (*CJn* I.36) to bring a new element into the complex, the contrast between "new covenant" and "old letter." In the remainder of the section, Hebr 8:5 and 10:1 appear along with references to Galatians 4, Prov 8:9 and Rev 14:6, primarily to make the argument that just as the law contains shadows of good things to come, so the gospel itself contains both easily intelligible teachings and mysteries towards which the believer needs to advance. The section finishes with a citation of Rom 2:28–29, where the assumed distinction between Jews and "Jews in secret" (i.e. Christians) is used to explain a distinction between Christians at more elementary and more advanced levels, as a basis for Origen's assertion that like Paul (1 Cor 9:20, Acts 16:3), it is necessary to "act as a Christian both spiritually and bodily," for the benefit of more "fleshly" believers. In this context, although the oppositions are intact, the explicitly disinheriting emphasis is in abeyance. This difference may be due to the change in rhetorical setting; *CJn*, unlike *Peri Archon*, was written for supporters, not detractors, who were fully in sympathy with Origen's aims and method.[45]

In sum: I suggest that, in *Peri Archon* (and subsequently in *CJn*), "real Jews" are not in view. The disinheriting Paul is a by-product of Origen's central task: building a coherent Christian philosophy in opposition both to detractors within the more conventional Alexandrian church, and to the assertions of heterodox Christians, primarily followers of Marcion and Valentinus. The insistence that spiritual and not fleshly Israel are the true inheritors of the promises of scripture, the "spiritual law," functions together with the establishment of Paul as the apostolic authority for Origen's allegorical method of reading, in this rhetorical task. On the one hand, Origen claims the (Jewish) scriptures as the legitimate property of Christians (not Jews), against Marcionite rejection; on the other, he enlists Paul as spiritual reader against differing Valentinian and Marcionite images of the authoritative Apostle, while at the same time countering the anti-Pauline sentiment of other groups by casting Paul's words (and method of understanding the Jewish scriptures) as like the words of God. As the *Commentary on John* illustrates, however, this constructed Paul can stand independent of the polemical necessity that brought him to life; in *CJn*, "Israel according to the spirit" has become the accepted and expected substitute for "Israel according to the flesh."

III. "Jewish Literalism" in the Caesarean Homilies[46]

In *CJn* VI.76, written soon after his move to Caesarea, Origen makes the programmatic statement that when interpreting "the history" (that is, the philological meaning of the [OT] text), the Christian interpreter should first inquire regarding the teaching known "among the Hebrews." This statement should be noticed as a significant addition to (if not departure from) Origen's earlier programmatic statements about interpretation in *Peri Archon*. Both his Caesarean commentaries and his sermons make clear that he followed his own advice, as his philological interpretations from this period contain frequent references to teachings known "among the Hebrews." It seems clear that this designation in the Caesarean works indicates interpretations gleaned from rabbinic scholars.[47]

Origen invokes interpretations "from the Hebrews" at the exegetical stage that Torjesen designated the first and second exegetical steps. Thus, like the biblical versions and Philo, rabbinic readings may also be brought to clarify the meaning of the text, and occasionally to expand the platform of the literal meaning for spiritual interpretation. Origen often grounds his authority for citing "Hebrew" interpretations in personal encounters with Jewish interpreters, positioning himself as an authoritative tradent of "Hebrew" traditions.[48] Occasionally the weight of the Hebrew tradition is deployed explicitly against heterodox exegesis.[49]

However, at the transition to exegetical step three, the establishment of the spiritual meaning, the constructed Apostle of *Peri Archon* re-enters the picture. Rom 7:14 and 1 Cor 10:18 recur frequently, usually in combination with another verse such as I Cor 10:11, Hebr 8:5 or 10:1, Rom 2:28/29. These verses may be used to ground a statement to the effect that "these things were written (also) for us," *without* the explicit corollary that they were *not* written for the Jews.[50] On occasion, however, the verses are used with the full negative rhetorical regalia that we saw in *Peri Archon*. Such is the case, for example, in *Gen. hom.* III.4–6, which treats the circumcision of Abraham.[51] Section 3 of the homily establishes the text to be considered, first by citing in brief the significant events (for this sermon) of Genesis chapters 12–17 (exegetical step one), and then by discussing the significance of the narrative sequence (exegetical step two).[52]

Section III.4 makes the transition to the meaning beyond the literal by asking a rhetorical question: Could it really be that the omnipotent God, ruler of heaven and earth, in making a covenant with the holy Abraham, actually intended that the central meaning of this covenant should be circumcision of his foreskin? The exegetical problem, acknowledges Origen, is Gen 17:13: "My covenant shall be *upon your flesh*." Origen's implied answer is "No, of course not!" – it would be beneath God's dignity to be so obsessed. However, says Origen, "these indeed are the only things in which the masters and teachers of the synagogue place the glory of the saints."[53] The phrase "masters and teachers of the synagogue," associates contemporary Jewish interpreters with the literalism we have already seen excoriated in *Peri Archon*.

The remainder of sections 4–6 is construed as a dispute between the Jews and the Church. The Church's "honorable" spiritual understanding of true circumcision as circumcision of the heart, built upon Paul's teaching in Phil 3:2–3 and Rom 2:28–29, is brought as a "more appropriate" (*dignius*) understanding of circumcision among the "saints and friends of God" than "a pruning of the flesh" (*carnis obtruncatio*).[54] At III.5, Origen begins his spiritual interpretation in earnest. Asking for the prayerful help of his hearers, he states that the exegetical task at hand is that of refuting not only "the Jews" but also some Christians (such as the Ebionites) who continue to insist on observance of physical circumcision.[55] He then brings forth further scriptural passages which use circumcision/uncircumcision in a figurative sense.[56] At each juncture he expresses and refutes supposed objections by "the Jews" and sets out the difficulties these passages would cause the Jews if they read them the way they read this story of Abraham.

Interestingly, when Origen discusses Jer 6:10, he refuses to "permit" the Jews to "take refuge in our allegories which Paul taught."[57] The construction acknowledges that Jewish interpreters would read the passage figuratively, but it claims figurative interpretation as the exclusive prerogative of the Church, originating with Paul. At the end of this anti-Jewish-interpretation section, Origen again acknowledges that Jews would read these passages figuratively: "But if you refer circumcision of lips to allegory and say no less that circumcision of ears is allegorical and figurative why do you not also inquire after allegory in circumcision of the foreskin?" (*quomodo non et in circumcisione praeputii allegoriam requiritis?* Baehrens I, 45.19–20). In this argument, Paul appears as the originator of the right and reasonable method of reading such texts, even as Origen admits that his opponents on their own initiative would adopt such right and reasonable (and non-literalist) techniques.

The remainder of section 5 and section 6 give "more fitting," figurative and moral interpretations of circumcision of the ears, lips, flesh and heart, based primarily on texts from the Jewish scriptures. At the end of section 6, Origen again attacks his rhetorical Jewish opponent:

> Compare, if you please, this our account with your Jewish fables (cf. Tit 1:14) and disgusting stories (*Confer, si placet, haec nostra cum vestris Iudaicis fabuils et narrationibus foetidis*). . . . Do not even you yourself perceive and understand that this circumcision of the Church is honorable, holy, worthy of God; that that of

yours is unseemly, detestable, disgusting, presenting a thing vulgar both in condition and appearance? "And," God says to Abraham, "circumcision and my covenant shall be in your flesh" (Gen 17:13). If therefore, our life has been such that, properly joined together and united in all its members so that all our movements are performed according to the laws of God, truly "the covenant of God will be in our flesh."

The switch between second and first person is revealing, here, along with Origen's closing appeal to a church "united in all its members." The "disgusting" rhetoric is most likely aimed, again, not at "real Jews," but this time at the "Ebionites and others" who practice physical circumcision as Christians. The sermon's conclusion, section 7, presents an exhortation, drawn mainly from Paul, to let the covenant of Jesus Christ be "in our flesh," and so returning to and dispensing with the problematic Gen 17:13.[58] Thus, similar to what we found in *Peri Archon*, the rhetorical thrust against the Jews is sharpened precisely in a situation when the real target is opposing views within the church.

However, the disinheriting Paul can easily be turned directly against contemporary Jews, as this passage from the twelfth homily on Jeremiah illustrates. Fairly early in the sermon, we meet 1 Cor 10:11, as Origen reassures his readers that these words are meant spiritually for them (section 3). However, this spiritual meaning is related to an unfortunate literal sense directed against the Jews as well. In section 6, we learn that Israel's punishment brings about the salvation of others (invoking Rom 11:11); therefore, since God is good, he says, "I shall not spare, and I shall not have pity on them [Israel] in their destruction" (13:14). Section 13 (the final section of the homily) interprets Jer 13:17: "If you do not listen in a hidden manner, your soul will wail before the face of violence"):[59]

> ... If I listen to the Law, either I listen to it in a hidden manner, or I do not listen to it in a hidden manner. The Jew does not listen to the law in a hidden manner. Therefore he is outwardly circumcised, not knowing that "he is not a Jew, who is one outwardly, nor is circumcision that which is outward, in the flesh" (Rom. 2:28). But he who listens about circumcision in a hidden manner, is circumcised in secret (Rom 2:29). ... The ordinary Jew ('Ο δὲ πολὺς οὗτος Ἰουδαῖος) therefore killed the lord Jesus and is today responsible for the murder of Jesus because he did not listen to either the law or the prophets in a hidden manner. ...

Here, the citation of Rom 2:28–29 comes to describe the reading practices that led to and *continue* to lead to the murder of Jesus. Later in the section, Origen goes on to relate this insight on sinful Jewish reading to the "Jewish condition" of his day, compared with that of former times:

"and your eyes shall drop tears because the Lord's flock has been crushed" (Jer 13:17, end). If the Lord's former flock has been crushed because "they judged themselves unworthy" (cf. Acts 13:46), how much the more should the "wild olive branch" (Rom 11:17) fear being crushed if it fails in love and faith. The rhetorically presumed permanent destruction of the Jewish people provides the object lesson to the "luke-warm" among Origen's flock. Although Origen is not the first to level the charge of murdering Jesus,[60] this passage contains an ominous concatenation of the themes of past and continuing responsibility for that murder, permanent disinheritance from being God's flock, and consequent lowly political estate, all founded here on Jewish inability (or stubborn refusal?) to interpret scripture properly.

IV. Conclusions

Origen's synthetic reading of Paul in *Peri Archon* succeeds beyond Paul's own intention, in aligning the Jews as a people with "the letter that kills" (2 Cor 3:6). In *Peri Archon*'s theological picture, the Jews distort even the legitimate meanings of the "bodily sense" of scripture; what is more, since the true promises of scripture deal with spiritual and not historical realities, the Jews never have been the true heirs to these promises. The true heirs are "Israel according to the spirit." In the more complex cultural situation of Caesarea, Origen learns to value traditions "from the Hebrews" as tools toward clarifying the philological sense of the text. Nevertheless, his hermeneutical method, which ultimately controls his deployment of exegetical materials, continues to be driven by the polemical and Pauline-based opposition between literalist (Jewish) and spiritual (Christian, Logos-centered) interpretation. Scholarly contacts with rabbis and the usefulness of rabbinic interpretation notwithstanding, the "masters and teachers of the synagogue" continue to appear as Origen's interpretive arch-enemies, and "Jewish interpretation" remains synonymous with literalist reading, alienated from and deleterious to the spiritual sense when mistaken for the deepest meaning of scripture.

Origen's positive/negative "rhetorics of Jewish interpretation" has a dual rhetorical function which serves a single hermeneutical aim. In Alexandria, especially in *Peri Archon,* the rhetorical opposition between Israel according to the flesh and Israel according to the spirit functions primarily, I have argued, to rescue the "Old Testament" from Marcionite dismissal and Gnostic distortion. In Caesarea, this rhetorical construction comes to serve a different primary purpose. The Caesarean works presume the hermeneutical replacement of fleshly Israel by spiritual Israel, a replacement which is only tentatively proffered in *Peri Archon*. Origen's invocation of "Hebrew" exegetical authorities domesticates "useful" Jewish interpretation, making him the

authoritative tradent of "Hebrew" exegesis to his Christian flock. His
dismissal of the "masters and teachers of the Synagogue" as proponents
of "Jewish literalism" at the same time delegitimizes contemporary
rabbinic interpreters (and "the Synagogue" as their locus of operation)
as authorities whose teachings and practices his congregants might
follow. In both cultural situations, Origen's rhetorics of Jewish interpretation: 1) creates the theological basis for a unified hermeneutical
approach to the Old and New Testaments; and 2) functions to control
the appeal of external beliefs and practices for insiders, for those within
Origen's church.

The authoritative Paul who emerges both in *Peri Archon* and in subsequent exegetical works is more consonant with (and probably influential in shaping) the emerging patristic mindset of the early third century
than with the first century Apostle. The Paul who disinherits literalist
"Israel according to the flesh" in favor of "Israel according to the spirit"
provides a consistent (if unfortunate!) theological platform for the
attempts of later Christian writers to come to terms with the refusal of
the Jews to stay disinherited.

---

[1] To cite just three examples: Krister Stendahl, *Final Account: Paul's Letter to the
Romans* (Minneapolis: Fortress, 1995); Stanley Stowers, *A Rereading of Romans:
Justice, Jews and Gentiles* (New Haven: Yale University Press, 1994); John Gager,
Reinventing Paul (Oxford and New York: Oxford University Press, 2000). I want
to offer a special note of thanks here to Professor Stendahl, from whom I have
long benefitted as student and as reader, and whose *Paul Among Jews and Gentiles*
first articulated for me the urgency of the task of rethinking Paul (*Paul Among
Jews and Gentiles and Other Essays* [Philadelphia: Fortress, 1976]).

[2] This schema is laid out in chapter two of my dissertation, *"Peri Pascha*: Passover
and the Displacement of Jewish Interpretation Within Origen's Exegesis" (Th.D.
diss., Harvard University Divinity School, 1997).

[3] Origen went to Rome in ca. 215, for perhaps two years. For the chronology of
Origen's life and works see Pierre Nautin, *Origène: Sa vie et son oeuvre*
(Christianisme Antique 1; Paris: Beauchesne, 1977); Joseph W. Trigg, *Origen: The
Bible and Philosophy in the Third-Century Church* (Atlanta: John Knox, 1983;
London: SCM, 1985) essentially adopts Nautin's chronology for the English-
reading public. While in Rome, Origen may have heard Hippolytus speak (cf.,
Jerome, *Vir. ill.* 61). Aside from that, we know no specifics of the visit. However,
during the second century, Rome became the home of both Marcion and Valentinus,
and important successors of theirs. It was also, at the turn of the second century,
home to a feisty group of "adoptionist" Christians who, among other things,
admired the text-critical practices of Galen and produced numerous and
contradictory editions of biblical texts (see Eusebius, *EH*, V.28) Robert M. Grant,
Heresy and Criticism: The Search for Authenticity in Early Christian Literature
(Louisville: Westminster/John Knox, 1993), devotes the bulk of his book (chapters
three through seven) to heterodox critics based in Rome. All of Origen's
Alexandrian commentaries – on Psalms, Genesis, Lamentations, the Gospel of
John – as well as his text critical apparatus, the Tetrapla/Hexapla, can be cast as
responses to the heterodox critical challenge Origen might have met on this trip.

[4] Nautin has argued on the basis of internal evidence that Origen preached all of
his sermons during one three-year stint in Caesarea, which he dates to about 239–
242 (*Origène*, 389–409, esp. 403–405). This contradicts the picture presented by
Eusebius, who has Origen preaching throughout his career but only allowing his

sermons to be recorded during his last years in Caesarea (after about 245; *EH* VI.36). Nautin's reconstruction is in the main persuasive, and seems to accord well with various developments in Origen's exegetical practice.

[5] Eusebius says that in his *Homilies on the Letter to the Hebrews*, Origen expresses doubt that the letter was actually written by Paul himself, and suggests that a close disciple was the author (*EH* VI.25). However, *Peri Archon* contains no such reservations. Here, Origen explicitly cites Paul or "the Apostle" when quoting passages from Hebrews. I use the term "Paul" in this paper to refer to Origen's literary construction, rather than the leaner Paul of modern scholarship.

[6] See Trigg, *Origen* (London and New York: Routledge, 1998), 15.

[7] Nautin, *Origène*, 420, 423–24, summarizes indications within Origen's writings of growing opposition to his multi-level hermeneutic within the Alexandrian church. At the same time, his reputation was such that Origen began to be summoned to other parts of the Empire to consult with interested secular authorities; not long before writing *Peri Archon*, he travelled to Arabia at the behest of the provincial governor (cf. *Origène*, 420–21, and the chronological table, 410).

[8] The fact that Origen was invited to preach there by the bishops of Caesarea and Jerusalem only made matters worse. See Nautin, *Origène*, 427–431 for a summary of the events, charges, and counter-charges that eventually led to Origen's banishment from Alexandria, spearheaded by Demetrius.

[9] English translations are drawn, with occasional modifications, from G. W. Butterworth, *Origen: On First Principles* (Introduction by Henri de Lubac; New York: Harper and Row, 1966; repr. Gloucester, MA: Peter Smith, 1973). Butterworth gives separate translations of the available Greek fragments alongside the Latin. These are most extensive for Books III and IV; I cite the Greek and its translation whenever possible. I refer to the critical edition of Henri Crouzel and Manlio Simonetti, *Origène: Traité des principes*, 5 vols. (SC 252, 253, 268, 269, 312; Paris: Cerf, 1978–1984); vol. 1 contains the text of Books I and II, vol. 3 the text of books III and IV.

[10] It seems unlikely that the Alexandrian Jewish community, which had been essentially destroyed in the Jewish revolts under Trajan, had become a strong presence once more by Origen's day. The only allusions to contemporary Jews in Origen's Alexandrian writings are references to his "Hebrew teacher," who seems to have been a Jewish convert to Christianity, transplanted from Palestine to Alexandria. (The biographical detail is supplied by Origen's later mention of this figure in *Jer. hom.* 20.2.) Only in the Caesarean works do "Hebrews" and "Jews" receive frequent mention.

[11] *Peri Archon* contains more references to Origen's Paul than to all the other New Testament writings combined. Within these references, the most numerous are to 1 Corinthians, with Romans a close second. See the scriptural index in Butterworth, *First Principles*, 340–342. *Biblia Patristica* (*Biblia Patristica: Index des citations et allusions bibliques dans la littérature patristique* [6 vols. and supplement; Paris: CNRS Editions, 1975–1995]) has a few more citations, but not enough to change the general trend.

[12] *Peri Archon* I.Preface.1.16–17: *Vnde sufficere aestimo uno hoc Pauli testimonio debere nos uit ex epistula, quam ad Hebraeos scribit. . .* The Hebrews passage speaks of Moses, and closes with the words, "accounting the reproach of Christ greater riches than the treasures of Egypt." Obviously, Origen uses this quote because of the direct link between Moses and Christ.

[13] *Peri Archon* I.Preface.1; Butterworth, 1; Crouzel and Simonetti, 1:76–79.

[14] In *Peri Archon* II.4–5, Origen develops at some greater length this Paul who defends the unity of the law and the revelation in Christ; see discussion below.

[15] Rom 7:14 appears only in allusions in *Peri Archon*, (I.Preface.8; IV.2.4 in alliance with Hebr. 10:1). Occasionally in later works it appears in full Pauline dress as an authorizing statement, e.g. *Ex. hom.* II.1–2. In *CMt.* XI.14 (on Mt 15:10–20),

Origen juxtaposes Rom 7:14, 12 with 2 Cor 3:6 to contrast Jesus' spiritual interpretation of the law with the Pharisee's 'death-bringing' one; he extends the Pharisees' practice to the mistaken (contemporary) notions of "the Jews" on holiness.

[16] Cf. Ptolemy, *Letter to Flora*; critical edition: Gilles Quispel, *Ptolémée, Lettre à Flora: Analyse, texte critique, traduction, commentaire et index grec*, (2nd ed.; SC 24 *bis*; Paris: Cerf, 1966); English translation in Bentley Layton, *The Gnostic Scriptures: A New Translation with Annotations and Introductions* (Garden City: Doubleday, 1987), 306–315. Layton speaks of the role of Paul as a foundational authority for Valentinian tradition (303). Ptolemy offers a multi-level hermeneutic for the books of Moses, based on a notion of multiple authorship (for which he names "the Savior" as primary authority). He asserts that the ritual laws have only a symbolic meaning now, naming Paul as the source of this teaching and citing 1 Cor 5:7. Then he notes that Paul also taught the threefold division of the law: Eph 2:15 speaks of the part of the law which is now to be abolished and Rom 7:12 denotes the part of the law which is "not interwoven with the inferior" and continues to stand, "fulfilled" by the Savior (Mt 5:17; see *Letter* 33.5.8–15, 33.6.4–6).

[17] Trigg, *Origen*, 33. See *Peri Archon* IV.2.4. Origen gives Prov 22:20–21 as his scriptural basis for the threefold division of the levels of scriptural meaning.

[18] See Karen Jo Torjesen, *Hermeneutical Procedure and Theological Method in Origen's Exegesis* (Patristische Texte und Studien 28; Berlin: De Gruyter, 1986), 43 and notes thereto, who argues that these terms represent stages rather than fixed states, against a background of mixed opinion in prior scholarship.

[19] Annewies van den Hoek, "The Concept of σῶμα τῶν γραφῶν in Alexandrian Theology" (*StPatr* 19 [1989]: 250–254), traces to Philo the application of the term σῶμα to the scriptures, but observes that it is Origen who transforms the concept of the "body" and "soul" of scripture into a hermeneutical construct central to (Christian) scriptural interpretation.

[20] *Hermeneutical Procedure*, 68–69, with a clearer summary statement on 138. It should be noted that all of the texts analyzed by Torjesen were written following *Peri Archon* and after Origen's move to Caesarea. The paucity of Alexandrian period writings mitigates against drawing firm conclusions, but it appears that the basic exegetical framework was already in place in the earlier Alexandrian works, although perhaps less rhetorically elaborate than in those written after *Peri Archon*.

[21] In *Contra Celsum* VII.20, Origen invokes Philo (under the rubric "some of our predecessors") as the source of his own hermeneutical premise that "the law has a twofold interpretation, one literal (πρὸς ῥητόν) and the other spiritual (πρὸς διάνοιαν)." Philo uses these technical terms as rhetorical markers throughout his work; see *Spec.* I.287 for a statement of the hermeneutical relationship between them. For *Contra Celsum*, see Marcel Borret, ed., *Origène: Contre Celse* (5 vols.; SC 132, 136, 147, 150, 227; Paris: Cerf, 1967–1976); ET: Henry Chadwick, *Origen: Contra Celsum* (Cambridge: Cambridge University Press, 1965).

[22] Torjesen, *Hermeneutical Procedure*, 144. These are the terms, suggests Torjesen, by which Origen distinguishes the spiritual sense in general from the literal meaning of the text. The transitional marker ἀναγωγή is particularly important, as indicating "meaning which leads the soul upward;" she notes that it is not used to describe an exegetical procedure prior to Origen: "This implies that Origen developed and introduced a term to express the theological character of exegesis because the available hellenistic terms were inadequate" (144, n. 107).

[23] Ibid., 145. We might understand τὰ πνευματικά as deriving from Paul; in addition to Rom 7:14, note 1 Cor 2:13, another favorite authorizing prooftext.

[24] *Hermeneutical Procedure*, 41–43. Pagan grammarians likewise understood their task as moving from textual criticism to the "lesson" of the text; Origen has transformed the pagan procedure by casting it in a Christian theological

framework. For a study of Origen's exegetical practice within its Hellenistic context, see Bernhard Neuschäfer, *Origenes als Philologe* (2 vols.; Schweizerische Beiträge zur Altertumswissenschaft 18; Basel: Friedrich Reinhardt, 1987).

[25] Cf. IV.2.4, where Origen quotes 1 Cor 10:4 to prove that Christ is the spiritual reality of which the Septuagint's historical narratives are the figures.

[26] Origen's disparaging use of "Hebrews" here is an anomaly. In his Caesarean works, he consistently uses "Hebrew/s" as a term of exegetical authority, generally to introduce a rabbinic interpretation, while "the Jews" and other circumlocutions signal polemical contexts. In *Peri Archon*, this rhetorical distinction has not yet been worked out.

[27] This is a standard Christian polemical reading of this verse, found also, for example, in Justin (cf. *Dialogue with Trypho* 52–54; 120.

[28] 1 Cor 1:29, the text under transformation, reads: ὅπως μὴ καυχήσηται πᾶσα σάρξ ἐνώπιον τοῦ Θεοῦ. "No flesh," meaning no human being, becomes "no Jew."

[29] In *Peri Archon* I.1.2, Origen quotes 2 Cor 3:6 and 15–17, in opposition to Christians who understand literally the biblical metaphors that describe God. Cf. also III.5.1, where Origen calls the letter itself a "veil for profound and mystical doctrines." Neither of these contexts is directed explicitly against Jews.

[30] *Peri Archon* IV.2.6: πνευματικὴ δὲ διήγησις τῷ δυναμένῳ ἀποδεῖξαι, ποίων ἐπουρανίων ὑποδείγματι καὶ σκιᾷ οἱ κατὰ σάρκα Ἰουδαῖοι ἐλάτρευον, καὶ τίνων μελλόντων ἀγαθῶν ὁ νόμος ἔχει σκιάν. The translation is slightly altered from Butterworth.

[31] At its first appearance, in Book I.1.4, Hebr 8:5 is combined with Jn 4:21–24 to show that "those who worshiped in Jerusalem" worshiped neither in spirit nor in truth. See also II.6.7. At IV.3.12 Hebr. 8:5 is used more strictly as a hermeneutical principle.

[32] Origen gives one further example, Rom 11:4, quoting 1 Kings 19:18, to show that not only the books of Moses, but also "the rest of the history" may be subjected to the same kind of figurative interpretation.

[33] As we recall, this is the type of error for which Origen has faulted the gnostics and simple Christians, although they are not here identified by either label. Grant cites this passage as reflecting some of the criticisms set forth by the Marcionite Apelles (*Heresy and Criticism*, 76).

[34] These labels surface frequently in Origen's broadsides against "Jewish interpretation" (e.g., *Lev. hom.* IV.7, where he applies them to the "Jewish teachers' " literal reading of Lev 6:8; and through the remainder of this section of *Peri Archon*). It seems, too, that they figured in Marcionite criticism of the Jewish scriptures themselves; cf. Origen's *Gen. hom.* II.2, where he invokes a Jewish tradition in answer to Apelles' criticisms of the story of Noah's ark, and expresses the hope that his argument will suffice "against those who endeavor to impugn the Scriptures of the Old Testament as containing certain things which are impossible and irrational" (. . .*adversum eos dicta sint, qui impugnare scripturas veteris testamenti nituntur tamquam impossibilia quaedam et irrationabilia continentes*). Note that, on the one hand, Origen exculpates the scriptures of charges of irrationality brought against the text itself, by making such passages the "stumbling blocks" which point to the higher meaning; on the other hand, he retains these terms for his own polemic against the reading practices of the Jews.

[35] These are the setting of a boundary for travel on the Sabbath, and a discussion of what constitutes carrying. Rulings related to both of Origen's examples may be found in mishnaic sources (on boundaries, *m. Sotah* 5:3; *m. Eruvin* 4:3, 5, 7, 8; 5:7, 9; on carrying, *m. Shabbat* 6:2, 10:3).

[36] Translation slightly altered from Butterworth.

[37] It is not likely that Origen learned these interpretations from actual Jewish teachers. Both the polemical designations ("those of the circumcision," "the teachers of the

Jews") and the inclusion of the teaching of Dositheus the Samaritan on the Sabbath, to say nothing of the historical setting of *Peri Archon*, make it likely that Origen has inherited this set of examples from traditional Christian anti-Jewish polemic.

[38] Most of the examples are taken from the gospels, from sayings of Jesus (Mt 5:28–29, 39; Mt 10:10/Lk 10:4) The single example given for the Apostle is Paul's directive in 1 Cor 7:18, that one who is circumcised should not try to "remove the marks of circumcision" (ἐπισπάομαι). Origen finishes his discussion of this "impossibility" (and closes section 3) with reference to the "shame" (ἀσχημοσύνη) which is felt by most people to attach to "having been circumcised" (περιτετμῆσθαι). Thus, the rhetorical implication of the section is that in the New Testament itself, problematic aspects of the literal meaning are somehow connected to the shameful practices of "those of the circumcision."

[39] Origen sets his interpretation of this verse explicitly against that of the Ebionites, who "suppose that Christ came especially to the Israelites after the flesh" (IV.3.8). It appears from his manner of highlighting the verse that this was a key prooftext for some "Ebionite" Christians to validate their (continuing) assumption of Jewish practices.

[40] IV.3.8: . . .εἰ Παύλου ὡς θεοῦ ἀκούμεν καὶ σοφίαν φθεγγομένου.

[41] The lengthy remainder of chapter three goes on to suggest the typology implied by other historical place names and persons in scripture (sections 9–11), as well as the Exodus from Egypt (sections 12–13). The concluding sections 14–15 offer some remarks on the awesome task of trying to fathom the highest spiritual meanings of scripture. These sections assume the substitution of "Israel according to the spirit" for "Israel according to the flesh."

[42] The extant Greek text stops at the end of IV.3.11, which means that this discussion and etymology exist only in Rufinus' translation. The same etymology appears earlier in Rufinus' translation in section eight, in place of the citation of Romans 9:8 ("it is not the children of the flesh that are the children of God"), which is found in the Greek. The form of the citation in IV.3.8 mirrors that of *Num. hom.* 11.4. Whether or not the earlier allusion has been added, it is interesting that both contexts make or presume a connection between the negatives of Rom 9:6, 8, and the Philonic etymology. In Philo's works this definition is often associated with the notion of descent into and exodus from Egypt as an allegory for the journey of the soul, as it is here in *Peri Archon* IV.3.12.

[43] "Origen on the Jews," in *Christianity and Judaism*, ed. Diana Wood (Studies in Church History 29; Oxford: Blackwell, 1992), 1–13; see 10–13, esp. p. 12. McGuckin draws attention to Origen's theological construction of anti-Judaism by highlighting Origen's reshaping of New Testament polemical passages on Jews and Judaism. He concludes that Origen has "edited out" positive NT references to Jews, particularly in his appropriation of Paul.

[44] C. Blanc, ed. and trans. *Origène: Commentaire sur Saint Jean*, 5 vols. (SC 120, 157, 222, 290, 385. Paris: Cerf, 1966–1992. Translations of Book I are taken from Trigg, *Origen*, 104–149.

[45] The commentary was commissioned by Origen's patron and student Ambrosius, "truly a man of God and a man in Christ, hastening to be spiritual and no longer fleshly" (*CJn* I.9, translation slightly altered from Trigg). Ambrosius, who considered himself to have been rescued by Origen's thoughtful Christianity from the lure of gnosticism, requested Origen to write the commentary for his students, in refutation of the commentary recently written by the Valentinian Heracleon.

[46] Most of Origen's exegetical works – commentaries, treatises, *scholia* (exegetical notes on individual biblical verses) – were aimed at scholarly readers and students. His sermons were delivered orally to the more intellectually mixed audience of the Caesarean congregation; stenographers took notes of these oral performances, which then were (more or less) edited into the form of the written homilies that remain to us. Thus the homilies had a double rhetorical life as oral presentations

(to potentially widely diverse audiences) and as study documents. See Trigg, *Origen: The Bible and Philosophy*, 176–177.

⁴⁷ The most complete recent discussion of the connections between Origen's citations and known rabbinic traditions is found in N. R. M. De Lange, *Origen and the Jews* (Cambridge: Cambridge University Press, 1976). On pp. 25–32, De Lange discusses the connotations of the term "Hebrew" as used in Origen's exegetical works.

⁴⁸ In, e.g., *Ex. hom.* V.5; *Ezek. hom.* IV.8; *Isa. hom.* IX.1, he says he has "heard a Hebrew expound" a particular tradition; in *Gen. hom.* II.2; *Sel. in Ex.* 10:27; *Sel. in Ps.* (*PG* XII.1080 C) he says "has learned" from a Hebrew, or that a Hebrew has transmitted a tradition to him.

⁴⁹ A textbook example is *Gen. hom.* II, on Noah's ark where interpretations "from the ancients/Hebrews" are brought against the criticisms of the Marcionite Apelles (cited by name).

⁵⁰ For, example, *Ex. hom.* II.1, using Rom 7:14 and 1 Cor 10:11; *Ex. hom.* 8:2 using 1 Cor 10:18 and Rom 2:29. It is interesting that in the latter context, Origen does *not* make an explicit negative statement about the "Jews according to the flesh."

⁵¹ Critical edition: W. A. Baehrens, ed., *Origenes Werke 6, Homilies zum Hexateuch in Rufins Übersetzung*, I: *Die Homilien zu Genesis, Exodus, und Leviticus* (GCS 29; Leipzig: Hinrichs, 1920). The English translation is taken, with modifications as noted, from *Origen: Homilies on Genesis and Exodus*, trans. Ronald E. Heine (FC 71; Washington: Catholic University of America Press, 1982).

⁵² Origen pays special attention to the fact that after leaving his father's house (Genesis 12) Abram merits being called both "Abraham"(Gen 17:5) and "presbyter" (Gen 18:11), and notes that these appellations coincide with his acceptance of the covenant and of circumcision.

⁵³ Baehrens I, 43.7–15: . . . *requirere volo, si omnipotens Deus, qui coeli ac terrae dominatum tenet, volens testamentum ponere cum viro sancto, in hoc summam tanti negotii collocabat, ut praeputium carnis eius ac futurae ex eo sobolis circumcideretur. . . . Hocine erat quod »coeli ac terrae Dominus« ei, quem e cunctis mortalibus solum delegerat, aeterni testamenti munere conferebat? Haec enim sunt sola, in quibus magistri et doctores synagogae sanctorum gloriam ponunt.*

⁵⁴ Origen supports his citations of Paul by quoting Ezra 44:9 and Jer 9:26, both of which contrast uncircumcision of the flesh and uncircumcision of the heart.

⁵⁵ The Latin verbal form translated as "refuting" is *revincendi*; Origen construes the exegesis throughout in disputation mode. Twice in the very short space of this transitional passage, Origen alludes to some Christians, as well as the Jews, as those whose exegetical understanding he must refute. At the end of section 6, Origen indicates that his preceding figurative interpretation should serve to confound all those (both Jew and Christian are implied) who trust in circumcision of the flesh, as well as edifying the Church.

⁵⁶ Specifically Jer 6:10 (uncircumcised ears); Ex 4:13, 10, conflated with 6:30 (uncircumcised lips).

⁵⁷ Baehrens I, 45.3–4: *Confugere enim tibi ad allegorias nostras, quas Paulus docuit, non permitto.*

⁵⁸ The exhortation presents a string of quotations recast as appropriate in the first person singular or plural: 1 Jn 4:2, 1 Cor 4:20, Col 3:5, 2 Cor 4:10, 2 Tim 2:12, Rom 6:5, 19; Gal 2:20, 6:17; Rom 8:35, 10:9–10; Mt 5:16, Gal 1:5 (doxology). The next to last sentence mentions distinguishing "ourselves" from the Jews, "who think they confess God with the mark of circumcision alone, but deny him with their deeds."

⁵⁹ LXX: ἐὰν δὲ μὴ ἀκούσητε, κεκρυμμένως κλαύσεται ἡ ψυχὴ ἡμῶν ἀπὸ προσώπου ὕβρεως. Origen reads the κεκρυμμένως as going with ἀκούσητε, but the sense of LXX and Hebrew is "if you do not listen, my soul will wail in secret . . . ."

⁶⁰ Cf. Melito of Sardis, *Peri Pascha*, par. 96, where deicide is specified.

A Response: Origen's Christian Platonist Readings of Romans

Peter Gorday

———— ◆ ————

I. In this paper the author offers a sketch of the way in which Origen seems to have adapted, first in the *Peri Archon*, and then in the commentaries of his Caesarean period, the language of Pauline antithesis for his own scriptural hermeneutic. [She lists these as flesh/spirit, letter/spirit, etc., but for a specifically Origenian formulation see also *ComRom*, I.1 (Praef.), ed. Hammond Bammel, p.41, 11. 93-98, as well.] Beginning with comments in the preface and in the fourth book of *Peri Archon*, she shows how Origen engaged in "transformative readings" of various Pauline texts. Examples are Heb. 11.24-26 (PA I, pref. 1.16-17) on the way in which Christ speaks through Moses, or Rom. 7.14 (PA I, pref. 8, IV. 2.4) where Paul affirms the "spiritual" nature of the Law, and I Cor. 2.6f (PA IV. 2.4) where the mature believer is the one graced with spiritual, rather than carnal, knowledge. The upshot for Origen in the use of such passages was not only the strong assertion of Paul's apostolic authority, but also his own three-fold biblical hermeneutic of body/soul/ spirit, which served to exalt the "spiritual sense" of Scripture at the expense of the "literal sense." The problem with this literal sense, typical of Jews, heretics, and many well-intentioned, but ignorant ("simple") believers, was, for Origen, in its obtuseness to the central dogmas of God and Christ and the Church. A critical element thus in Origen's appropriation of Paul was the use of texts which could be seen to imply a disparagement of this "literal" sense of Scripture, numerous passages such as Rom. 2.28-29 ("true Jew" and "false Jew"), Rom. 9.6 (Israel "according to the flesh," and "Israel according to the spirit"), Gal. 4.26 (the earthly Jerusalem and the Jerusalem above), etc., serving the purpose nicely. Ultimately, argues Ruth Clements, Origen settled on I Cor. 10.18 and the contrast of "Israel according to the flesh" and "Israel according to the spirit" as "his hermeneutical key" and the "unique exegetical move" of his project. In doing so, he disinherited, with great and clear decisiveness, the Jews as readers of the Scriptures.

Indeed, the thrust of the author's argument is the claim that Origen accomplished this disinheritance of Jewish interpretation by means of a conscious rhetorical strategy. With his artful use of Paul he was able both to appropriate Jewish exegesis of Scripture in order to refute competing Gnostic interpretations, but also to depreciate that same Jewish exegesis finally as "literal" and thus unworthy of the higher spiritual reading. This strategy, begun in *Peri Archon* and continued in the Commentary on John, then remerged in the commentaries of the Caesarean period, where Origen showed signs of contact with contemporary Jews. The hallmark of the strategy repeatedly was to engage in a polemic against Jewish literalism, which is then a foil for mounting a simultaneous strike against heretics or lukewarm believers, who can be accused of being "Jews." Thus, a "dual rhetorical function" served for Origen a "single hermeneutical aim," that of rescuing Hebrew Scripture from heretics, as well as from contemporary Rabbinic interpreters, by exposing through the contrast of fleshly Israel and spiritual Israel the errors contained in literal readings of Scripture. Origen had thereby established a powerful way of reading Scripture, a way which served purposes both of internal social control, as well as of external defense – just the tool, in short, for centuries of ecclesiastical tyranny!

II. Now, what seems to me most true and most helpful in Ruth Clements' argument is its sense for the way Origen's hermeneutic of Scripture consistently, and with discernible continuity, shapes his entire work. There is the implication at least that its influence on later Christian interpretation has been massive (witness Henri de Lubac's work). Origen truly stands in the middle of the headwaters of the "spiritual" interpretation of Scripture and the countless debates, for better or worse, engendered by the concept. Equally compelling is her awareness that Origen's hermeneutical theorizing and application somehow grows out of, even as it seriously modifies, Paul's own theological agony about how to read scripture. Origen's hermeneutics, however esteemed, are certainly an attempt to be faithful to Paul and his convoluted reflection about "Israel." Reading Israel in Romans, and throughout Paul's letters, seems to have been just as important and pressing for Origen as it is, for quite different reasons, for modern interpreters.

Ruth Clements makes, as well, an original contribution, it seems to me, with her development of Origen's polemical context and his consequent rhetorical strategizing to meet the demands of that context. His use of various terms to disparage and dismiss adversaries is vivid, rich, and pointed, often cutting in multiple directions simultaneously. She is absolutely right in contending that he "disinherits," and I might say "dis-entitles," his opposition. There is no question but that he was engaged, as were all parties at the time, in a battle for control of the interpretation of Scripture. This is the period of the creation of Scrip-

tural canons for both Christian and Jewish communities, with the en-
tailed process, as well, of establishing norms of interpretation. Intricately involved, in addition, were the disputes about orthodoxy shaking
both the Christian and Jewish communities. A great many polemical
things were said in the heat of conflict (and domestic conflict is the
worst), with denunciations hurled in all directions. A great deal of
smoke was generated by these forest fires, and the modern historian
must not be misled by its thickness into taking everything at face value.

The author is also quite right, nonetheless, in (what I think is) her
determination to hold Origen accountable for what is at times his
massive and contemptuous dismissal of Jewish interpretation and
practice. She gathers abundant testimony to this side of Origen's
expressions, though, in the process, she then chooses to downplay the
possibility that at other times, and on certain levels, Origen operated in
the posture of authentic (not feigned!) gratitude to Jewish wisdom precisely as Jewish. She somewhat saves Paul himself from anti-Jewish
indictment by suggesting that Origen's picture of the Apostle is purely
and simply part of a patristic construct, but she does not acknowledge
that Origen's struggle with the "letter" is also in part Paul's as well, as
I believe it was.

In fact, both Paul and Origen stood in a deep stream of literary and
theological development that swirled around issues of the truth-status
and correct interpretation of "classic" texts. Origen's hermeneutic is
not a piece of anti-Jewish argument in unambiguously simple terms, but
rather was part-and-parcel of the widespread grappling for typological
models of scriptural interpretation, so that authoritative texts would
"live" for present, and ever-changing, contexts. An arch-figure in the
Jewish portion of this history is Philo of Alexandria – an obvious influence acknowledged by Clements, but quickly minimized. Origen was in
this regard preceded in the Christian orbit by Irenaeus of Lyons, as
well as a series of Gnostic and Jewish-Gnostic interpreters, and
then paralleled later by the Antiochene interpreters, beginning with
Diodore of Tarsus, who were in their own way just as committed to
symbolic exegesis. What we can see is that the development of these
symbolic and allegorical types of interpretation was not just an effort to
dismiss and disinherit, but also a means of "making meaning" in the
light of current experience. Here the Rabbis were just as inclined to
engage in typology and scholastic extenuation of the texts as anyone
else. It is important to see that at the same time Origen dismissed Jewish interpretations as "literal," he borrowed from them, and, even more,
engaged in forms of interpretation shared by all, even if they came to
different conclusions. I believe that he in fact recognized elements of
kinship here, and thus was quick to acknowledge shared horizons
between "Moses" and "Christ," particularly at the level of ethical inter-

pretation, when circumstances warranted (as in the *Contra Celsum*).

In an even larger perspective, moreover, there is the question of Origen's Platonism (and some would say his Gnosticism as well). These obviously are major players in any assessment of his view of the status of the "literal sense" of Scripture. I have argued elsewhere that in fact, and within the parameters of Platonism, he has profound respect for the "literal sense." At the risk of great oversimplification, he was constantly faced with the problem of dealing with the fact that "higher" levels of reality can be experienced only in, through, and by means of concrete embodiments. All of his manifest conflict with Valentinian Gnosticism makes sense only in terms, as Clements acknowledges, of his determination to uphold free will, but the essential import of embodied existence with its moral drama is thereby necessarily included as well. A major portion of Origen's use of Paul in Romans, as this appears in *Peri Archon*, is in III.1, with its elaborate exposition of the theme of God's hardening of Pharoah's heart. Drawn both from Exodus and Romans, the theme allowed Origen to argue his case for the nature of divine *pronoia* and *paideusis* both in generating the terms of moral evil and in holding humans accountable for it. God's punishing of Pharoah stands, thought Origen, as a kind of window into the mysterious working of divine grace as it interacts with human freedom. But, this is tantamount to saying that the drama of the soul and its transformation is central to Origen's hermeneutic.

Thus, as his Platonism suggests, and as his actual exegetical practice testifies, with its ever present concern for the moral import of Scripture, Origen seems to have focused not on dogmas for their own sake, but for their moral value (in the sense of the building up of the soul). Here he learned constantly from the Rabbis (his use of the wisdom literature is omnipresent), even as he attempted to wrest Scripture away from them. Technically, therefore, it may be correct to say, as Clement does, that the literal sense represents literalism and the "muffling" of the Logos in no other way.

I suspect that we cannot ourselves read Israel in Paul, or in Origen, apart from our current context. Today, everything is sharply, very sharply, polarized, as daily reports remind us, and a deeply anti-Jewish Origen makes sense. Some years ago, however, and from Jerusalem University, a Jewish scholar, Ephraim Urbach, argued that Origen, in his allegorical interpretation of the Song of Songs in terms of the journey of the soul toward God, had learned deeply from the Caesarean Rabbis [Script. Hieros. 22 (1971), 247-275]. The mood was more irenic, more conciliatory, when Urbach wrote, and an ecumenical, more inward, spirit reigned. Hopefully, those times will return, with added justice, and with the advantage of all that we have learned in the meantime from interpreters of Origen like Ruth Clements.

SEVEN

Jews and Gentiles in Origen's *Commentarii in Epistulam Pauli ad Romanos*

Sze-kar Wan

———— ◆ ————

In spite of his penchant for what modern critics would call wild allegorization, Origen's discussion of Jews and gentiles in his *Commentary on Romans* is surprisingly sensitive and historical. Commenting on the phrase, "to the Jew first, then the Greek" (Rom 2:10), for example, Origen argues that even though Jews and gentiles are ultimately judged by the same criterion of faith in Jesus Christ, Jews nevertheless stand in priority over the gentiles because of the glory, honor, and peace which came into the world through their reception of the Law from God. By their possession of the Law, Jews must be rewarded somehow if they hold fast to it – even though they still could not receive eternal life because they do not have faith in Christ. Thus begins Origen's nuanced discussion of the relationship between Jews and gentiles in his *Commentary on Paul's Epistle to the Romans*. This paper will attempt to trace Origen's view of the Jewish-gentile relationship through an examination of a few of the key passages in the *Commentary*. Because of the restricted scope of this paper, what conclusion it can draw will of necessity be limited.

Priority of the Jews
"To the Jew first, then to the Greek"
(Romans 2:9b-10)

Commenting on Paul's oft-repeated phrase in Romans, "To the Jew first, then to the Greek," which is used twice in succession in Rom 2:9b-10, Origen first affirms the priority of the Jews in *Heilsgeschichte* by citing Rom 3:2 ("First, to them [*viz.* the Jews] were the words of God entrusted") and Bar 4:4 ("Blessed are we, Israel, because we know what please God"). Then he makes a distinction between "knowing God" and "knowing the *will* of God" based on the Parable of the Watchful Servants:

> "The servant who knows the will of his master and does not do it
> will deservedly receive great beatings" (Luke 12:47) – that is the
> Jews. "He who does not know him" – the Greek, that is, the gen-
> tile – will receive little beating" (v. 48a). There is a difference, there-
> fore, between knowing God and knowing the will of God. Even the
> gentiles can know God "from the creation of the world through
> the creatures that were made and his eternal power and divinity"
> (Rom 1:20). His will, however, cannot be known except through
> the Law and the Prophets.[1]

That would explain why Paul would assert that the Jews would receive
punishments, inasmuch as they would also receive rewards, before the
gentiles in Rom 2:9b-10.

This priority granted to the Jews establishes a foundation of respect
for the Jews that is characteristic of Origen's efforts in the *Commentary*
in general. In the immediate context it is used to refute a *naive* identification of "Jews" as unbelievers and "Greeks" as believers. "If he [prob-
ably meaning the Apostle Paul] were to call 'Jews'," Origen continues,
"those who are still under the Law and are not coming to Christ and
'Greeks' Christians from among gentiles who believe, he would contradict the meaning of the whole mystery (*totum mysterium*)."[2]

It is not immediately clear what Origen means exactly by *totum
mysterium* in this context. Theresia Heither is of the opinion that the
phrase represents "the essential kernel of revelation, in this case the
message of Paul,"[3] which is true in general but does little to illumine
the passage in question. An examination of Origen's ensuing discussion,
however, would lead one to understand it as an embodiment of an overall vision in which the "true Jews" reveals their heretofore hidden identity. Contrary to expectation, Origen does not discuss first the identity
of the "Jews," focusing instead on who "the first" are: "In what manner, then, are they called 'the first'?"[4] Origen's answer consists of a
series of citations from Scripture. From his use of Mt 20:16 ("The first
shall be last"), Mt 23:38 ("See, your house is abandoned as your
desert"), and the episode of the fig tree in which Jesus curses the tree to
permanent fruitlessness (Mt 21:19), he be accused of toeing the traditional *heilsgeschichtliche* line, explaining how the Jews have lost their
primary position as the first recipient of God's promise of salvation to
the gentile latecomers. His allusion to the story of Jacob and Esau (Gen
25:23) and Jacob's stealing of the first-born blessing from Esau in
Genesis 27 would seem to confirm this suspicion.[5] Two considerations,
however, argue against this reading. First, Origen does not identify
"the first" as "the Jews" throughout his citations. Second, when he does
make the identification of "the Jews," they are actually identified as
"Christians": "If, however, he names us 'Jews,' that is us Christians and
those from all races who believe, whom he says to be 'Jews in secret'
(Rom 2:29), then it remains that he calls the gentiles 'Greeks' who do

not yet believe."[6]

In this highly nuanced discussion of "Jews" and "Greeks," Origen appears to be answering several questions at the same time. On the one hand, he dismisses the facile identifications of "Jews" as non-Christians and "Greeks" as Christians. He does so by openly calling Christians "Jews" and by appealing to Paul's formulation, "Jews in secret." It would stand to reason that Origen is here arguing against a contemporary position that sees Judaism as *passé* and that it has been replaced by Christianity. Such a supercessionist view of Judaism can be easily ascribed to Marcion and his followers. Against this view, Origen insists that there are unbelievers among both Jews and gentiles.[7] Among the Jews, especially, if they could not come to Christ because of pressure from their community, they could still receive rewards provided they perform good deeds. They will not receive eternal life, for they believe only in God but not Christ; nevertheless "glory, honor, and peace" (Rom 2:10) for their works cannot perish.[8] This hedging in regard to the fate of the Jews, if one could hazard a guess, might represent a stage in the early church, at least in Origen's immediate circle, in which mission to the Jews was alive and well and which caused Origen to expect Jewish converts into the church. The parallel case of identifying "Greeks" as potential converts, when the mission to gentiles was obviously being carried out in earnest,[9] would seem to strength this case.

On the other hand, Origen lifts the Jewish-gentile distinction out of the historical realm into a much higher plane of identification. Seizing Paul's phrase "Jews in secret," Origen applies it to all Christians, thus coopting such terms as "Jews," "Judaism," "Israel" into the Christian vocabulary. As a result, Origen often answers critics who suggest that Paul was denigrating the Jews by posing whether, indeed, these criticisms by the Apostle ought not be directed against the church itself.[10] In this regard it is not clear whom Origen identifies "the first" to be. While the term appears to be referring to the Jews who came first in salvation history, it is not impossible that Origen purposely leaves the phrase ambiguous, so that one could with equal persuasiveness identify "the first" as Christians, members of the church who could easily be replaced by latecomers. The first could become last and Christians could lose their positions in the church.

Who is a True Jew?
"If you call yourself a Jew" (Romans 2:17-24)

When the true identity of the Jew is so fluid, it becomes difficult to assess Origen's statements on this issue with accuracy. To illustrate this problem, it is instructive to consider his many-faceted answers to the question, Who are the true Jews? In a lengthy disquisition on Rom

2:17-24, where Paul details the shortcomings of "the Jew." Origen first notes that Paul does not actually say, "You are a Jew" but "You *who call yourself* a Jew" in v. 17.[11] This distinction signals to him that there must be a difference between the true Jew and the one who only claims to be so. Once this is established, "Jew" can have three different identifications: as the historical Jews; as Christians who through the true circumcision, baptism, can claim to be true Jews; and as "the heretics," Christian teachers who fail to reveal the truth hidden in Scripture.[12] This division into different levels of identification should not surprise anyone familiar with Origen's exegesis, which spans the literal and allegorical, and covers everything in between. What is surprising, however, is how stereotypical, and generally ahistorical his criticisms of the historical Jews are.

The Jews' fundamental mistake, Origen contends, is that they adhere totally – but merely – to the letters of the Law. From this they conclude that they know the will of God and could boast of the ability to know and differentiate the good from the bad. Such arrogance leads them to presuming to be leaders of the blind and light to darkness. In support of these accusations, Origen cites Mt 15:14 and 6:23, but offers no independent proof otherwise. The Jews, continues Origen, presume to be teachers of the foolish and teachers of children. They publicly expounds on all things but have no real possession; that is why, according to Origen, the Apostle Paul says of them, "You teach others, but you do not teach yourself" (Rom 2:21).[13]

So far these criticisms of the Jews are remarkable only for their strictly conventional character. Other than their supposed fault of confining themselves to the literal Law – which represents a typical Origenism, the shortcomings of the Jews consist of nothing more than the standard anti-Pharisaic statements compiled from the Gospels and a repetition of Paul's enumeration of the Jews' sins in Rom 2:17-24. Origen adduces no anecdotal illustrations, no corroboration, no contemporary arguments.

His explanation of Paul's reproach that the Jews preach against stealing, but themselves steal, and that they preach against adultery, but themselves commit adultery (Rom 2:21-22) does deviate from this pattern somewhat. But even here, one sees only standard criticisms typical of most Christians, with a twist unique to Origen. The Jews "steal" in that they "suppress the arrival and presence of Christ which has radiated in the whole world," and they "commit adultery" in that they "tempt the people of God in the synagogue to commit adultery by introducing a perverted and adulterous word of teaching."[14] This is so, because they stick to the letters of the Law, seeing only the external and missing the truly essential, to the detriment of not seeing Christ in it. In support of his argument, Origen once again turns to Scripture, this time citing Ps 45:14 and Jer 13:17.[15]

The gravest "sin" of the Jews, then, according to Origen, is what stands behind Paul's word in Rom 2:23: namely, they abhor idols but themselves rob temples. This really means they "desecrate the true temple of God, which is Christ Jesus." They demolished the temple of God, but it was re-erected in three days, echoing the sentiments expressed already in John 2:19. Furthermore, they "steal from the message from the Law and the Prophets which foretell Christ," and they "hide it, so that people could neither hear nor believe in it." This, to Origen, is what Paul means in truth by their robbing the temple and defiling the temple of God.[16]

Through all this, Origen's Jewish interlocutor might as well be a make-believe figure fabricated with straws from the Gospels. Even the Jews' lack of allegorical imagination which prevents them from seeing and believing in Christ, a result of Origen's well-known need to raise interpretation to a higher, more spiritual level, is supported by a citation from Scripture: "If [a Jew] believed in Moses," paraphrasing John 5:46, "he would also believe him about whom Moses had written."[17] It is fair to say that, while Origen's criticisms of the Jews are less than complementary, they remain focused on the single point of departure between Jews and Christians: the Jews' failure to acknowledge Jesus as the Christ. He reuses standard apologetic arguments developed already in late-first-century Gospel accounts. The Gospel of John, in particular, seems useful to him, perhaps because of the bitter parting of the ways between the Johannine community and the local synagogue that stands behind that Gospel. Otherwise, Origen does not add other anti-Jewish arguments that he himself might have developed, or that might have become familiar to his immediate circle.

By contrast, the second and third identifications of "the Jew," as "Christian" and "heretic" of his day, lead Origen to rather detailed criticisms of his contemporaries. When applied to the Christians, Paul's criticisms of hypocrisy take on new meanings. A Christian teacher, writes Origen, should not demand discipline and chastity from his students, when he himself is afflicted with intemperance and lustfulness, maybe even inflamed with secret passions. To such people, Paul's statement becomes highly appropriate: "You teach others, but not yourself. You preach, 'Thou shalt not steal,' yet you yourself steal. You say, 'Thou shalt not commit adultery,' yet you yourself commit adultery."[18] Thus far, Origen's criticisms of the Christian seem general enough; intemperance, lustfulness, passion, and so on, appeared on every ancient catalogue of vices. But Origen continues with something far more concrete: "When, *as it often happens,* the gifts offered to God or a donation given to the poor has been misappropriated as one's own profit," then it is perfectly legitimate to use the Apostle's word, "You abhor idol worship, yet you rob the temple."[19] Such an illustration does not appear to be a mere generalization of vices, but represents a common, but real, problem in the second-and third-century church, that took almsgiving as part of its ministry to the poor. One could only surmise that such acts of avarice must have been frequent and when they were caught it would bring public shame to the church, something to which Origen appears to allude in the ensuing lines.[20]

Origen, however, reserves the most severe, also the most concrete, criticisms for "the heretics," who are most probably his detractors in the church. These appear to be literalists who are most different from him in exegetical method. He imputes to them stealing and adultery, because they suppress the words of God by pilfering their "inner sense" (*intellectum*) of Scripture through an "perverse interpretation," and because they introduce an "adulterous understanding of faith" (*adulterinus fidei sensus*) into the church, Christ's bride, in the royal chambers.[21] They rob the temple of costly vessels, furthermore, when they steal the "pearls of true faith from the Holy Scripture." Thus the name of God has been blasphemed among the gentiles, when they soil the pure and precious teachings of the church with erroneous teachings that are heretical and adulterous.[22]

One can conclude, then, that Origen was in contact with Christian and what he calls "heretical" errors of his days, errors that he intentionally applies the Pauline rhetoric to correct. These errors include unedifying ethical problems, church practices, abuse of authority entrusted to leaders of the church, as well as theological misappropriation and misinterpretation. His criticisms of these errors reflect a lively controversy in a real community in which Origen was actively engaged. In contradistinction, his criticisms of Judaism of his day appear to lie on a different plane. They seem theoretical and academic, reflecting a position removed from any active engagement. It would not be accurate to say that Origen has no criticism of Judaism in the *Commentary*: he criticizes the synagogue for its overdependence on the literal sense of Scripture, which results in refusing to acknowledge Christ. But other than this broad issue, Origen seems unwilling or unable to name synagogue abuses of his days. He resorts to generalizations and well-established stereotypes found in Christian writings for his illustrations, but otherwise could muster no more than the standard controversy over the person of Christ and the Jews' inability or unwillingness to read Scripture allegorically, that is Christologically. One is drawn irresistibly, therefore, to the conclusion that Origen was not engaged in any real controversy with his contemporary Jews. While he seems to keep alive the hope that they ought to recognize Jesus as Christ, he holds them in fundamental respect and esteem.[23]

What is True Circumcision?
"Circumcision of the heart" (Romans 3:29)

This tentative conclusion can be corroborated by an examination of Origen's different understandings of circumcision. In a massive excursus on the question of circumcision, Origen entertains three questions: (1) Does the commandment of circumcision in Genesis have any intrinsic value in its literal sense? (2) If it does, to whom is the commandment given and how should they obey it? (3) Does the commandment of circumcision have any transcendent, spiritual meaning beyond its literal sense?[24] To the first question regarding the intrinsic value of circumcision, Origen is unreservedly positive. He quotes at length, approvingly, the institution of circumcision in Gen 17:9-14 and God's injunction to Moses in Lev 12:1-4 that all male children be circumcised on the eighth day. He even defends the circumcision against gentile charges that it is no longer valid after Christ and against a possibly Marcionite rejection of it.[25] We can be confident of the intrinsic value of circumcision because "our Lord and savior" approved of it for coming not only from Moses but from the Father (John 7:22-23). Origen's defense of circumcision, however, should not be taken to mean any affinity or sympathy with Judaism; it is more likely part and parcel of his defense of the status of the Jewish Scripture, what eventually became his Old Testament, against his detractors.

In answering the second question, whether circumcision is still valid only for Jews, or whether it is also valid for gentile believers, Origen insists that only the physical descendants of Abraham are obligated to follow God's commandment of circumcision. God commanded Abraham in Genesis 17 to circumcise only those born in his household, even those brought into the household like slaves and bondservants (vv. 7-12), but those not part of the household are under no such obligation (vv. 12-13).[26] Origen furthers his exegesis by adducing a host of passages from Leviticus and Numbers,[27] demonstrating that, in times even before Christ, non-Jews were never required to go through circumcision. This elaborate appeal to Scripture might seem excessive. A part of this is probably owed to Origen's source, in this case Philo of Alexandria, but it is more likely motivated by his concern for the continual validity of Scripture.

What Origen is after ultimately is, of course, a spiritual understanding of circumcision. Here he follows Philo rather closely. Circumcision signifies, rather than the mere ridding of the foreskin of the flesh, a cutting away of vices and harmful desires. It is properly, therefore, a circumcision of the heart, citing Jeremiah for support.[28]

Throughout this allegorical interpretation of circumcision, however, Origen takes great care not to denigrate physical circumcision. Even as he uses it to set up an allegorical interpretation, he goes out of his way to affirm its value. In his exegesis of Rom 15:8-12, focusing especially on v. 8, "Christ has become a minister of circumcision regarding the truth of God, in order to establish the promises of the patriarchs," Origen comes up with a double meaning for circumcision. His final aim is to demonstrate that the essential and true circumcision is baptism into the death of Christ. But just as circumcision does not totally destroy the flesh but preserves it at the end, true circumcision means dying *and* rising with Christ. But even as Origen trains his allegorical sight on his final goal, he begins his exegesis with an affirmation of Christ's own physical circumcision. Christ himself was circumcised as a Jew, so as to fulfill God's commandment to Abraham, that through his seed – that is Christ – all peoples of the world will receive blessings (Gen 22:18). Those who remain under the Law, that is all Jews, can with good conscience continue their observance of the Law.[29]

How Shall They be Saved?
"I want you to understand this mystery"
(Romans 11:25)

Herein lies the ambiguity of Origen's position. While he affirms the superiority of the Jewish Law, which might represent a good in itself, he is bound still to the criterion of faith in Christ as the ultimate court of appeal. But in this regard, Origen could be said to have understood Paul perfectly, for the apostle was wrestling with the same ambiguity. Just as Paul pronounced it a "mystery" how his own kinsfolk will be saved in the endtime (Rom 11:25), Origen too argues that Israel will ultimate receive God's promise, once the full number of gentiles have come in. Origen makes his case by relying on an ingenious interpretation of Deut 32:8-9, which in the LXX reads:

ὅτε διεμέριζεν ὁ ὕψιστος ἔθνη,
ὡς διέσπειρεν υἱοὺς Αδάμ,
ἔστησεν ὅρια ἐθνῶν
κατὰ ἀριθμὸν ἀγγέλων θεοῦ,
καὶ ἐγενήθη μερὶς κυρίου λαὸς αὐτοῦ Ιακωβ,
σχοίνισμα κληρονομίας αὐτοῦ Ἰσραηλ.

When the Most High allotted the gentiles,
when he dispersed the sons of Adam,
he set boundaries of the gentiles
according to the number of *the angels* of God,
And his people Jacob became the lot of the Lord,
Israel his shared inheritance.

The crucial reading for Origen is "the angels" of God (MT reads "the Israelites"), the number of whom corresponds to the allotment of the shares given to the gentiles according to this passage. By the same token, the share of Israel remains fixed and has already been promised to all the Jews from the start. If the children of Israel held onto their share, says Origen, "it would not be possible for us gentiles to share in God's inheritance and succeed in the right of his prerogative."[30] That is why God allows a few, though certainly not all, of the members of Israel to become blind, to come under the influence of a few evil angels, with the result that they were eventually cheated out of their rightful inheritance. God could have prevented all this – so as to preserve the original allotment – but he did not, so as to preserve human freedom. At the end, some children of Israel lost their share, but their loss also created an opportunity for the gentiles and, through the gentiles, the rest of the world, so that they now have access to God's original promise. But the shutting out of the children of Israel is only temporary. When the full number of gentiles have come in, when this brief window for the rest of the world once again closes in the eschaton, Israel will return to the Lord. Thus will the first become last, for Israel who had priority in the first place, will once again claim its original inheritance in the endtime.[31]

While Origen's exegesis might leave room for much doubt, in a circuitous way, Origen has most appropriately expressed Paul's ambivalence and ambiguity towards the fate of Israel. Paul refuses to spell out the role of faith in Christ in Rom 11:25-27, falling back on the fuzzy logic of the "mystery." Origen, through an ingenious exegesis, consigns the problem to mythology. But the results are the same: both express God's faithfulness to the original covenant he established with the Jews; both give priority to the Jews in the history of salvation; both celebrate the entry of the gentiles into God's covenant; both lament the price of Israel's temporary hardening of hearts—though in Paul's case it was a matter of Israel's self-will, whereas in Origen's, unsuspecting Israel was deceived by scheming angels; and both look forward to the endtime, when Israel returns to its original heritage, once the full number of gentiles have come in.

Conclusion

The sensitivity to the Jews displayed throughout this work leads one to suspect strongly that Origen was in touch with a certain segment of the historical Jewish communities when he was writing his *Commentary to Romans,* namely the academy where other Jewish exegetes lived. It has been suggested before that Philo of Alexandria might have greatly influenced Origen. This remains a real possibility; but dependence on Philo alone cannot explain Origen's generally high esteem for Judaism, or his extensive knowledge of Jewish practices. In light of this commentary, but also his other works, notably his *Commentary on the Song of*

Songs, it is far easier to envision the possibility that Origen was engaged in a lively dialogue with his contemporary Jewish exegetes.

As for his view of the relationship between the church and synagogue, Origen remains steadfastly Christocentric, in spite of his obvious sympathy for Judaism overall. He faults the Jews for failing to rise to the spiritual level of Scripture, thus resulting in failing to see the messiahship of Jesus. But it should be emphasized that his attitude towards his Jewish interlocutors closely corresponds to his hermeneutical principles. Just as his devotion to spiritual exegesis never leads him to reject the literal meaning of Scripture, his Christocentrism never causes him to denigrate historical Judaism. Even as he is quick to criticize Judaism for not recognizing the Messiah, he is equally quick to defend it against Marconites, Gnostics, and pagans. In Origen's conception, the church-synagogue relationship resembles, more like sibling rivalry than competing religious systems.

---

[1] *Commentarii in epistulam ad Romanos* (hereafter CER) 2.7; Origen, *Commentarii in epistulam ad Romanos*, tr. and ed., Theresia Heither (6 vols.; Freiburg, etc.: Herder, 1990-1999), 1.208.15-23 (hereafter Heither). I am responsible for all translations except when noted to the contrary.

[2] CER 2.7 Heither 1.210.1-4. Here and elsewhere, Origen seems to structure his exegetical discussion of Rom 2:9b-10 -by means of a series of questions. The whole discussion of the identities of "Jew" and "Greek" is prefaced by a formulaic introduction to the problem: Verum quoniam et ad poenam et praemium Iudaeos praefert et Graecos postponit apostolus, requirendum est, quos hic Gaecos, quos Iudaeos velit intelligi [*sic*] ("In fact, as to why in regard to both punishment and praise the Apostle places the Jews before the Greeks, it is necessary to inquire [zhtevon *vel sim.*], whom he understands the Greeks, whom he understands the Jews"); Heither 1.208.24-210.1. After this opening introduction, he asks about who "the first" are (Quomodo enim illi primi dicentur, "In what manner, then, are they called 'the first'; line 5) and proceeds with the discussion thereafter (lines 5-16). He next entertains the question how could the Apostle Paul grant unbelieving gentiles a salvation by means of their good work ("sed quomodo apostolus tantam spem gentibus nondum credentibus ponit, cum ecclesiatica regula videatur obsistere, "but how can the Apostle give such a hope to the gentiles who do not yet believe, when it appears to contradict the ecclesiastical rule?" lines 17-19), followed by his answer (CER 2.7 Heither 1.210.19-212.5).

[3] CER 2.7 Heither 1.210 n. 21.

[4] CER 2.7 Heither 1.210.5.

[5] CER 2.7 Heither 1.210.5-16.

[6] CER 2.7 Heither 1.210.13-16.

[7] CER 2.7 Heither 1.214.10-11.

[8] CER 2.7 Heither 1.214.11-20.

[9] CER 2.7 Heither 1.214.21-216.15.

[10] CER 2.13 See, e.g., Heither 1.254.5-260.24. Cf. also C. P. Bammel, "Die Juden im Ršmerbriefkommentar des Origenes," ed. H. Frohnhofen, *Christlicher Antijudaismus und judischer Antipaganismus: ihre Motive und Hintergrunde in den ersten drei Jahrhunderten* (Hamburg: Steinmann & Steinmann, 1990), 145-151; cf. 146, 149 n. 1.

[11] CER 2.11 Heither 1.238.21-22.

[12] CER 2.11 Heither 1.240.11-248.8.

[13] CER 2.11 Heither 1.240.14-242.2

[14] CER 2.11 Heither 1.242.3-6.

[15] CER 2.11 Heither 1.242.6-10. On lines 11-14, Origen repeats his explanation of the Jews' "adultery." It consists of their introducing "an adulterous sense" to them (=synagogue?).

[16] CER 2.11 Heither 1.242.15-21.

[17] CER 2.11 Heither 1.244.1-2.

[18] CER 2.11 Heither 1.244.23-246.2.

[19] CER 2.11 Heither 1.246.3-6.

[20] CER 2.11 Heither 1.246.6-11.

[21] CER 2.11 Heither 1.246.16-19.

[22] CER 2.11 Heither 1.246.21-26.

[23] This tentative conclusion based on a limited survey of Origen's *Commentary on Romans* accords well with that of N. R. M. de Lange, *Origen and the Jews: Studies in Jewish-Christian Relations in Third-Century Palestine* (Cambridge: Cambridge University Press, 1976), 133-35; which is based on a much broader study of Origen's other works. See the similar conclusion by Heither 4.246-47 n. 39; and her *Translatio religionis: Die Paulusdeutung des Origenes* (Köln & Wien: Böhlau Verlag, 1990), 176-87. De Lange's judgment that Origen "inveighs at length against the Jewish practice of circumcision" (*Origen and the Jews*, 90; 189 n. 9) might be an overstatement as regards the *Commentary on Romans*.

[24] CER 2.13 Heither 1.262.1-296.19. This analysis owes much to Heither's helpful summary of Origen's views of circumcision in terms of these three questions; see 1.49-52.

[25] CER 2.13 Heither 1.262.26-264.13. Heither (1.50) is of the opinion that the second position belongs to the Gnostics, which is entirely possible. Origen's description of his opponent's view is sketchy at best: ita ut putarent haec non esse boni Dei mandata ("Thus they impute that it [*viz.* circumcision] is not mandated by the good God"; CER 2.13 Heither 1.264.11-12).

[26] CER 2.13 Heither 1.264.14-266.11.

[27] CER 2.13 Heither 1.266.13-278.15.

[28] CER 2.13 Heither 1.278.16-296.15.

[29] CER 10.8 Heither 5.200.19-204.25.

[30] CER 8.12 Heither 4.302.1-3.

[31] This represents Origen's summary found in CER 8.12 Heither 4.302.4-24. The much lengthier exposition of the same passage is found in CER 8.9 Heither 4.264.21-274.29. See summary in Bammel, "Die Juden," 149-50.

A Response to Ruth Clements and Sze-kar Wan: Will the Real Paul Please Stand Up!

Charles H. Cosgrove

———— ◆ ————

I want to begin by thanking Prof. Clements and Prof. Wan for their essays, which have helped me understand Origen better and have stimulated my thinking immensely. Since I understand our journey of reading Romans through history and cultures as above all an exploration in hermeneutics, I will focus my response on this subject, beginning with some general remarks about Origen and premodern interpretation of scripture.

Origen and Premodern Hermeneutical Assumptions

In a study of the concept of scripture in Jewish and Christian antiquity, John Barton sets forth four widely shared assumptions about what it means for a writing to be "scripture."[1] James Kugel has recently identified a very similar set of assumptions for ancient Jews and Christians.[2] The following are my own formulations of these principles, based on Barton's four and with one addition.

Five Premodern Hermeneutical Assumptions with their corresponding hermeneutical imperatives (or "rules").

I. A scriptural writing is an important text, deep in meaning, containing no trivialities. Read it as profound.

II. A scriptural text is not ephemeral but addresses every generation. Read it as relevant to your own situation.

III. A scriptural text is internally consistent. Read it in unifying (harmonizing) ways.

IV. A scriptural text is cryptic, full of mysteries, with many layers of meaning beyond its surface sense. Read it according to interpretive methods appropriate to uncovering its hidden meanings.

To these, I would add a fifth common assumption:

> V. A scriptural writing is not a profane text, meant for everyone, but an arcane text, a writing for those given the eyes to interpret it, those to whom it belongs as scripture. Read it from the circle of insiders. (If scripture is also for outsiders, they are dependant on insiders.)

Prof. Clements identifies various passages in Paul's letters that Origen invokes in *Peri Archon* as hermeneutical keys. It is illuminating to ask how far Origen's hermeneutical principles correspond to the widely shared assumptions I have just listed. The following enumeration, based on Prof. Clements' paper, summarizes Origen's hermeneutical principles and correlates them with the Five Premodern Hermeneutical Assumptions.

Origen's Hermeneutical Principles

1. Scripture is written "for our sake" (1 Cor. 10:11)

    This correlates with II but qualifies it. If scripture is written for us, it remains relevant to us generation after generation. Does this principle of relevance apply also for the generations of Israel before the revelation of Christ (according to Origen or the historical Paul)?

    This also correlates with V. Scripture is written for "us," that is, for the church of Jesus Christ, which has the keys to the spiritual interpretation of scripture. Jews and non-Christians are outside the circle of this "us." Heretics are also largely outside.

2. Scripture has a hidden spiritual sense, beyond its literal ("bodily") meaning, that must be interpreted spiritually (figuratively, allegorically).

    In Origen this is variously described. The Law is a "copy" of heavenly things and a "shadow of things to come;" it must be interpreted figuratively (based on Heb. 8:5 and Col. 2:16-17). To understand the Law means not observing its literal requirements, but comprehending the allegories in what is written (based on Gal. 4:21ff.). The whole Law is spiritual, containing spiritual meaning that only the few can grasp (based on Rom. 7:14).

    All of this correlates with IV.

3. Clinging to the literal sense apart from or against its spiritual sense distorts the literal sense (which is to lead to the spiritual). The letter thus distorted "kills." (based on 2 Cor. 3:6)

This assumes IV and works out one of the relations, as Origen sees it, between the patent and the hidden meaning of scripture.

4. God has placed *skandala* in the literal sense as signs that scripture is not to be read only at the literal level (and that some passages have no viable literal sense).

    This principle depends on II. and III.

5. Jews are the hermeneuts of literalist interpretation; Christians are the hermeneuts of spiritual interpretation, which gives proper place to the bodily, soulish, and spiritual senses of scripture.

    Some carnal or heretical Christians are also literalists. Some Jewish scholars are very helpful guides to the bodily meaning of scripture and also to the soulish (moral) sense.

    The hermeneutical principle here is that proper interpretation of scripture depends not only on hermeneutical theory, in an abstract sense, but also crucially on the identity and character of the interpreter. Being part of the community of Christ and being a spiritual person are necessary (if not sufficient) conditions for understanding scripture fully and truly.

    This correlates with V and works out a subordinationist dichotomy within the circle of insider hermeneuts. In some sense, Jews are insiders – the scriptures were written for them or at least "to" them.[3] But they are not insiders in the fullest sense. Moreover, their hermeneutical vantage point is subordinate to the superior hermeneutical position of the church.

Modern(ist) Hermeneutical Principles in Churchly Interpretation of the Bible

Modern historical-critical scholarship, including churchly historical-critical scholarship, has for the most part rejected premodern hermeneutics. Historical scholarship has affirmed a set of counter-principles, a hermeneutics that challenges the Five Premodern Assumptions. What follows are my formulations of these modern hermeneutical principles with some observations suggesting that there may, in fact, be less distance between modern churchly, historical scholarship and premodern exegesis than one commonly assumes (an observation that others have also made in recent years).

Five Modern(ist) Hermeneutical Principles

I[m].   A scriptural writing is a writing like any other, which may
        contain profundity and triviality, along with everything in
        between. Read scripture "like any other book."

        In practice, most churchly historical critics have operated with a
        presumption of significance and have looked for significance
        and profundity.

II[m]. A scriptural text is a historically contingent writing, dependant
        for its meaning on its original setting, applying directly only to
        its original hearers, and relevant (if at all) only indirectly and
        analogically to later generations. Read scripture for its original
        meaning and honor that original meaning in making any ana-
        logical connections with your own time and place.

        In practice, this has often cast the churchly historical critic in the
        role of umpire, declaring some churchly interpretations "safe"
        and others "out."[4] The base runners in this game have often
        ignored (and resented) these self-appointed referees.

III[m]. A scriptural text is as likely as any other writing to display both
        internal consistency and internal contradiction and
        disjointedness. Read scripture without harmonizing.

        In practice, reading scripture without harmonizing is part of the
        churchly scholar's strategy for dismantling the quasi-premodern
        approaches to scripture that students bring to college, university,
        and seminary. It is also one of the ways that churchly scholars
        find hidden meanings in biblical texts, but here "hidden" refers
        to meanings that can be discovered only through rather arcane
        historical methods, including meanings belonging to earlier lay-
        ers of the tradition.

IV[m]. A scriptural text communicates in ordinary ways, by the logic of
        conventional language and the common genres of its original
        socio-linguistic contexts. Read scripture like you would any
        other book (see I[m] above).

        In fact, churchly historical critics don't usually read scripture
        (only) like any other book. Consider how they have typically
        interpreted Genesis 1. The critical commentaries are not inter-
        ested in exploring the facticity of the story of creation, the de-
        gree of correspondence (if any) between the literal meaning of
        the text and a referential external world or set of actions. Nor is
        the churchly critical commentator interested primarily in the
        literal meaning in itself (as a literary sense). As James Barr has
        observed, the literal level of the story is important because it

provides clues to the *theology* of the story. Barr suggests that this makes churchly critical scholarship closer to allegorical exegesis than to literalist or historical exegesis.[5] I agree, especially, where the theological meaning of the text is set forth with the help of traditional Christian concepts.

Something quite akin to Origen's hierarchy of scriptural senses is in evidence here. Taken literally, the creation account presents a *skandalon* for the modern interpreter. But we don't reject the literal level. We do justice to the "letter" by pressing on to the theological intent, which is *more than* and *other than* the letter, although it can be discovered only *through* the letter.[6]

V^m. A scriptural writing is open to correct interpretation by anyone (regardless of their spiritual or religious identity) who knows the original languages of the Bible and can read the Bible in its (reconstructed) ancient historical setting. Read scripture from the historically reconstructed vantage of ancient readers.

Practically speaking, this has meant–and generations of seminary students have experienced it as – a privileging of the scholarly guild of biblical interpreters as the insiders who possess the keys to interpretation. In this perspective, the rest of the church is a bit like the simple Christians in Origen's construction – both insiders and outsiders, able to interpret at a rudimentary level but certainly subordinate in status as hermeneuts.

Origen's Spiritual Hermeneutic

Prof. Clements makes the astute comment that Origen's use of Paul in *Peri Archon* to develop a distinctively Christian hermeneutic is revealing not only for what Origen draws on in Paul but also for what he passes over (Clements, 2). Examples are Rom. 1:17 (the priority of the Jew), 3:2 ("they have been entrusted with the oracles of God"), and 11:1-2, 26-28 (God "has not rejected his people," the Jews, but will save "all Israel" in faithfulness to the irrevocable promises made to the Jewish people). Origen's "transformative" exegesis, it seems, distorts the historical Paul.

I agree that much of what Origen does with Paul's teaching about Israel exceeds the bounds of what today counts as reasonable historical-critical interpretation. But there is more than one reasonable way to read Paul historically and some of Origen's anti-Jewish interpretations are not too far from some historically defensible ways of interpreting Romans. Some very able Pauline scholars continue to argue the traditional view that in Paul's understanding the new people of God (the church of Jews and gentiles) supersedes ethnic Israel and in effect becomes the new Israel.[7] This line of exegesis goes against the grain of another emergent scholarly view that the Jews remain God's people Israel, *post Christum,* and continue to have their own, valid way from God (a *Sonderweg*) alongside the way of Christ for the church.[8] I don't think the debate over these two readings of Israel in Paul can be settled exegetically. Romans is susceptible to more than one reasonable historical-critical interpretation.[9] I will come back to this after looking at an ostensibly hermeneutical statement in Romans that Origen does not mention in *Peri Archon* and does not take hermeneutically in his commentary on Romans.

I have in mind Rom. 3:19: "We know that whatever the law says it says to those under the law." The context is Paul's quotation of a string of denunciations taken mostly from the Psalms (Rom. 3:10-17). These show that all are under sin, Jews and gentiles. If the law speaks here as the Psalms and some of the prophets, then Paul is using the term "law" (*nomos*) in the sense of scripture (a common way of speaking about scripture in his day). I paraphrase Paul's hermeneutical principle as follows: "Whatever scripture says it says to those under the authority of scripture." As it happens, the passages Paul quotes are, in their original contexts, denunciations of *gentiles*, not Jews. Paul invokes his hermeneutical principle to justify applying these words of scripture to Jews as well.

In his commentary on Romans, Origen does not interpret "law" in this passage (Rom. 3:19) as scripture.[10] He argues that law here must mean "natural law," since only natural law applies to both Jews and gentiles. Why? Is it because he cannot accept the claim that everything the law as scripture says applies to those under the law? I find some support for this conjecture in Prof. Clements' observation that, for Origen, the promises in scripture were never meant for Jews but were always meant for Christians.[11]

On the other hand, I can imagine ways in which Origen might have construed *nomos* as scripture in Rom. 3:19 and still have worked out an interpretation that preserves the hermeneutic by which he effectively reads the Jewish people out of the promises and denies them identity as God's people. His reading of scripture depends on a set of theological convictions that he claims to find in scripture but finds there with the help of those same convictions. Moreover, the theological convictions include his hermeneutic, as Prof. Clements shows (especially with reference to Origen's interpretation of 1 Cor. 10:18). Origen's theological opposition between fleshly Jews and spiritual Christians is part of what we might call "the rule of faith" as he understands it, at once a doctrinal and a hermeneutical guide.

Prof. Clements observes that for Origen the spiritual sense of scripture is primarily about "the doctrines about God and his only-begotten Son."[12] A superficial reading of Origen might give the impression that, in his hermeneutic, allegorical exegesis is the only avenue to discovering these doctrines. But, by his own claim, he already knows these doctrines from the apostolic teaching of the church, especially in the Gospels and Paul.[13] His allegorical exegesis is the way in which he discovers Christian doctrine in those parts of scripture where it is *not* express, but hidden, especially in the Law.[14] Thus, the content of the spiritual teaching exists, for Origen, at a *plain sense* level in at least some parts of the apostolic writings.

Prof. Wan puts his finger on the crucial point when he observes that for Origen allegorical interpretation is *christological* interpretation. This insight deserves further exploration. As far as I can see, Origen invokes the plain sense of explicit christological statements in the apostolic writings as revelation of spiritual doctrines. In the express christological statements of the apostolic writings, the "plain sense" is the "literal sense," if by literal one means the conventional, grammatical sense. This plain/literal sense *is* the spiritual sense. Origen's interpretation of Rom. 9:5 is a good example of this.[15] Origen follows a grammatical construal that takes the phrase ὁ ὢν ἐπὶ παντῶν θεὸς εὐλογητὸς εἰς τοὺς αἰῶνας as an appositional statement modifying Χριστος and, therefore, as clearly asserting Christ's identity as God. Origen does not distinguish the plain-sense, literal meaning here from a hidden, spiritual meaning. The reason is that in this case the plain sense is the unveiled spiritual meaning, that in turn becomes the hermeneutical key to spiritual interpretation of the Law.

If a christological rule of faith guides Origen's spiritual exegesis, do any other convictions or sensibilities inform his hermeneutical judgments? If I read them rightly, both Prof. Clements and Prof. Wan are suggesting that it is not antisemitism, born of conflicts with and personal animosity toward Jews, that leads to Origen's anti-Jewish exegesis. It is rather the logic of his theology that leads to anti-Jewish interpretations, a theology that he inherits from and shares with many other early Christian thinkers. This is a significant judgment. I read its implications as follows. It is important to distinguish the political meaning of theological anti-Judaism in Origen from theological and cultural anti-Judaism (*cum* antisemitism) in the modern era. We can make this distinction without "excusing" Origen's statements about Jews and Judaism..

I assume that all interpreters are guided by many convictions that are not expressly theological but shape their theological judgments. Sometimes we acknowledge these convictions; often we don't. Much of the time, we are not fully aware of them. The deepest of these convictions function as "rules of recognition"[16] for judging what we can accept as true or divine, including which interpretations we are ready to accept as valid for faith and practice. It would be a difficult, but enormously instructive, project to identify the rules of recognition in Origen that do not belong expressly to his rule of faith (but no doubt shape it). Let me illustrate what I have in mind with one example. Prof. Clements notes that Origen defends his interpretation of true circumcision in Rom. 2:28-29 and Phil. 3:2-3 by describing it as *dignius*. I am not sure how much freight to pack into this translation term, but it strikes me that it implies a kind of "rule of recognition" for what counts as a valid interpretation of scripture. We might formulate it this way: A scriptural writing is a good and virtuous text, teaching nothing undignified or dishonorable. We should read it for virtuous meaning. What counts as "dignity" for Origen? Clearly, however we might define it precisely (if it can be precisely defined), it is part of the cultural knowledge that he takes for granted as manifestly true. In the same way that we "know" that torture is cruel *and therefore immoral* (people in Origen's time would not have understood this conviction of ours), so Origen "knows" that bodily circumcision is shameful.

It is not only Origen who brings a sense of what is morally good to the process of discriminating between interpretations of an authoritative text. We all do, and today some advocate that we *should*, that is, that moral-theological criteria *ought* to guide churchly adjudications between competing interpretations of scripture.[17] Parallel views can be found in contemporary jurisprudence, particularly in the area of constitutional law. Two contemporary examples come to my mind – one from law and the other from theology. Both are especially *apropros* of our reading of Origen. The legal example is the late Justice William Brennan's claim that the Supreme Court should treat the U.S. Constitution as a document designed to promote human dignity and should read it accordingly.[18] Brennan's notion of dignity as a substantive hermeneutical norm is not the same as Origen's notion of "dignity" (*dignatio?*); but both are operating with their own best sense of what their culture (or subculture) esteems as human dignity, and using that sense to adjudicate between competing interpretations of authoritative texts. My other example is the argument by Pauline scholar Lloyd Gaston that if a Judaism-affirming interpretation of Paul is *possible*, then it is also *necessary*, after Auschwitz.[19] Gaston does not say but his argument implies, for me, that the "rule of faith" by which the church reads Paul and makes judgments between competing possible interpretations ought to include the conviction that the Jewish people are and remain Israel *post Christum*, and that their way in the Torah is God's good and life-giving way for them. Auschwitz as history and symbol creates for Gaston and many others of us a kind of "rule of recognition" for judging theology and discriminating between competing interpretations of scripture.

Will the Real Paul Please Stand Up!

There is a famous scene in the film *Annie Hall*, where the character played by Woody Allen is with Annie in line at a movie theater. Behind them a man is pontificating on film criticism and modern media theory. Allen fumes in irritation. When the man begins invoking Marshall McLuhan, Allen steps over to a poster and pulls from behind it the real Marshall McLuhan (Marshall McLuhan playing himself!) who proceeds to tell the annoying man, "You know nothing of my work. . . ." Many modern interpreters reading Origen would like to summon the real Paul into Origen's text to tell Origen, "You know nothing of my work. You have completely misunderstood me." Prof. Wan's reference to "what modern critics would call wild allegorization" in Origen's reading of Paul and Prof. Clements' comment that Origen's "synthetic reading of Paul . . . succeeds beyond Paul's intention"[20] are reminders that it is almost impossible today to speak about the way premodern interpreters read Paul without assuming that the real Paul is the historical Paul (in the modern sense of that term), and that "we" have a pretty sure grasp on that historical Paul. My guess, however, is that if Origen were with us today, he would like to step into the hallway and bring in the real Paul to tell us moderns (present company excluded) that we know nothing about how to read scripture, and for that reason know nothing about how to read Paul.

I should stress that neither Prof. Wan nor Prof. Clements uses the term "real Paul." But both do seem to operate with a distinction between the historical Paul and Origen's Paul (which may or may not be the same thing as a distinction between "the real Paul" and other Pauls). In any case, Origen would see the way we differentiate between his Paul and ours as a disagreement over who has a better way of getting at the *real* or *true* Paul. That Paul, for Origen, includes but is *more than* the historical Paul's "intentions" in his letters. For Origen, the real Paul is what Paul's letters say *as scripture* revealing the *intentions of the Logos*, the divine Author.

Since Origen is not here to defend himself, and Paul is not likely to descend from heaven to instruct us, I'm going to conclude by giving a short little speech in the name of Origen about how to read Paul. And, so as not to give offense, I'm going to address this speech to an anonymous New Testament scholar, whom I'll call Professor Hans Bibfeldt:[21]

> Professor Bibfeldt, your business card describes you as a Professor of New Testament Studies, but as far as I can tell, you don't make the *theological concept* of a "New Testament" determinative for how you read the New Testament or the rest of scripture. You claim to recover the real historical Paul and often appeal to him as an authoritative voice of the church's scriptures, a corrector of bad popular theology. Well and good, but how can you claim to be a faithful interpreter of Paul, and invoke Paul for your own theol-

ogy, when you don't read scripture the way Paul read scripture? How can you appeal to Paul's letters as scripture, when you don't read those letters the way they read scripture? Why don't you read scripture christologically? Are you deaf to Paul? And why do you think the burden of proof is on me to prove that I'm not such a bad exegete after all, that I can and do read scripture at least sometimes, sort of, the way you do? Isn't the burden of proof rather on you to show that the Bible read differently than the Bible reads itself, and a canonical Paul read according to a different hemeneutic than Paul himself uses, somehow gets us to the *real* Bible and the *real* Paul?

I've given this speech to myself as well. It spurs me on to build hermenuetical bridges to premodern interpreters like Origen without burning the bridges that connect me to modernity. That's a tough challenge. I'm grateful for the two papers that have caused me to think about it afresh.

---

[1] John Barton, *Holy Writings, Sacred Text: The Canon in Early Christianity* (Louisville, KY: Westminster John Knox Press, 1997), 134-145.

[2] James L. Kugel, *Traditions of the Bible: A Guide to the Bible as It Was at the Start of the Common Era* (Cambridge, MA and London: Harvard University Press, 1998), 14-19.

[3] See n. 11 below.

[4] I owe this figure to Wayne Meeks, "On Trusting an Unpredictable God: A Hermeneutical Meditation on Romans 9-11," in *Faith and History: Essays in Honor of Paul W. Meyer*, ed. John T. Carroll, Charles H. Cosgrove, and E. Elizabeth Johnson, 105-24 (Atlanta: Scholars Press, 1990). Meeks suggests that historical criticism should give up its role as "umpire," acknowledge that ahistorical "charismatic" readings have their place, and adopt a role of "standing up for the past in a dialogue between Then and Now" (119).

[5] James Barr, "The Literal, the Allegorical, and Modern Scholarship," *Journal for the Study of the Old Testament* 44 (1989): 12-13.

[6] By "letter" I have in view the original, literal sense that ancient readers would have found in the story. They would have assumed that the text is talking about what God factually did. They would not have raised our scientific questions as a point of *skandalon*, but some of them, such as Origen, did discover problems at the literal level of purported facticity. These *skandala*, Origen says, are reminders that the text has other, non-literal meanings.

We sometimes use the term "myth" in a positive sense to describe a text that lets itself be interpreted beyond the letter in ways that are significant, even profound, not only for ancient people but for us, too.

[7] E.g., N. T. Wright, *The Climax of the Covenant: Christ and the Law in Pauline Theology* (Edinburgh: T. & T. Clark, 1991; Minneapolis: Fortress Press, 1992), 245-51.

[8] E.g., Franz Mußner in many essays and books, beginning with his first important statement, "'Ganz Israel wird gerettet werden' (Röm 11,26)," *Kairos* 18 (1976): 241-55; see also Lloyd Gaston, *Paul and the Torah* (Vancouver: University of British Columbia Press, 1987) and Stanley K. Stowers, *A Rereading of Romans: Justice, Jews, and Gentiles* (New Haven, CT: Yale University Press, 1994).

[9] On the question of the *Sonderweg* for Israel and how the church should deal with competing plausible interpretations, see Cosgrove, "Advocating One Reasonable Interpretation of Paul Against Other Reasonable Interpretations: A Theological

Approach to the Sonderweg Question," in *Another Way? Pauline Soteriology for Jews and Gentiles in Romans*, ed. Robert Gagnon (Grand Rapids, MI: Wm. B. Eerdmans, forthcoming).

[10] *Origenes Commentarii in Epistulam ad Romanos*, vol. 2, ed. Theresia Heither (Freiburg: Herder, 1992), 82-87.

[11] Perhaps Origen was not consistent on this point. He claims that the promises were really meant all along for the church, and yet, when he treats Rom. 11:25ff., he speaks of the promises being for Israel, as Prof. Wan points out. Origen's ambivalence surely grows out of the fact that he must acknowledge that the Law was given "to" Israel, even though he wants to claim that the ancient scriptures' promises, in their highest sense, were always meant for the church.

[12] Clements quotes this phrase from *Peri Archon* IV.2.7.

[13] Clements does not emphasize this point, but it is implied by her discussion.

[14] Allegorical exegesis probably also serves as a kind of dialogue with scripture by which Origen works out his own distinctive understanding of the apostolic doctrines. If he finds there what he is looking for, this may not be too much different than the brilliant way in which Alexandre Kojève found his own philosophy in (by commenting on) Hegel (in notes and transcripts of lectures published originally in French under the title, *Introduction à la Lecture de Hegel*). Even if the historical Hegel is distorted in Kojève's reading, Hegel the text was somehow indispensable to the philosophical discoveries Kojève made. Kojève reading Hegel is just one of many examples of creative misreading in which a text is the indispensable basis of discoveries that transcend its original (or authorially intended) sense.

[15] *Origenes Commentarii in Epistulam ad Romanos*, vol. 4, ed. Theresia Heither (Freiburg: Herder, 1994), 140-141.

[16] Space does not permit me to define how my use of the expression "rule of recognition" relates to its antecedents in Christian hermeneutics (I have in mind the *regulae cognoscendi* of Matthias Flaccius Illyricus) and in jurisprudence (notably in the work of English legal theorist H. L. A. Hart).

[17] For a survey, see Cosgrove, *Appealing to Scripture in Moral Debate: Five Hermeneutical Rules* (Grand Rapids, MI: Wm. B. Eerdmans, 2002), 154-80; idem, *Elusive Israel: The Puzzle of Election in Romans* (Louisville, KY: Westminster John Knox, 1997); idem, "Advocating One Reasonable Interpretation of Paul against Other Reasonable Interpretations;" Daniel Patte, *Discipleship according to the Sermon on the Mount: Four Legitimate Readings, Four Plausible Views of Discipleship, and Their Relative Values* (Valley Forge, PA: Trinity Press International, 1996); Robert C. Tannehill, "Freedom and Responsibility in Scripture Interpretation, with Application to Luke," In *Literary Studies in Luke-Acts*, ed. Richard P. Thompson and Thomas E. Philips, 265-78 (Macon GA: Mercer University Press, 1998).

[18] William J. Brennan, Jr., "The Constitution of the United States: Contemporary Ratification," in *Interpreting the Constitution: The Debate over Original Intent*, ed. Jack N. Rakove (1990). I give a brief discussion of Brennan's view of Constitutional interpretation in my article, "The Declaration of Independence in Constitutional Interpretation: A Selective History and Analysis," *University of Richmond Law Review* 32 (1998): 142.

[19] Lloyd Gaston, "Paul and the Torah," in *Antisemitism and the Foundations of Christianity*, ed. Alan T. Davies (New York: Paulist Press, 1979), 67.

[20] Clements, 173.

[21] Son of Franz Bibfeldt, the theologian.

Irenaeus's and Origen's Treatment of Paul's Epistle to the Romans: An Assessment

Dieter Georgi

———— ◆ ————

Given the many interesting and meaningful observations in papers and responses for the seminar, I limit myself to some contextual and atmospheric observations that might be helpful for the discussion. Dr. Bassler mentions in her response the ghastly events of Sept. 11 as bearing hermeneutical relevance. I want to take that point some steps further. These events hint at a complex issue that at the present time seems to be completely out of the purview of the Christian West and limited entirely to the world of Islam, namely, that of *martyrdom*. The two persons that are in the center of this seminar's discussion and their contexts, however, prove that the early church produced martyrological ideas, motivations and practices that were, respectively are, not too different from the urges of the suicidal assassins of Sept. 11, 2001.

This equation might upset at first sight, yet critical historians and theologians will agree that the adulation of martyrdom in the early church and the enthusiastic readiness of early Christians to die the martyr's death were obviously suicidal, and this not merely occasionally but 'en masse.' But murder? Yet, what is the glorification of blood and gore in the preaching and teaching of the early church other than the exaltation of butchery and the encouragement to have it carried out? Within the biographical context of Irenaeus there is the long report on the martyrs of Lyon given by Eusebius in the fifth book of his Church History. This account is engulfed in slaughter, terror and suicidal urges of the victims, turning active instigators into actors who change the will of the torturers and those of the executioners into their own. But this is not yet all.

There are two further aspects always overlooked in the generally venerating portrayals of early Christian martyrdom in the common histories of the church. The first one is the denunciatory purpose and effect of the heresiomachic literature of the early church. The authors of these works must have known that the Roman police would have taken these

206

writings as excellent sources for their investigative and persecuting efforts. The defamatory qualities of these writings *adversus haereses* augmented the dangerous aspects of all those holding the caricatured opinions and being identified with the denounced evil practices, that also the Roman authorities would also have been dead set against. The fact that the heresiomachic literature is written for public consumption proves that one did not mind the police and the courts having easy access to it. The intentionality of these authors therefore cannot be excluded. The deadly persecution of heretics by the forces of the state in the time Constantine onward made merely more obvious what had been the opinion and intention of church leaders before.

There is even another murderous aspect generally overlooked in the discussion of martyrological literature, in particular its Christian examples. Scholarship, curiously enough, has overlooked the fact that nowhere in the martyrologies is anything said about police-hearings, nor about what those victims answered when they were asked by the police and the court about names, locations, practices and rites – questions that were definitely raised. This is, for instance partly documented in the famous reports of Pliny – and they were required by procedural rules anyhow. Another clue is the reference to acts of torture before the execution. Since the martyrs allegedly confessed readily to being "Christiani," the torture could not aim at bringing that out but must have aimed at further information. A further hint in this direction is found in the case of the martyr Sanctus from Vienna as reported in the martyrology of Lugdunum. Of him we hear that he confessed right away and readily "Christianus sum." Nevertheless he was further tortured many a time never saying anything more than the confession mentioned, not even his name, nor those of his people or his place of origin. He did not reveal his social status (slave or free), nor did he give away any other personal data. Only from Gnostic circles is such silence known. They seem to have been prepared for such investigative hearings and trained in how to evade precise answers, if necessary, through outright lying, all of this for the purpose of protecting people, community and cult. The "catholic" heresy-fighters turned this evidence into the defaming lie that the Gnostics shied away from martyrdom. From Basilides on, we have evidence that for Gnostics subversive protest against state and society was in order, indeed a fundamental necessity, and persecution and martyrdom a matter of course. Yet there was no reason to play along with the powers' game and actively thirst for martyrdom. If it would come, one would be ready for it, but without any direct or indirect assistance to the persecutors, judges or hangmen from the victims, even less an endangering of fellow-believers or the community, its cult and theology. What if the Christian Gnostics had learned such evasiveness and the use of code language from Paul, the author of Romans?

On the other hand, the silence about the investigative procedures of Roman police and courts, and about the reactions of arrested members of the "catholic" branch of the church, calls for the conclusion that these people did not mind betraying the names of their fellow-believers and other data relevant for the police. Such an assumption is not unrealistic, given the high value put on martyrdom. Being arrested and tried would be a safe way to heaven – just as the Islamic "martyrs" believe today. Irenaeus puts a high value on martyrdom. He had relations to victims of persecution already in Asia Minor, and according to the report about the (48) martyrs in Lyon, mentioned above, Irenaeus, meantime removed from Asia Minor to Gaul, was considered by these Celtic martyrs as their man, as the proper successor to their martyred bishop. The report does not give any clues what "denominations" these martyrs came from. No theological classifications are intimated. With all probability "heretics" were among them. As one reads Irenaeus, one needs to acknowledge that the segregation of the heretics had not happened, and did not occur even after the persecution. Irenaeus has to acknowledge the existence of "heretics" in his environment. Anyway, there is no justification for the common claim that Irenaeus in his *Adversus haereses* described reality. Whatever Irenaeus says seems to be much less definitive than usually assumed. The chances are much higher that everything he describes as factual, is merely alleged, is rather wishful thinking, a reality he wants to be, but that is not yet.

A major question I have with respect to Irenaeus' surviving writings discussed in the seminar is this: whether the martyrs that called for his elevation would have been happy about the two books that are objects of our study now. The position that Irenaeus sets forth there would not have put Roman police or courts on alert, but rather would have put them to rest. Was that intentional? There does not seem to have been a persecution in Lyon after that in 177 / 78. Jerome's hint that Irenaeus died as a martyr has little evidence in its favor. If Gnostics alone were persecuted, neither Irenaeus nor any of our "catholic" sources would have mentioned them. Concern for sons and daughters of the devil were not necessary.

Unlike Irenaeus, Origen had been tortured and victimized by Roman persecutors several times. He definitely eulogized martyrs and martyrdom. The question whether he died in prison is undecided. Origen, son of a martyr, was certainly imprisoned toward the end of his life. Still, Origen, as little as Irenaeus, had any room for protective means and training of believers against persecutors, means such as evasiveness and outright lying, or the use of code-language.

Common to both authors and the writings discussed is an antiheretical perspective, yet with a rather ironical twist, in as much as both are anything but paragons of "orthodoxy" such as the later church wanted and wants them to be, but bordered on what the later church would call heresies. Irenaeus leaned towards the Montanists. Although in his remaining works his enthusiasm and chiliasm are reduced, the latter still informs his understanding of history, and contributes to its isolation, schematization and mythification. Even more obvious is the distance of Origen from later orthodoxy, in particular from what the Western church understood by orthodoxy. Origen was even a condemned heretic. Irenaeus and Origen shared the irony of being a "blend" of "orthodox" and "heretical" with another person later viewed as a major producer of orthodox ideas, Tertullian. In his case, too, the fact that he later joined the same so-called heresy that Irenaeus had flirted with, Montanism, usually treated as a marginal accident in the history of Christian theology. All of this points to the fact that any treatment such persons as interpreters of scriptures should look at them and their works as representatives of phenomena in flux, in this entirely comparable with Paul and his writings.

This is already sufficient warning against the common treatment of both authors. They are forced into the very artificial and abstract Procrustesbed of an allegedly consistent development of theology within the early church, a development that was anything but consistent, but very colorful and turbulent instead. They do not fit that procrustean arrangement. Such an approach does not recognize that a fixed and firm Christ-oriented theology did not exist yet at that time – although both, Irenaeus and Origen, would have loved to have had such a theology, and would have referred to it if it had existed. All general claims about and references to these and other authors, later claimed as "catholic," provide no real proof, but are merely emphatic asseverations. In fact, they relate to a theology highly in motion, and they do this by way of experimentation and trying out certain directions, not with any consistency, but very much in a trial and error fashion.

Their approach was anything but innocent or apolitical, but rather highly politicized. This politicization applies to the debate about the canon issue, too, in which both authors were involved as well. Because of this highly politicized situation and the motives of the authors, the stratification of facts became very important. In this process, claims become substitutes for facts, and exegesis worked often enough as producer, conveyer and deliverer of political arguments and "virtual" facts, contrary to reality.

Therefore, the observation of resemblances between Irenaeus' (and Origen's) hermeneutical and argumentative patterns and those of modern exegetes should not simply be made, but should be more profoundly scrutinized. There are certainly some things in common, but the situation and the purpose of modern scholarly exegesis in many ways are very far removed from those of Irenaeus and Origen. The political

standing of contemporary scholarly exegetes in church and society today is very isolated. Presently, the only ones who have opportunities to
connect – are extremely conservative exegetes – since much of the power-
structures in West and East are very conservative with society too.

The representatives of dialectical theology had such influence for a
relatively short time, first as exegetes of the dissident movement against
Hitler, and then, for twenty years at most in the context of the restoration of church and theology in post-war Germany. As soon as such
exegetes turned against that restoration, as, for instance, Ernst
Käsemann did, the church turned against them.

The dialectical theologians in general, and Ernst Käsemann in particular, had this in common: that they practiced targetshooting in their
environment like sitting ducks, because enemies were and are essential
for their understanding of theology and church, not merely ordinary
adversaries, but true heretics. The dialectical theologians and the ancient heresiomachs were obsessed with the concept of holy writ too,
although both groups knew better – namely, that this concept stood on
feet of clay. Irenaeus and Origen, as well as the dialectical theologians,
used exegesis of alleged "holy writ" for doctrinal purposes. Their concept of doctrine, however, is very different. In the case of Irenaeus and
Origen, the targetshooting was part of the creation of a new world. In
the case of Käsemann and his likes, this world is no longer new. Despite
their schematized, cardboardlike character, Irenaeus' and Origen's targets, the Gnostics, were more real than Käsemann's "enthusiasts".
Whereas Irenaeus and Origen knew their own religious environment
which was still close enough to that of Paul, including the Gnostics,
Käsemann in his commentary on Romans does not want to know the
Gnostics anymore, and his religio-historical analysis is wooden at
best. The reason for this woodenness connects him again with the
schematizations of Irenaeus and Origen. These schematizations are
done for the alleged purpose of a higher degree of theologization. In the
case of Origen, who had a very lively exchange with and knowledge of
Jews, not only in Caesaria but also in Alexandria, and then in Caesarea
and Jerusalem again, it is a tragedy that this experience and the knowledge that accompanied it did not really influence his interpretation of
Romans. A de-historicized concept of theology was the cause of that.
The models for the abstraction of Irenaeus and Origen were the Pastoral
Epistles, although Origen's concept of theology should have been
lightyears removed from that of the author of the Pastorals.

An additional point needs to be made with respect to the comparison
of Käsemann with Irenaeus and Origen: Käsemann's political naiveté
and his ignorance of strategy are stunning. His belief in the lasting
force of scholarly arguments is moving in its innocence. Not only
Irenaeus and Origen but also the author of the Pastorals, so much hated
by Käsemann, were politically more astute and shrewd than the father

of Elisabeth Käsemann, murdered by the Argentinian security forces. When this murder struck Käsemann was his commentary on Romans was more or less finished. The last phase of Käsemann's life remained practically unreflected in literature.

Despite the lengthy deliberations about New Testament texts, and those of Paul in particular, and those of Origen, of course, vastly more than those of Irenaeus, the argumentative pattern and, to a certain degree, the results are similar to those of Pastoral Epistles: it is the high grade of abstraction from the movement and life of the real texts. In the case of Origen, this is especially tragic, because he proves a few times, for instance in some interspersed treatments of certain psalms, that he is still prepared to demonstrated an awareness of texts as living phenomena. But in general, his exegesis taskes the form of the presentation of more or less elaborate theological essays, for which the Pauline text, often simply paraphrased, gives merely the excuse. Irenaeus, of course, is the father of prooftexting, to a degree even unknown in Pharisaic-rabbinic exegesis. Even in that respect the Pastorals, and most probably Polycarp, had instigated Irenaeus, and has inspired all fundamentalism ever since. In the papers for the seminar, Irenaeus' ingenuous invention of a hermeneutical/doctrinal masterkey for the interpretation of all of scriptures, no matter what text or what document, is touched upon. This invention allows him to transform any text in the Bible into an arbitrarily exchangeable pattern that can fit anywhere. Origen does not go that far. Despite his speculative passion, he still has respect for the individuality of texts and documents. His portrait of Romans is definitely different from that of the Gospel of John, and not only because the one is an epistle and the other a gospel.

It is very surprising, however, that the argument implied in the Pastorals and made again and again by Irenaeus, that the Gnostics had no respect for texts and that their exegeses were sham and bogus has been repeated ever since. The extant textual traces of Gnostic exegesis speak against that conclusion, and also what we learn generally about the exegetical activities of persons like Basilides. The claim that they did not respect the First Testament is proven wrong, too, by the vestiges we have of their elaborate interpretations of the First Testament. The most extraordinary phenomenon in this respect is Marcion, whose Antitheses seemed to be built to a large extent on exegeses of the Septuagint. I mention this here, because despite of the belittinglings and denunciations of Gnostic exegeses by people like Irenaeus and Origen, the church definitely knew of them and reacted to them, most often without direct reference, as fathers in the texts dealt with in the seminar papers.

Another point regarding the relevance of silence is the problem of Rufinus' translation of Origen's commentary on Romans. It represents a shortened text. What did he leave out and why?

This needs to suffice. I am thankful for the instigation which the papers and responses have given me for further thinking. In concluding my observations, I want to make a more general remark concerning the present emphasis on the contextuality and subjectivity involved in the reading of texts. Such insights are meaningful, and it should not be forgotten that they are found already in Marxist and in Heideggerian hermeneutics. However, this emphasis on the relativism of exegetical pursuits and insights should not blind us to the fact that approaches to Paul like those of Irenaeus and Origen turned Paul upside down and robbed him of his identity, and also obscured the understanding of the first readers of the texts. Is there a justification for such drastic revisions, even outright burials? Do authors have no dignity of their own? Are the texts which they have written a free-for-all for everyone? Should exegetes not take into account that these are human-rights issues too? Should liberation theology in our times not call for a liberation of the fettered, disenfranchised dead as well, that is, of those who were not allowed by later generations to say what they wanted to say? Do not exegetes disown and kill Paul one again by the monuments erected above him and in his alleged favor? Exegesis that respects human rights is not so much interested in political correctness as in passionate political engagement on behalf of human rights and human beings all across the board and through all times.

Contributors

———— ◆ ————

IKATHY L. GACA is Associate Professor of Classics at Vanderbilt University. She is the author of *The Making of Fornication: Eros, Ethics, and Political Reform in Greek Philosophy and Early Christianity* (2003) and of a number of articles and reviews. She received her Ph.D. in Classics at the University of Toronto and held the Hannah Seeger Davis Postdoctoral Fellowship in Hellenic Studies at Princeton University.

L. L. WELBORN is Professor of New Testament and Early Christian Literature at United Theological Seminary in Dayton, Ohio. He is the author of *Politics and Rhetoric in the Corinthian Epistles* (1997), *Paul the Fool of Christ: A Study of 1 Corinthians 1-4 in the Comic-Philosophic Tradition* (2005), and co-editor (with Cilliers Breytenbach) of *Encounters with Hellenism: Studies in 1 Clement* (2003).

HALVOR MOXNES is Professor of New Testament in the Faculty of Theology at the University of Oslo, Norway. He is the author of *Theology in Conflict: Studies in Paul's Understanding of God in Romans* (1980) and *Putting Jesus in His Place: A Radical Vision of Household and Kingdom* (2003).

MICHAEL JOSEPH BROWN is Assistant Professor of New Testament and Christian Origins at the Candler School of Theology, Emory University in Atlanta. He is the author of *What They Don't Tell You: A Survivor's Guide to Biblical Studies* (2000), *Blackening of the Bible: The Aims of African American Biblical Scholarship* (2004), and *The Lord's Prayer through North African Eyes: A Window into Early Christianity* (2005).

SUSAN L. GRAHAM teaches theology and Scripture at Saint Peter's College, Jersy City. A specialist in early Christian biblical interpretation, she is author of *'Zealous for the Covenant': Irenaeus and the Covenants of Israel* (forthcoming). She co-authored (with Michael Signer) "Jewish Exegesis" in Charles Kannengiesser's *Handbook of Patristic Exegesis* (2003) and has written several articles on Irenaeus, including "Structure and Purpose of Irenaeus' *Epideixis*" (2001), "The Next Generation: Irenaeus on the Rebellion in the Wilderness of Paran" in *Israel in the Wilderness* (ed. Kenneth Pomykala and Robert Kugler, forthcoming), and "Irenaeus and the Covenants: Immortal Diamond," *Studia Patristica* (forthcoming).

D. JEFFREY BINGHAM is Chair and Professor of Theological Studies at Dallas Theological Seminary. He is the author of *Irenaeus's Use of Matthew's Gospel in* Adversus Haereses (1995) and several articles and essays on Patristic theology and interpretation of the Bible. He also serves as general editor for the monograph series, The Bible in Ancient Christianity (Brill).

JOUETTE M. BASSLER is Professor of New Testament at Perkins School of Theology, Southern Methodist University. She has served as co-chair of the SBL Pauline Theology Group (1990-95), editor of the *Journal of Biblical Literature* (1995-99), and New Testament Editor of the *Harper Collins Study Bible*. In addition, she has served as editor of one, and contributor to several, of the volumes in the *Pauline Theology* series. She is the author of *Divine Impartiality: Paul and a Theological Axiom* (1982), *A Commentary on 1 Timothy, 2 Timothy, and Titus* (1996), and numerous articles including "Epiphany Christology in the Pastoral Letters" in *Pauline Conversations in Context* (ed. J. Capel Anderson, et al., 2002), "Grace: Probing the Limits,'" *Interpretation* (2003), and "Limits and Differentiation: The Calculus of Widows in 1 Tim. 5:3-16" in *A Feminist Companion to Pauline Thought* (ed. A.-J. Levine, 2003).

CHRISTOPH MARKSCHIES is Professor of Early Church History (Patristics) at the Humboldt University in Berlin. His numerous publications include *Die Gnosis* (2001) and *Arbeitsbuch zur Kirchengeschichte* (1995).

RUTH A. CLEMENTS received her doctorate in Christian Origins from the Harvard Divinity School (1997). She is Director of Publications for the Orion Center for the Study of the Dead Sea Scrolls and Associated Literature at the Hebrew University of Jerusalem. She is also a John W. Kluge Fellow at the Library of Congress, where she is pursuing research for a study on biblical interpretation and the separation of early Christianity and rabbinic Judaism.

PETER GORDAY is a clinical staff member with the Georgia Association for Pastoral Counseling and priest-associate at St. Anne's Episcopal Church in Atlanta. He is the author of *Principles of Patristic Exegesis: Romans 9-11 in Origen, John Chrysostom, and Augustine* (1983) and *Ancient Christian Commentary on Scripture: Colossians, 1-2 Thessalonians, 1-2 Timothy, Titus, Philemon* (2000).

SZE-KAR WAN is John Norris Professor of New Testament at Andover Newton Theological School. He is the author of *Power in Weakness: Conflict and Rhetoric in Paul's Second Letter to the Corinthians* (2000) and co-editor of *The Bible in Modern China: The Literary and Intellectual Impact* (1999). He was selected as a 2001-2002 Henry Luce III Fellow in Theology for a project on Paul's Epistle to the Romans.

CHARLES H. COSGROVE is Professor of New Testament Studies and Christian Ethics at Northern Baptist Theological Seminary in Lombard, Illinois. He is author of *Appealing to Scripture in Moral Debate: Five Hermeneutical Rules* (2002), *Elusive Israel: The Puzzle of Election in Romans* (1997), and *The Cross and the Spirit: A Study in the Argument and Theology of Galatians* (1988), and the editor of *The Meanings We Choose: Hermeneutical Ethics, Indeterminacy, and the Conflict of Interpretations* (2004).

DIETER GEORGI is emeritus Professor of New Testament at the University of Frankfurt, Germany. His numerous publications include *The Opponents of Paul in Second Corinthians* (1986), *Remembering the Poor: The History of Paul's Collection for Jerusalem* (1992), and *The City in the Valley* (2005).

Index of Scriptural References

————— ◆ —————

103:30	127		**Baruch**	
105:20-21	6-7		3:20-4:1	97
			4:4	184
Proverbs			4:36-5:9	128
3:5	70			
3:6	70		**Ezekiel**	
3:7	70		23:46-49	29n.15
3:12	70		27:13	29n.13
3:23	70		28:25-26	128
8:9	169		37:12-14	128
22:20-21	176n.17			
	Isaiah		**Hosea**	
3:16-25	29n.15		2:25	94
6:12	127		10:12	169
9:11	29n.13			
10:22-23	94, 95		**Joel**	
11:6-9	127		3:5	29n.13
26:19	127		4:2-6	29n.13
30:25-26	127			
31:9-32	127		**Habakkuk**	
43:18-21	105		2:4	72
53:1	56			
54:11-14	127		**Malachi**	
58:14	127		1:2	102
65:1-2	78			
65:17-25	127		**Matthew**	
66:18-19	29n.13		5:5	128
66:22	127		5:16	179n.58
			5:17	176n.16
Jeremiah			5:17-48	96
2:4-5	7, 9, 28n.9		5:28-29	178n.38
2:8	100		5:39	178n.38
2:13	21, 32n.40		6:23	187
6:10	171, 179n.56		10:10	178n.38
9:26	179n.54		12:5	128
13:17	172, 173, 187		15:10-20	175n.15
16:14-15	128		15:14	187
23:7-8	128		15:24	167
23:13	100		20:16	185
31:10-14	128		19:29	76
38:31-34	94, 95, 105		21:19	185
			22:31	149n.4
Lamentations			22:31-32	168
5-5	161		22:32	89, 102
			22:37-40	95

Index of Patristic Sources

—— ◆ ——

Index of Greek, Roman, and Jewish Sources

———— ◆ ————

Index of Names

━━━━━ ◆ ━━━━━

Index of Modern Authors

——— ◆ ———

Printed in the United States
70733LV00002B/589-600